W9-CHC-102

THE
UNITED
KINGDOM

THE
UNITED
KINGDOM

by
Charles F. Pfeiffer

BAKER BOOK HOUSE
Grand Rapids, Michigan

PHOTOLITHOPRINTED BY CUSHING - MALLOY, INC.
ANN ARBOR, MICHIGAN, UNITED STATES OF AMERICA
1970

INTRODUCTION

The three generations from Saul to Solomon cover about a century, yet they witnessed the growth and decay of a people whose very history is considered sacred by Christians and Jews throughout the world. Egypt was no longer a major power, and the threat of Assyria to the smaller states of western Asia was still future. Smaller states, including Israel, had an opportunity to develop during the time of this power vacuum.

Saul's court at Gibeah was humble by any standards. Solomon's at Jerusalem was known throughout the Near East for its splendor. Materially, Israel made greater progress during these three generations than at any comparable age of her history. Spiritually, however, our appraisals must be qualified. While a splendid Temple with elaborate rites had been built during the reign of Solomon, idolatry was rampant and the king himself was accused of idolatry.

All three of Israel's kings began well, and all three ended tragically. Saul's disobedience, David's sin in the matter of Bath-sheba and Uriah, and Solomon's idolatry left their mark upon king and people. The nation was not without a prophetic voice to call for repentance and trust in Israel's God, but Israel's political success had within it the germs of failure. With the death of Solomon the kingdom was shattered, never to be united again.

In writing about this interesting, if sometimes frustrating, period of Israel's history the author has relied heavily on our major source of information — the Biblical text itself. The bibliography will indicate secondary sources, to which credit for numerous insights is acknowledged. Thanks are due to the Baker Book House and its efficient staff, particularly Mr.

Cornelius Zylstra, editor. Photos have been generously made available by those acknowledged in the text. It is the author's hope that the reader will find, as he did, lessons of human sin and divine grace in studying this period of the history of Israel.

Charles F. Pfeiffer

Central Michigan University
Mt. Pleasant, Michigan

CONTENTS

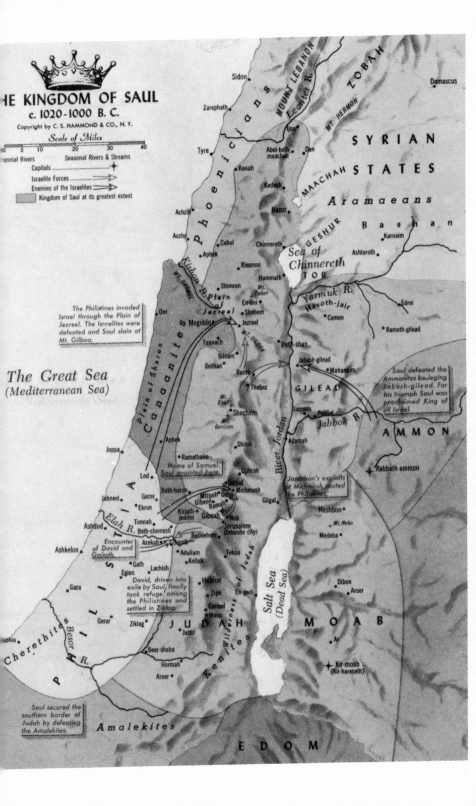

THE KINGDOM OF SAUL
c. 1020-1000 B.C.

Copyright by C. S. HAMMOND & CO., N.Y.

Scale of Miles
0 5 10 20 30 40

Perennial Rivers   Seasonal Rivers & Streams
Capitals
Israelite Forces ....
Enemies of the Israelites ....
Kingdom of Saul at its greatest extent

The Philistines invaded Israel through the Plain of Jezreel. The Israelites were defeated and Saul slain at Mt. Gilboa.

Saul defeated the Ammonites besieging Jabesh-gilead. For his triumph Saul was proclaimed King of all Israel.

Jonathan's exploits at Michmash routed the Philistines.

Home of Samuel. Saul anointed here.

Encounter of David and Goliath.

David, driven into exile by Saul, finally took refuge among the Philistines and settled in Ziklag.

Saul secured the southern border of Judah by defeating the Amalekites.

The Great Sea
(Mediterranean Sea)

ZOBAH
Damascus
Sidon
Zarephath
MOUNT LEBANON
Leontes R.
MT. HERMON
SYRIAN STATES
Tyre
Ijon
Dan
Abel-beth-maachah
MAACHAH
Aramaeans
Kanah
Kedesh
Bashan
Karnaim
Achzib
Cabul
Hazor
GESHUR
Ashtaroth
Accho
Aphek
Chinnereth
Sea of Chinnereth
TOB
Phoenicians
Rimmon
Hammath
Kishon R.
Mt. Carmel
Shimron
Mt. Tabor
En-dor
Yarmuk R.
Havoth-jair
Edrei
Dor
Plain Jezreel
Shunem
Jezreel
Camon
Ramoth-gilead
Megiddo
Mt. Gilboa
Beth-shan
Taanach
Jabesh-gilead
Mahanaim
Ibleam
Dothan
Bezek
GILEAD
AMMON
Plain of Sharon
Thebez
Succoth
Mt. Ebal
Shechem
Peniel
Jabbok R.
Gerizim
River Jordan
Adamah
Rabbath-ammon
Joppa
Shiloh
Canaanites
Aphek
Ramathaim
Ophrah
Lod
Bethel
Michmash
Heshbon
Beth-horon
Mizpeh
Geba
Gezer
Gibeon
Ramah
Gilgal
Jabneel
Ekron
Kirjath-jearim
Gibeah
Nob
Mt. Nebo
Timnah
Jerusalem (Jebusite city)
Medeba
Ashdod
Elah R.
Beth-shemesh
Azekah
Socoh
Bethlehem
PHILISTIA
Ashkelon
Gath
Lachish
Adullam
Tekoa
Egion
Keilah
Salt Sea (Dead Sea)
Dibon
MOAB
Gaza
Hebron
Aroer
Gerar
Ziph
En-gedi
Ziklag
Jattir
Carmel
Maon
JUDAH
Wilderness of Judah
Kenites
Ar
Kir-moab (Kir-hareseth)
Cherethites
Besor R.
Beer-sheba
Hormah
Aroer
Amalekites
EDOM

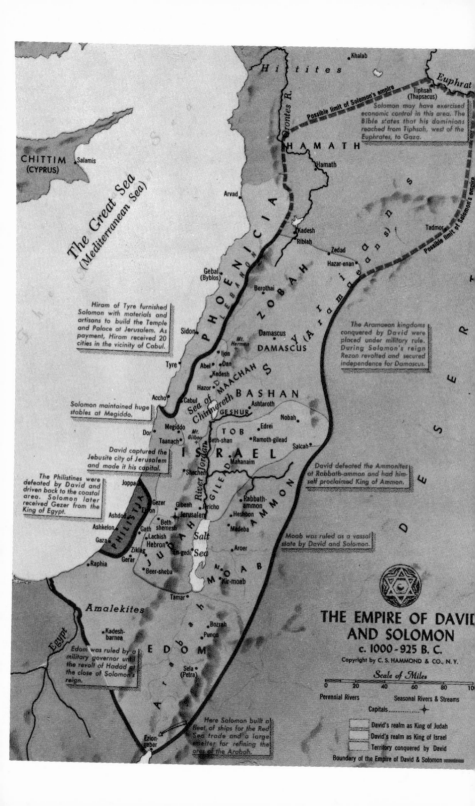

Khalab

H i t t i t e s

Euphrat

Orontes R.

Tiphsah
(Thapsacus)

Possible limit of Solomon's empire

Solomon may have exercised
economic control in this area. The
Bible states that his dominions
reached from Tiphsah, west of the
Euphrates, to Gaza.

H A M A T H

Hamath

CHITTIM
(CYPRUS)

Salamis

Arvad

Kadesh

Riblah

Zedad

Tadmor

Possible limit of Solomon's empire

The Great Sea
(Mediterranean Sea)

Gebal
(Byblos)

Berothai

Hazar-enan

P H O E N I C I A

Z O B A H

Y (A r a m a e a n s)

D E S E R T

Hiram of Tyre furnished
Solomon with materials
and artisans to build the Temple
and Palace at Jerusalem. As
payment, Hiram received 20
cities in the vicinity of Cabul.

Sidon

Mt.
Hermon

Damascus

DAMASCUS

The Aramaean kingdoms
conquered by David were
placed under military rule.
During Solomon's reign
Rezon revolted and secured
independence for Damascus.

Tyre

Ijon

Abel

Dan

Kedesh

D

Accho

Hazor

Cabul

M A A C H A H

Sea of
Chinnereth

B A S H A N

Ashtaroth

Nobah

Solomon maintained huge
stables at Megiddo.

Dor

Megiddo

Mt.
Gilboa

GESHUR

T O B

Edrei

Salcah

Taanach

Beth-shan

Ramoth-gilead

I S R A E L

David captured the
Jebusite city of Jerusalem
and made it his capital.

Mahanaim

David defeated the Ammonites
at Rabbath-ammon and had himself proclaimed King of Ammon.

The Philistines were
defeated by David and
driven back to the coastal
area. Solomon later
received Gezer from the
King of Egypt.

Joppa

Shechem

G I L E A D

River Jordan

Rabbath-
ammon

A M M O N

Gezer

Gibeah

Jericho

Heshbon

P H I L I S T I A

Ashdod

Ekron

Beth-
shemesh

Jerusalem

J U D A H

Medeba

Moab was ruled as a vassal
state by David and Solomon.

Ashkelon

Gath

Lachish

Salt

Hebron

Aroer

Gaza

Ziklag

En-gedi

Sea

Gerar

M O A B

Raphia

Beer-sheba

Kir-moab

Amalekites

Tamar

Egypt

Kadesh-
barnea

Bozrah

Punon

THE EMPIRE OF DAVID
AND SOLOMON
c. 1000 - 925 B.C.

Copyright by C. S. HAMMOND & CO., N. Y.

E D O M

Edom was ruled by a
military governor until
the revolt of Hadad at
the close of Solomon's
reign.

Arabah

Sela
(Petra)

Scale of Miles

0   20   40   60   80   100

Perennial Rivers

Seasonal Rivers & Streams

Capitals

Here Solomon built a
fleet of ships for the Red
Sea trade and a large
smelter for refining the
ores of the Arabah.

Ezion-
geber

David's realm as King of Judah

David's realm as King of Israel

Territory conquered by David

Boundary of the Empire of David & Solomon

1

SAMUEL, THE KINGMAKER

The period when charismatic leaders known as Judges exercised civil and military power in Israel came to a close with the career of Samuel, who served as a transition figure. He was the last of the Judges (I Sam. 7:15), a priest (I Sam. 2:18; 7:9), and a prophet (II Chron. 35:18). During his lifetime the more or less independent tribes of Israel, joined together with common traditions and a common loyalty to Yahwah, were forged into a nation under a king, Saul, and subsequently David.

Samuel was born during the judgship of a priest, Eli, who ministered at the "house of God" at Shiloh. During the early days of the conquest of Canaan the Tabernacle was set up at Shiloh, a town located on the east side of the highway that leads from Bethel northward to Shechem (Josh. 18:1; Judg. 21:19). During the period of the Judges, Shiloh was the principal sanctuary of the Israelites (Judg. 18:31). As time went on the sanctuary became a permanent structure, so that Eli is described as priest at the "temple of Yahweh" (cf. I Sam. 1:9). Living quarters were maintained for the priest's family, and here young Samuel first came to know the crisis that faced Israel.

Shiloh has been identified with modern Seilun, a place of ruins on a hill nine miles north of Bethel. Danish excavators, working at Seilun during campaigns from 1926 to 1929, and again in 1932, have found evidence that the city was destroyed, presumably by the Philistines, about 1050 B.C. While there are evidences that Shiloh was later occupied by Israelites (I Kings 11:29; 14:2), its destruction by the Philistines was considered by later prophets to be a warning for all time that Yahweh was a holy God. Jeremiah warned the people of Jerusalem, "Go now to my place which was in Shiloh, where I made my name dwell at first, and see what I did to it for the wickedness of my people Israel" (Jer. 7:12).

Eli appears in the Biblical record as a weak man, whose sin was in his failure to discipline his sons more than in overt acts of his own. Hophni and Phineas, Eli's sons, are described as "men of Belial" (I Sam. 2:12), thoroughly unprincipled men whose sole concern was their own lust. So greedy were they that they seized animals as they were being offered as sacrifices to Yahweh, insisting that the priest had the right to take all that he desired (I Sam. 2:13-17). They also indulged in indiscriminate sexual relations at the very shrine of Yahweh (I Sam. 2:22), which the Bible regards as evil in itself, and wicked because of its association with the Canaanite fertility cult which had been the source of a series of tragedies for Israel during the period of the Judges. Canaanite temple prostitutes served the function of insuring fertility to lands, animals, and humans. The God of Israel, Himself, brought fertility, and any compromise with Canaanite religion was regarded as infidelity to Yahweh. The reader of the Bible concludes that the religious life of Israel was at a low ebb at the time of Samuel's birth.

Samuel's parents, Elkanah and Hannah, were pious Ephraimites. Elkanah's other wife, Peninnah, had borne children, but Hannah was childless. Feeling that this was a cause of reproach, she went to Shiloh and there vowed that if Yahweh were to grant to her a son, he would be dedicated to God's service. Although Eli first accused Hannah of drunkenness, he later realized that she was praying to Yahweh from the depths of a grieved heart. As she finished her prayer, he said, "Go in peace, and the God of Israel grant your petition which you have made to him" (I Sam. 1:17).

After Samuel, the child born to Hannah, was weaned, his mother took him to Shiloh and left him in the care of Eli. Each year Hannah would make her pilgrimage to Shiloh. There she would see her son and bring to him the garment which she had made for him since the last visit (I Sam. 2:19). The tenderness of the family of Samuel stands out in contrast to the callousness of Eli's sons.

We read of two warnings that Eli's sons would die because of their sins. First a nameless "man of God" told Eli that his descendants would have their priesthood taken from them, and that a faithful priest would take their place. The line of Eli came to an end when Abiathar was replaced by Zadok early in the reign of Solomon (I Kings 2:35). The death of Hophni and Phineas was the more immediate judgment on the house of Eli.

The second warning came through the child Samuel. The Biblical writer artfully describes the voice in the night which aroused young Samuel, causing the lad to hasten to Eli for directions. The third time Samuel appeared, Eli sensed that Yahweh, Himself was speaking to the lad. Eli told Samuel to go back to bed with the counsel that, if the voice call again, the lad should reply, "Speak, Lord, for thy servant hears" (I Sam. 3:9). So it happened, and Yahweh revealed to Samuel the judgment soon to fall on Eli's house. Eli, himself, accepted the message with equanimity, apparently resigned to the prophesied end.

As Samuel grew he became recognized as a leader in Israel. He served as a prophet, with his headquarters at the shrine at Shiloh. At this time the Philistines encamped at Aphek, doubtless planning to take over the entire land from the Israelites. In an initial battle, the Israelites were defeated. The elders of Israel determined to put Yahweh to the test. They took the sacred ark from the shrine at Shiloh and brought it to the battlefield, accompanied by Hophni and Phinehas, the two sons of the priest Eli. The Israelites felt that the presence of their cult object would insure victory, but the fighting was hard, and the result was a resounding victory for the Philistines. The ark was taken as a trophy of war, and Hophni and Phinehas died on the field of battle.

When aged Eli learned what had happened, he too died. Perhaps he suffered a heart attack. The Biblical historian says that he broke his neck as he fell. As a final act in the tragedy, the wife of Phinehas died in giving birth to a child whom she named Ichabod ("no glory"), with the pathetic cry, "The glory has departed from Israel" (I Sam. 4:21).

Israel's fortunes had reached a new low. For the moment it appeared that the Philistine victory was absolute. The old order was gone, yet Samuel lived to breathe fresh hope into his beaten people.

In the meantime the Philistines were to learn that Israel's God was not a commodity to transport from place to place. If Israel was wrong to ascribe magic to the ark, the Philistines were also wrong to assume that they could make the ark into a good luck charm in their temples. They took the ark to the temple of their God Dagon at Ashdod. Dagon was a Canaanite god of grain who was adopted by the Philistines as one of their chief deities. When the ark of Yahweh was placed in Dagon's temple it seemed evidence of a great Philistine victory, but when the

Philistines entered a day later and found the image of Dagon on the ground before the ark, its head and arms severed from its trunk, they were moved with fear. Next they suffered the pains of bubonic plague and their bodies began to swell (I Sam. 5:6). The ark, which first appeared as a symbol of victory, now appeared to be a herald of death.

For seven months the ark remained in the Philistine country. From Ashdod it was sent to Gath, and from Gath to Ekron. Plague and panic continued, however, and the Philistine diviners urged that the ark be sent back to Israelite territory. As an offering to the God of Israel they prepared "golden tumors and golden mice" with the hope that this gift would appease the God of Israel. This would also involve imitative magic. By sending away the replicas of the "mice" (probably rats) and the tumerous growths, they hoped to rid their land of the plague which is usually spread by rats.

The advice of the Philistine diviners was taken. The ark was placed on a cart, drawn by two cows. The Philistines followed the carts as far as the borders of Beth-shemesh, then they turned back, satisfied that the ark had arrived in Israelite territory. The Levites at Beth-shemesh were thankful to have the ark

Site of Ancient Beth-shemesh. *Courtesy, Gerald Larue*

Mizpah, where the Philistines were repulsed by the Israelites under the spiritual leadership of Samuel. *Courtesy, Matson Photo Service*

back, and they sacrificed the cows to Yahweh. Some of the men of Beth-shemesh, however, irreverently looked into the ark, and died as a result. The people of Beth-shemesh began to fear for their safety with the ark in their midst. They sent it on to Kiriath-jearim where it remained until the time of David. Abinadab of Kiriath-jearim consecrated his son Eleazar to serve as custodian of the sacred ark.

Samuel appealed to the Israelites to rid themselves of the pagan cults associated with Baal and Astarte. These deities had been objects of worship during the days of the Judges, and they still held an attraction for the Israelites. The people gathered for a solemn religious occasion at Mizpah. They confessed their sins and offered sacrifices to Yahweh. The Philistines, however, learning of the gathering of Israelites at Mizpah, prepared to attack. Samuel rallied the Israelites and put the enemy to flight. In gratitude to God for giving them the victory, the Israelites named the battle sight Eben-ezer ("stone of help"). In the aftermath, Israel was able to regain cities lost to the Philistines and to enjoy peace with the other inhabitants of Canaan, called collectively the Amorites (I Sam. 7:5-14).

Samuel's leadership brought spiritual and material blessing to Israel, but as he grew older his people expressed concern for the future. The sons of Samuel were not of their father's caliber. As judges they were willing to accept bribes and pervert justice. The elders of Israel, conscious of continuing threat from the Philistines, decided that they must ask Samuel to anoint a king for them.

In theory Israel had been a theocracy, with Yahweh acknowledged as king. In practice, to be sure, the situation often was one of anarchy, with every man doing what was right in his own eyes. When the elders demanded a king of Samuel, he was understandably disturbed. He warned the Israelites of the perils of kingship — military conscription, high taxes, slavery — but they insisted that they would not be satisfied without a king. Slowly Samuel came to see that it was the theocracy that was being rejected, not his own ministry. Yahweh, Samuel was convinced, would give a king to Israel.

2

THE PHILISTINE THREAT

The crisis which precipitated the desire for kingship in Israel came during the latter part of the eleventh century B.C. Following the death of Joshua, Israelite tribes were content to trust Yahweh as their divine king. In times of crisis, charismatic leaders known as Judges were able to lead the tribes into victory. The Canaanite wars were thus ended, and threats from the Moabites, Ammonites, and other transjordanian peoples were effectively met. Troubles persisted, however, from the Philistines who had entrenched themselves along the coastal plain of southern Canaan.

We first meet the Philistines among the Sea People who invaded Egypt during the eighth year of Ramesses III (ca. 1188 B.C.). During the latter half of the second millennium B.C. there were extensive population movements in southeastern Europe and the eastern Mediterranean. This is the period of the fall of Troy (perhaps around 1200 B.C.) and the end of the Hittite Empire in Asia Minor. Merneptah and Ramesses III were able to turn back the Sea People from Egypt, but the Philistines (Egyptian *prst*) were successful in occupying the coastal regions of southwestern Canaan.

Before their settlement in Canaan, the Philistines had been in Crete (Jer. 47:4; Amos 9:7). Their name appears to have been of Indo-European origin. To the Israelites they were "uncircumcised" strangers who sought to prevent Israel from occupying her land. Their culture was that of the Cretan Minoans and the Greek Mycenaeans. Once in Canaan, however, they very quickly adopted Canaanite customs. We find the Canaanite god Dagon occupying an important place in Philistine religion.

When we first meet the Philistines we find them organized in city-states, each ruled by an overlord who is known as a *seren*. The title is related to the Greek *turannos,* the word for an ab-

Ramasses III reviewing prisoners and spoil from Libya. During his reign threats to Egypt came also from the "Sea Peoples," including the Philistines. *Courtesy, Oriental Institute, University of Chicago*

solute ruler which ultimately produced the English word "tyrant." The lords of the Philistines met in common council and policies of mutual concern were there determined (I Sam. 29:1-7). The Philistine strongholds were the cities of Ashkelon, Ashdod, Ekron, Gaza, and Gath. They were successful in winning many of the older Canaanite peoples to make common cause with them against the Israelites.

Our knowledge of the material culture of the Philistines comes in large measure from Medinet Habu in Egypt. A palace relief depicts captive Philistine warriors wearing a kilt similar

Philistines in Egypt. Captive Philistines are depicted on the north wall of the Medinet Habu temple in Egypt.
Courtesy, Oriental Institute, University of Chicago

to those used by other Aegean peoples. They are wearing a head-
dress with plumes and chin straps.

The distinctive Philistine ships depicted at Medinet Habu
have straight masts rising from the center. The keel is curved,
and there is a high stem and bow. Philistine wagons and chariots
are also depicted. From the Bible we know that the Philistines
had a monopoly on the use of iron (I Sam. 13:19-22). Until the
victories of David, the Israelites were dependent on the Philistines for such metal as they used — a fact which gave the Philistines a distinct military advantage.

Archaeologists are able to trace the patterns of Philistine expansion through the discovery of their pottery at sites in the
hill country known as the Shephelah and in the Negev. After
about 1150 B.C. the Philistines exerted pressure on the tribes
of Dan and Judah which claimed much of their territory. Had
they succeeded, the Philistines would have extended their supremacy over all of Canaan, with the resulting destruction of
Israelite distinctiveness. Well-trained, well-equipped Philistines
might be expected to annihilate the Israelite tribal confederacy
in short order. Many in Israel feared this very thing, and it was
from them that there arose a clamor for a king.

The fortunes of the Israelites reached their nadir when the
Philistines struck at Aphek in the coastal plain near Joppa.
After an initial defeat, the Israelites brought their sacred ark
from Shiloh in the hope that Yahweh's presence would insure
victory. The ark had no magical effect. Israel's army was routed.
Eli's sons, Hophni and Phinehas, were killed. The ark was taken
as a trophy of victory by the Philistines.

A Danish archaeological expedition worked at Shiloh during
the years 1930-32, uncovering evidence that the city was destroyed about 1050 B.C. Centuries later, the prophet Jeremiah
warned the people of Jerusalem that Yahweh had permitted
the shrine city of Shiloh to fall (Jer. 7:12, 14; 26:6, 9) and the
city of the later Temple must not expect deliverance. The Bible
is reticent concerning the destruction of Shiloh (cf. Ps. 78:60),
but there can be no doubt that it was a bitter moment to Israel.

With its central shrine destroyed, its priesthood killed or
dispersed, and its armies routed, Israel seemed to have reached
the end. Philistine garrisons occupied strategic sites throughout
the land. Israel would either end her history ingloriously or rise
to meet the crisis.

3

SAUL: ISRAEL'S FIRST KING

Samuel was reluctant to introduce kingship into the life of Israel. Yet the times were such that he could not refuse. A loose confederation of tribes could not stand before the Philistines. Something new was needed, and Samuel was willing to anoint a king.

Saul, the son of Kish of the tribe of Benjamin, would become a charismatic leader in his own way. Benjamin was a small tribe, and a Benjaminite would not be the object of jealousy that a man from Judah or Ephraim might become. Saul possessed a commanding figure, "from his shoulders upward he was taller than any of the people" (I Sam. 9:2). A leader of men was expected to have appropriate physical characteristics, and Saul had them.

The Biblical historian tells us that Saul was anointed secretly by Samuel before he was introduced to the people through a public act of bravery. Kish, Saul's father, was a wealthy man whose asses had strayed away. Saul and his servant searched for them throughout Benjamin with no success. Finally the servant suggested that they consult a "man of God" who might be able to tell them where to find the lost animals.

Saul and his servant entered the city and met Samuel, who had been prepared by Yahweh for this encounter. Samuel assured them that the asses had been found. Then he urged them to join in the sacrifice at the high place, where the best portion had been reserved for Saul. The next morning Samuel anointed Saul as king of Israel and sent him on his way.

Saul emerged as an able leader in a difficult time. He found Israel a loosely-organized group of tribes with a common religious loyalty. Shiloh had been a religious center for the tribes since the days of Joshua, but the city had been destroyed by the Philistines. Happily the tribes rallied to the old shrine at Gilgal,

Gibeah of Saul, known today at Tel el Ful. This was Saul's home and the seat of his government. *Courtesy, Matson Photo Service*

The Citadel of Saul at Gibeah, as reconstructed on the basis of archaeological research.

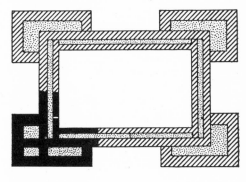

perhaps to be identified with Khirbet el-Mefjer, two miles north-east of ancient Jericho.

As leader of a united Israel, Saul's first challenge was to meet the threat of the Ammonites against Jebesh-gilead (I Sam. 11:1-4). Messengers hurried to Gibeah, a town in Benjamin three miles north of Jerusalem, where Saul lived. While the men of Jabesh lamented the plight of their city, Saul was stirred into activity. He sacrificed a "yoke of oxen" and sent pieces throughout the tribes of Israel. This was a call to arms against the Ammonites, Israel's enemy to the east. The call was answered, and Saul led his people to victory. The men of Jabesh-gilead would never forget what they owed to Saul. All Israel gathered at Gilgal to offer thanks for victory, and there Saul was publicly acclaimed as king (I Sam. 11:14-15).

Having dealt a decisive blow against the Ammonites, Saul turned to the more difficult task of challenging the Philistines who were harrassing Israel from the west. Making Gibeah the seat of his government, Saul prepared to assault the Philistines at Michmash, located nineteen hundred feet above sea level on a hill north of the Wadi es-Suwenit on the east slope of the central mountain range. The enemy had been raiding Israelite territory from the Michmash stronghold, and Israel seemed powerless to do anything about it.

The bravery of Jonathan, Saul's son, changed the tide of the Philistine war. Under cover of darkness, Jonathan and his armorbearer climbed down the rock Seneh, on which Geba was built, stole through the Philistine encampment in the pass, and climbed the rock Bozez on top of which stood Michmash, the Philistine headquarters (I Sam. 14:4-15). Jonathan threw fear into the enemy camp and roused his fellow Israelites to action. The result was more than a local victory for Israel. As the Philistines were defeated, Israelites came out of hiding and joined forces in pursuing the enemy out of the hill country as far as to Aijalon in the Shephelah.

The Philistine threat was not ended, but Israel was able to hold its central strongholds against its enemies throughout Saul's reign. Future battles were fought along the traditional Israelite-Philistine borders, not in the heartland of Israel. Other enemies also threatened — Amalekites from the south, Edomites and Moabites from the southeast, and Arameans from the north. Except for the Phoenician on the northwest, Israel was surrounded by a ring of active foes.

Although successful in battle, Saul is remembered more for his failures than for his victories. Samuel had been reluctant to anoint a king for Israel, and we may suspect that he was never really enthusiastic about kingship. No doubt he was grateful for Saul's leadership against Israel's foes, but it was not long before a serious rift developed between the prophet and the king.

During the preparation for battle with the Philistines at Michmash, Saul understandably wanted sacrifices made to insure success. Time was rapidly passing and Samuel did not appear. Finally Saul felt he could wait no longer. He took matters into his own hands and offered the burnt offering. When Samuel appeared he denounced Saul for his rash act: "You have done foolishly; you have not kept the commandment of the Lord your God, which he comanded you; . . . your kingdom shall not continue" (I Sam. 13:13-14). While we may be sympathetic with Saul for acting in an emergency, his act was condemned because he failed to observe the limited nature of monarchy in Israel. Unlike absolute monarchs, the Israelite king was subject to the law of God. The king must not usurp the position of the priest. The circumstances are different from those of our day, but there was a distinct separation between "church" and "state." Priests and kings were anointed to serve the Lord, but their functions were distinct.

The final breech between Samuel and Saul followed the Amalekite war. Samuel, as God's spokesman, ordered Saul to exterminate the Amalekites, who had taken advantage of Israel's pre-occupation with the Philistines to make raids regularly across the southern border. Saul was successful in his campaign, but he spared the Amalekite king, Agag, and spared the best of the sheep and the cattle.

In a dramatic encounter with Samuel, Saul stated that he had obeyed the command given by the prophet. Samuel asked, "What then is this bleating of the sheep in my ears, and the lowing of the oxen which I hear?" (I Sam. 15:14). Piously, Saul protested that he had saved the best of the sheep and the oxen "to sacrifice to the Lord your God." The explanation was not satisfactory. As a simple matter of fact, Saul had not obeyed God, Samuel said:

> "Has the Lord as great delight in burnt offerings and sacrifices, as in obeying the voice of the Lord?
>
> Behold, to obey is better than sacrifice, and to hearken than the fat of rams.

For rebellion is as the sin of divination, and stubbornness is an in-
iquity and idolatry.
Because you have rejected the word of the Lord,
He has also rejected you from being king. (I Sam. 15:22-23).

Saul acknowledged his sin and begged forgiveness, but Samuel
would not be appeased. Agag, not knowing of the attitude of
Samuel, felt that he was now safe. Samuel asked that he be
brought in, whereupon "Samuel hewed Agag in pieces before
the Lord at Gilgal" (I Sam. 15:33). The breach was now complete. Samuel did not see Saul again until the day of his death.

The last years of Saul are marked by personal tragedy. Our
focus of attention turns to the attractive young son of Jesse,
David, who is destined to become Saul's successor. Saul hears the
crowds crying, "Saul has slain his thousands, and David his ten
thousands" (I Sam. 18:7) and he is understandably jealous. During these years Saul suffered periodically from mental illness,
described in Biblical language as "an evil spirit from the Lord"
which tormented him. Forsaken by Samuel and eclipsed by
David, Saul's condition grew progressively worse. Saul determined to do away with David, and he was prepared to stoop to
any depth to do it. He attempted to pin David to the wall with
his spear (I Sam. 18:9-16). David succeeded in evading Saul, but
the king next exerted every effort to persuade David to marry
Michal, his daughter. In this way he would be able to use Michal
in getting at David. When a marriage was planned, Saul mag-
nanimously demanded no present "except a hundred foreskins
of the Philistines" (I Sam. 18:25). In this way Saul hoped that
David would meet death at the hand of the enemy. Saul's purposes were thwarted, however. David was successful in killing
two hundred Philistines, and he claimed Michal as his wife.
Saul grew increasingly bitter.

Saul next sought to get at David through his son, Jonathan.
From Saul's point of view, Jonathan should have been jealous
of David. Saul's son should expect to succeed him on the throne,
and David would be an obstacle. Yet Jonathan and David became the best of friends, and Jonathan tried to persuade his
father to desist from his plan to kill David. Saul probably promised in good faith (I Sam. 19:6), but jealousy soon got the better
of him and Saul again tried to pin David to the wall with his
spear (I Sam. 19:10). David escaped and Saul sent messengers to
David's house to apprehend him. Michal warned him of danger

and let him down through the window. Thus David again
eluded Saul.

Jonathan risked his own life in attempting to reason with his
father. Saul in his disturbed state cast his spear at Jonathan,
but happily he was no more successful in hitting Jonathan than
he had been in aiming at David (I Sam. 20:33). David knew he
could not return to Saul's court, and we follow him from place
to place as he seeks to elude the demented king. The priests at
Nob provided food for David, and gave him the sword of
Goliath which had been kept there (I Sam. 22). When Saul
learned of the help they had given to David he had them
murdered in cold blood.

Only the Philistinees could profit from Saul's senseless pursuit
of David. In a cave at En-gedi, David and his men had the opportunity to kill Saul, but David simply cut off the skirt of
Saul's robe as evidence that the king was in his power. On another occasion, in the Wilderness of Ziph, David and Abishai,
Joab's brother, actually entered the camp of Saul and took the
king's spear and a jug of water while Saul and Abner were sleep-
ing. Saul had many evidences of David's concern for him, and
he did admit, "I have done wrong...I will no more do you
harm" (I Sam. 27:21). Nevertheless David did not feel he could
trust Saul. So he fled to Achish, the Philistine king of Gath.

Mount Gilboa, site of the battle during which Saul and
Jonathan died at the hand of the Philistines. *Courtesy,
Gerald Larue*

The Impressive Mound of Beth-shan, held by the Philistines during the time of Saul. The men of Jabesh-gilead
rescued Saul's body from the walls of Beth-shan. *Courtesy,
Religious News Service*

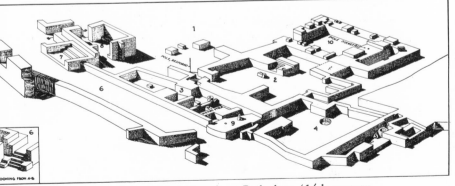

Drawing of the Mekal Temple at Beth-shan (14th century
B.C.). The Philistines hanged the body of Saul on a wall
at Beth-shan. *Courtesy, University Museum, Philadelphia*

Saul, however, grew more and more despondent. The Philistines were able to make major gains. God seemed to have forsaken Saul completely, for he could get no communication by dreams, by Urim, or by prophets. Samuel had died, and Saul still respected his memory. Although mediums had been outlawed Saul made his way to the village of Endor in order to contact a woman who reputedly had power to communicate with the dead.

The medium was reluctant to contact the dead, but Saul in disguise assured her that she would not be harmed. Samuel appeared, frightening the woman and telling Saul that he would be in the realm of the dead on the next day. The practice of sorcery and necromancy was forbidden in Israel, but the author of I Samuel indicates that desperate Saul received a message from the netherworld that pronounced his doom.

At Mount Gilboa the Philistines fought the Israelites, divided as a result of Saul's pursuit of David. Saul himself was severely wounded and three of his sons, including Jonathan, were killed. Saul asked his armorbearer to strike the fatal blow lest the Philistines claim credit for killing him. When the armorbearer refused, Saul fell on his own sword.

The Philistines found the body of Saul and took it to Bethshan. Saul's armor was placed in the Ashtoreth temple, and his body hanged on the walls of the city as a warning to others who might rebel against the Philistines. As one crowning act of homage to Saul, the men of Jabesh-gilead risked their lives to take the body from the wall. Then, to prevent it from falling into the hands of the Philistines again, they cremated the body. There is something fitting in this act of valor for Saul began his career by rescuing Jabesh-gilead from humiliation at the hand of the Ammonites.

4

DAVID: THE MAN AFTER GOD'S OWN HEART

The book of Ruth provides us with an introduction to the
career of David, Israel's second king, and the king through
whom the messianic line would continue. In seeking to show
that Jesus of Nazareth was Israel's Messiah, Matthew asserted
that Jesus was the "son of David, son of Abraham" (Matt. 1:1).
The Messiah had to be of the seed of Abraham, and he had to
trace his lineage through the king with whom Yahweh had
made an everlasting covenant (II Sam. 7). Yet Ruth shows that
David himself had a Moabitess in his ancestry. This is one of
many reminders that the Jew, no more than any other people,
can boast of racial purity.[1] Ruth had accepted the God of Israel
as her God. Although born an alien, through faith in Israel's
God she had become a part of the people of Israel, and an an-
cestress of Israel's greatest king.

The Biblical historian gives us a threefold introduction to the
young David. When we first meet him, the boy is tending the
flocks of his father Jesse, a Bethlehemite. When Samuel came to
Bethlehem with his horn of oil, prepared to anoint the one
whom Yahweh might designate as Saul's successor, he went to
the house of Jesse. David's seven older brothers successively
passed before Samuel, but none of them proved to be Yahweh's
choice. It was only after he made further inquiry that Samuel
learned of the youngest son, David, who was tending the sheep.
When he was brought in, Yahweh instructed Samuel to anoint

---

1. Tamar, Rahab, Ruth, and Bath-sheba are alluded to in Matt. 1:2-6. The
writer seems to be self-consciously stating that the Davidic, Messianic line
was not characterized by a so-called racial purity.

him as the king designated to replace Saul on the throne of Israel.[2]

The anointing of David was done in secret. Saul was still on the throne and we can assume that he would have reacted immediately had he known that Samuel had anointed a successor. Since this was unknown to Saul, the historian can tell us of how, in very favorable circumstances, David was introduced to Saul's court (I Sam. 16:14-22).

The latter years of Saul's life were tragic, indeed. The Biblical historian says, "the Spirit of the Lord departed from Saul, and an evil spirit from the Lord tormented him" (I Sam. 16:4). Saul had a mental illness which plagued him from this time until the time of his death. The rift between Samuel and Saul may have helped to unbalance the king. In any event, the king's counsellors learned of the youthful David whose ability to play the lyre might have a wholesome effect upon the disturbed king. David was brought to Saul's court where he served both as court musician and armorbearer to the king (I Sam. 16:14-23).

Following the stories of David's secret anointing, and of his introduction to the court of Saul, we have the account of young David proving his bravery on the battlefield against the hated Philistines (I Sam. 17). Saul and the Israelite army, including Eliab, Abinadab, and Shammah — three of David's brothers — were fighting the Philistines in the Valley of Elah. A Philistine champion, Goliath of Gath, challenged the Israelites to produce a man who would come to fight him in single combat. The outcome of the war would be determined by the contest (I Sam. 17:8-10).

According to the record in I Samuel, Jesse sent his youngest son David to the battlefield with provisions for his older brothers who were fighting the Philistines. Young David was horrified to find the Israelites cringing before the enemy, and volunteered to accept Goliath's challenge. With no weapon but his sling, David met the challenger, felled him, and cut off Goliath's head with his own sword. In II Samuel 21:19 we read that a man

---

2. The law of primogeniture prevailed in Israel. When, however, the first-born does not become the chief heir, this fact must be accounted for, hence the Biblical stories of younger sons surpassing their elder brothers. The stories of Jacob and Esau (Gen. 25; 27), and of Joseph and his brothers (Gen. 37) illustrate the fact that younger brothers often eclipse their elder brothers. When the law of primogeniture is violated, an explanation is given.

named Elhanan slew "Goliath the Gittite," and many scholars have concluded that the deeds of a lesser Israelite hero have been transferred to David. John Bright suggests that "Elhanan and David were the same person, the latter name being perhaps a throne name."[3] David must have performed some conspicuous act of heroism to win the love and loyalty of Israel, and the Goliath episode would provide the basis for the public acclaim he later received.

Following his victory over Goliath, David enjoyed the closest of relations with Saul and his family. Saul looked upon David as a brave and loyal Israelite, and insisted that the young man stay with his court. Soon Saul's attitude would be one of bitter hostility, but for the moment David was highly esteemed by king and people alike.

A particularly close relationship developed between David and Jonathan, Saul's son. Jonathan truly loved David, and his loyalty continued even when he realized that David was to become heir to the throne which he might hope to occupy. Jonathan and David both proved their bravery on the field of battle, and both proved themselves to be above petty jealousy.

Saul, however, soon came to see David as a threat to his throne and dynasty. The mental illness which had afflicted Saul earlier grew worse, and the king seemed to be wholly consumed with his passion to kill David. In the meantime David was growing ever more popular with the people in view of his success against Israel's enemies.

Fearing what might happen if he personally harmed the idol of the crowds, Saul determined to maneuver David into a situation in which he would die at the hand of the Philistines. When Saul learned that his daughter Michal was in love with the young hero, he took it as an opportunity to strike at David. When arrangements were made for a wedding, David protested that he was a poor man and could not hope to give the customary marriage present to the bride's father. Saul, in apparent magnanimity, insisted that he wanted nothing but "a hundred foreskins of the Philistines" (I Sam. 18:25), hoping that David would be killed in the process of killing Philistines. David, however, killed two hundred Philistines and claimed Michal as his wife.

---

3. John Bright, *A History of Israel,* pp. 171-172.

David's continuing victories, and the popularity that attended them, brought Saul to the place where he determined to act decisively. The king dispatched messengers to David's house, but Michal warned him of danger and David was able to flee. Michal fooled her father's messengers by placing an image and pillow on the bed, making it appear that David was sick in his bed (I Sam. 19:13). When Saul learned of the deception, Michal told her father that David had threatened her so that she had to let him escape.

The fleeing David made his way to Samuel at Ramah in the mountain country of Ephraim. Saul learned of the whereabouts of David and sent messengers to take him. Samuel and the prophets with him were engaged in the ecstatic dancing early associated with the prophetic gift (I Sam. 19:20-24), and Saul's messengers were caught up in the enthusiasm. After a second and a third group were affected similarly, Saul personally went to Ramah where he too, joined the prophetic frenzy. In this way David was again protected from Saul's plan to have him killed.

From this time on until the death of Saul, David was a fugitive. At Nob, near Jerusalem, David secured the co-operation of Ahimelech and the priests who gave him bread and a sword. Flight from Saul took him to the Philistines. Achish, king of Gath, recognized David and the fugitive feigned madness in order to save his life (I Sam. 21:10-15). We next find David in Adullam, southwest of Bethlehem. Here he gathered a band of four hundred men, including men of his own family and outlaws who wished to escape from society. David arranged to have his parents stay in Mizpah of Moab while he sought to protect himself from Saul. The unfortunate priests at Nob were slaughtered because of the help they had given David.

When Keilah in the Shephelah, southwest of Bethlehem, was attacked by the Philistines, David and his men moved in to rescue the Israelites there. It is a mark of the impotence of Saul's defense policies at the time that David's outlaw force, rather than Saul's regular army, brought relief to the city. David was not safe in Keilah, however. Abiathar, using his priestly ephod,[4] told David that Saul would pursue him to Keilah and the men of Keilah would surrender David to his enemy.

---

4. The ephod, here, is the box which contained the sacred lots. These were consulted to give "yes" or "no" answers to questions proposed to the priest who used them.

Nob, home of the priests.
Courtesy, Matson Photo Service

When Pursued by Saul, David had to flee for refuge in the Judean Wilderness, seen here from Mount Nebo. To the left, center, we see the northern end of the Dead Sea. *Courtesy, Matson Photo Service*

Again we find David fleeing to the wilderness area east of the central mountain range. The inhabitants of Ziph reported David's presence in their territory, southeast of Hebron, to Saul. David moved farther south to the Wilderness of Maon, where Saul caught up with him. As Saul and his men were closing in on David, a messenger brought word of a Philistine attack (I Sam. 23:24-29). Again David fled from Saul, this time making his way to En-gedi, an oasis near the center of the western shore of the Dead Sea. Here Saul entered the cave where David and his men were hiding. David cut off the skirt of Saul's robe, but he did not take advantage of the opportunity to kill his enemy. In spite of all that Saul did to David, David respected Saul's office and would not lift a hand to harm him (I Sam. 24:1-7).

As David called after Saul, confronting the king with evidence that he was at the mercy of David in the cave, Saul acknowledged in apparent penitence, "You are more righteous than I; for you have repaid me good, where as I have repaid you evil" (I Sam. 24:12). David vowed that he would not exact vengeance from Saul and his descendants. Saul in his madness might rage against David, but the Biblical historian makes it clear that David is God's elect. Nevertheless David treats Saul and his family with respect, and during Saul's lifetime, David did not lift a hand against him. There is no reconciliation, however. David returned to his mountain stronghold, and Saul went home to Gibeah. If chastened, it was a temporary feeling.

While David was in the En-gedi area, the prophet Samuel died. Samuel had been involved in Israel's political history since his youth, and he had become the grand old man of Israelite life. David, in particular, would have looked upon him as a source of strength. In the divided state of the nation, it is noteworthty that "all Israel assembled and mourned for him" (I Sam. 25:1). The prophet was buried in his house at Ramah, traditionally identified with a hill five miles northeast of Jerusalem known as Nebi Samwil ("the prophet Samuel"). The mosque at Nebi Samwil, one of the highest points in Palestine, is supposed to contain the tomb of Samuel. It does bear witness to the fact that Moslem as well as Christian and Jew honor Israel's kingmaker.

Following Samuel's death, David and his followers moved farther south to Maon, south of Hebron. There David and his men continue to live as outlaws, demanding and receiving provisions

from those among whom they live. To be sure, they would sometimes serve as a police force, protecting their neighborhood from
intruders (I Sam. 25:21). Here we meet the churlish Nabal and
his discreet wife, Abigail. Nabal was a wealthy sheikh who refused
to acknowledge any obligation to David. At the time of sheep-
shearing it was usual to give something to needy neighbors, and
David sent ten of his young men expecting gifts from Nabal.
Wandering groups such as David's retinue represented a real
danger in an area, and when they did not resort to plunder
they expected some sort of tribute. Nabal treated the request
of David's young men contemptuously, with the rhetorical question, "Who is David? Who is the son of Jesse? There are many
servants nowadays who are breaking away from their masters.
Shall I take my bread and my water and my meat that I have
killed for my shearers, and give it to men who come from I do
not know where?" (I Sam. 25:10-11). David was angered at this
response, and he prepared to attack and plunder Nabal and his
household.

When Abigail learned what had happened she immediately
sought to rectify matters. She had appreciated the presence of
David and his men, and she feared the consequences of their
anger. Sending her young men on ahead, Abigail mounted her
ass and approached David with a gift of fig cakes, raisins, bread,
wine, sheep, and grain (I Sam. 25:18). As she approached David,
Abigail took upon herself the blame for David's young men returning empty handed. Nabal had lived up to his name; he was
a fool. Abigail should have known of David's demands, but she
was ignorant of them. Now she wished to make amends, thereby
preventing David from shedding innocent blood (I Sam. 25:23-
31). The speech is moving and appropriate. David had spared
Saul. His hands were not blood-stained. For him to have re-
taliated in anger after Nabal's foolish remarks he would have
harmed his own chances for influence throughout Maon. David
accepted the gifts and the council of Abigail.

When Abigail returned home she found Nabal drunk; so she
delayed telling him what she had done. The next morning Nabal
learned what his wife had done in presenting gifts to David.
Nabal's "heart died within him" (I Sam. 25:37), perhaps a reference to a heart attack. Ten days later Nabal was dead.

When David heard of Nabal's death, he sent for Abigail
and married her. This wise and beautiful widow brought her
own loyalty, and there can be no question that the whole of

Maon would look upon David with greater sympathy because of his marriage to Abigail. Saul had given Michal, David's first wife to another, but David had also married Ahinoam of Jezreel. Ahinoam was the mother of David's firstborn, Amnon (II Sam. 3:2), and Abigail bore his second son, Chileab (II Sam. 3:3).

A second time we read that the Ziphites betrayed David's presence to Saul (I Sam. 26). David's spies reported the arrival of Saul, and with his nephew Abishai, David stole into the camp of Saul and stole his spear and a jug of water. Then, from the opposite mountain, David taunted Abner for not remaining awake to protect his master, Saul. Again Saul recognized that David had spared his life, but there was no reconciliation.

Since it was impossible to evade Saul forever in Israel, David decided to move into the Philistine country. There were dangers in such a move, for the Israelites might accuse him of selling out to their perennial foes. Yet the Biblical writer makes it clear that David's loyalty never waivered. Although a vassal of Achish of Gath for a year and four months, David only attacked peoples such as Geshurites, Girzites, and Amalekites. The Philistines thought he was attacking the neighboring Israelites, but David was careful to avoid hostile contacts with his own people (I Sam. 27:8-12). Achish trusted David implicitly, but the other Philistine leaders were suspicious (I Sam. 29:1-4). This proved providential, for the Philistines were preparing for battle with Saul and his forces.

When David returned to Ziklag he found that the Amalekites had burned the city and had taken the women and children captive. David's men were prepared to revolt, but David trusted his God for strength and determined what action had to be taken. He consulted his priest, Abiathar, who counseled him to pursue the enemy with the assurance that he would rescue Ahinoam and Abigail and the others who had been taken captive. Again providence was working for David. His men came upon an Egyptian slave who had been abandoned by the Amalekites after their raid, presuming that the slave was about to die. David's men gave the slave nourishment, and he served as their guide, directing them to the camp of the Amalekites.

David came upon the Amalekites in a surprise attack and liberated the people of Ziklag who had been captured. The four hundred camel riders comprising the Amalekite cavalry escaped, but the rest of the Amalekite army was annihilated. All of the spoil of war was claimed by David (I Sam. 30:20). On the return trip to Ziklag, David met the two hundred of his men who were too exhausted to join the expedition against the Amalekites. In spite of the counsel of some of his men, David insisted that those who had stayed at home should have their share of the spoil (I Sam. 30:21-25). While not obligated to do so, David sent a share of the spoils to the cities of Judah which had suffered periodically from Amalekite raids. This demonstrated David's loyalty to his own people, in spite of the fact that he had been recently a vassal to the Philistines.

David was not present at the fateful battle on Mt. Gilboa. There Saul and Jonathan met their death and Israel went down in defeat. David expressed his grief in a poetic dirge, quoted by the author of II Samuel from an ancient poetic epic known as the Book of Jasher (II Sam. 1:18). There is irony in the fact that David's bitter enemy — King Saul — and his best friend, Jonathan, died together. Yet David chose to forget the difficult years with Saul, and recall the brave warrior of earlier and happier times. There can be no question that David's grief was genuine. Yet we must note that the death of Saul made it possible for David to become king, even if the initial phase of his kingship was limited to the south.

Hebron, twenty-eight miles south of Jerusalem was David's first capital.

The men of Judah proclaimed David king in Hebron, while the partisans of the house of Saul acknowledged Saul's son Eshbaal, or Ishbosheth, as king of the north. Saul's commander Abner was loyal to Ishbosheth in the early days of his reign. The forces of Joab, David's general, and Abner tangled at Gibeon. A tournament seems to have been arranged between the opposing forces, the outcome of which would determine whether David or Ishbosheth would be acclaimed king (II Sam. 2:12-17). The result was a bloody draw, for the twelve partisans of David and the twelve partisans of Ishbosheth slaughtered one another. In the battle that followed David's forces prevailed.

David's forces soon gained the upper hand in battle with the forces of Ishbosheth. Asahel, a brother of Joab, David's commander, pursued Abner who was loyal to Saul's son Ishbosheth. When Asahel insisted on taking Abner, Abner smote Asahel with the butt of his spear and killed him. Not only did David lose a loyal warrior, but Asahel's death produced a blood feud between Joab and Abner.

As David was growing stronger, troubles developed between Abner and Ishbosheth. Abner took one of Saul's concubines, and Ishbosheth interpreted the act as treason. A king's concubines were considered royal property, and a man who claimed the wives or concubines of a king could be considered a claimant to the throne. When Ishbosheth took Abner to task for taking the concubine, Abner gave the king a tart reply and promptly prepared to shift his loyalty to David (II Sam. 3:6-11).

When Abner negotiated with David for a covenant. David insisted on the return to him of Michal, Saul's daughter and his first wife (II Sam. 3:14). This would strengthen David's claim to the throne of all Israel, for he would then be son-in-law to Saul. Michal's husband Paltiel was reluctant to part with her, and Michal, herself, had no desire to rejoin David. Abner, however, did as David had requested and brought Michal to him.

Abner then negotiated with the elders of Israel, including Benjamin, Saul's tribe, to persuade them to accept David as king (II Sam. 3:17-19). Having been successful, he journeyed southward to Hebron and told David that the northern tribes were prepared to enter a covenant with him and thus acknowledge him as their king.

Abner did not live to enjoy the position of prominence he doubtless hoped for in the court of David. Joab would naturally be jealous of Abner as a rival commander. Since Abner had killed Joab's brother Asahel, Joab felt justified in murdering Abner (II Sam. 3:26-30). The people of the north would be understandably bitter at the death of Abner, but David made it clear that he had no part in it. David mourned for the fallen Abner, and insisted that Joab alone would bear the curse for the horrible deed. The death of Abner might have alienated the northern tribes, but David was successful in convincing them that he was in no way responsible for the tragedy.

Soon after Abner's death, Ishbosheth himself was murdered. Rechab and Baanah, professional soldiers and captains of guerilla bands, stole into the king's chamber and murdered Ishbosheth. They brought his head to David at Hebron, hoping for a reward. Instead David ordered that Rechab and Baanah be put to death for their crime.

Real and potential enemies of David had been removed one by one, but David was never personally responsible for their death. David mourned for Saul, for Abner, and for Ishbosheth as though they had all been loyal to his cause. There is no reason to see hypocrisy in this. David's conduct at this time of his life won the hearts of friend and foe alike. The hand of God might be seen in preparing the way for David to rule over all Israel, but David never forced or hurried the hands of providence.

After David reigned for seven years as king over Judah, the northern tribes assembled at Hebron and entered into covenant to make David king of all Israel. The two parts of the land — north and south — would split permanently after the death of Solomon. At the beginning of David's reign we see that the sections were conscious of distinctive institutions and rights. David was king of the south, and the north acclaimed him as king after the death of Ishbosheth. The union was in the person of David. It persisted through the career of Solomon, but no longer.

Hebron was a satisfactory capital for Judah, but a united monarchy demanded a headquarters farther north. The Jebusite enclave at Jerusalem was a final vestige of Canaanite control of Israel. It was centrally located and had not been incorporated into Judah or Benjamin, the tribes on its borders. It seemed ideally located for a capital. The details of the capture of Jerusalem-Jebus are difficult to follow because of problems in the Biblical text and its interpretation. David's men seem to have stormed the water shaft, overwhelmed the Jebusite guards

stationed at its upper end, and conquered the city.[5] Tradition
seems to have regarded the capture of the shaft as the decisive
event in the capture of the city.

We have no record of David's treatment of the Jebusites, but
we may assume that he spared them and permitted them to live
in safety in his kingdom. The captured city was not incorporated
into the tribal territories but remained a royal city, "the city of
David." David was concerned about its defenses. On the long
north side of the city hill he built the Millo, perhaps a raised
platform or terrace of filled-in masonry. The north was the one
direction from which the city was vulnerable, and special pre-
cautions had to be made for its defense.

Soon after David united the kingdom under his personal rule,
the Philistines began to give him trouble. They had profited
from the controversies between partisans of Saul and David and
wanted to keep the Israelites weak. David, however, was emerging as a force to be reckoned with, and the Philistines attacked
at the valley of Rephaim, southwest of Jerusalem. David was victorious, and he took away the idols of the Philistines as they had
once taken the ark of Yahweh, God of Israel (II Sam. 5:21).
While we do not have details of David's wars with the Philistines, there is evidence that they ranged over a wide area in
central and southern Palestine. On one occasion, while the
Philistines were occupying Bethlehem, David expressed his wish
to drink water from the Bethlehem well. As a youth he had
known that well, and in a moment of nostalgia he craved its
water. Three of his warriors actually broke through the enemy
line, took water, and brought it to David. Moved by their
loyalty and courage, David poured it out as an offering to the
Lord (I Chron. 11:17-19). Such acts of understanding generosity
endeared David to his warriors.

David planned to make Jerusalem the religious as well as the
political capital of his empire, so he ordered that the ark be
taken from the house of Abinadab at Kiriath-jearim and brought
to Jerusalem. While passing over the threshingfloor of a man
named Nacon, Abinadab's son Uzzah reached out to steady the
ark which appeared to be moving from the cart on which it was
carried. Uzzah died on the spot, for his well-meaning act
was considered irreverent because he had dared to touch the

5. Cf. J. Simons, *Jerusalem in the Old Testament,* Leiden: E. J. Brill, 1957,
pp. 165-173.

sacred ark (II Sam. 6:6-11). David was angry, and probably frightened at the swift retribution meted out to Uzzah. Instead of bringing the ark to Jerusalem, he left it with a man named Obed-edom. During the three months it was with Obed-edom, prosperity came to his house. David then decided to bring the ark to Jerusalem.

The procession to Jerusalem was a noisy and colorful one. David, himself, joined in the procession, dancing and leaping in a frenzied march. Michal, Saul's daughter, was horrified at her husband's lack of dignity, and she told him so. She may have been filled with resentment at being torn from her former husband, Paltiel (II Sam. 3:15-16), and at the decline in her family's fortunes since her father's death. Michal may also have been angered to discover that she was but one of David's many wives. In any event. David resented her criticism. Her's was a difficult burden to bear, for she died childless.

The arrival of the ark in Jerusalem was a happy occasion. Special sacrifices were offered and food was distributed among the crowds (II Sam. 6:18-19). The ark had at last found a home. It moved from place to place during the wilderness wandering, and even in the Promised Land it had no permanent resting place until David brought it to Jerusalem.

The next logical act for David would be to build a magnificent Temple to house the sacred ark. This he purposed to do, and Nathan, the prophet, was enthusiastic in approving the venture. David had built a sumptuous mansion for himself, and it seemed inappropriate to permit the ark to remain in a humble tent.

Yet Yahweh intervened to tell Nathan that he did not wish David to make him an house; conversely Yahweh wished to build David a house (II Sam. 7:11). To be sure, there is a play on the word "house" here. David purposed to build a dwelling-place; Yahweh will build a dynasty. The ideas are interrelated, however, for David's son (Solomon) will build a house for Yahweh. Yet the emphasis is on God's promise to David. David's children will rule after him. On occasion they will sin, and be punished, but the dynasty will not end as Saul's dynasty ended (II Sam. 7:14-15). David, in gratitude, accepted God's promise and covenant.

Following the establishment of the ark in Jerusalem, and Yahweh's covenant with David, we read of yet other victories of David over his foes. Not only must he continually fight the Philistines, but Moabites, Arameans, and Edomites stir up trouble (II Sam. 8). David occupied Damascus in Syria and pushed back the boundaries of his sphere of influence to the Euphrates River. Toi of Hamath, one hundred twenty miles north of Damascus, offered loyalty and tribute to David.

On the personal side we find David remembering his friend Jonathan and showing kindness to his son Mephibosheth. Mephibosheth, as a descendant of Saul, might have aspired to kingship. Yet David would note that he was a cripple, hence hardly one to lead a revolt. There is no reason to doubt that David was really anxious to show kindness to this son of his best friend. The restoration of Saul's lands, and a subvention from the royal treasury for support were the least that David could do for this crippled prince (II Sam. 9:9-13).

David's career, like that of Saul, ended in a series of personal tragedies which affected the fortunes of his people as well. The turning point was the sin which he committed with Bath-sheba (II Samuel 11). The armies of David, under Joab, were fighting the Ammonites east of the Jordan River, but the king himself remained in Jerusalem. This fact suggests that the once mighty warrior was growing careless. Others faced danger while he enjoyed the comforts of home. Worse yet, as he observed the beautiful Bathsheba, wife of one of his soldiers, Uriah the Hittite, he lusted after her and ordered that she be brought to him. They had sexual relations, and in due time David learned that she was pregnant.

Black as David's sin was in the first instance, his efforts to cover it were still blacker. The king invited Uriah to come home for a period of rest. A loyal soldier is entitled to some time away from the battle field. David hoped that Uriah would go to his home, have sexual relations with his wife, and then assume that the child which she would bear was his own. The plot was fiendishly clever, but Uriah failed to cooperate. As a soldier he knew that his companions at the front were dying. It was inappropriate, he felt, to go home to his wife. Perhaps he believed that sexual relations with his wife would weaken him, and incapacitate him for the tasks ahead. Some have suggested that he was suspicious of David's motivation. In any event, by refusing to go home, Uriah signed his death warrant.

Since Uriah would not go home, David resorted to a new stratagem. He dispatched a message to his field commander, Joab: "Set Uriah in the forefront of the hardest fighting, and then draw back from him, that he may be struck down and die"

(II Sam. 11:15). This was murder just as truly as if David had personally killed Uriah with his own sword.

The order was carried out. Joab placed Uriah in the place of greatest danger, and in the fighting that took place outside Rabbah — modern Amman, the capital of Jordan — Joab was killed. A messenger brought David word that the fighting had gone against his armies. The people of Rabbah had tried to lift the siege, and many Israelites were killed — including Uriah.

David's response was the height of hypocrisy: "Do not let this matter trouble you, for the sword devours now one and now another; strengthen your attack upon the city, and overthrow it" (II Sam. 11:25). Wars involve casualties. Such is life! Try harder next time. All will be well. David's plans were working according to schedule.

There can be no question that David's two-fold sin — murder and adultery — is one of the blackest recorded in or out of the Bible. David was not acting as "the man after God's own heart" but as an absolute tyrant who used his power to cater to his own lusts. He was no better than others of his or later ages who are corrupted with power. We are shocked not at his sin, which was common enough, but at the fact that it was David who committed such sin. We expect better things of our Biblical heroes.

Yet here is where we see the Biblical concept of kingship in action. That a king committed adultery and tried to cover it with a murder was not unique to Israel. That a prophet challenged that king and pronounced the judgments of Yahweh upon him because of his sins — and lived to see another day — was unique. The king was Yahweh's anointed. He was not above law but was subject to the Law of God. Nathan, the prophet, addressed the king in the language of parable. In a certain city there was a rich man who had large flocks and herds. Near him lived a poor man who had only one lamb, which he and his family loved as a pet. A stranger visited the rich man, but he was unwilling to take of his abundant flocks to feed the guest. Instead he took the poor man's lamb and prepared it as a meal. David in anger stated that the rich man, utterly devoid of pity, deserved to die. Nathan quietly replied, "You are the man."

Nathan declared that David would suffer as a result of his sin. The sword would not depart from David's house. Tragedy would stalk his days (II Sam. 12:10-15). The child about to be born to Bath-sheba would die. And so it happened. Although

David fasted and prayed, refusing to eat food or to accept consolation, his child died on the seventh day.

After the ordeal of losing their first child, David and Bathsheba had a child that lived — Solomon, later to become king. Yet the prophecies of Nathan were to come true. One of David's sons, Amnon, raped his half-sister Tamar, the sister of Absalom. When he then rejected her, she told her brother Absalom, who plotted revenge. During festivities at the time of sheep-shearing, Absalom had his servants strike and kill Amnon (II Sam. 13:23-29). Then Absalom fled to the home of his maternal grandfather, remaining at Geshur for three years.

Finally Joab determined to arrange a reconciliation between David and Absalom. He arranged with a woman of Tekoa to come to David with a story about a widow whose sons had quarreled until one son killed the other. She feared to surrender the murderer lest her entire family be obliterated (II Sam. 14:5-7). David immediately became interested in the woman's problem, and promised assistance. As he continued talking with her he realized that Joab had arranged for the interview as a means of asking David to welcome back Absalom. The king accepted the message, and promptly ordered that Absalom be permitted to return to Jerusalem (II Sam. 14:23-24).

Absalom lived in his own house in Jerusalem for two years before he saw his father, David. During this time he probably conceived the idea of revolt. He was a fine looking young man, and he consciously tried to win the favor of the people. As David was once the young, glamorous warrior in contrast to the older Saul, now David is of the older generation and Absalom captivates the people. He sympathized with people who felt they were wronged, and hinted that he would give them justice if he were only king (II Sam. 15:1-6). After four years he felt strong enough to plot a coup. He found a following at Hebron, which may have resented the fact that David had moved his capital to Jerusalem. David's counselor, Ahithophel, joined the forces of Absalom. The king and his retinue including the palace guard and the priests and Levites left Jerusalem, crossing the Kidron with David. David, however, ordered that the ark be returned to Jerusalem, an act which indicated that he hoped to return. Continuing to flee from Jerusalem, he encountered Shimei of the house of Saul who taunted the king, counting his troubles a just recompense for the blood of the house of Saul (II Sam. 16:5-8). David did not punish Shimei, humbly accepting his abuse.

As David was reaching the Jordan, Absalom was entering Jerusalem in triumph. Following the counsel of Ahithophel, Absalom publicly took his father's concubines, a dramatic way of laying claim to the throne (II Sam. 16:20-23). Then he rejected Ahithophel's advice that he strike at David immediately. Hushai, really on David's side, suggested that Absalom gather an army of men from Dan to Beer-sheba — a policy that would take time and give David an opportunity to prepare his forces (II Sam. 17:11-12). When Hushai's counsel was accepted, Ahithophel hanged himself in disgrace (II Sam. 17:23).

During Absolom's Revolt David crossed the Jordan River as he fled from Jerusalem. The scene above is near the natural crossing point east of Jericho.

Finally Absalom felt that he was ready to pursue David across the Jordan. Amasa was commander of Absalom's forces, and Joab remained loyal to David. Finally the two armies met in the Forest of Ephraim. David was torn between emotions of love for a son and desire to protect his throne. He wanted victory, but he gave orders that Absalom not be personally harmed (II Sam. 18:5). As it happened, Absalom's mule passed under the branches of an oak tree, and Absalom's head was caught in the oak. The young man who reported the incident to Joab did not know what to do, but Joab did not hesitate. He took three darts in his hand, and thrust them into the heart of Absalom (II

Sam. 18:14). Then Joab sounded the trumpet. Absalom was buried under a heap of stones, and a messenger brought word of the victory to David. David, however, was brokenhearted at the message of Absalom's death. In anguish he cried, "O my son Absalom, my son, my son Absalom! Would I had died instead of you, O Absalom, my son, my son!" (II Sam. 18:33).

David and the armies had proved victorious, but the moment of triumph lost much of its joy because of David's attitude. Finally Joab warned David of the seriousness of the situation. Men had risked their lives on David's behalf, and the king was acting as though he would have preferred that they die and his rebellious son live (II Sam. 19:1-8). Joab told David frankly that he should appear before the people or he would lose their loyalty. The king accepted the rebuke.

With the knowledge that Absalom was dead, the tribes of Israel acquiesced in the rule of David. Problems and rivalries between north and south were to flare up periodically, but David's throne had been preserved. He was magnanimous in treating the partisans of Absalom in an effort to recover a degree of normalcy (II Sam. 19).

After the revolt of Absalom we find a Benjaminite named Sheba leading an uprising against David. Sheba was from Saul's tribe, and he was one of the Benjaminites who rejected David's rule. Sheba sounded the cry of independence and war, "We have no portion in David, and we have no inheritance in the son of Jesse; every man to his tents, O Israel!" (II Sam. 20:1). Judah remained true to David, but Sheba found a large following in the north. David called upon Amasa, who had replaced Joab as David's commander, to assemble the men of Judah to put down the revolt. Amasa, however, delayed in collecting the forces of Judah; so David called upon Abishai, Joab's brother, to take to the field against Sheba. Joab, of course, soon took the initiative himself, joined by David's guard of Cherethites and Pelethites. Amasa joined the fighting men at the great stone in Gibeon, but Joab would not tolerate his presence in the camp. Taking Amasa by the beard as though to kiss him, Joab struck Amasa to the ground with one fatal stroke of his sword.

With his rival gone, Joab and Abishai pursued Sheba. Amasa's dead body was left in a field by the side of the road with a garment thrown over it, and the warriors continued northward until they came to Abel of Beth-maacah where Sheba had taken refuge. While Joab and his men were battering the wall of the city in order to take Sheba, a wise woman called down from the city to suggest a way of saving Abel. She offered to throw the head of Sheba to Joab, and he agreed to spare the city under those. terms. She lived up to her bargain, and Sheba was murdered and decapitated in Abel.

Abel had been an oracle city in years before the time of David. The wise woman declared, "They were wont to say in old time, 'Let them but ask counsel at Abel'; and so they settled a matter" (II Sam. 20:18). Debir, in the Judean hills, seems to have had a similar reputation, for the name itself means "oracle." Like the Greeks of historical times, the ancient Canaanites evidently had holy places to which they went for an answer to their problems. On occasion at least, the oracle was a wise woman whose knowledge of human nature equipped her to render decisions in perplexing situations. Here the wise woman was instrumental in saving her own city from destruction at the hand of Joab and his forces.

The next tragedy to face David was a famine which persisted throughout the land for three years. During this time David learned that Saul had not kept the covenant made between Joshua and the Gibeonites (cf. Josh. 9:3-27). Saul had broken the agreement and murdered a number of the Gibeonites. David concluded that the famine was a punishment for this act of Saul, and he set about to make expiation. All of nature would be out of joint until the wrong had been righted; so the Gibeonites demanded that seven members of the family of Saul be executed (II Sam. 21:6). Mephibosheth, the son of Jonathan, was spared but seven other members of the house of Saul were hanged (II Sam. 21:7-10).

The hanging took place at the beginning of the barley harvest, in late April or May. The bodies of Rizpah's two sons and the five others of Saul's family were exposed, unburied for the entire summer until the autumn rains came. In honor to the dead, Rizpah watched over the bodies to preserve them from the birds and animals which would normally devour the dead. Exposure was evidently part of the expiation demanded by the Gibeonites, but David was moved by the loyalty of Rizpah and ordered a proper burial. The bones of those who had been hanged, along with the bones of Saul and Jonathan taken from Jabesh-gilead were buried in the family tomb of Kish, Saul's father (II Sam. 21:10:14).

The wrath of God which resulted from David's census comes

at the close of a series of tragedies which plagued David's last days (II Sam. 24:1-17). With the aid of Joab and the army the entire land "from Dan to Beer-sheba" on both sides of the Jordan was covered in nine months and twenty days. Joab reported that there were eight hundred thousand fighting men in Israel, and five hundred thousand in Judah — round figures, of course.

A census was never popular in the East. It had as its purpose the gathering of information for purposes of military conscription and taxation, neither of which were popular with the people. After taking the census, David had an uneasy conscience (II Sam. 24:10) fearing that he had done wrong. The prophet Gad confirmed the fact that he had yielded to temptation and suggested that God's judgment would come upon him in one of three ways. The land might experience three years of famine, or David might flee three months before his enemies, or pestilence might come upon the land for three days (I Sam. 24:12-13). Trusting the mercy of the Lord rather than the wrath of his enemies, David accepted a period of pestilence which filled the land and threatened Jerusalem itself. When the messenger of the Lord was at the threshingfloor of Araunah, his hand was stayed and the plague ended. Then Gad, the prophet, told David to erect an altar of Araunah's threshingfloor. David purchased the threshingfloor and the animals for the sacrifices which he made, and the plague ended.

The site of Araunah's threshingfloor later became the site of Solomon's Temple. David thus prepared the way for the building of the Temple, although it was his son Solomon who would see the sacred structure rise.

The last days of David were marked by senility. Abishag, a young girl from Shunem in the Plain of Esdraelon was brought to the court to care for the king. Sexually he was impotent, so Abishag cannot be considered one of David's wives. During the period of David's senility the final contest for the throne took place. Solomon emerged successful, with David's blessing.

5

SOLOMON IN ALL HIS GLORY

As David reached senility, the factions in his court at Jerusalem were giving serious thought to the question of succession.
David's oldest living son, Adonijah, seemed to be the logical
choice. Joab, David's general, and the priest Abiathar were
among those who were prepared to anoint Adonijah. There
were important segments of the court that were not included in
these plans. Benaiah, commander of David's personal body-
guard, wielded considerable power. Nathan, David's court
prophet and personal counselor, was not ready to support
Adonijah, preferring Solomon, the surviving son of Bath-sheba.

While the partisans of Adonijah were offering sacrifices, preliminary to the anointing, Nathan made his way to Bath-sheba
to warn her of the impending coup. Although Nathan had denounced David for his affair with Bath-sheba, he now sided
with her in her desire to see Solomon on the throne of Israel.
In spite of the way in which David's relation with Bath-sheba
had begun, the king seems to have developed a close relationship with her, and even Nathan had come to accept her. Bath-
sheba reminded David that he had vowed that her son Solomon
would succeed to the throne (I Kings 1:17). Adonijah might be
expected to purge the land of all possible rivals, with the result
that Bath-sheba and Solomon would be killed (1:21).

When Nathan gave further details concerning Adonijah's
plans, David determined to act at once. Zadok the priest and
Nathan the prophet were instructed to bring Solomon to the
Gihon, now called the Virgin's Fountain, a short distance north
of En-rogel, "Job's Well," where Adonijah's partisans were assembled. A curve in the valley of the Kidron made it impossible
for the two groups to see one another, but they were well within
earshot of one another. With the aid of Benaiah and the royal

guard, Zadok and Nathan anointed Solomon, and the assembled crowd cried out, "Long live King Solomon" (1:39). The scene was joyful, with singing and the playing of instruments to commemorate the occasion.

Around the bend in the valley, however, the partisans of Adonijah heard the sound and puzzled over its meaning. Finally Jonathan, Abiathar's son, arrived with news that King David had ordered the anointing of Solomon as king. Adonijah realized that he could not hope to stand against the forces of David, so he rushed into the temple and sought sanctuary at the altar. A person touching the projections from the altar ("horns") was not supposed to be slain, and Adonijah determined to stay in the sanctuary until he would get a promise of safety from Solomon. Solomon was cautious, stating that Adonijah would not be harmed as long as he behaved himself (1:52). For the moment Adonijah felt that he was safe.

David died shortly after Solomon took the throne. In his old age a girl from Shunem had been brought to minister to the king. Had he been younger he might have married her, but the Biblical writer tells us "the king knew her not" (1:4), i.e. he had no marital relations with her.

Whatever his motives, Adonijah certainly showed a lack of judgment in approaching Bath-sheba and asking her to intercede with Solomon to permit him to marry Abishag. Such a request could be interpreted as a claim to the kingdom, for a king normally laid claim to his predecessor's harem. Solomon put the worst possible construction on the request, and in anger said to Bath-sheba, "Ask for him the kingdom also . . . !" (2:22). Solomon sent Benaiah, captain of the guard, to kill Adonijah.

Since Abiathar was a priest, Solomon did not order his execution for having taken Adonijah's side. Abiathar had been an honored priest during David's reign, and Solomon was content to banish him to his estate in Anathoth, about three miles north of Jerusalem. Joab, however, did not fare so well. Realizing that Solomon was purging the partisans of Adonijah, Joab fled to the altar and sought sanctuary. Benaiah hesitated to strike him down at a holy place, but Solomon showed no mercy. For justification he could invoke the law of blood revenge. Joab had slain Amasa, one time leader of Absalom's army, and Abner, Saul's commander who had shifted allegiance from Saul's son,

Ishbosheth, to David. At Solomon's command Benaiah killed Joab and succeeded him as commander of the army. Zadok, who had sided with Solomon against Adonijah, became High Priest in place of the deposed Abiathar.

The purge continued as Solomon sought to limit the movements of Shimei, the Benjaminite who had accused David of complicity in the extermination of Saul's house (II Sam. 16:5-8). David, who had not lifted his hand against any of the house of Saul, spared Shimei, but Solomon restricted him to Jerusalem. When Shimei pursued two fugitive slaves to Gath he incurred the wrath of Solomon. Again Benaiah was dispatched to execute an offender. Solomon had purged his realm of real and imaginary foes. Presumably he could now rule without fear.

The personal life of Solomon is full of those contradictions which plague us all. At times he seems a saint, and at other times a scoundrel. History has dealt kindly with Solomon; perhaps too kindly. We choose to remember him as a man of wisdom, forgetting that he was a man of his age and that in many facets of his life he exhibited the worst features of life as it was lived three millennia ago.

Solomon's domestic life is a case in point. Early in his career he married an Egyptian princess (I Kings 3:1), no mean accomplishment in itself. In a day when Egypt was stronger and Israel weaker, a Pharaoh might take an Israelite girl into his harem, but he certainly would not have given one of his daughters to an Israelite king. During the reigns of David and Solomon, Israel reached its highest level of international prestige. At such a time marriage can become a matter of diplomatic convenience: "Solomon made a marriage alliance with Pharaoh" (I Kings 3:1). This was not Solomon's only "marriage alliance." We are told that he had "seven hundred wives, princesses, and three hundred concubines" (I Kings 11:3). A large harem was the result of such alliances, and it also suggests the oriental grandeur which had come to mark Solomon's court. The king of a major state must have a harem worthy of his position. The larger it was, the more prestige would be accounted to the monarch. In simple language, a large harem was a status symbol, and Solomon was interested in status. It is hard to realize that only three generations passed between the days when Saul reigned from his humble court at Gibeah, to the magnificence of Solomon in all his glory. Externally these were years of progress, yet trouble was already on the horizon. Solomon's wives came from many nations, and they worshiped many gods. As a kind husband, Solomon permitted them to build shrines to their deities. Before long we find Solomon, himself, enmeshed in idolatry.

If Solomon puzzles and annoys us with his large harem, he pleases us with his quest for wisdom. As a young king he offered sacrifices to his God at Gibeon. In a dream, Solomon heard the voice of the Lord saying, "Ask what I shall give you" (I Kings 3:5). Solomon is at his best in his reply. He acknowledged the blessings of God upon him, his own inexperience: "I am but a little child," and his lack of knowledge: "I do not know how to go out or come in" (I Kings 3:7). In humility he prayed, "Give thy servant therefore an understanding mind to govern thy people, that I may discern between good and evil" (3:9).

From this time on, Solomon's wisdom became proverbial. The Near East had had a long tradition of Wisdom Literature stretching back to the Egypt and Mesopotamia of the third millennium B.C. Yet, the Biblical historian tells us, Solomon's wisdom "surpassed all the wisdom of all the people of the east, and all the wisdom of Egypt" (4:30). Traditionally the books of Proverbs, Ecclesiastes, and the Song of Solomon have been attributed to him, although the hand of other wise men is occasionally evident in them.[1]

The practical nature of the wisdom Solomon sought is evident in the story of two harlots who had each given birth to a child. One of the infants died, but both women claimed the surviving child as her own. Solomon suggested a solution: "Divide the living child in two and give half to the one and half to the other." One of the women was content to accept the king's solution to the problem, but the living child's mother suggested that the child be given to the other woman, and not slain (3:16-28). The woman who showed concern for the child above her own rights proved to be the mother of the child, and Solomon ordered that the child be given to her.

---

1. Proverbs 25:1 tells us that proverbs attributed to Solomon were gathered into collections as late as the time of Hezekiah. Proverbs 30:1 and 31:1 name Agur and Lemuel (or Lemuel's mother) as authors of collections of proverbs.

That the fame of Solomon spread to distant lands is evident from the story of the visit to Solomon's court of the Queen of Sheba, a land in southern Arabia about twelve hundred miles from Jerusalem. This queen from the area that we know as Yemen was doubtless willing to make the long journey to Jerusalem in order to meet Israel's wise king and to negotiate trade agreements with him. The queen brought a large caravan bearing spices, gold, and precious stones for Solomon. In return, Solomon dealt generously with her, giving her all that she might desire when she returned home. Solomon showed his wisdom in the answers he gave to her hard questions, and the queen observed, "The report was true which I heard in my own land of your affairs and your wisdom, but I did not believe the reports until I came and my own eyes had seen it; and, behold, the half was not told me; your wisdom and prosperity surpass the report which I heard" (9:6-7).

Tradition has added to the story of Solomon and the Queen of Sheba. Ethiopian legend tells of a child of Solomon and the Queen of Sheba who became king and established a Davidic dynasty in Ethiopia. The legend suggests the close connections which existed in antiquity between southern Arabia and eastern Africa. Arabian legends name the Queen of Sheba, Bilqis.

King Solomon was an able organizer, and he gave a form to the political life of Israel such as it never had before. In his court we find the chief priest, royal scribes or secretaries, a recorder, a military commander, a palace governor, the chief of the corvee (forced labor batallions) and other priests and counselors (I Kings 4:1-6).

The country was divided into twelve administrative districts, each of which had a governor who was responsible for providing for the royal household one month a year. The twelve districts did not follow the older tribal lines, a fact which may indicate that Solomon wished to break down old tribal loyalties in the interest of a strong centralized government.

Although best known for the Temple which he built, Solomon built and enlarged many other structures in Jerusalem and elsewhere. He spent thirteen years on his palace and administrative complex (I Kings 7:1-12). Solomon expanded the Jerusalem fortifications and built fortresses in strategic parts of

Storage Pit at Megiddo. Note the stairs which circle down the side. *Courtesy, Oriental Institute, University of Chicago*

Megiddo, overlooking the Esraelon Valley was one of the cities fortified by Solomon. *Courtesy, Oriental Institute, University of Chicago*

the country. Hazor held the key to the far north, and Megiddo protected the Esdraelon Valley. The fortress at Gezer overlooked the Aijalon and the Sorek valleys.

After twenty years of major construction work, Solomon found it difficult to pay his debts. As time went on he found it increasingly difficult to pressure the people into paying higher taxes, and tribute from subject states became increasingly hard to collect. In his extremity Solomon had to cede twenty cities in Galilee to Hiram of Tyre for a cash consideration (I Kings 9:10-14).

Solomon is not remembered as a warrior, but he did give considerable attention to problems of defense. Not only was Jerusalem fortified, but Solomon developed a chain of cities along the perimeter of Israel to provide defense against raids from Israel's neighbors. Hazor in Galilee faced Aramean territory; Meggiddo faced the main pass through the Valley of Esdraelon; Gezer, Beth-horon, and Baalah guarded the western approaches to Israel from the maritime plain, and Tamar, south of the Dead Sea faced Edom (I Kings 9:15-19).

From these strongholds, Solomon could easily maneuver his forces to meet external threats or internal emergencies. In earlier days the mountainous terrain of Israelite territory discouraged the use of chariots. Canaanites found them useful on level ground, but Israelites felt no need for them. With the annexation of Canaanite city-states into Israel, Solomon determined to develop chariot warfare as part of his defense system. We read

Stables at Megiddo, reconstructed. Many scholars date them from the time of Solomon. *Courtesy, Oriental Institute, University of Chicago*

that he had fourteen hundred chariots and twelve thousand horsemen stationed in Jerusalem and in the chariot cities (I Kings 11:26). Excavations at Megiddo have brought to light stables for four hundred fifty horses, along with city fortifications and the governor's residence. Similar installations have been discovered during excavations at Hazor, Taanach, Eglon, and Gezer. Evidence suggests that Solomon maintained a large standing army as part of his military strategy.

Solomon's age was one in which Israelite trade and commerce flourished by land and sea. Ezion-geber served as the terminal port for trade with southern Arabia (I Kings 9:26-28). This port at the north end of the Gulf of Aqabah, contained a copper and iron smelting refinery, was strongly walled, and located two and one-half miles west of the old city of Elath, modern Aqabah. This site, now known as Tell el-Kheleifeh, stood in the path of winds which howled down the Arabah Valley and provided a

Copper Mining in Wadi Arabah, south of the Dead Sea, was a major industry during the days of Solomon. *Courtesy, Israel Information Service*

natural draft for firing the furnaces. Ores were mined in the Arabah valley which is still rich in copper.

Hiram of Tyre assisted Solomon in building and maintaining a merchant fleet. The Phoenicians of Tyre were old hands at sea trade, for their principal cities were on the Mediterranean coast and Tyrian mariners early built ships and set out for the islands and coastlands bordering the Mediterranean. It was these very mariners who taught their Greek counterparts the use of the alphabet. The best known of their colonies was Carthage, in Africa, which vied with Rome at a later day for control of the Mediterranean.

With Hiram's help, Solomon developed a fleet which brought gold, sandlewood, and precious stones to Jerusalem (I Kings 10:11). Solomon had to import horses for his chariotry. These came from Egypt and from Kue in Cilicia, southeastern Asia Minor. Rulers of the neo-Hittite principalities of northern Syria looked to Solomon for their horses and chariots (I Kings 10:29).

Solomon's merchant fleet went on long journeys, bringing back such exotic items as ivory, apes, and peacocks (or baboons, in an alternate translation). Ships left the port at Ezion-geber and visited the coastal ports of Africa where such items were secured by trade. The Biblical writer tells us that ships returned with these items but once in three years (I Kings 10:22).

More regular was the tribute in silver, gold, garments, myrrh, spices, horses, and mules which tributary kings brought annually to Solomon's court (I Kings 10:23-24). From the standpoint of material grandeur, the era of Solomon was never to be equalled in the history of Israel.

There is, however, a negative side to all of this. Like Saul and David, Solomon was to experience a series of tragedies during the closing years of his reign. His wives and concubines influenced him in the direction of idolatory, so that Solomon, himself, came to worship the gods of the Sidonians, the Ammonites and the Moabites (I Kings 11:5-8). A crowning insult to Yahweh, God of Israel, was the erection of a shrine for the god Molech on the Mount of Olives, east of Jerusalem. The worship of Molech was associated with the sacrifice of children in fire (cf. Lev. 18:21; II Kings 23:10).

During this period of decline we find the beginning of disintegration within Solomon's empire. Hadad, a member of the royal family of Edom, had fled to Egypt when David conquered

Edom, but he returned to lead a revolt against Solomon in the
interest of Edomite independence (I Kings 11:14-22). Rezon, an
Aramean, set up an independent kingdom at Damascus in Syria.
He was successful in defying Solomon, outlived the Israelite
United Kingdom and established his own dynasty in Damascus.

Even more threatening was Jeroboam the son of Nebat who
was in charge of the forced labor units from the Joseph tribes
— Ephraim and Manasseh. On day a prophet named Ahijah from
Shiloh met Jeroboam on the road. The prophet took his garment,
tore it into twelve pieces and gave ten of them to Jeroboam. In
explanation he stated that God was about to tear the kingdom
from Solomon and give ten of the twelve tribes to Jeroboam
(I Kings 11:30). Ahijah, like others who remembered the happier
days before Solomon's court had taken on a cosmopolitan air,
felt that God was about to judge the king for his idolatry.

When Solomon learned of Jeroboam's ambition he determined
to kill him, but Jeroboam fled to Egypt where Shishak was king.
At the beginning of Solomon's reign a Pharaoh of Egypt had
given his daughter as Solomon's wife. Now a Pharaoh offered
refuge to Solomon's enemy. Egypt had seen a change of dynasty, and relations between Israel and Egypt had seriously
deteriorated.

The kingdom held together to the end of Solomon's life, but
the king who was noted for his wisdom brought the kingdom
to the verge of bankruptcy. Within a short time after Solomon's
death the prophecy of Ahijah was fulfilled and the Davidic dynasty was limited to the south. Solomon was the last king of
the United Kingdom.

6

SOLOMON'S TEMPLE

The crowning achievement of Solomon's reign was the construction of a Temple to the God of Israel. David had made Jerusalem his political and religious capital, and had directed that the sacred ark he brought to the Holy City. During the days of wilderness wandering the Israelites had used a portable shrine, the Tabernacle, as their sanctuary. Now that they were settled in their land, a permanent shrine seemed to be demanded.

Between the fourth and the eleventh years of his reign, Solomon supervised the construction of a small but elegant Temple. Like the Tabernacle which preceded it, the Temple was not designed to accomodate worshipers. Its inner shrine was regarded as God's Throne Room, and it was entered but once a year — on the Day of Atonement — by the High Priest. Priests had access to the outer shrine — the Holy Place — where they would replenish the supplies of oil, incense, and bread.

Since the site of Solomon's Temple has been occupied through the centuries, archaeological studies of the site have not been made. Some light on Syro-Palestinian temples has come from the discovery of an eighth century B.C. temple at Tell Tainat, ancient Hattina, in Syria. The basic ground plan of the Tainat temple is similar to that described in I Kings.

Solomon drew upon his alliance with Hiram of Tyre to procure skilled Phoenician workmen (I Kings 5:6). A contingent came from Gebal (Byblos) to assist in the work. Thirty-thousand Israelites were used in procuring materials (5:13). At the time the Temple was built, Israel enjoyed the prestige and wealth of a nation to which tribute was paid by subject states. No expense was spared in building the Temple. The use of forced labor, however, became very unpopular and it added to Solomon's heartaches during the closing years of his reign.

Northwest Corner of the Temple Area. In New Testament times the Tower of Antonia was located here. *Courtesy, Matson Photo Service*

The Temple was a long, narrow structure, about one hundred feet long and thirty feet wide. At the front was a vestibule, or entrance hall with windows, the number and size of which is not specified. Beyond the vestibule was the Holy Place which was the main room of the Temple. Next, in the form of a perfect cube of twenty cubits in each direction, was the inner shrine, the Most Holy Place.

Around the entire structure, except the vestibule, were side chambers, arranged in three stories. We are not sure how these were divided into rooms, but Temple treasures were assuredly kept in these chambers. The Temple was approached by ten broad steps, with two landings in the flight providing space for ceremonial processions. To the right and the left of the steps were two free standing pillars called Jachin and Boaz. Jachin means "he [God] establishes," and Boaz means, "In Him [God] is strength." The significance of the names for the pillars has been debated, but scholars are not agreed. The pillars were cast in the clay of the Jordan valley, and made of burnished copper. According to the Biblical text they were nearly forty feet high, with a diameter of about six and one-half feet. They appear to have been hollow, with the metal four fingers (about three inches) thick.

The basic material for the Temple was white limestone, finished at the quarries by Hebrew and Phoenician laborers (I Kings 5:18; 6:7). The interior walls were covered with cedar, and the floor with boards of Cyprus so that no stone could be seen from the inside. According to the English translations, much of the cedar wood was overlaid with gold (6:21), but W. F. Stinespring is probably right in suggesting that inlay rather than overlay is intended.[1] Ivory inlay is well known from excavations at Samaria, and it is likely that similar techniques were used with gold. The inside walls were carved with figures of cherubim, palm trees, and flowers (6:29).

There was no door to the vestibule, but large elaborately decorated doors opened into the Holy Place (6:33-35). A smaller double door, with similar decorations, opened into the Holy of Holies (6:31-32). Within the Holy of Holies were two huge cherubim of gold-trimmed olivewood. They were each ten cubits high, with a wingspread of ten cubits. They faced the front so that a wing of each cherub touched the wall, and the other two

---

1. "Temple, Jerusalem," Interpreter's Dictionary of the Bible, IV, p. 537.

wings touched in the center of the room. Beneath these wings
the ark of the covenant was placed (8:6-7).

Within the Holy Place we find a number of articles of gold.
Here was the golden Altar of Incense standing before the steps
to the Holy of Holies. Five lampstands stood on each side of the
entrance to the Holy of Holies, and nearby stood the table for
the "Bread of the Presence" or "shewbread." Fresh loaves of
bread were brought to the sanctuary each sabbath, and the old
loaves were eaten by the priests.

Outside the Temple proper, but within the court we find the
great altar for burnt offering, made of bronze, and the huge
basin known as the "molten sea" with a capacity of two thousand
baths, or approximately ten thousand gallons. The molten sea
was ten cubits (about seventeen and one-half feet) in diameter,
thirty cubits in circumference, and ten cubits deep. It was a
handbreadth thick, and was decorated with two rows of gourds
all the way around. The cup-like brim resembled the flower of
a lily.

This huge basin rested on twelve bronze bulls, arranged in
groups of three, each facing one of the four points of the com-
pass. The author of II Chronicles (4:6) suggests that the molten
sea was a place for ceremonial washing by the priests as they
prepared to minister in the Temple. Modern scholars see a cos-
mic symbolism in the molten sea, suggesting that water or the
sea is frequently a source of life in Near Eastern mythology.
The bulls on which the basin rested may also be likened to
representations of the fecundity principle in the Baal cult. In
view of the Phoenician artisans and craftsmen who assisted in
the building of the Temple, such symbolism may have been
intended. The faithful Yahwist in Israel, however, would have
rejected pagan symbolism, and would have seen the molten sea
as a laver of cleansing for the priest as he would prepare to enter
the Sanctuary.

We also find ten highly ornamented bronze wagons, on each
of which was mounted one of the ten lavers, or wash basins, in
the Temple court. Each of the lavers had a capacity of forty
baths (about two hundred gallons). These would serve the
priesthood in their ceremonial washings (I Kings 7:27-39).

The splendor and artistry of Solomon's Temple suggests the
prestige which Israel enjoyed during the Solomonic age. King
Hiram of Tyre sent an architect-artisan, also named Hiram (I
Kings 7:13) to the court of Solomon to work on the Temple. He

cast the bronze pillars, the molten sea, and other furnishings of the Temple in specially suited clay found in the Jordan Valley between Succoth and Zarethan. Seven years of Solomon's career were spent in the building of the Temple which stood as the center of religious life in Judah until the destruction of Jerusalem by the forces of Nebuchadnezzar in 587 B.C.

7

ISRAEL AND THE PHOENICIANS

The northern coastal regions of the Syria-Palestine area, comprising such cities as Tyre, Sidon, and Byblos, were known in ancient times as Phoenicia. The name is the Greek equivalent of the word Canaan, which appears in the form *kinahhu* in the Nuzi texts, with the meaning, "purple." Greek *phoinix* has the same meaning. When used of the Phoenician people it refers to the industry of dyeing fabrics with purple derived from the murex shellfish, which is indigenous to the area which we know as Phoenicia. Since the area was divided into independent city states, our texts are more apt to speak of Tyrians or Sidonians than Phoenicians or Canaanites, yet the culture was sufficiently homogenous to warrant consideration in its own right.

Geography made the life and goals of the Phoenicians differ in a marked degree from that of other Semitic peoples of the Near East, including the Israelites. The distinctive area of the Phoenician cities was bounded by the Lebanon Mountains to the east, and the Mediterranean to the west. The distance between mountains and sea varies from seven to thirty miles. Northern and southern boundaries varied, but Phoenicia was always a narrow strip of land with small valleys bringing water from the mountains, making the land the most fertile of the entire Near East, as visitors to Lebanon observe today.

Rocky promontories stretch into the Mediterranean, and the Phoenicians frequently used them for building cities with harbors that might face both north and south. Roads were difficult to build in this rocky terrain, but sea travel was always at hand, and the Phoenicians excelled as mariners. Instead of building a land empire, thus clashing with Israelite and Philistine goals, the Phoenicians colonized the islands and coastlands of the Mediterranean. Best known of these colonies was Carthage in North

Africa which challenged Roman control of the Mediterranean at a much later time. Vergil in his Aenead has Aeneas forsake Dido of Carthage because destiny has called him to become the ancestor of the Romans in Italy. Dido's curses upon him form a rationale for the subsequent hatred between Carthaginian and Roman. Like other Phoenicians (Canaanites), the Carthaginian pantheon included the god Baal. The great Hannibal had a name comparable to Biblical Hananiah, the former meaning "Baal has been gracious," and the latter, "Yahweh has been gracious."

It was during these journeys of Phoenician mariners that the Semitic alphabet was passed on to the Greeks, another seafaring people. The Greeks modified the Semitic alphabet for their own purposes and, with later modifications, this alphabet is used throughout the West today. Even the Russian alphabet is derived from the Greek, introduced as it was by missionaries in the process of bringing Christianity to the slavic peoples.

Although the extent of arable land was limited, the Phoenicians grew figs, olives, grapes, and wheat. The date palm was abundant in ancient times, as were the cedars which were famous throughout the Near East. Expeditions came from Egypt and Mesopotamia to procure this fine wood for use in temples, palaces, and sacred barges. The cedars are nearly depleted, and the state of Lebanon is preserving the remaining groves as state property.

Phoenician history must be reconstructed from a variety of ancient sources. While we have a corpus of ancient Phoenician inscriptions, they do not enable us to recognize any coherent pattern. They mention individual rulers of Phoenician cities and, on occasion, dynastic successions. Dedicatory inscriptions appear on Phoenician monuments, and the protective deities are frequently invoked. Tenth century Byblos provided many such texts, but on the whole information is scanty.

Although writing in the first century of the Christian era, Josephus quotes valuable matter for understanding Phoenician history from Menander of Ephesus. Menander quoted from a work known as the Annals of Tyre, and his references relate events from the tenth to the eighth centuries, and from the sixth century B.C. Compared with Biblical material and other ancient sources, these quotations appear to be accurate.

Egyptian and Assyrian texts provide a further source of information. The Assyrian annals describe the subjugation of

Phoenician cities during campaigns of the Assyrian kings in western Asia. The Egyptian tale of Wenamun shows that Egyptian prestige had suffered greatly in Phoenician by the middle of the eleventh century B.C.

The invasions of the Sea Peoples, peoples from the Aegean area, about 1200 B.C. had important results throughout the eastern Mediterranean. The Hittite Empire of Asia Minor fell, as did the Phoenician states of Aradus and Sidon. The Egyptian Empire entered a period of weakness from which it never fully recovered, and Assyria was confined within her borders. With the major powers at least temporarily checked, the smaller Hebrew, Aramaean, and Phoenician states emerged as independent units, sometimes co-operating and sometimes fighting one another.

The leading Phoenician cities of the time were Aradus, Byblos (Gebal), Sidon, Tyre, and Akko. The term "Sidonians" is used both in the Old Testament and in Homer for the Phoenicians in general, leading to the conclusion that Sidon was the dominant city of the period. Josephus states that Sidon was defeated by the king of the Ascalonians — Askelon being a Philistine city, and Philistines were among the "Sea Peoples" — at a date which seems to have been shortly after 1200 B.C. According to Josephus, the defeated Sidonians fled to the area of Tyre and founded the city. While Tyre is known to have existed prior to this time, it is possible that the city had been sacked by the Sea Peoples and was rebuilt by the Sidonians. Sidon was the principal Phoenician city until about 1000 B.C., after which Tyre came to dominate the area.

While we might expect that Philistines, Phoenicians, and Israelites would be major rivals in the Syria-Palestine area, the Bible indicates friendly relations between Israel and Phoenicia. It is possible that David included portions of the Phoenician coast in his kingdom.[1] That Tyre remained independent, however, is obvious from the fact that Hiram, its king, provided David with craftsmen and cedar wood for his palace (II Sam. 5:11).

Our knowledge of relations between Hiram and David's successor, Solomon, are more complete. The Annals present Hiram as a builder in his own right. He is said to have enlarged the city

---

1. The census account of II Sam. 24:6-7 mentions the regions of Tyre and Sidon.

and to have built new temples to Melqart (Heracles) and Astarte. An impressive golden column was erected in the temple
of Baal Shamem (Zeus Olympus). A war was fought with Kition,
the Phoenician colony of Cyprus, because its inhabitants refused
to pay tribute.[2]

When Solomon determined to build a Temple to Yahweh, he
drew upon the experience of Hiram and requested cedar and
fir trees for use in its construction (I Kings 5:1-11). For his part,
Solomon provided wheat and oil as payment to the Tyrian king.
Evidently Solomon found himself unable to provide adequate
payment for the materials and artisans which Hiram provided,
for he ceded twenty Galilean cities to the Tyrians (I Kings
9:10-14).

The fact that Solomon enlisted the cooperation of Hiram in
sending ships from Ezion-geber into the Red Sea and beyond, is
testimonial both to the wealth of Solomon's kingdom and the
maritime skill of the Phoenicians. Israel was basically a land
state, and it was prudent of Solomon to enlist the aid of the seafaring Phoenicians in his commercial venture to the land of
Ophir (I Kings 9:26-28). The location of Ophir is much disputed, with India, southern Arabia, and Somaliland in Africa
being suggested. While it is unlikely that Solomon's ships traded
directly with India, they brought back exotic products including
gold, silver, ivory, and apes (I Kings 10:22). Such items may
have been secured in Africa or southern Arabia.

The combined Israelite-Tyrian expeditions were evidently
successful, for we are told that the ships went forth once in three
years. We must assume that such cooperative ventures ended
during the last years of Solomon when his kingdom began to
disintegrate. During the period of the Divided Kingdom, Tyre
remained a potent force. The marriage of Jezebel, daughter of
Ittobaal of Tyre, to Ahab, the son of Omri of Israel, precipitated
the religious conflict during which Elijah emerged as the prophet
of Yahweh.

---

2. Josephus, *Contra Apion*, I, 118.

8

BABYLONIA AND ASSYRIA

Shortly after the reign of the famous lawgiver, Hammurabi (*ca.* 1728-1686 B.C.), the Old Babylonian Empire came to an end. The Hittite Empire was extending eastward and southward from its strongholds in central Asia Minor and, under Mursilis I, reached as far as Babylon (1530 B.C.). While Babylon was destroyed, and its first dynasty ended, the Hittites were unable to follow up their victory. Dynastic struggles at home forced Mursilis to return with such booty as he could take with him, only to be assassinated by his brother Hantilis.

Babylon was never incorporated into the Hittite Empire, but Mursilis' raid opened the way for a people from the Zagros Mountain region, the Kassites, to assume power. Kassites had looked upon the fertile Tigris-Euphrates area as ripe for occupation for some time. The Hittites had weakened Babylon to the point that the Kassites found little resistance as they took over. Agum II, a Kassite king, occupied Babylon and extended his power up the Middle Euphrates as far as Hana, and claimed the territory of Gutium in the hills to the east of Assyria.

The culture of the Kassites was inferior to that which had developed in the Tigris-Euphrates valley since the time of the Sumerians. A period of cultural lag followed, but the Kassites soon learned to adopt and adapt the superior culture of the land they had come to occupy. Kassite Babylon adopted the Semitic Akkadian language of the Old Babylonian Empire, and the cuneiform script which had first been introduced into southern Mesopotamia by the Sumerians prior to 3000 B.C.

The Amarna letters, discovered in Egypt in 1887, show that Akkadian cuneiform was the lingua franca of the Middle East during the Amarna Age — the fifteenth and fourteenth centuries B.C. The letters contain correspondence between the Egyptian Pharaohs Amenhotep III (1406-1370 B.C.) and his son

Amenhotep IV, Akhenaten (1370-1353 B.C.) on the one hand, and the kings of the Hittites, Mitanni, Assyria, and Kassite Babylon, along with princees of the city states of Syria and Palestine on the other. If the Kassites added little to Babylonian culture, at least they preserved what they inherited.

While the Kassites were consolidating control in Babylonia, farther north in Assyria and adjacent lands a people known as Hurrians (Biblical Horites, Gen. 14:6; Deut. 2:12) came to exercise a dominant position. As early as the third millennium B.C. Hurrians had migrated southward from the Caucasus Mountain region into the mountains north of Assyria. By the time of Sargon of Akkad (*ca.* 2360 B.C.) there was a Hurrrian kingdom centered at Urkish, a city in the Habur region west of Assyria. By the time of the Third Dynasty of Ur (*ca.* 2060-1950 B.C.) Hurrian names appear in texts from Dilbat, near Babylon. During the centuries that followed, evidence of Hurrian names appears in documents from Nuzi and Arrapkha in the area east of Assyria near modern Kirkuk, and in the Syrian cities of Qatna, Alalah, and Ugarit. Mari, on the Middle Euphrates, has yielded a number of ritual texts in the Hurrian language.

During his raid on Babylon, the Hittite ruler Mursilis I fought Hurrian princes along the upper Euphrates. After his death, dynastic confusion weakened the Hittite cause with the result that a major Hurrian state known as Mittani developed in the Habur River area of northern Mesopotamia. The Hurrians were the nucleous of the Mittani population, although an Indo-Aryan warrior caste ruled the region. The old Indian gods Mitra, Varuna, Indra, and the Nasitiyas were worshipped at Mitanni. Hurrian and Aryan lived together in peace. There was intermarriage between the two groups, and Hurrians are found among the ruling class.[1]

By the time of the Mitannian ruler Saushsatar (*ca.* 1450 B.C.), a contemporary of Thutmose III of Egypt, Mitanni extended from Nuzi, east of the Tigris, westward to northern Syria, and perhaps as far as the Mediterranean. Assyria was a part of the Mitannian Empire, and the rulers of Mitanni brought booty from the Assyrian cities to their capital city. A letter from Tushratta of Mitanni to Amenhotep III of Egypt states that Ishtar of Nineveh had expressed a desire to visit the Egyptian

---

1. See R. T. O'Callaghan, *Aram Naharaim* (Rome: Pontifical Biblical Institute, 1948), pp. 51-92.

court again, mentioning a former visit in the days of one of
Tushratta's predecessors. The goddess Ishtar was a favorite
throughout Mesopotamia. The fact that a Mitannian ruler could
send her image to Egypt is ample evidence of the power of
Mitanni during the Amarna Age.

The Kassites of Babylon appear to have been mild rulers, with
the result that the land was not rent with inner dissention. Assyria (a vassal of Mitanni) and Elam continued to threaten
Babylon, but internal unity was a help in international relations. A Kassite princess was sent to the court of Amenhotep
III to secure an alliance with Egypt. Kurigalzu, king of Kassite
Babylon during the Amarna Age, conducted successful campaigns against Elam, over a potential enemy. He also is known
for temple restoration at the old cities of Erech, Ur, and Eridu
with histories going back to Sumerian times. At Aqarquf, near
Baghdad, the visitor may still see the remains of a fortified capital built by Kurigalzu.

By the time of Kurigalzu, Mitanni had passed the zenith of
its power. With the accession of the powerful Hittite ruler
Shuppiluliuma (*ca.* 1390 B.C.), Mittanian power began to decline. Pro-Egyptian and anti-Egyptian factions vied for power.
Since Egypt and the Hittites vied for control of Syria and Palestine, Mitanni was in a potentially dangerous position. Tushratta
of Mitanni, mentioned in the Amarna letters was pro-Egyptian
in his sympathies, but his younger brother, Artatama, became
ruler of a break-away section of the kingdom in the old Hurrian
homeland south of Lake Van. Artatama was pro-Hittite in his
loyalties.

Tushratta looked in vain to Egypt for aid. Shuppiluliuma
annexed the Hurrian states of north Syria, erstwhile vassals of
Egypt or Mitanni. Around 1350 B.C. Tushratta was murdered
by a son supporting the party of Artatama and the Hittites. In
name the kingdom would continue, but in fact Mitanni had
ceased to matter in world politics.

The practical demise of Mitanni brought the possibility of
independence and power to Assyria. A measure of freedom came
during the days of Tushratta, when Mitanni was threatened
with inner dissention. Burnaburiash II, a successor of Kurigalzu
on the throne of Babylon, complained when Ashur-uballit I of
Assyria had an ambassador accepted at the Egyptian court. With
Assyria's independence from Mittani an accepted fact, Babylonia
evidently hoped to exercise suzerainty over her neighbor to the

north. Babylon's protest was in vain, and an alliance between Assyria and Babylon was established by the marriage of Ashur-uballit's daughter to Kara-indash, son and heir of Burnaburiash.

With Assyria's growth in power, Shuppiluliuma evidently saw the wisdom of preserving Mitanni as a buffer zone. The Hittite ruler assisted Matiwaza, heir to Tushratta, to regain the contested throne of Mitanni. With the loss of Assyria to the east, and Carchemish in the west, Mitanni was now relatively small and insignificant in world politics. The name Hanigalbat is usually used of this successor state to the once powerful Mitannian kingdom. Three Hurrian princes of Hanigalbat are known, and all had to defend themselves against the expanding Assyrian state. Adad-nirari I (1307-1275 B.C.) conquered Shatturara I of Hanigalbat and made him his vassal. Shattuara's successor revolted, but he was reconquered. Shalmaneser I (1274-1245 B.C.) conquered Shattuara II, and Hanigalbat became an Assyrian province. About 14,000 prisoners were deported from Hanigalbat, a fact of significance because it illustrates the Assyrian policy of deportation later used against the Israelites in the days of Sargon II.

Tukulti-Ninurta I (1244-1208 B.C.) continued the policies of conquests in the north and west, accompanied by extensive deportations. Most significantly, Tukulti-Ninurta conquered Babylon, bringing it under Assyrian control for the first time. The Assyrian appraisal of the event is given in an Assyrian work known as the *Epic of Tukulti-Ninurta*. It recounts how Enlil — the great god — had chosen Tukulti-Ninurta to overthrow Kashtiliash IV, the Kassite king of Babylon who had broken his oath and, in consequence, was deserted by the gods.

Assyrian administrators found their way to Babylon, and Assyrian control was established with a firm hand. The statue of Marduk, god of Babylon, was taken to Ashur and Babylonian religious customs began to appear in the north. The Babylonian New Year's festival, known as the *akitu*, was introduced to Ashur, and the name of Marduk, along with other gods, appears increasingly in Assyrian personal names.

While Tukulti-Ninurta achieved a military victory over Babylon, it may be argued effectively that Babylon achieved a cultural victory. The religious ideas of the south penetrated Assyria, and the rugged Assyrian peoples began to develop a cosmopolitan attitude toward religion and life.

Important changes were taking place throughout the Near

East during the closing years of Tukulti-Ninurta's reign. The
Sea Peoples were conquering Asia Minor, bringing the Hittite
Empire down to defeat. Assyrian sources of metal in the old
Hittite lands were cut off. A century of warfare had caused severe
economic strain. Troubles were brewing in Assyria, with the
result that Tukulti-Ninurta was murdered by a son, Ashur-nadin-
apli (1207-1204 B.C.). During this period of Assyrian confusion
and weakness, Babylon assumed control of the land. An anti-
Babylonian revolt brought Assyrian independence under another
son of Tukulti-Ninurta, Enlil-Kudur-usur (1197-1193) B.C.).

Around 1192 B.C., an Assyrian nobleman who had been living
in Babylon, backed by the Kassite king of Babylon, seized the
throne of Assyria. Ninurta-apal-Ekur (1192-1180 B.C.) maintained independence of Babylon, but Assyria was now reduced
geographically to its homeland. Tribesmen were free to loot
and pillage the mountainous territory east of Assyria.

Tukulti-Ninurta's attack had wrought havoc on Babylon, and
the resulting internal dissension brought about the overthrow
of the Kassite dynasty. After a period of confusion, a native
Babylonian dynasty known as the Second Dynasty of Isin, came
to power. Ashur-Dan I (1179-1134 B.C.) was ruler of a weakened
Assyria. After his death the Babylonians were able to secure
the Assyrian throne for their protégé Ninurta-tukulti-Ashur who
restored the statue of Marduk to Babylon. Tukulti-Ninurta's
victory had secured the image for Assyria, but its restoration
symbolized the return of Marduk to his own land, Babylon.

The most important king of the Second Dynasty of Isin was
Nebuchadrezzar I (1124-1103 B.C.). As a strong ruler, Nebuchadrezzar maintained firm control of his homeland and embarked
on an expansionist foreign policy. The Elamites had been
perennial foes of Babylon, and in one of their raids they had
taken a statue of Marduk. Nebuchadrezzar mounted a campaign
against the Elamites. After an initial defeat, Nebuchadrezzar
assisted by an Elamite defector, Ritti-Marduk, gained a significant victory. The statue of an Elamite god was captured by
the Babylonians, and brought back to Babylon along with the
statue of Marduk. A cuneiform inscription notes special privileges granted to Ritti-Marduk in exchange for his aid. Nebuchadrezzar had penetrated deep within Elamite territory, gaining
his final victory on the banks of the Ulai River, near Susa.

Another foe of Babylon, the Lullubi, occupied the territory
northeast of Babylon. Nebuchadrezzar was able to subdue

them, along with Kassite tribes of the mountains. These were related to the Kassites who had earlier established an alien dynasty in Babylon.

The forceful Nebuchadrezzar maintained control over Assyria until the reign of Ashur-resh-ishi (1133-1116 B.C.) who strengthened Assyrian prestige and power throughout the Near East. Both Assyria and Babylonia were facing new threats from the west when Aramaean tribes threatened the trade routes leading to the Syrian coast and Anatolia. Ashur-resh-ishi boasted of victories over an Aramaic tribe known as the Ahlamu. An inscription describes the Assyrian king as "the one who crushes the widespread forces of the Ahlamu." Ashur-resh-ishi also conducted campaigns against tribes in the eastern mountain districts — the Lullubi, the Quti and their allies. Here Assyrian and Babylonian interests clashed. Nebuchadrezzar's heavy siege engines were no match for the chariots of Ashur-resh-ishi. Assyria was the victor and Nebuchadrezzar's successors had to fight to protect their own land against the Assyrians.

Ashur-resh-ishi was succeeded by an able son, Tiglath-pileser I (1115-1077 B.C.). The Assyrian war machine of later centuries drew its inspiration from Tiglath-pileser. Shortly after his accession a people known as Mushku (Biblical Meshech) pushed southward from eastern Asia Minor and invaded the Assyrian province of Kummuh. Tiglath-pileser reacted forcefully, decisively defeating the Mushku and punishing all who had assisted them. Succesive campaigns brought Assyrian power into the areas north, northeast, and northwest of the Assyrian homeland, penetrating deep into Asia Minor.

Tiglath-pileser had more troubles from the west than he did from the north. Population pressures following the invasions of the Philistines and other Sea Peoples made basic changes in the ethnic make-up of western Asia. About this time the kingdom of Saba (Biblical Sheba) emerged as a power in southern Arabia, possibly causing other southern tribes to migrate northward. Assyria would ultimately conquer most of western Asia (the Jerusalem area being a notable exception), but it would take many frustrating campaigns to do so.

The Assyrians never acknowledged defeats, and their annals are not always reliable. Nevertheless the royal scribes give us a good picture of the way in which an Assyrian ruler depicts himself. Here is Tiglath-pileser's boast:

I am Tiglath-pileser, the legitimate king, king of the world, king of
Assyria, king of the four parts of the earth, the courageous hero guided
by the oracles of Ashur and Ninurta, the great gods his lords; he who
has overcome his foes. ... At the command of my lord Ashur, my hand
conquered from beyond the lower Zab river to the upper sea that lies
to the west. Three times did I march against the Nairi countries. ...
I made bow at my feet thirty kings of the Nairi countries, and took
hostages from them. I received as tribute horses broken to the yoke. I
imposed upon them tribute and gifts. Then I went to the Lebanon. I
cut cedar timber for the temple of Anu and Adad, the great gods my
lords, and brought it away. I conquered the entire Amurru country. I
received tribute from Byblos, Sidon and Arvad.[2]

Tiglath-pileser claims that he crossed the Euphrates twenty-
eight times to attack the Aramean peoples and their allies. His
victories made possible a thriving trade along the time-honored
trade routes, now in Assyrian hands. The resulting wealth enabled the king to be generous in building and restoring temples, thus assuring a favorable place in history. For recreation
he hunted lions, bisons, and elephants, and collected exotic animals in his personal zoo.

After the reign of Tiglath-pileser I, however, Assyrian fortunes sank until the accession of Adad-nirari II. The years from
1077 to 911 B.C. saw Assyria quiescent — and it was precisely at
this period that Israel emerged as a potentially powerful state.
A power vacuum in the Near East made possible the glories of
the court of a Solomon, but three generations after the establishment of the Israelite monarchy.

Babylon's history paralleled that of Assyria. A chronicle dated
around 990 B.C. says that, "for nine years successively, Marduk
did not go forth, Nabu did not come." The reference is to the
annual New Year's feast, when Marduk was taken in solemn
procession to a shrine outside the city, and when Nabu of
Borsippa visited him on his return. While the sequence of kings
is known, the history of this period is obscure. During the days
of the Assyrian ruler Ashur-rabi II (1010-970 B.C.) the Arameans
were able to occupy Assyrian settlements on the Middle
Euphrates (including Pitru, Biblical Pethor). This complicated
trade, for even in times of peace customs duties had to be paid
to large numbers of small independent states. Assyria, for the
moment, was contained.

---

2. James Pritchard, *Ancient Near Eastern Texts,* pp. 274-275.

9

PEOPLE ON THE MOVE

The thirteenth century B.C. saw mass movements of Indo-European peoples in southeastern Europe, with important results for western Asia, including Palestine. Dorians, Aeolians, and Ionians occupied the Greek mainland, the Aegean islands, and western Asia Minor. The older Mycenaean culture, best known as the Achaeans in Homer's account of the Trojan War, was now past. The Trojan War was fought around 1270 B.C. The historical kernel behind the legendary accretions probably reflects the struggles among the peoples of the thirteenth century. Shortly after 1200 B.C. the Hittite Empire was defeated and the Sea Peoples, as the Egyptians called them, fled eastward along the coast of Asia Minor, and southward through Syria and Palestine to threaten Egypt itself. By sea and by land they challenged the power structure of the lands of the Fertile Crescent and Egypt.

About 1174 B.C. the Egyptian Pharaoh Ramesses III defeated the Sea Peoples in land and sea battles. The threat was a real one for the invaders had come to stay. They brought their women and children in wheeled carts drawn by humped oxen, as we can see depicted on the temple walls at Medinet Habu. Among the tribes of Sea Peoples we find the Tjekker, who later are found at the Palestinian port of Dor, and the Peleset, the Philistinees who settled in southern Palestine and struggled with the Israelites during the days of the Judges and the early period of the monarchy.

Ramesses III in a speech to his sons and courtiers described his response to the attack of the Sea Peoples:

> The foreign countries made a plot in their islands. Dislodged and scattered by battle were the lands all at one time, and no land could stand before their arms, beginning with Khatti (e.g. the Hittites), Kode, Carchemish, Arzawa, and Alasiya (Cyprus)... A camp was set up in one place in Amor, and they desolated its people and its land

as though they had never come into being. They came, the flame prepared before them, onwards to Egypt. Their confederacy consisted of Peleset, Tjekker, Sheklesh, Danu, and Weshesh, united lands, and they laid their hands upon the lands to the entire circuit of the earth, their hearts bent and trustful. . . . But the heart of this god (Ramesses III, the divine Pharaoh), the lord of the gods, was prepared and ready to ensnare them like birds. . . . I established my boundary in Djahi (i.e. Palestine and Syria), prepared in front of them the local princes, garrison commanders, and maryannu (chariot warriors). I caused the river mouth to be prepared like a strong wall with warships, galleys, and skiffs. They were completely equipped both fore and aft with brave fighters, carrying their weapons and infantry, of all the pick of Egypt, being like roaring lions upon the mountains; chariotry with able warriors, and all goodly officers whose hands were competent. Their horses quivered in all their limbs, prepared to crush the foreign countries under their hoofs.[1]

Ramesses likened himself to Mont, the god of war, and boasted of his complete victory:

As for those who reached my boundary, their seed is not. Their hearts and their souls are finished unto all eternity. Those who came forward together upon the sea, the full flame was in front of them at the river-mouths, and a stockade of lances surrounded them on the shore.

In gory detail Ramesses glories in the defeat of the foe:

A net was prepared for them to ensnare them, those who entered into the river-mouths being confined and fallen within it, pinioned in their places, butchered and their corpses hacked up.

Following the victory of Ramesses III we find the Peleset (Philistines) settling in force in southern Palestine, to become the foes of Israel within a short time. The Bible places the home of the Philistines in Caphtor (Deut. 2:23; Jer. 47:4; Amos 9:7), usually identified with Crete, the center of the Minoan culture, one of the most advanced cultures known during the first half of the second millennium B.C.

About the same time that Sea Peoples were storming the gates of Egypt and the Hittite country, other Indo-European peoples were moving southward from the region of the Caspian Sea to become the Madai (Medes) and Parsua (Parthians) of later history. These and kindred tribes were able to gain control of the regions later known as Persia, Afghanistan, and Turkistan.

The Indo-European migrations had little direct affect on Mesopotamia. Kassites from the Zagros Mountain region ruled Babylon for four hundred years with little concern for problems in the west. Farther north, the Semitic Aramaeans took advantage of the confusion to move into the Syrian hinterland

---

1. W. F. Edgerton and J. A. Wilson, *Historical Records of Ramesses III* (Chicago: University of Chicago Press, 1936), p. 42.

and establish a number of petty kingdoms which, collectively, threatened the larger states, particularly Assyria. Israelites at the same time were establishing themselves in the area west of the Jordan which would be the nucleous for the kingdom of Saul, David, and Solomon.

Aside from the Biblical records and Assyrian Royal Inscriptions we have little documentation for the period immediately prior to the establishment of the monarchy. About 1190 B.C. the Hittite archives at Boghazkoy came to an abrupt end. The successors of Ramesses III were impotent rulers, and by the dawn of the eleventh century, Egypt separated into two rival kingdoms.

When our documentation improves, about 900 B.C., we find a new power structure throughout western Asia. Aramaean states are thriving from the Lebanon to the Zagros mountain regions. Damascus is the center of a major Aramaean state with which Israel will have frequent contact. The Philistines are settled on the southern coast of Palestine, while the Phoenicians (as the Canaanites of the area were called by the Greeks), occupied the northern Mediterranean coast with major port cities at Tyre, Sidon, and Arvad.

The contribution of the Phoenicians to subsequent history was both positive and negative. On the positive side is the alphabet, a distinct improvement on earlier hieroglyphic and cuneiform systems of writing. When Greek mariners learned the alphabet from their Phoenician counterparts, the west began its journey into literacy. Similarly the Aramaeans took the alphabet eastward, although cuneiform writing continued to be used in some places until the time of Christ.

The negative influence of the Phoenicians is well documented in the Biblical records. These are the people of Baal, and the Phoenician wife of Ahab, Queen Jezebel, is the one who tried to eliminate Yahwism from Israelite religious life. The fertility cult associated with Baal and his consort reaped the just scorn of Israel's prophets.

The Phoenician cities had excellent harbors, and the abundant timber on the mountains to the east helped make of the Phoenicians a nation of seafarers. With the collapse of the Mycenaean Empire, the eastern Mediterranean was open to mariners of all nations, and the Phoenicians of Tyre, Sidon, and Arvad began to sail the Mediterranean with timber, wine, oil, and the luxury goods of Phoenicia. The purple dye, extracted by the Phoenicians from the murex shellfish, was particularly prized, and royalty in many lands attired itself in the expensive purple of Sidon. Intricate embroidery work was another Phoenician specialty.

Phoenician artisans are not known for their originality, but they learned quickly to imitate the best designs and materials that flowed through their busy ports. They cut jewels and ivory for export and fashioned vessels of translucent glass.

Phoenician influence throughout the eastern Mediterranean was greatest between the ninth and the sixth centuries. David and Solomon used Phoenician artisans and materials in their building operations. The islands of the Mediterranean and the coastlands of northern Africa and southern Europe were dotted with Phoenician colonies. Malta, Sicily, Spain, and — most important of all — Carthage had major Phoenician settlements.

Carthage is remembered because of its battles with Rome in a series of "Punic" (i.e., Phoenician) Wars. Here many heroes had Semitic Phoenician names, such as Hanabal ("The grace of Baal"), comparable to Biblical Hannaniah ("The grace of Yahweh"). Vergil in his *Aeneid* explained the hostility between Carthage and Rome in terms of a love affair between Dido, queen of Carthage, and Aeneas, a Trojan hero who visited Carthage during his journeys following the destruction of Troy. Destiny called Aeneas to leave Dido and move on to Italy where his descendants would become the mighty Romans. As Aeneas prepared to leave, Dido cast herself upon a funeral pyre, calling down curses upon her erstwhile lover and asserting undying enmity between her people and his. Although entirely fictious, Vergil's story underscores the rivalry between the Romans and Tyre's most illustrious daughter city, Carthage.

10

EGYPT

The power vacuum which made possible the rise of Israel as an independent state was as obvious in Egypt as it had been in Mesopotamia. Ramesses III had responded vigorously to threats from the Sea Peoples but his successors left no lasting mark on the pages of history. Eight more Egyptian Pharaohs bore the name of Ramesses, but the reigns of all but two (Ramesses IX and Ramesses XI) were very short. The tendency was to live in the Delta, leaving Thebes to the complete control of the Amun priesthood. Egypt conducted no campaigns into Asia during this period, and even Sinai is not mentioned after the reign of Ramesses VI. Egypt retreated into an isolation which Thutmose III or Ramesses II would have had difficulty understanding. Cyril Aldred observes, "She escaped the transfusions of new blood and ideas, such as rejuvenated the peoples of Canaan and created the vigorous Phoenician city-states. Thereafter she lived on, a Bronze Age anachronism in a world that steadily moved away from her."[1]

Egypt, like many nations, thrived on adversity but could not stand success. Egyptians came to desire genteel vocations. The priest and the scribe were honored, yet their work had neither danger nor drudgery associated with it. An Egyptian could seek such a job and fill or create a comfortable bureaucratic office that he might pass on to his son. The army could be left to mercenaries — Nubians, Sudanis, Libyans and others.

As Egypt's Twentieth Dynasty dragged to a close (*ca.* 1075 B.C.) Egypt was virtually two lands with the High Priest at Thebes ruling southern or Upper Egypt, and the Pharaoh ruling in and over the Delta. The Philistines were in control of

---

1. *The Egyptians* (New York: Frederick A. Praeger, 1963) p. 139.

the coast of Palestine, and the Phoenicians had become masters of the sea. Unemployment among the mercenary soldiers increased the lawlessness of the times, and famine caused by a succession of years in which the Nile did not provide adequate water for irrigation, made things worse. Dishonesty was rampant among officials who tried hard to cover their mismanagement of men and material, and the poorer classes resorted to strikes and violence to relieve their hunger.

The tombs of the Pharaohs, once reverenced as manifestations of god on earth, were now pillaged systematically and with the connivance of the officials. Of thirty tombs in the Valley of the Kings, only that of Tut-ankh-amon was preserved, and that probably by accident because the entrance to the tomb was concealed behind debris.

After the death of the last of the Ramesides, the country fell into its natural halves. The fiction of a united Egypt might be observed, but Upper Egypt was clearly a theocracy under the priests at Thebes, and Lower Egypt had a succession of ineffective rulers.

Shortly after 950 B.C. a family of Libyan descent which had settled at Herakleopolis succeeded to the throne. They were in no sense invaders, but probably the descendants of captured prisoners or voluntary settlers who were assigned land on condition that they obligate themselves to perform military service. The founder of the dynasty was Sheshonq (Biblical Shishak, I Kings 11:29-40) who harbored Jeroboam as a fugitive from Solomon. About 925 B.C., after the division of the kingdom, Sheshonq invaded Palestine, subdued Judah, and took Temple treasures as tribute (I Kings 14:25-26). The Libyan dynasty offered the hope of fresh vigor on the throne of Egypt, but Egypt was never to recover the glories of her past when Egypt ruled western Asia from Egypt to the Euphrates. It was in her period of decline that the Israelite kingdom came into being.

AFTERWORD

Israel developed into an important nation in the ancient Near East during a period when there was no major power that dominated the scene. Following her glorious New Kingdom, when Egypt ruled the East, Egyptian power gradually was lost. Dreams of restoring that power challenged Pharaohs of the first millennium B.C., but with no permanent results. Assyria was developing into an important state in Mesopotamia — a state which would incorporate most of western Asia during the centuries which would follow — but in the days of David and Solomon she was no threat. Political tensions developed among the smaller states of western Asia — Philistines, Phoenicians, Arameans, Moabites, Ammonites, Edomites, and Israelites — but neither the Nile nor the Euphrates gave any real concern.

It was during this time of a power vacuum that Israelite military power reached its zenith. David unified the country and made Jerusalem its capital. Solomon built its Temple during his days of wealth, but seeds of decay were soon evident. With Solomon's death the kingdom was divided, never to be united again.

The period of Israel's political power was not, however, the period of Israel's great contribution to religion and culture. Other nations produced rulers who defeated enemies and ruled in the style of David and Solomon. Israel's uniqueness was in her prophetic spokesmen who dared to challenge erroneous, if popular, views. A Nathan in the court of David was such a person. Nathan made it clear that his royal title and office did not give David license to break the Law of God. In later centuries an Amos, a Hosea, an Isaiah, a Jeremiah and their like, dared to insist that Yahweh demanded more than ritual conformity — that a heart devoted to Yahweh's will and moved with compassion toward all of Yahweh's creatures was essential. Jonah must be concerned even about the wicked city of Nineveh. This was the prophetic message. God would one day vindicate the righteous. The world would experience renewal and regeneration in a day when the earth would be filled with the knowledge of the glory of Yahweh as the waters cover the sea. This was the prophetic hope.

The sin of David and the material splendor of Solomon's court did not give much hope for better things in themselves. The prophetic response, however, gave occasion to the faithful to hope for better things. David's sin would be punished, but David's line would be preserved. The Lord's anointed, the Messiah would come as "the son of David, the son of Abraham" (Matt. 1:1).

BIBLICAL HISTORY

Albright, W. F., "The Biblical Period," from *The Jews: Their History Culture and Religion,* Louis Finkelstein, ed. (Harper, 1960). Published separately as *The Biblical Period from Abraham to Ezra* (Harper Torchbooks, 1963).

——, *From the Stone Age to Christianity* (Doubleday Anchor Books, 1957).

Anderson, B. W., *Understanding the Old Testament* (Prentice-Hall, 1957).

Baron, Salo Wittmayer, *A Social and Religious History of the Jews,* I (Columbia University Press, 1952).

Bright, John, *A History of Israel* (Westminster, 1959).

Buck, Harry M., *People of the Lord* (Macmillan, 1965).

DeVaux, Roland, *Ancient Israel: Its Life and Institutions* (Mc-Graw-Hill, 1961).

Gordon, Cyrus H., *The Ancient Near East* (Norton, 1964).

Gottwald, Norman K., *A Light to the Nations* (Harper, 1958).

Heinisch, P., tr. W. Heidt, *History of the Old Testament* (Ecumenical Press, 1952).

Kaufmann, Yahezkel, "The Biblical Age" in *Great Ages and Ideas of the Jewish People,* Leo W. Schwarz, ed. (Random House, 1956).

Lods, A., *Israel* (Kegan, Paul, Trubner and Co., 1932).

Maly, Eugene H., *The World of David and Solomon* (Prentice-Hall, 1966).

Neher, Andre et Renee, *Histoire Biblique du Peuple d'Israel* (Adrien-Maisonneuve, 1962).

Noth, Martin, *The History of Israel* (Harper, 1958).

——, *The Old Testament World* (Fortress Press, 1966).

Oesterley, W. O. E., and Robinson, Theodore, *A History of Israel* (Oxford, 1932).

Orlinsky, Harry M., *Ancient Israel* (Cornell University Press, 1960).

Pederson, J., *Israel* (Branner, 1940).

BIBLICAL GEOGRAPHY

Pfeiffer, Charles F., *Baker's Bible Atlas* (Baker Book House, 1961).

ANCIENT NEAR EASTERN HISTORY

Bury, J. B., Cook, S. A., and Adcock, F. E., *The Cambridge Ancient History*, III (Cambridge, 1953).

Hall, H. R. H., *The Ancient History of the Near East* (Methuen, 1950).

Moscati, Sabattino, *Ancient Semitic Civilizations* (Elek Books, 1957).

———, *The Face of the Ancient Orient* (Doubleday Anchor, 1962).

———, *The Semites in Ancient History* (University of Wales, 1959).

Pareti, Luigi; Brezzi, Paolo; and Petech, Luciana, *The Ancient World* (Volume 2 of the UNESCO *History of Mankind* series, Harper and Row, 1965).

Schwantes, Siegfried, *A Short History of the Ancient Near East* (Baker, 1965).

ARCHAEOLOGY

Adams, J. McKee, *Biblical Backgrounds*, revised by Joseph A. Callaway (Broadman, 1965).

Albright, W. F., *The Archaeology of Palestine* (Penguin, 1960).

Barton, G. A., *Archaeology and the Bible* (American Sunday School Union, 1937).

Finegan, Jack, *Light from the Ancient Past* (Princeton, 1959).

Kenyon, Kathleen, *Archaeology in the Holy Land*, 2nd edition (Praeger, 1966).

———, *Beginning in Archaeology* (Praeger, 1953).

McCowan, C. C., *The Ladder of Progress in Palestine* (Harper, 1943).

———, *Man, Morals, and History* (Harper, 1958).

Pfeiffer, Charles F., ed., *The Biblical World* (Baker Book House, 1966).

Pritchard, James B., *Archaeology and the Old Testament* (Princeton, 1958).

Thompson, J. A., *Archaeology and the Old Testament* (Eerdmans, 1960).

Unger, M. F., *Archaeology and the Old Testament* (Zondervan, 1954).

Wright, G. E., *Biblical Archaeology* (Westminster, 1957).

JERUSALEM

James, E. O. (Forward by), *Jerusalem: A History* (Paul Hamlyn, London, 1967).

Kenyon, Kathleen, *Jerusalem: Excavating 3000 Years of History* (McGraw-Hill, 1967).

Kollak, Teddy, and Pearlman, Moshe, *Jerusalem: A History of Forty Centuries* (Random House, 1968).

Parrot, Andre, *The Temple of Jerusalem* (S.C.M. Press, 1957).

Pfeiffer, Charles F., *Jerusalem through the Ages* (Baker, 1967).

Simons, J., *Jerusalem in the Old Testament* (Brill, 1952).

Vincent, L. H., and Steve, A. M., *Jerusalem de l'Ancien Testament* (J. Gabalda, Paris, 1954, 1956).

INDEX

**Resolutions and decisions of the
Communist Party of the Soviet Union**

General Editor: Robert H. McNeal

**Resolutions and decisions of the
Communist Party of the Soviet Union**

Volume 2
The Early Soviet Period: 1917–1929

Editor: Richard Gregor

University of Toronto Press

© University of Toronto Press 1974
Toronto and Buffalo
Printed in Canada

ISBN 0–8020–2157–3
LC 74–81931

Editor's Preface

Russian terms are translated if a generally accepted English form exists, but are transliterated otherwise. In the latter case the term (e.g., oblast) is treated as an anglicized expression, without hard and soft signs (except in titles), to simplify the appearance of the text. The index of the volume provides parenthetical translations of transliterated terms. Translations of periodical titles appear with the first occurrence of a given title.

Document numbers are supplied by the editor of the volume; a prefix such as "2." indicates the volume number in the present series. Throughout the book such a decimal number implies reference to a document number.

Square brackets [] enclose material added by the editor of this volume, while parentheses appearing in documents are in the original Russian text. Brackets are used in titles of documents if the original version of a given resolution lacked any definite title. Ellipses (...) indicate omissions of part of the original document by the editor, unless otherwise specified.

To assist the reader in identifying changes in successive versions of the party Rules, bracketed notes are inserted with each article, indicating whether it is a new, revised, or unchanged article with respect to the previous version of the Rules. Since this volume contains three successive versions of the Rules (1919, 1922, 1925), and there is considerable repetition of articles from one version to another, the full text of all articles is provided only in the first (1919) version. Thereafter articles of the Rules that repeat an article from the previous version are covered with a cross-reference to the previous version.

At the end of each document or group of documents adopted at a given meeting source attributions are provided. On the left the earliest published source that was accessible to the editor is cited; with a few exceptions all were consulted by the editor. On the right the location of the material in the standard Soviet reference work is cited: *Kommunisticheskaia Partiia Sovetskogo Soiuza v rezoliutsiiakh i resheniiakh s''ezdov, konferentsii i plenumov TsK* (Communist Party of the Soviet Union in Resolutions and Decisions of Congresses, Conferences and Plenums of the Central Committee), 8th edition, Moscow, 1970–1972 (hereafter abbreviated *KPSS v resoliutsiiakh*). Not all documents published in the present work appear in *KPSS v rezoliutsiiakh*, so citations of this source do not appear in every case. All dates cited are in the new style.

Most of the documents carry a date when passed by the appropriate organ. In a few instances the exact date could not be established.

The editor of the present volume made a number of changes in the original translation for reasons of consistency, accuracy, and to suit his own taste.

The end of each set of documents emerging from a congress, conference, or Central Committee plenum is indicated by the following symbol: ※.

Contents

The Early Soviet Period
1917–1929

Introduction

'You are no longer an underground party but a government of a vast country,' pleaded Leonid Krasin with the top party leaders, at the XII Party Congress in 1923, in a vain attempt to make them break loose from their conspiratorial mentality.[1]

In this one sentence Krasin accurately described the problem which confronts any successful revolutionary movement, i.e., a transition from a revolutionary party to a governing party – a metamorphosis which requires a good deal of political sophistication and restraint. It is easy for revolutionary leaders, during their struggle for power, to decide on the adoption of almost any means to accomplish the desired, and often utopian, ends. It is far more difficult for them, when successful in seizing power, to prevent such means from becoming the ends, especially if their original expectations have not materialized.

Lenin, the founder of the Soviet state, is a classical example of such a failure in transition from a revolutionary to a statesman precisely because of his obsession with ultimate goals. Lenin believed that he could not be squeamish about the choice of means if he was to defeat the capitalist order and establish the communist millenium.

Only a few months before the Bolshevik Revolution, Lenin published what is sometimes, and erroneously, considered one of his major works, *The State and Revolution*. In it he argued that once the capitalist state was destroyed by a violent revolution, the socialist state, an absolutely complete democracy, would wither away. This state was so constituted that 'it begins to wither away immediately, and cannot but wither away.' During the transitional period 'no special machinery for repression' would be required because a large majority of the population would enjoy democratic rights.[2]

---

1 *Dvenadsatyi s''ezd RKP(b), 17–25 aprelia 1923 goda, Stenograficheskii Otchet* (Moscow, 1968), 124; hereafter cited as XII Congress.

2 V.I. Lenin, *Polnoe sobrania sochinenii* XXXIII (55 volumes; 5th edition, Moscow 1963–65), 5–119; hereafter cited as Lenin 5. (The various Soviet editions are not consistent in the usage of either arabic or roman numerals for volume numbers. Roman numerals are used throughout this work).

But before this happened the revolutionary party could not rely on democratic methods and had to be so organized as to withstand tsarist oppression and persecution. Lenin described how this was to be accomplished in 1902, long before he wrote *The State and Revolution*, in a pamphlet entitled *What Is To Be Done* which turned out to be his lasting legacy to the Soviet regime. His own assessment of the relative merits of the two works became clear only six months after the revolution, when in an argument with Bukharin at the VII Congress, in 1918, he flatly stated that 'to announce in advance the withering away of the state would be a violation of historical perspective.'[3]

Both the validity and permanence of his assessment, as well as the failure of the leninist experiment, become obvious when we realize that more than half a century after Lenin enunciated his visionary principles in *The State and Revolution*, the Soviet Union is still run on the basis of the means elaborated in *What Is To Be Done*. The majority support which Lenin expected from the international proletariat and which was to compensate for his domestic political weakness, did not materialize and, as a result, the conspiratorial party of the revolution became a conspiratorial party of legitimacy.

It was a problem which some marxist contemporaries of Lenin, such as Georgii Plekhanov or Rosa Luxemburg, and indeed even some close collaborators of Lenin, saw quite clearly. The outcome of Lenin's programme would be, as Plekhanov prophetically stated, not socialism but civil war and authoritarian communism.

The mark of a true statesman is his ability to compromise with others. Lenin chose to cling to power alone at all cost rather than to compromise and combine with the other socialist parties in Russia to form a workable majority rule. The supremacy of the Bolshevik Party had to be secured, opposition without as well as within the party had to be eliminated, the population had to be neutralized and ultimately terrorized, and party control had to spread into all walks of life. But in the process even the party itself was destroyed, the dictatorship of the proletariat became the dictatorship of the party, the dictatorship of the party became that of the Central Committee and ultimately of one man, as Trotsky, in one of his better moments, so accurately predicted in an argument with Lenin after the II Congress.

In a vicious circle, the centralization of power with its consequent concentration of decision making in a few hands, was directly responsible for the inability and unwillingness of the leaders to address themselves to the question of orderly leadership succession which, in turn, made the perpetuation of the Byzantine conspiratorial mentality inevitable.

---

3 *Sed'moi ekstrennyi s"ezd RKP(b), Mart 1918 goda, Stenograficheskii otchet* (Moscow, 1962), 162; hereafter cited as VII Congress.

There is evidence that towards the end of his life, in 1922, Lenin began to have doubts about the system he created, but by then it was too late. The result was that Lenin earned the dubious distinction of having laid the foundations for the first totalitarian state. This is not to suggest that the moment Lenin seized power he became an all-powerful dictator. In fact, at least within the party, he had to rely for a time more on persuasion than on force to carry the day. It was not until 1921 and the X Congress that the necessary prerequisites were established for the silencing of the opposition within the party. Even so, it took Lenin's successor, Stalin, until the 1930s to emerge as the undisputed ruler of the Soviet Union.

Apart from the obvious personal imprint that every leader puts on policy, Stalin did not contribute in any appreciable way to the Soviet political system. He merely took over where Lenin left off and became more intolerant of and more brutal to any opposition, more suspicious of any one who as much as hinted at disagreement with his policy, and less scrupulous in elimination of real or imaginary adversaries. Under Stalin, in the words of Leonard Schapiro, the party truly became one man.

ORGANIZATION AND ROLE OF THE PARTY

In a fundamental way the organization and the role of the party were outlined by Lenin in 1902 in *What Is To Be Done* and subsequently during the critical debates at the II Congress in 1903. Lenin's justification of his elitist approach was plausible when looked at from the standpoint of the situation in Russia at the time. The party membership had to be small, Lenin argued, because in an autocratic state the more membership was confined to professional revolutionaries, the more difficult it would be to destroy such an organization. To be sure, combined with this practical argument was the arrogant, vanguard assumption that the proletariat could not look after its own interests and thus it fell to the party, as the repository of ultimate wisdom, to assume this task on behalf of the workers. The workers, according to Lenin, if left to their own devices, would acquire only trade union consciousness and would fight only for immediate material gains. Consequently, socialist theory, which arose independently of the spontaneous growth of the working class, had to be, as it were, superimposed on the proletariat: 'it (spontaneity) overwhelms political consciousness,' he argued, 'and makes people get carried away by the argument that a kopek added to a ruble is worth more than any socialism or politics.'[4]

Lenin's views met with strong opposition on the part of many Russian Social Democrats who claimed that this type of organization contradicted all democratic principles. Lenin's impatient, but again plausible, retort was that the charge was foreign because under autocracy one could not rely on

4 V.I. Lenin, *Sochineniia* IV (30 volumes; 2nd edition, Leningrad-Moscow, 1926–32), 380–1, 383–5, 389; hereafter cited as Lenin 2.

democratic principles; it confused the Western situation with the Russian one.[5]

Given these views, it is small wonder that Lenin refused to collaborate, on an equal basis, with the other socialist parties in Russia after the seizure of power. At the II Congress of Soviets on 7 November 1917, the other socialist parties disassociated themselves from the Bolshevik seizure of power, condemned it as a 'military coup d'état,' which it was, and insisted on the formation of a broadly based government including all socialist parties. To add weight to their opposition to the coup, most of the socialists decided to leave the Congress in the belief that the Bolsheviks would be unable to govern on their own. Needless to say, this left the Bolsheviks in control of the governing apparatus and the anti-bolshevik socialists ended up, as Trotsky suggested, in the garbage can of history. However, at the same time, the refusal to co-operate with the other socialists put the party into a position not dissimilar to that of the pre-revolutionary time and, given Lenin's determination to hang on to power at all cost, made the perpetuation of the means of *What Is To Be Done* inevitable. This does not mean that the Bolshevik Party as a body was opposed to a coalition with the other socialists. There were, in fact, several prominent Bolsheviks, Kamenev and Zinoviev among them, who were in favour of it and indeed were even prepared to exclude both Lenin and Trotsky from such a government to make a coalition possible (2.1, 2.2, 2.3).

But Lenin prevailed, the supremacy of the party (in the sense of legitimacy) with respect to the rest of the country was theoretically established, and before too long applied in practice. It took but a small and easy step to carry this policy to its logical conclusion and apply the principle of elitism to intra-party decision making as well.

For more than a year after the seizure of power no special attention was paid to the organization of the party. The reasons are not difficult to fathom. A good part of the first six months was spent in securing peace with Germany and living from day to day, never knowing whether or not the regime would survive. Only a year after the Brest-Litovsk peace, and by then in the midst of a civil war, did the leaders begin to occupy themselves more systematically with organizational problems; however by now they had eighteen months of leadership experience behind them.

Until then the decisions were made, for all practical purposes, by two men – Lenin and Sverdlov – who, when they felt the need, consulted with a few other leading party members. Even the Central Committee ceased, for all practical purposes, to exist during this time.[6] This type of leadership

5 Lenin 2, IV, 456, 466–7; see also *Vtoroi s"ezd RSDRP, Iiul-Avgust 1903 g.* (Moscow, 1933), 417–23.

6 *Vos'moi s"ezd RKP(b), Mart 1919 goda, Protokoly* (Moscow, 1959), 23, 164; the charge was made by Osinsky and admitted by Lenin. Hereafter cited as VIII Congress.

obviously suited Lenin's temperament, but the organization was too haphazard to allow for proper implementation of top level decisions. Consequently, at the VIII Congress in 1919, a resolution was passed, subsequently incorporated in the party Rules of 1919, 1922, and 1925, which addressed itself to the problem (2.9, 2.10, 2.31, 2.52).

The new organizational set-up provided for a yearly congress (from the XV Congress, every two years), which was described as the highest party organ. Among its functions were approvals of the political and organizational reports of the Central Committee, revision of the party Programme, elections of the Central Committee and later also of the Central Control Commission, and a definition of the tactical line on current problems. In between the yearly congresses, a provision was made for a pre-congress conference whose functions were not defined except that it was to serve, along with the Central Committee, as a sort of a credentials committee for the next congress.

The delegates to the congresses and conferences were to be elected by local party conferences, primarily on the oblast and guberniia levels. However, party members from various non-party organizations, such as the armed forces or the trade unions, also participated. They were to be elected by the party fractions in these organizations. The delegates were of two types: those with a deciding vote and those with a consultative vote, a somewhat euphemistic description of delegates with a vote and those without a vote. While the latter could not vote, they were allowed to participate in the debates. It is not entirely clear on what basis the distinction between the delegates was made. It is of some interest that at the VII and VIII congresses and at the VIII Conference, before the passage of the Rules, none of the Central Committee members had a deciding vote and it may well be that this was a deliberate distinction, as it were, between the executive and the legislative branches, providing for accountability of the Central Committee to the congress or conference.

Later, in 1921 the practice was developed that, if a delegate represented solely the Central Committee, he received only a consultative vote; if a Central Committee member represented also a local party conference then he received a deciding vote.[7] Beginning with the IX Conference, the principal Central Committee members, in most instances, were also elected by local conferences and thus had a deciding vote, and the above distinction was therefore of no great practical value.

There were exceptions, however. After 1924, opposition members, on the verge of elimination, but not yet expelled, appeared at congresses and conferences, as delegates with a consultative vote. For instance, at the XV Congress, Kamenev and five others, appeared 'on the decision of the

[7] *Desiatyi s"ezd RKP(b), Mart 1921 goda, Stenograficheskii otchet* (Moscow, 1963), 640, note*; hereafter cited as X Congress.

Central Committee' as such delegates. On other occasions, the decision may have been quite deliberate on the part of the member concerned. For example, at the XI Congress, Stalin attended as a delegate with a consultative vote, probably because he wished to appear aloof from the anticipated stormy session on the control commissions, which by then served him as a tool in his consolidation of power. Or, at the XIV Conference, Stalin, Zinoviev, and Kamenev attended as delegates with a consultative vote, probably by mutual agreement, to postpone what turned out to be the inevitable split of the troika. With regard to those delegates who were not Central Committee members, it may be assumed that the original intention was to nominate for elections the more prominent members of the local organizations and, in order to increase the sense of participation, allow others to be present without a vote. With the increasing control of the local organizations by the central organs, however, it became the practice to nominate the reliable members for delegates with a vote and the less reliable for delegates without a vote.[8]

Each congress and conference also approved its own procedural rules, which included the provision that any group of forty delegates had the right to submit co-reports to the official ones. The exceptions were the VII Congress and the IX Conference at which it was decided that any ten delegates could do so. In the latter case, the original proposal was thirty but on the motion of Sapronov the number was reduced to ten.[9] On one occasion (strangely enough at the X Congress, which put the lid on all opposition), the oppositionists did not muster the required forty signatures but the delegates nevertheless voted to let them proceed.[10] The practice was terminated with the XIV Congress in 1925.

The party Rules also provided for two plenums of the Central Committee each month and later, in 1922, for one plenum every two months. The Central Committee, chosen by the congress, was to deal with questions which did not require immediate attention concerning various party institutions as well as other Soviet and social organizations. It also controlled the treasury, and approved decisions of the conferences (2.10, 2.35).[11] Although the Central Committee supposedly functioned even before the passage of the Rules, its meetings were infrequent and very few could be called plenums. More often than not, they were rump gatherings, usually a

---

8 See Riazanov's remarks at the X Congress, 400.

9 *Deviataia Konferentsia RKP(b), Sentiabr' 1920 goda, Protokoly* (Moscow, 1972), 3; hereafter cited as IX Conference.

10 X Congress, 234.

11 The Central Committee function to approve conference decisions, announced at the XII Congress, although continued, was not incorporated in the 1925 party Rules.

combination of some Politburo and Orgburo members.[12] After the VIII Conference, the Central Committee meetings were designated as plenums and probably were such.

Further, the Rules established three additional party organs, whose members were appointed by the Central Committee, to deal with political and organizational matters on a day-to-day basis. These were the Politburo, whose function was to be political work, the Orgburo, for general direction of organizational work, and the Secretariat, for current organizational and executive work. It is difficult to determine what the situation was before the passage of the Rules. A Politburo had been established previously, shortly before the seizure of power, on 23 October 1917, although it is not clear that it actually functioned. Later, in December 1917, a buro of the Central Committee was established which may have functioned in such capacity or that of the Orgburo. At any rate, it is likely that informal meetings of the top leaders between 1917 and 1919 were called Politburo or Orgburo meetings.[13] Below this upper structure were the lower local party organs, organized hierarchically on the basis of the unitary principle – 'one centralized party and side by side with it – a federation of states,' as Zinoviev put it (2.9).[14]

In addition to these organs, the leadership subsequently established three other institutions to serve as controlling agencies: the Central Control Commission and local control commissions, the Revision Commission, and the Workers' and Peasants' Inspectorate or Rabkrin, the last more a governmental rather than party organ.

The Central Control Commission, founded at the IX Conference in 1920, was to be directly responsible to the Central Committee. Its original task was to serve alongside the Central Committee to fight bureaucratic excesses and to receive complaints against party members or organizations as well as to implement strict party control. They were to hold joint meetings with the Central Committee when necessary, within the framework of their jurisdiction. Subsequently control commissions were also established on local levels and given the right to participate, with a consultative vote, in joint meetings with their counterpart party committees (2.12, 2.15, 2.31). Dispute commissions were also established in the armed forces to function as military investigation apparatus of the Central Control Commission (2.48).

It was on the basis of the IX Conference resolution that the so-called

12 *Izvestiia tsentral'nogo komiteta RKP(b)*, nos 1–11, 28 May 1919 – 31 December 1919; hereafter cited as ITSK.
13 VIII Congress, 25, 26, 184, 273; see references by Lenin, Zinoviev, and Kamenev to Politburo and Orgburo before these organs were established.
14 VIII Congress, 286.

Joint Plenum of the Central Committee and the Central Control Commission came into being already before the X Congress, although not under that name. The joint sessions appeared under different labels until October 1923 when the term joint plenum was used for the first time and continued to be referred to by that name.

The joint sessions were by no means automatic. For example, between the X and XI congresses in 1921 and 1922 there were fifteen Central Committee meetings of which only one was joint, or between the X Congress in 1921 and the XVI Congress in 1930 there were eighty-seven Central Committee meetings of which thirteen were joint. Until 1925 and the XIV Congress, the joint plenums were called only when the subject matter on the agenda fell within the official jurisdiction of the Central Control Commission. It was at that time that this organ received formal recognition in the amended party Rules and the Central Control Commission members were granted a deciding vote at the joint meetings. At the same time, the presidium of the Central Control Commission was given the right to send three members to Politburo and five to Orgburo meetings, although with a consultative vote only, thus incorporating a resolution of the XII Congress (2.35, 2.52). At the XV Congress the number of the Central Control Commission presidium members with the right to attend Politburo meetings was raised to four members and four candidates.

The Revision Commission or Revkom served as a tool of the Central Committee primarily in the sphere of decisions on directives of a financial nature and was to report any short-comings to the Central Committee (2.12, 2.27).

The Workers' and Peasants' Inspectorate or Rabkrin was really a parallel organisation of the Central Control Commission on the governmental level and its primary concern was the administration of the economy. Its commissar was Stalin. Ultimately, as a result of one of Lenin's last recommendations, the two were fused into one organization (2.35, 2.42).

This organizational form was described as democratic centralism, although the meaning of the term is not clearly defined and left interspersed in the three sets of Rules of this period. Essentially it meant 'regular military discipline' under which all decisions of the higher bodies had to be first carried out and only then could be appealed (2.9). Ominous as this already sounded, it still did not correspond to reality – which turned out to be even more stringent.

The jurisdictions of the various bodies were not adhered to and often completely ignored. Some of these inconsistencies were clearly associated with various power struggles. Others, however, are more difficult to explain. For example, the congress, a supreme organ of the party according to the Rules, was by-passed in 1919 and 1922; and the Rules were passed by the VIII and XII conferences respectively. The conference, as we saw, was an organ barely mentioned in the Rules. In contrast, the XIV Conference discussed certain amendments to the Rules, but the actual resolution on these was passed by the XIV Congress. To be sure, the congresses or conferences had no real power, but in the early years, they at least provided some opportunity for a free debate. While irregularities in the elections of delegates and attempts at curtailment of criticism occurred from the beginning, until the X Congress both elections and debates appear to have been more or less open. However, even then the leadership was already protected by the power of the Central Committee to exclude delegates elected to the congresses. The relative free expression of opinion which these bodies provided for was, however, never translated into any real power. On occasion the delegates to one of these bodies may have prevailed against the official stand of the leadership which manifested itself in the passing of a resolution. The implementation of such a resolution would be a different matter – it was simply ignored by the leaders or interpreted in such a way that it turned to their advantage. The X Congress with its outlawing of opposition within the party made even these instances of short-lived opposition triumphs unlikely, but it still did not provide for adequate control over the selection of delegates on the local levels. As a result, at the XI Congress a decision was made giving the Central Committee power to authorize the guberniia committees (gubkoms) to select delegates by means other than elections. The control over the guberniia organizations was further tightened at the XII Conference when the new Rules specified that the appointment of the gubkom secretary had to be confirmed by a higher party organ, which in this instance meant the oblast committee. Both, in turn, were directly responsible to the Central Committee and had to report to it on all of their activities (2.31).[15] In this way the Central Committee exercised a very effective control over the guberniia organizations and in 1922 it meant, in practice, that the power was exercised by the General Secretary. It even appears that this institutionalization of Central Committee control was actually a recognition of an already existing reality. The method of selecting rather than electing delegates was introduced already before the XI Congress. About fifty delegates from the Samara guberniia were selected by the plenum of the guberniia committee instead of elected by the guberniia conference. In this case, as the mandate commission report of the XI Congress put it, 'the Central Committee allowed it as a result of those objective conditions in which the Samara guberniia found itself' –

15 *Odinnadsatyi s''ezd RKP(b), Mart-Aprel' 1922 goda, Stenograficheskii otchet* (Moscow, 1961), 320, 369–70; hereafter cited as XI Congress; *XIV s''ezd Vsesoiuznoi Kommunisticheskoi Partii*(b), *18–31 dekabria 1925 g., Stenograficheskii otchet* (Moscow, 1926), 883; hereafter cited as XIV Congress.

a rather oblique reference to the fact that Samara was a stronghold of the Workers' Opposition and had elections been held, the delegation would have been composed of the (by now outlawed) oppositionists. While this practice was admitted at the Congress only in the one instance it was used elsewhere as well at the time.

Even if the original party Rules had been strictly adhered to, it is doubtful that the congresses and conferences would have become powerful bodies. One meeting a year, and later every two years, lasting barely more than a week, was hardly sufficient for serious deliberations, especially under a regime which took it upon itself to pass decrees on every conceivable aspect of human activity. Nevertheless, up to and including the X Congress, the opposition could air their grievances more or less unhindered and, although the resolutions passed under opposition pressure were ignored, Lenin ruled, for the most part, by his prestige and by his considerable talents of persuasion.

The real power was vested from the start in the central organs of the party – the Central Committee, the Politburo, the Orgburo, and the Secretariat. However, hard and fast evidence as to which of these bodies prevailed at any one time is hard to come by. We can only infer from the respective frequency of their meetings or from the charges made by the oppositionists and from the occasional admissions by the leadership as to what happened. It appears from the opposition charges that between 1920 and 1921 the Central Committee exercised a great deal of power in its own right. At the IX Conference accusations were made that the Central Committee ceased to be a guiding organ and became one of administration and execution usurping all power of decision and creating a situation which some of the critics called one of the verkhy and nizy or the top echelons and the underlings.[16]

The charges of centralization and the resulting verkhy and nizy relationship between the respective party organs were quite justified. The party Rules recognized that problems facing local organizations had to be solved autonomously according to local needs. Yet, when local organizations attempted to do so pressures from the centre were applied and local interests ignored. In the early years such pressures were usually justified by military and other similar requirements. Later on, no justifications were used, and even this kind of criticism was labelled anti-party activity and dealt with accordingly.[17] However, the disciplinary provisions of the party Rules could be interpreted as giving the central organs precisely such power (2.31).

16 IX Conference, 156, 164.
17 X Congress, 45–6; XIV Congress, 85.

Perhaps the most glaring example of this attitude was Stalin's treatment of the Georgian central committee through his henchman in Georgia, G.K. Ordzhonikidze. Since the local Georgian central committee was not fully amenable to Stalin's demands, it was dismissed and a new one appointed in its place. The members of the old Georgian central committee were systematically being discredited and persecuted. This was 'truly a rare instance in the life of our party,' remarked Makharadze, a Georgian delegate to the XII Congress, although he knew very well that similar interventions took place before and elsewhere.[18]

At any rate, the Central Committee's predominance lasted from about September 1920 to some months after the X Congress when the centre of gravity shifted to the Politburo.[19] This trend to even greater centralization was influenced by the introduction of the NEP with all its concomitant dangers of bourgeois influence, at least as Lenin and some of his followers saw it.

This picture is confirmed by the frequency of the high organs' meetings. For example, we saw above that the opposition charged, and Lenin admitted, that the Central Committee as such, for all practical purposes, did not function up to December 1919. This is supported by the fact that it only met six times between March and December 1919, while the Politburo and Orgburo had 29 and 110 meetings respectively. During this period there were also 19 joint Politburo-Orgburo meetings. From December 1919 to September 1920 the Central Committee met only nine times while the Orgburo and Politburo met 77 and 64 times respectively. On the other hand, between September 1920 and March 1921 the Central Committee held 24 meetings, almost one a week, while the Orgburo and Politburo held 47 and 26 sessions respectively. The Central Committee held its own until August 1921. Between May and August 1921 it held nine meetings and the Orgburo and Politburo 48 and 39 respectively. However, between September and December 1921 the Central Committee met only 5 times while the Orgburo and Politburo met 63 and 44 times respectively.[20] By 1921, the Politburo, in conjunction with the Orgburo, also appeared to control party fractions in

18 XII Congress, 171–2.

19 ITSK, 18 September 1920 – January 1922, nos 22–37.

20 The figures are compiled from ITSK, nos 1–11, 28 May 1919 – 31 December 1919; nos 12–26, 14 January 1920 – 20 December 1920; nos 27, 28, 31–36, 27 January 1921, 5 March 1921, 20 July 1921 – 15 December 1921; no. 37, January 1922; the figures for the period from 6 March 1921 to 1 May 1921 were not published. They ceased to be published altogether after January 1922 although no. 40, March 1922 issue gives data for the previous year, the totals of which do not seem to correspond to the figures which appeared in the individual issues between March 1921 and March 1922.

non-party organizations, cancelling elections and appointing their own men to these.[21]

The centralization was made easier by the atmosphere which the leadership created and under which even party members in responsible positions became unwilling to make decisions. The result was that even the pettiest matters were submitted to the Politburo for final approval. The situation went so far that the Politburo had to make a decision on whether or not to buy tinned meat from a French exporter, as Lenin sarcastically observed at the XI Congress. Although this state of affairs was solely of his own making, he apparently became quite concerned about it and urged the liberation of the Politburo from petty detail.[22] His concern, of course, was not with the division of power but rather with the division of labour, and in any case, it appeared too late.

Lenin was no longer in full control and Stalin, due to his membership in the Politburo and Orgburo and due to his control of the Secretariat, was beginning to consolidate power in his own hands. Stalin acknowledged at the XIII Congress the concentration of power in the Politburo and Orgburo up to that Congress by confessing that the Central Committee plenum delegated all authority in decisions of basic problems to the Politburo, 'the infallible pope,' as Lutovinov described it. Stalin assured the Congress that this was no longer the case and the centre of gravity once again moved from the Politburo and Orgburo to the Central Committee.[23] Somewhat delicately he refrained from mentioning the enormous power concentrated in his own Secretariat.

Stalin's growing power did not escape the attention of some party members and both he and the Secretariat were beginning to get their share of criticism from the still vocal opposition at the XI Congress (although formally he did not become Secretary General until after the XI Congress in April 1922). Paradoxically, on this occasion, only a few months before he came to the conclusion that Stalin was a most undesirable leader, Lenin came to Stalin's defence arguing that 'in order to be able to apply control, it is necessary to have in the lead a man with authority, otherwise ... we shall drown in petty intrigues.'[24]

With official recognition of the existing situation, manifested by the appointment of Stalin as General Secretary in April 1922, the fate of the

21 XI Congress, 127–8.

22 XI Congress, 33–5, 43.

23 Trinadsatyi s''ezd RKP(b), Mai 1924 goda, Stenograficheskii otchet (Moscow, 1963), 121; hereafter cited as XIII Congress. For Lutovinov's remarks see XII Congress, 115–16.

24 XI Congress, 61, 143.

party was sealed – by then it was truly reduced, as Kosior remarked, even before the event, to 'loading firewood and sweeping streets.'[25]

The Secretariat, controlling all party appointments, made it possible for Stalin gradually to staff all decision-making bodies with his own supporters. In this venture he was greatly assisted by Lenin's recommendations on the enlargement of the Central Committee (see below headnote to XII Congress). Although, as the headnotes below indicate, it took Stalin some time before he emerged as the undisputed leader, by the time of the XIV Congress, the Secretariat became almost an all-powerful organ, interfering constantly with the work of the other leading organs, by combining policy and organization within its jurisdiction.[26]

This does not mean that the Central Committee became a useless organ. There was indeed truth in Stalin's statement on the shift of gravity from the Politburo to the Central Committee plenum. In the Politburo Stalin had to rely on various combinations with members who were not his underlings, whereas he could put more reliance on the Central Committee or the joint plenum thanks to their enlargement with his own supporters. In his struggle for power he used the plenums, especially the joint ones with the Central Control Commission, to eliminate all three successive opposition groups. In addition, since October 1923, Stalin used to enlarge the plenums and joint plenums by inviting to their meetings his supporters from various other party organizations or from the Revkom, in an obvious desire to give the resolutions emanating from these bodies the appearance of widest possible support.

The Central Control Commission alone, in its own right, also became an important tool in Stalin's struggle for power. As we saw above, this organ was established at the IX Conference and its origin is closely linked to opposition charges and discontent at that time. The establishment of the Central Control Commission may have looked like a victory in the opposition's fight against abuses on the part of the party bureaucrats. It was not a victory of long duration. Before long, these organs turned into instruments of the leadership solely for the enforcement of discipline in the party as well as in the Soviet organs (2.35), fighting the opposition and actively participating in purges and verifications of party members. In fact they were regarded by some party members as a form of a criminal investigation section and in reality became almost an adjunct of the OGPU. After 1925, under Stalin's guidance, and in violation of party Rules, they extended their jurisdiction and participated in much of the Central Committee's political work.[27]

25 XI Congress, 143.
26 XIV Congress, 274, 335.
27 XI Congress, 167; XIII Congress, 266, 298; XIV Congress, 525, 602, 572–3.

In the final analysis, during Stalin's ascendancy to power, the respective use of these organs depended on the particular issue to be decided. So long as Stalin was assured of a majority, in combination with one or another group in the Politburo or Orgburo, he did not hesitate to work through these bodies. If he was not assured of a majority he resorted to the use of the Central Committee or the joint plenum. This was the case during his alliance with Zinoviev and Kamenev. As we have seen, Stalin announced at the XIII Congress in 1924, that decision-making power shifted from the Politburo and Orgburo to the Central Committee. What he failed to divulge at the time was that in the summer of 1923, Zinoviev, although still allied with Stalin, took steps to limit the General Secretary's power (see headnote to XIV Congress) which resulted in the appointment of Zinoviev, Trotsky, Kamenev, and Korotkov to the Orgburo and which were also a clear indication to Stalin that his position in the Politburo was precarious at the time. Although the change in the Orgburo composition was of no practical significance because Stalin had unlimited control over the Secretariat, this development nevertheless forced him to turn to the larger bodies, safely packed with his underlings (although in one instance he experienced some difficulties even there; see below p. 305). In 1928 Stalin used similar tactics when he embarked on the collectivization policy and the elimination of Bukharin.

PARTY COMPOSITION

The elitist character of the party, postulated by Lenin in 1902, was maintained after the revolution, the party membership remaining a fraction of the total population. However, the party did not remain one of the professional full-time apparatchiks of the pre-revolutionary period. This group, of course, continued to be the most important one in the party, but was greatly outnumbered by those whose work occupied them otherwise, whether in the government proper, in the trade unions, or in general work in factories, offices, etc. At the time of the XIII Congress there was one apparatchik for every twenty-two members of the party and at the time of the XIV Congress one apparatchik for every forty party members.[28]

To keep the party in this privileged position the leaders had to pay special attention both to its composition as well as to the removal of undesirable elements from its ranks. While in the pre-revolutionary period keeping the size of the membership under control did not present a special problem, the situation changed with the seizure of power when, for obvious reasons, it became an advantage to be a party member. In 1917, before the seizure of power, the leaders encouraged a growth in membership which resulted in an increase from 23,600 to 115,000 members between January

28 XIV Congress, 81, Molotov's report.

1917 and January 1918[29] The checks and verifications of the prospective members had not yet reached their later thoroughness and, as a result, the party was penetrated by a number of 'careerists.' It is not certain that in the inital stages the leaders were particularly worried about this problem. Their main concern may have been solely an increase in membership. This attitude seems to have prevailed until some time after the outbreak of the Civil War when the increasingly more non-proletarian character and composition of the party came under attack. In an attempt to rectify the situation the first re-registration of party members was carried out (2.19). During this period, in 1918 and 1919, the percentage of workers (in terms of social origin) dropped from 60.2 per cent in 1917 to 56.9 per cent in 1918 and 47.8 per cent in 1919; the percentage of peasants increased from 7.6 per cent in 1917 to 14.5 per cent in 1918 and to 21.8 per cent in 1919. The percentage of white collar workers and others dropped from 32.2 per cent in 1917 to 28.6 per cent in 1918 and rose to 30.4 per cent in 1919. However, the re-registration was not a success – the percentage of workers further decreased in 1920 to 43.8 per cent, that of the peasants and white collar workers and others again rose to 25.1 per cent and 31.1 per cent respectively.[30] Consequently, the IX Conference in 1920 resolved that formalities for the admission of workers had to be reduced to a minimum and raised for all other categories (2.12). The leaders, while wishing for an increased percentage of workers, i.e., the urban proletariat, did not appear at this time to be especially concerned about the peasant representation in the party as about that of the white collar workers. This was indicated by their stated intention to put emphasis in admissions particularly on young workers and peasants (2.12).

The party Rules of 1919 passed by the VIII Conference introduced a new stage to the admission into the party, namely the so-called candidacy. From then on anyone wishing to join the party had to serve a period of candidacy no less than two months for workers and peasants and no less than six months for all others. Candidate members were accepted upon the recommendation of two party members of six months standing after such recommendation was checked by the appropriate local party committee (2.10).

By March 1921 the party, with 730,000 members (the division into full members and candidates is not available for this period), reached its

---

29 *Bolshaia sovetskaia entsyklopedia* XI (1st edition, Moscow, 1930), column 531; hereafter cited as BSE, the BSE figures cannot be considered fully reliable. For difficulties connected with the data compilation see T.H. Rigby, *Communist Party Membership in the USSR, 1917–1967* (Princeton, 1968), 59ff; hereafter cited as Rigby.
30 BSE, column 533.

peak in membership since the revolution. The sharp increase resulted again in a decrease of workers to 41.0 per cent in 1921 and in an increase of peasants to 28.2 per cent in the same period. The percentage of white collar workers and others dropped to 30.8 per cent in that time.[31] This phenomenon, in combination with the transition from War Communism to the New Economic Policy, brought about further demands for tightening of admission rules and of the party composition, and together with opposition criticism and the Kronstadt rebellion, culminated in the announcement at the X Congress of the first general purge and verification of party members, with the result that more than 200,000 were expelled.[32] Almost all of these came from the categories of the peasants and white collar workers and others mainly in the candidate rank.

By the beginning of 1922 the membership was 518,300 of whom 410,400 or 77.7 per cent were members and 117,900 or 22.3 per cent were candidates (1922 is the first year for which candidate figures are available). On the basis of social origin the percentage of workers rose to 44.4 per cent and that of peasants and white collar workers and others dropped to 26.7 per cent and 28.9 per cent respectively.[33]

The party organizations were instructed that in the future the sole criteria for the assessment of each prospective member's qualities were to be his devotion to the working class and to the proletarian revolution. Subsequently, at the XI Congress in 1922, the admission rules were further amended to make it more difficult for 'not purely proletarian elements' to enter the party (2.22, 2.25). The new Rules passed by the XII Conference and a resolution of the XII Congress respectively addressed themselves again to this question and decided that while the party had to admit members from all walks of life, the percentage of industrial workers actually engaged in production (so-called bench workers) had to be raised systematically and only in conjunction with that raise would acceptance of other categories be regulated and organized. It was stressed that only a proletarian composition of the party could be the best guarantee against the dangers of the NEP. As a result, until the XIII Congress, only industrial workers from the ranks of the candidate members were to be admitted to full membership and the candidacy of all others was to be extended by one more year. On the basis of the new 1922 Rules the candidates for admission were divided into three categories: workers, Red Army men of working class or peasant origin; peasants (apart from those in the Red Army);

31 BSE, column 533.

32 *Kommunisticheskaia Partiia Sovetskogo Soiuza v rezoliutsiiakh i resheniiakh s"ezdov, konferentsii i plenumov TsK* 11 (8th edition, Moscow, 1970), 211–12; hereafter cited as *KPSS*.

33 BSE, columns 531 and 533.

others. In line with the new party policy on composition, the first category of course received preferential treatment (2.31, 2.35, 2.39).

The new admission policy was not a success; the number of full members steadily fell from 410,400 in 1922 to 350,000 in 1924. The number of candidates for the same period rose insignificantly from 117,900 to 122,000. Nor did the proletarian content reach the desired heights, and it was once again decided to reduce admission requirements for workers. As a result, more detailed admission rules were presented to the XIV Conference in 1925 and subsequently confirmed by the XIV Congress which incorporated them in the 1925 party Rules (2.46, 2.52). Throughout the whole period the party also carried out several re-registrations to eliminate the remaining 'undesirable elements.'

These changes were part of a new recruitment drive, the so-called Lenin Enrolment of 1924 and 1925, launched after Lenin's death, to attract industrial workers into the party. As a result, from 1924 onwards the number of full members increased from 350,000 to 1,089,661 in 1929 and that of candidates rose from 122,000 to 442,686 during the same period. During the same time, the percentage of workers increased from 44.0 per cent to 61.4 per cent and that of the peasants decreased from 28.8 per cent to 21.7 per cent. The percentage of white collar workers and others decreased from 27.2 per cent to 16.9 per cent.[34] The two drives under the Lenin Enrolment also somewhat changed the character of the party in another way in that the percentage of full members between 1924 and 1926 decreased from 74.2 per cent to 59.2 per cent and that of candidates increased from 25.8 per cent to 40.8 per cent.[35]

Increase in the percentage of workers during the period 1924–29 was not consistent. For example, in 1927 the workers' percentage dropped from 56.8 per cent in 1926 to 55.7 per cent in 1927 which affected primarily some local organizations (2.57).[36] In 1927, however, a new recruitment drive was launched, the so-called October Enrolment, and the workers' percentage continued to rise from 55.7 per cent to 56.8 per cent in 1928 and to 61.4 per cent in 1929. The percentage of peasants rose from 19.0 per cent to 22.9 per cent and dropped again to 21.7 per cent during the same time. These increases took place at the expense of the white collar workers and others who dropped from 25.3 per cent to 20.3 per cent in 1928 and to 16.9 per cent in 1929.[37]

On the eve of the collectivization of agriculture, the Central Committee, in an obvious desire for better control of the countryside at that crucial time, issued instructions for the drafting into the party not only of industrial workers but also of agricultural and farm workers (2.64), with the result

34 BSE, columns 531 and 533.   36 BSE, column 533.
35 BSE, column 531.   37 BSE, column 533.

that by January 1930 the party had 1,674,910 members of whom 1,182,320 or 70.6 per cent were full members and 492,590 or 29.4 per cent were candidates. Of the total, 65.3 per cent were workers, 20.2 per cent were peasants (the last figure was a relative percentage decrease but an absolute increase), and 14.5 per cent were white collar workers and others.[38] At the same time, the residue of unreliable elements – those suspected of op-positionist tendencies – had to be removed and as a result the second general purge of this period was carried out (2.68).

With regard to nationality, the Russian element predominated out of proportion to its population size. In 1927 Russians constituted 65.0 per cent of the party although they formed only 52.9 per cent of the total Soviet population. Conversely, Ukrainians were only 11.7 per cent of the party although their share in the population was 21.2 per cent. On the other hand, small groups prominent in the leadership, such as Armenians, Georgians, Jews, Latvians, and Poles, held a disproportionate percentage of the party membership when compared to their respective populations.[39]

INSTRUMENTS OF POWER

The gigantic task facing the small leadership of a small party becomes more apparent when we consider the control which the leaders set out to exercise over non-party institutions. In a system which aspired to dominate all public and increasingly even private activity this implied total control.

In the initial stages the leaders seemed to realize that the small party apparatus had to limit itself to a guiding role; that problems, in a country as vast and varied as the Soviet Union, had to be solved on the basis of local needs; that the higher party organs could not and should not become victims of bureaucratism, i.e., bogged down in the morass of detailed decision making; and that a clear division of labour had to be maintained (2.9, 2.10, 2.11, 2.25). Party guidance was to be exercised through party fractions in all non-party organizations under the control of a correspond-ing party committee (2.10).

However, given the centralization of the party organization, it was not surprising that similar developments took place with regard to the relationship of the leading party organs to the non-party institutions. The first target became the soviets – the governmental institutions proper. For some time after the revolution the soviets were, for all practical purposes, ignored by the leading party organs and, although party fractions had been established in them, both were as a rule by-passed. This downgrading of the soviets and their party fractions aroused the ire of the Democratic Centralists and Workers' Opposition and the issue was aired at the VIII and

38 BSE, column 532.
39 BSE, columns 537 and 538; Rigby, 366.

IX Conferences. The leaders made promises of reform incorporated in a resolution (2.12) but it remained a dead letter.

By the time of the XI Conference in 1921 the situation changed, not to the extent that the soviets acquired power but to the extent that their leading organs were under tight control of the leading party organs and in turn fully controlled the local soviets. In other words, they were beginning to be used as proper transmission belts for party decisions. Already at the X Congress Lenin reminded his listeners that 'as a ruling party we could not but merge the party leadership with the soviet leadership – they are merged and will remain so.'[40] In this way a twofold system of control over the soviets was established: a vertical one through the party fractions in the soviets from the highest to the lowest which was abolished in 1925 (2.52), and a horizontal one through party organizations on corresponding levels of the soviet organizations. In addition, the party organizations were, of course, subject to a vertical type of control by higher party organs. Not to leave any loopholes, the control commissions and Rabkrin saw to it that all decisions of higher bodies were properly implemented.

As we saw above the inability of the leadership to break loose from the confines of this conspiratorial mentality became a target of Leonid Krasin's criticism at the XII Congress in 1923. Krasin, who was a Commissar of Foreign Trade, had been arguing for some time for more freedom in decision making for the specialists in the soviet organizations, but the effort only brought him an accusation of menshevism from Zinoviev and an assurance that the party 'was competent to do anything.'[41]

The specialists, on Lenin's insistence, had been employed in these agencies since 1920. However, they were completely controlled by centrally appointed party members and were in reality merely carrying out the leading organs' orders (see below pp. 100 and 188).[42] The system did not live up to Lenin's expectations. He returned to the theme at the XI Congress chiding his followers 'who do not know that they do not know' for unwillingness to learn trade and so on.[43] However, he was unwilling or unable to draw the one logical conclusion – namely to ease the central party control, although, as we saw above, he came to be very acutely aware of its short-comings.

The trend continued until the XIV Congress when Molotov proudly informed the delegates that all boards in the people's commissariats were almost exclusively staffed by party members, as were the directorates of

40 X Congress, 27.

41 XII Congress, 47, 124.

42 *Deviatyi s''ezd RKP(b), Mart-Aprel' 1920 goda, Protokoly* (Moscow, 1960), 162; hereafter cited as IX Congress.

43 XI Congress, 18.

banks, heavy industry, and trade organizations. This development was speeded up during the period between the XIII and XIV congresses when the number of party members in all administrative-economic commissariats increased two and a half times.[44] Admittedly, this was the period of the Lenin Enrolment and some of the experts in these organizations may have been recruited into the party. However, as the leading party organs had clearly established the practice of vetoing elections within the party fractions in non-party organizations and filling them with their own appointees, the result was that important positions in these fractions were always held by party members, who could be relied on to carry out the orders from the centre, thus leaving no room for individual initiative.

Communist overcrowding also took place in vtsik, the supposedly legislative body of the soviets, and also in the local soviet executive committees, supposedly legislative local bodies. Controlled as these bodies were, vertically and horizontally, the leadership came to the view that it could afford to allow some non-party members to be elected to these organs. According to Molotov, at the XIV Congress, the Central Committee, in a 'deliberate policy to increase the non-party element,' issued directives that vtsik should be composed of up to 30 per cent of non-party workers and peasants.[45] The latter belonged to the so-called non-party 'aktiv,' i.e., those who showed loyalty to the regime and participated in one form or another in public life. The very fact that the leadership could determine the percentage of these shows the complete control which it exercised over these institutions.

Practically identical developments took place in all other spheres. The leadership was very much aware that if the youth of the country was not effectively harnessed into the service of the party, the regime's chances of survival would be slim indeed. Consequently, work among youths and its indoctrination became of utmost importance. The vehicle through which the leaders set out to accomplish this task was to be a theoretically independent organization of a communist character – the Communist Youth League, or Komsomol.[46]

During the Civil War the Komsomol, like other groups controlled by the party, was successfully mobilized into the struggle against the Whites.[47] With the advent of the NEP, however, a reaction set in. The NEP was regarded by many young people as the betrayal of socialist principles; in

44 XIV Congress, 72.

45 XIV Congress, 66.

46 *KPSS o Komsomole i molodezhi: Sbornik rezoliutsii i reshenii s"ezdov, konferentsii i postanovlenii TsK, 1917–1958* (2nd edition, Moscow, 1958), 4–5; hereafter cited as *KPSS o Komsomole*.

47 *KPSS o Komsomole*, 35.

addition, with increased unemployment, the economic situation of young people deteriorated, the membership of the Komsomol fell appreciably, and anti-party tendencies became more evident. The party leadership answered with closer supervision of the Komsomol by the party through drafting of party members into the Komsomol and vice-versa (2.28 and 2.36). In order to prepare children for the work in Komsomol, a children's organization, the so-called Young Pioneers, was established and put under the guidance of Komsomol. It was up to the party, however, to help the Komsomol with the consolidation of 'revolutionary pedagogic forces around the children's communist movement' (2.36). During the period of the NEP, Komsomol, like the party, had the task of counter balancing bourgeois influences through propaganda and education. But it was not until the preparation of the Five-Year Plan that, like other party instruments, it came into its own. The grandeur of the plan appealed to the youthful imagination and temperament and Komsomol was effectively integrated into its implementation (2.61).[48]

The most intriguing problem facing the leaders was the question of the trade unions, especially since there appeared several divergent views within the party on this issue. The control of the trade unions was a subject of heated debates beginning with the IX Congress and continuing at the X and XI congresses (see below pp. 99, 114–17, 153). The debate was closely connected with Lenin's insistence on running industrial plants on the basis of so-called 'one-man management' since the beginning of 1918 and just as firmly opposed by the trade unions who repeatedly rejected any such notion.[49]

Given the beliefs of the leaders, the dilemma was quite genuine. As Bukharin asked at the IX Congress – was it possible to set the trade unions as independent organizations against the political organization of the working class – the party and the Soviet government?[50] The answer was obvious: the Soviet state was an all-encompassing form of workers' organization; the trade unions were a workers' organization, thus it would be absurd and a deviation from marxism to admit any possibility of opposition among them (2.11). The problem was not, as Bukharin pointed out, whether or not the trade unions should become governmental organs – they were already proceeding in that direction. The problem was how speedily they should get there.[51] The trade union controversy assumed such proportions that candidates for election to the X Congress were running on the basis of the trade union platforms (see below pp. 114–17). Three platforms emerged at the Congress: that of the Workers' Opposition favouring full autonomy for the trade unions, that of Trotsky and Bukharin, advocating trade union

48 *KPSS o Komsomole*, 233–6.   50 IX Congress, 214.
49 IX Congress, 584, note 9.   51 IX Congress, 219–20.

merger with the state (since the IX Congress Bukharin had become more radical on the issue and teamed up with Trotsky), and Lenin's Platform of Ten, which stood between the two extremes, urging caution and warning that a rapid conversion of the trade unions into state institutions would be a major political mistake (2.16). While the Lenin resolution of the X Congress was more moderate in its tone than Bukharin's at the IX Congress, Lenin, after having had more time to reflect upon the possible pitfalls of the NEP, swung towards the more radical view at the XI Congress. Absurd or not, marxist or not, Lenin was forced to admit a contradiction. While the task of the unions, so his resolution went, was defence of the toiling masses' interests, they could not refrain, on the other hand, from using pressures as participants in state power and as builders of the national economy (2.24).

At any rate, before the XI Congress, possibly out of concern that the more moderate tone of the resolution of the X Congress not be misunderstood, Lenin saw to it that the trade unions followed the official line. When the party fractions in the unions did not elect members who were deemed entirely satisfactory by the leading organs, they were simply dismissed and the Politburo nominees appointed.[52] In one instance this was admitted by Molotov at the XI Congress. The particular case concerned the central committee of the party fraction in the Metal Workers' Union which, at its congress in May 1921, nominated a majority of candidates from the ranks of the former Workers' Opposition 'thus giving it a one-sided character.' The Central Committee of the party intervened (which it had the right to do under the party Rules (2.10)), appointed its own nominees to the fraction's central committee who, by the mysterious logic of Soviet dialectics, were not 'one-sided,' and this made it possible for Molotov to assure the delegates of the XI Congress that such Central Committee interventions were no longer necessary.[53]

The appointment of party members from the centre to the leading organs of party fractions in the unions became a standard practice. Even this was not deemed sufficient and the overall communization of the unions followed the pattern established by the practice in the soviets. By the time of the XIII Congress in 1924, the presidiums of the central committees of the trade unions were composed of 97 per cent party members and, at the time of the XIV Congress in 1925, of 99 per cent party members.[54] Similarly, about 75 per cent of the delegates to the trade union congresses were party members.[55] Perpetuating the contradiction admitted by Lenin at the

52 XI Congress, 127–8.

53 XI Congress, 154.

54 XIV Congress, 58.

55 *Piatnadsatyi s"ezd VKP(b)*, I and II, *dekabr' 1927 goda* (Moscow 1961–62), I, 94; hereafter cited as XV Congress.

XI Congress, the trade unions, in an alleged workers' state, became their overseers instead of their protectors.

The leadership could not, of course, neglect the armed forces. The Red Army, at its inception, was not much of a fighting force, mainly because of bolshevik propaganda on peace before the revolution. Those who remained in the armed forces were imbued with an egalitarian spirit, elected their officers, and ran the army by committees. Recruitment was voluntary without compulsory service. It soon became clear that because of these and other organizational short-comings the armed forces would not amount to much for the defence of the revolution in the Civil War. Matters began to change with the appointment of Trotsky as commissar of war in March 1918. Trotsky centralized all activities of the army under the so-called Revolutionary Military Council, abolished the election of officers, introduced conscription, and against vocal opposition from some in the party drafted former tsarist officers into the services of the revolution. To guard against possible counter-revolutionary acts on their part, their families were held as hostages. In addition, the so-called political commissars were appointed to army units to check on counter-revolutionary activities but also to take charge of political propaganda among Red Army men. The commissars, as was explicitly stated, were not only direct representatives of the Soviet government but above all of the party, and to get full results from their work it was decided to speed up the establishment of party cells in the armed forces (2.8). The commissars had their own organization in the army which in 1919 became the Political Administration of the Army (PUR) responsible directly to the Central Committee. So long as Trotsky was in control it worked on its own. It was not until 1925 that Central Committee control, after Trotsky's fall from power, was put on a firm footing and the PUR became truly 'a military section of the Central Committee' (2.52). The dual command of the commissars and military commanders did not function smoothly, however. Although some compromises were arrived at (2.45), the problem was not solved until many years later.

Serious misunderstandings arose too between party members functioning in the armed forces and local party organizations. As a result a parallel party organization was established in the armed forces with defined roles and functions to minimize such frictions (2.19). In addition, the armed forces were also put under separate control of the OGPU.

The pre-revolutionary party Programme, which called for organization of the army on a territorial-militia basis, was put to rest at the VIII Party Congress because of the exigencies of the Civil War. At the IX Congress the issue was revived by Trotsky who wanted to apply the system, although under centralized control, to the solution of the industrial crisis. Trotsky's proposal called for a partial transition to militia formations in districts with the most solid proletarian population.

However, no measures were taken to implement Trotsky's plan and by 1921, after the revolts in the countryside and the Kronstadt uprising, it became a dead issue. At the X Congress in 1921 it was clearly stated that any agitation for a transition to a militia system was incorrect and dangerous in practice. The forms, methods, and speed of such a transition depended wholly on the international and domestic situation, on the length of the 'breathing space,' and on the mutual relations between the city and the village.

The motives behind the reluctance to decentralize the armed forces are not difficult to fathom. Any decentralization would have weakened direct party control and also endangered the security of the regime. The justification of the centralization of the armed forces was very much in tune with Lenin's other arguments. It was permissible to make demands for a transition to the militia system at a time and under the conditions of 'peaceful' capitalist development to take advantage of bourgeois legality, but when the class struggle assumed the proportions of a civil war the slogan of 'people's militia' lost all its meaning (2.8).

There was, of course, one other and all important instrument used with great effectiveness – the secret police. Various party resolutions have little or nothing to say on the subject which would be particularly revealing. The Cheka, as it was called at its foundation in 1918, as well as its successor, the GPU in 1922, and OGPU in 1924, were all dealt with primarily by the decrees of VTSIK, and OGPU also by the 1924 Soviet Constitution. As such it was under nominal governmental control of the Sovnarkom. Since the Sovnarkom and the VTSIK were under party control so was, of course, the secret police. This is evident from a few circulars issued by the Central Committee dealing with the secret police (2.53).

ECONOMIC AFFAIRS

Given the marxist point of view, the proof that Lenin seized power in the wrong country was perhaps nowhere more apparent than in the sphere of economic activity. He was, of course, aware of the dilemma. In 1917, before the seizure of power, Lenin observed that 'the party of the proletariat cannot set itself the aim of "introducing" socialism in a country of small peasantry so long as the overwhelming majority of the population has not realized the necessity for a socialist revolution.' The problem, as Lenin saw it, 'was not about promises of reform – these are empty words – the problem is to make the step which is necessary at this time.'[56]

Conscious as he was of this inconsistency, he never satisfactorily explained by what right he was then imposing the will of the small bolshevik

56 Lenin 2, XX, 119, 481.

minority on the 'overwhelming majority' who saw no need for socialism. He did attempt to justify the seizure of power by his belief in the, more or less, imminent outbreak of the international revolution. Lenin returned to this theme again, after the introduction of the NEP, but by then even he could not think of a proper justification for continued bolshevik rule; he only tightened the reins of power even further than before.

Aware as Lenin was, then, of the unsuitability of Russia for socialism, he did not contemplate any large-scale nationalization of industry immediately after the revolution. So far as it took place in 1918, nationalization was due to another factor: the additional takeovers of factories by workers were more a manifestation of their syndicalist tendencies than a reflection of official doctrine.[57]

The situation was not dissimilar in agriculture. In spite of the pre-revolutionary determination to nationalize land, the Bolsheviks shied away from it in practice after the revolution, and while they did abolish property in land, they distributed all of it to the peasants. In reality the peasants took the distribution into their own hands and were in fact sanctioned in doing so by the leadership. In this sense, the Bolsheviks adopted the land policy of the Socialist Revolutionaries as they themselves admitted (2.2), which made the legitimacy of their rule even more dubious.

Peasant ownership of land, in practice if not in theory, however, did not result in increased agricultural production. The reason was quite simple. The factories taken over by the workers ground to a standstill because of the inability of the workers to run them. This in turn brought about an acute shortage of consumer goods. The peasants, unable to buy anything, ceased to produce. This resulted in forced requisitions of grain by the leadership in order to feed the Red Army during the Civil War. In practice, as Lenin himself later admitted, it meant more often than not that the peasants were deprived not only of whatever little surplus they may have accumulated, but also of food for their own consumption.

Lenin's later explanations of this policy, which was generally referred to as the policy of War Communism, were contradictory. On one occasion, he argued that they had tried to organize a small-peasant country along communist lines, which he warned against in 1917. However by 1921 this was, in the absence of the international revolution, for all practical purposes, an admission that the bolshevik seizure of power was an error and that those in the party who opposed him at the time, as well as the Mensheviks and the Socialist Revolutionaries, were correct. On another occasion, and on safer ground, he claimed that the party had no other

---

57 Leonard Schapiro, *The Communist Party of the Soviet Union* (London, 1960), 191; hereafter cited as Schapiro.

choice, having been pushed into the forced requisitions policy by the circumstances of the Civil War.[58]

This method of taxation of the peasantry drove them beyond the limits of their endurance and in 1920 uprisings in the countryside took place against the Bolsheviks. While the uprisings were ruthlessly suppressed, Lenin learned his lesson. The international proletariat could no longer be relied upon in the foreseeable future and so only an agreement with the peasantry in Russia could save the socialist revolution under the conditions of 'capitalist encirclement.' The concrete result, the New Economic Policy (NEP), was the replacement of forced requisitions by the so-called tax in kind, and later by a monetary tax. Before long, as Lenin urged, the peasants were able to trade their surplus freely on the open market (2.17, 2.18, 2.34).[59]

While the NEP was originally directed towards the peasantry, its principles were soon extended to industry as well. To induce the peasants to produce and sell their products they had to be able to buy goods with their money. Consequently, industry had to have some incentives too. Lenin sought the solution in a partial return to capitalism. Some smaller industries were allowed to remain in private hands, some were leased to private individuals or co-operatives, while large industry remained nationalized. However, all now had to operate on the basis of the free trade principle. The NEP did not immediately solve the country's economic problems. While agricultural production made some progress, industrial production lagged considerably behind – resulting in large disparity between agricultural and industrial prices which Trotsky, at the XII Congress, termed the 'scissors crisis.' The problem was tackled through various monetary policies which considerably reduced the price disparity although they did not entirely remove it (2.18, 2.21).

By 1923, mainly under the influence of Bukharin who became the principal advocate of this policy, the bolshevik leaders accepted the inevitable, namely that the peasants had to be allowed to prosper so as to provide the sorely needed capital for industrialization (2.34).[60] However, some kolkhozes and sovkhozes were established in the early 1920s, although most agricultural production was based on the individual farmer until collectivization, when individual holdings were turned mainly into kolkhozes and some into sovkhozes (2.61, 2.62, 2.67).

The adoption of the NEP did not mean that the leaders abandoned all desire for central planning or their concern for heavy industry. In 1921 the so-called Gosplan was established. However, the role of the Gosplan in the

58 Lenin 5, LIII, 246–7; also Lenin 2, XXVI, 388; XXVII, 29.
59 X Congress, 36–8.
60 Schapiro, 275–6.

next few years was basic planning and it came into its own only with the era of the Five-Year Plans (2.21, 2.33).[61]

To realize the extent to which the NEP was an admission of defeat, it is instructive to compare that policy with a pre-revolutionary concept of Lenin's which he called 'the revolutionary democratic dictatorship of the proletariat and the peasantry.' This democratic dictatorship was to be the most advanced form of a left-wing bourgeois capitalist state under the political control of the proletariat.[62] On the economic side, it was to remain bourgeois capitalist; on the political side proletarian, drawing its support primarily (in addition to the proletariat) from what Lenin called the 'people par excellence,' that is, the small peasantry as the chief representative of the petty bourgeoisie. This was to be the last state before the dictatorship of the proletariat was accomplished. Neither Lenin nor his successors have admitted the practical identity of the NEP and the revolutionary democratic dictatorship. Instead, the NEP has been referred to as state capitalism under the dictatorship of the proletariat, although Lenin touched upon the problem at the XI Congress by reminding the delegates that the task before the party was 'to complete the bourgeois revolution to the end.'[63]

Although the one and only justification for the bolshevik seizure of power – the outbreak of revolutions in the capitalist countries – disappeared, and with it the one and only rationale for bolshevik rule, Lenin still did not explain by what right he was imposing his will on an unwilling 'overwhelming majority.' He did, however, succeed in buying their neutrality.

AGITATION, PROPAGANDA, CULTURE, EDUCATION
In addition to the centralization of control, to the retreats on the economic front, and to the use of terror to maintain themselves in power, the leaders resorted to a large-scale effort to win acceptance for their doctrine and policies. Apart from their obvious desire to convince the population about the correctness of the doctrine for its own sake, they also realized that this would facilitate the implementation of their decisions. Soon after the revolution they addressed themselves to the task of systematic indoctrination of the population. Through this indoctrination they attempted to

---

61 KPSS III, 504–23.

62 Lenin 2, VII, 197, 199–200.

63 XI Congress, 38; Lenin 2, XVII, 29; the NEP also found an advocate in Trotsky who was a few steps ahead of Lenin on this issue. At the beginning of 1920 he presented theses on "Fundamental Questions of Food and Land Policy" to the Central Committee which essentially proposed to implement what Lenin did under the NEP. At the time Trotsky's proposals were rejected as a denial of the leninist policy of the party 'in that period' (X Congress, 865, note 64).

penetrate all walks of life; considerable resources of the party were mobilized to fulfil this truly enormous task.

The kind of political indoctrination which the bolshevik leaders had in mind would have been a colossal enterprise even in a country with a literate population and developed communications. In a country such as Russia in the early 1920s, with a high rate of illiteracy and with poor communications, the task defied imagination. The extent to which the leaders succeeded is arguable. Since in 1926 the rate of illiteracy was still about 40 per cent it is doubtful that the indoctrination was an unqualified success during the 1920s.

Indoctrination must have been also made more difficult, even among those who were reasonably literate and receptive, by the policy switches of this period – from War Communism to the NEP, and from the NEP to the collectivization. The prolonged succession struggle, after Lenin's death, must have also contributed to the public's confusion.

To speed up the process as much as possible, formal education and indoctrination were combined in one wherever possible. Scientific socialism had to become an integral part of all cultural activity. School teachers had to regard themselves not only as agents of general but also of communist enlightenment. To ensure obedience of these directives they were controlled not only by their superiors but also by local party organizations.[64]

The same criteria were applied to the press. As early as 8 November 1917, one day after the seizure of power, the Military Revolutionary Committee Against Counter-revolutionary Agitation ordered the closing down of a number of non-communist newspapers and the following day the Sovnarkom adopted a resolution, 'On the Press,' which gave the government power to suspend newspapers and confiscate printing presses.[65] With the elimination of all anti-bolshevik opposition on the territory under bolshevik control in the summer of 1918, all non-communist newspapers were forced to cease publication. The local party organizations were charged not only with the revitalization of the party and soviet press, but party committees were also to give editors general political directives and watch closely that these were fulfilled.[66] In the initial stages these efforts left something to be desired, from the point of view of the leaders. This was so primarily because the party organizational problem had not yet been solved and a rectification of this situation was sought in the establishment of the Agitation and Propaganda section of the Secretariat of the Central Commit-

---

64 KPSS II 80–3.

65 Lenin 5, XXXII, 453, notes 24 and 25; see also 51–55 on Lenin's statements on the freedom of the press.

66 KPSS II, 84–6.

tee in September 1920. From rather inauspicious beginnings, the Agitprop developed into one of the major sections of the Secretariat. The press subsection of Agitprop was to exercise overall direction of all the provincial press and give them directions in accordance with the overall political and economic tasks of the party (2.20). After the introduction of the NEP, because of fear of the policy's bourgeois influence on the workers, especially because of what the leaders called their political illiteracy, agitation and propaganda were considerably widened (2.29). In 1924, when the party began to press for an increased influx of industrial workers into the party under the Lenin Enrolment, additional directives were worked out for Agitprop. While, in the meantime, the publication of party journals and newspapers increased, and the *Gleichschaltung* of the press became for all practical purposes complete, there was still a shortage of politically literate party members in factories and this interfered with Agitprop's work. It seems certain that the reasons behind the increased and by now all-encompassing party endeavours in the sphere of press and propaganda were, to a large degree if not totally, motivated by the continuing fear of the influence of the NEP on the population (2.24).

To improve the situation, every party member was duty bound to subscribe to and read the party press, and the number and quality of newspapers in non-Russian languages was to be raised and improved (2.29, 2.43, 2.44).

Apparently, enormous resources were channelled into this effort, since it was announced at the XIV Congress that the printing of newspapers in all languages increased in the previous year by 87 per cent and that of books by 66 per cent.[67] In the wake of the increase in the number of newspapers followed increased party control. The new party Rules of 1925 empowered the Central Committee to confirm all editors of major local party presses (2.52).[68]

At the same time Agitprop also increased its control over literature, although still professing its support for free competition in that sphere. A XIV Congress resolution introduced the beginning of so-called 'socialist realism' by stating that all writing had to have a 'social class' content with the exception of the 'literary form' which, together with style, would develop to match the epoch (2.47). By 1929, with the end of NEP and with the third revolution gathering momentum, Agitprop became one of the major tools of Stalin in his drive for industrialization.

The major publications during this period were the party daily *Pravda* (Truth), published since before the revolution in the name of the Central Committee, which served as an informational device for the whole party

67 XIV Congress, 82.
68 XIV Congress, 878–9.

membership but was directed to non-party readers as well. Its counterpart on the governmental level was a daily called *Izvestiia* (News), published by VTSIK. More specialized party publications, designed primarily for the use of the party apparatchiki, included the weekly *Izvestiia tsentral'nogo komiteta* (News of the Central Committee) and *Spravochnik partiinogo rabotnika* (Guide Book of the Party Worker). These two publications were devoted solely to the reporting of political and organizational activity of the party. Another publication of a more theoretical bent was the *Bol'shevik*, published by the Central Committee. There were other publications of a more historical character which published accounts, usually written by more prominent party members, of events in party history or episodes in party leaders' lives. The latter were usually of the hagiographic kind although many are an invaluable source of information. These publications included the *Proletarskaia Revoliutsiia* (Proletarian Revolution), *Krasnaia Letopis* (Red Annals), and *Krasnyi Arkhiv* (Red Archive).

OPPOSITION

A brief account of the various opposition groups is embodied in the head-notes to the congresses, conferences, and plenums. However, to understand these groups, they must be viewed from the perspective of what it actually was that they were in opposition to. We can safely start from the premise that they were all dedicated communists and that the differences which arose revolved not around basic questions of communism but rather on how to implement it. This is not surprising since the legacy which Marx left behind did not tell them how to build socialism in general, and in a predominantly peasant country in particular. Marx assumed that when a revolution took place in a country it would have been carried out by a proletariat which comprised the majority of the population and in that sense the dictatorship of the proletariat would have been a dictatorship of the majority. Some of the Bolsheviks were acutely aware of the situation in Russia at the time of the seizure of power and realized that it did not correspond to Marx's assumptions. This manifested itself in their insistence on coalition with the other socialist parties in order to form a majority rule (2.1). However, in a short span of time, they returned to the fold and from then on accepted unquestioningly the supreme role of the party over the rest of the country (as postulated by Lenin), to the exclusion of everyone else.

So far as can be judged, the major opposition groups which emerged after the revolution, the Democratic Centralists and the Workers' Opposition, as well as the later groups of Trotsky, Zinoviev, and Kamenev, their United Opposition, and finally Bukharin, never questioned the supreme role of the party, and all sanctioned Lenin's liquidation of the Mensheviks and Socialist Revolutionaries; nor did they raise a voice in protest to the brutal suppression of the Kronstadt uprising. As Shliapnikov, a member of the Workers' Opposition, reminded the delegates to the X Congress, at the same time as the cream of the Bolshevik Revolution, the Kronstadt sailors, were being slaughtered: 'we have no disagreements on the basic questions of our internal and external policies.'[69]

It was no secret at the time that there was no love lost between the Democratic Centralists and the Workers' Opposition, and one is forced to wonder if, had it been within their respective power, they would not have applied the same methods to each other as Lenin did to them both.[70] This was certainly true about the later oppositionists. Trotsky, Zinoviev, Kamenev, and Bukharin, all of whom ultimately ended up in opposition to Stalin, cheerfully sanctioned the destruction of the Workers' Opposition and the Democratic Centralists. Zinoviev, Kamenev, and Bukharin all had a major share in the destruction of Trotsky; Bukharin fully supported Stalin in his final elimination of the United Opposition of Trotsky, Zinoviev, and Kamenev. Consequently the question of what all the opposition activity was about cannot be avoided. In the initial stages the Workers' Opposition and the Democratic Centralists criticized the leadership for inefficiency, incompetence, bureaucratism, and generally for a lack of proper organization. For example, at the VIII Congress, Osinsky charged that there was no political line in the party, that general directives did not exist, and problems were solved, from case to case, by 'comrades in authority.' At the same Congress, even Vareikis, not a member of the opposition, complained that there were absolutely no communications to local organizations, there was no explanation of policy, no guidelines.[71] At the IX Conference, the inefficiency of the Secretariat in particular came under fire. Kotliar remarked that, when Stasova was the secretary, the whole organization plan could be found in her pocket, while under Krestinsky, it was lodged in the latter's extraordinary memory: 'that is not normal,' he complained. Sapronov's charges echoed those of the VIII Congress – local party organizations did not receive the Central Committee circulars – not even the *Izvestiia Ts.K.* Tomsky attributed it all to the fact that when 'Comrade Sverdlov died ... the whole gigantic archive of the Central Committee died with him.'[72] Similar charges of incompetence and inefficiency were level-

69 X Congress, 71.

70 See, for example, the statements by Osinsky and Rafail at the X Congress, 78 and 99 respectively.

71 VIII Congress, 28–9.

72 IX Conference, 108–9, 111, 120.

led at the Central Committee and the Orgburo at the IX Congress.[73] There
were also charges of a different nature, of course, referring primarily to the
lack of autonomy of local party organizations, or of the non-party institutions such as the trade unions or the soviets, or charges that the party was
being alienated from the masses.[74] On several occasions, the leadership
was even criticized for allowing the influx of 'foreign elements' into the
party which was losing its proletarian character.[75]

These accusations were remarkable for two reasons. All of them
were based on the assumption that there existed in Russia a dictatorship of
the proletariat in the original marxist sense and none of them questioned
the leninist premise of the supremacy of the party as a vanguard guiding
force. On the many occasions when the opposition complained about lack
of democracy and freedom, it was only within very narrow limits. This was
clearly put by V.V. Kosior, a follower of Trotsky, at the XII Congress,
when he complained about the leading group in the Central Committee
which carried out its own policy to the exclusion of all other party members: 'I understand,' said Kosior, 'why the working class in our country ...
has to apply excluding measures in relation to other classes in the struggle
for its dictatorship. But I do not understand why now, under conditions of
peaceful construction, this excluding law has to be applied to us?'[76]

Trotsky, Zinoviev, Kamenev, and Bukharin did not do better. It is
instructive to compare Trotsky's attack on Lenin, after the II Congress,
when he was isolated, with an answer which he gave at the height of his
power to some of the western delegates to the II Comintern Congress in
1920 who expressed alarm about the centralizing tendencies of the Bolsheviks: 'Today we received peace proposals from the Polish government.
Who decides this question? We have the Sovnarkom but they must be
subject to certain control as well. Whose control? That of the working class
as formless, chaotic mass? No. So we have called a meeting of the Central
Committee of the party in order to discuss the proposal and decide whether
or not to answer it.'[77]

It is almost unnecessary to comment on all these pronouncements
which speak for themselves. All the evidence points only in one direction –
the various opposition groups complained about centralization, lack of
democracy and freedom when they were excluded from power. This was

73 IX Congress, 48–9, 54.

74 IX Conference, 105.

75 See, for instance, Shliapnikov's remarks at the X Congress, 74.

76 XII Congress, 102–4.

77 Der Zweite Kongress der Kommunistischen Internationale, Protokoll der Ver-
handlugen vom 19. Juli in Petrograd und vom 23. Juli bis 7. August 1920 in Moskau
(Hamburg, 1921), 70ff.

rather shrewdly observed by Mikoyan, at the XIV Congress, when he remarked that 'when Zinoviev has a majority, he is for iron discipline, for submission. When he does not have a majority, if even for a minute, he is against it.'[78]

Differences on questions of democracy and freedom or on the role and organization of the party between Lenin and Stalin on the one hand, and the various opposition groups on the other hand, were those of degree but not those of kind. Like Lenin, all of them were intolerant of dissenting views and denied the right they claimed for themselves to others. In the last analysis, the only distinction between the oppositionists and Lenin or Stalin was that the former were not in power while Lenin and Stalin were. None of them understood that the fundamental condition of liberty is its universality.

CONCLUSION

A mere glance at the development of the party organization and policy shows that all the decisive steps were taken during Lenin's time and under Lenin's guidance. While Lenin's style of rule was different from that of Stalin, it nevertheless provided the organizational framework and indeed logically lent itself to the establishment of a vozhd, or leader, which Stalin was shrewd enough to see and exploit.

The fact that Lenin became aware of this danger belatedly and in vain attempted to warn the party against it before his death, does not change the situation. He still expected the party to be led on the basis of the elitist principle but by a collective rather than by one man. In a sense, this was yet another manifestation of his conceit and arrogance – he did not deem any one among his followers worthy and able enough to don his mantle.

We have seen that, although meeting with strong opposition, Lenin's justifications of the elitist party organization before the revolution had a ring of plausibility about them. We also saw that Lenin continued with that type of organization after the revolution. The question which then remains to be answered is why Lenin insisted on doing so.

The principal reason is that Lenin, because of his impatience, haste, and dogmatism, denied himself the luxury of a majority rule. He tried to console himself that the minority he would have to look to for support would be compensated by the electrifying 'spark' effect which the Russian revolution would have on the proletariat in the western countries, who would themselves rise, overthrow their bourgeois governments, establish dictatorships of the proletariat (and thus a sort of an international pro-letarian majority) on the coat-tails of which the Soviet regime would be

78 XIV Congress, 186.

able to survive, and with whose assistance it would be dovetailed into the march towards the classless society.

However, the revolutions in the West did not take place, as Lenin expected, and instead of compensating for this short-coming on the part of the western proletariat by making fresh approaches to the other socialist parties in Russia, he kept many of their leaders in jail and persisted in ruling alone with minority support.[79] This unwillingness to share power was in large part responsible for the Civil War and the foreign intervention.

Under the impact of the Civil War and the foreign intervention, and seeing that his original expectations were not about to come true, Lenin was forced to add to the doctrine. He took the occasion of the VIII Congress (at which he attempted to answer the charges of the German socialist, Kautsky, who labelled the Soviet regime a militarist one and not a socialist one) to postulate a state of affairs, known as capitalist encirclement, which was to guide him and his successors until the latter part of the 1950s. In his rebuttal to Kautsky, in defence of the Soviet military organization, Lenin argued that 'we live not only in a state but in a system of states, and the existence of the Soviet republic along with the imperialist states for a long time is unthinkable. In the end one or the other will conquer. And before this end comes, a whole series of the most horrible clashes between the Soviet republic and the bourgeois states is inevitable.'[80]

Combined with this postulated external danger was, of course, a later domestic one, as manifested by the NEP, which in fact was a policy of compensation for the lack of revolutionary activity in the West but which left the small party surrounded like an embattled garrison in the sea of petty bourgeois peasants. Determined to govern at all cost, Lenin then left himself no choice but to do so in a manner which did not allow for such luxuries as democracy, freedom, and tolerance.

On each occasion when Lenin met with criticism, he justified his style of rule by these postulates. At the VIII Congress, answering the charges of centralization, he dismissed them with the remark that 'during the Civil War one cannot do otherwise. If we did we would engage in half-way measures or parliament and in the epoch of dictatorship it is impossible to solve problems or administer the party or the Soviet organizations through parliamentary means.' To the charges that the Central Committee was not performing as it should, that it did not even bother to issue circular letters

79 In the one and only relatively free election in Russia under the Soviet system the Bolsheviks received about 25 per cent of the popular vote. These were elections into the so-called Constituent Assembly which took place at the end of 1917 and beginning of 1918. During its first, and last, session, the Assembly was dispersed by Lenin's Red Guards and its leaders imprisoned.

80 VIII Congress, 17.

and inform the party of its activities, he answered: 'One must bear in mind the conditions under which the work was carried out ... We were forced every day to give political directives on a variety of problems and only in exceptional cases, even rare cases, could we do so through the Politburo or the plenum of the Central Committee.'[81]

At the IX Congress, answering similar charges, he dismissed them as 'phrases about minority and majority, about democracy and freedom' which 'do not solve anything.' On the same occasion, during the debate on the trade unions, he rejected opposition pressure for a collective leadership in factories as a theoretical muddle with which the Central Committee could never get reconciled: 'Had we allowed in the basic questions of our military activity in our Civil War one tenth of such theoretical muddle we would have been beaten and it would have served us right.'[82] Some time before the X Congress, when criticized for intimidation and terrorizing, he answered: 'Look here, here we have a threat to the rule of the working class and to the dictatorship of the working class.'[83]

It cannot be denied that for more than three years of Lenin's rule the Soviet regime was under one or another form of attack. However, the situation was one of Lenin's own making – his determination to rule by or through a minority – and the charges against him were not concerned with that aspect but referred to his treatment of the party and its members. The Workers' Opposition and the Democratic Centralists, the principal opposition groups of his time, were no danger to the Soviet regime; in fact they demonstrated their loyalty to it by their unqualified support of Lenin at the X Congress during the Kronstadt uprising in 1921. Yet, a few days later that loyalty earned them the order of dissolution and a threat of expulsion from the party.

The explanation of Lenin's treatment of the party is twofold. First, he never succeeded in rising above his conspiratorial view of politics. To him the situation in the post-revolutionary period bore marked resemblance to that of 1902. He postulated a conspiracy, international and domestic, against the party and the regime, which (just as in 1902) could be fought only by conspiratorial methods. Any opening up of the party to discussion, free exchange of views, or decentralization would slacken its guard and expose it to infiltration and subversion from 'White Guards to Mensheviks.'

Secondly, we cannot separate the man from his policies. Making allowance for the inevitable exceptions, this is generally true of all political leaders in all political systems but especially of those in dictatorial systems where the constraints on their freedom of action are far smaller than in less

81 VIII Congress, 25–6.   83 X Congress, 28.
82 IX Congress, 21–2.

centralized ones. Consequently, it is very much open to question whether Lenin would have shown more respect for others had developments been different, had the Soviet regime come into existence under different and peaceful conditions, or whether he would have followed substantially different policies towards the party and its members. For Lenin to behave otherwise than he did would have been out of character – he was arrogant, utterly convinced about the correctness of his doctrine (no matter how much he may have distorted its original premises), and too intolerant of the views of others. In this respect, it is instructive to open at random any volume of Lenin's works, where one is at once struck by the extreme, polemical style of his writings and speeches and by the vitriolic attacks on all who disagreed with him even if only on minor points. Significantly, the same applies to Stalin – his technique, although cruder, more ponderous, and less sophisticated than Lenin's, was nevertheless pure, unadulterated leninism.

This side of his character must have figured prominently in Lenin's decision to embrace the marxist doctrine – it provided all the firm 'scientific' answers and may explain his behaviour (or Stalin's); for, in the last analysis, such behaviour is not surprising if a man believes himself to be in possession of the ultimate truth.[84] Indeed, so unshakable was Lenin's conviction of the rightness of his course that, foreshadowing Soviet attitudes fifty years later, he regarded anyone within the party who disagreed with him as insane or otherwise sick. For example, in his struggle with the opposition at the IX Conference he described their arguments as a 'manifestation of extreme fatigue reaching the point of hysteria.'[85]

Lenin was the mentor and Stalin the pupil who carried his master's legacy to its logical conclusion. The pages of history are full of accounts of atrocities committed in the name of high principles. The two bolshevik leaders were no exception. As difficult as it may be, to accept it, both, in their own ways, wished to serve what they regarded as the most worthy cause; and there lies one of the ironies of history, for there are no men more dangerous and more ruthless than those who 'know' how to save mankind.

84 Primarily due to the influence of Trotsky's writings, as well as because of the extent of Stalin's atrocities, it has come to be widely believed that Stalin was a power-drunk dictator, devoid of any ideological commitment. The opposite view, which I share, regarding Stalin's ideological commitment, is lucidly and convincingly argued by R.H. McNeal, 'Trotsky's Interpretation of Stalin,' in T.H. Rigby (ed.), *Stalin*, (Englewood Cliffs, 1966), 143–52. It should be noted that reference here is made to commitment, and not to Stalin's contribution to or understanding of the ideology.

85 IX Conference, 188; this was not an isolated example. For a witty and outstanding discussion of this leninist technique see Adam Ulam, *The Bolsheviks* (New York, 1965), 515–53.

Documents

Sessions of the Central Committee   11–15 November 1917

The Central Committee, the most authoritative party organ until November
1917 did not play as significant a role in the early days of the Soviet regime as
might have been expected. This may have been due to several reasons: first,
the difficulties which Lenin had with his fellow members of the Central
Committee regarding the seizure of power; second (perhaps following from
the first), the decision to put the organization of the seizure of power under
the so-called Military Revolutionary Committee of the Petrograd Soviet, of
which Trotsky was the chairman and which ceased to function only in the
latter part of December; and third, the chaotic situation of the first days after
the seizure of power which made it difficult for all the members of the Central
Committee to get together when required. It was for this last reason that the
so-called buro of the Central Committee was established. It consisted of
Lenin, Sverdlov, Trotsky, and Stalin (and later also Sokolnikov). Although it
was the duty of the buro to call to its meetings all Central Committee
members present in Petrograd at any one time, there is evidence that the
day-to-day business of the party was decided by Lenin and Sverdlov in the
name of the buro.

The first sessions of the Central Committee after the October Revolution
were absorbed by the question of including in (or continuing to exclude from)
the new government representatives of the other 'Soviet parties' (principally
the Socialist Revolutionaries and the Mensheviks).

On 11 November 1917 eleven members of the Central Committee (including neither the preoccupied Lenin and Trotsky nor Stalin) passed a series of
one-sentence resolutions concerning party policy on this question. The records of this session that survived are, according to the published Soviet
version, fragmentary and unclear. The following eight points may be regarded as a single resolution. The records on voting are confusing. Point 1
was said to be 'adopted unanimously,' while points 2–4 were 'adopted.'
The voting on point 5 was especially unclear. First, the figures 7 for and 3
against are given. Later during the meeting someone moved a roll call on
point 5 which was to include the votes of those who were absent. The motion
was carried but the vote was apparently taken at once and the opinion of the
absent members was not solicited. The vote was recorded as 4 in favour and 7
against. It may well be that the first vote was secret and that when it came to a

roll call three members changed their minds not wishing to be associated with a resolution which was so clearly directed against Lenin. Point six passed, 5–1 with 3 abstaining. No vote is recorded on points 7 and 8, though the implication seems to be that they passed.

2.1

[On the Soviet Parties and the New Government]   11 November 1917

1   The Central Committee recognizes the necessity of broadening the basis of the government and the possibility of changes in its composition.

2   [Text missing; it was proposed by Ia. A. Berzin (winter)]

3   The government was created by the [Soviet] Central Executive Committee and is responsible to it. *We shall not participate in a government which will include the right internationalists parties.*

4   The government approves the decrees on peace and land.

5   We are not issuing an ultimatum concerning entry into the government [Sovnarkom] of all Soviet parties up to and including the People's Socialists, *and we agree to renounce the candidacy* [as members of the Sovnarkom] *of Trotsky and Lenin if they* [the other socialist parties] *demand this*. [The word 'adopted' appeared after this sentence. In this context the intent of the reference to an 'ultimatum' is to state that the Bolsheviks do not insist on the exclusion from the government of other socialist parties, even the relatively right-wing People's Socialists. The statement is in the negative because it was being alleged, not without reason, that the Bolsheviks would not enter into any negotiations on a coalition unless certain parties were excluded in advance. The above italics are added by the present editor to designate material crossed out in the original record.]

6   The mutual right to veto the candidates [for membership in the government] who are advanced by (all participating parties is admissible as a point in the negotiations). [It would appear that the effect of such an agreement among the participating parties might well have been to exclude Lenin and Trotsky, as suggested by the italicized and crossed out portion of point 5 above.]

7   The [Soviet] Central Executive Committee should be replenished with representatives of the parties that left the congress in proportion to their numbers. [As the Bolsheviks proclaimed the seizure of power at the II All-Russian Congress of Soviets on 7 November, representatives of the other socialist parties, excepting the Left Socialist Revolutionaries, walked out in protest. The present point provides for the establishment of the authority of these parties in the Central Executive Committee of the Soviets.]

8   Representatives of the railroad workers [i.e., the trade union often called Vikzhel, which strongly favoured a coalition government], the postal-telegraph union and other similar organizations should be included in the [Soviet] Central Executive Committee.

Protokoly tsentral'nogo komiteta RSDRP(b), Avgust 1917–Fevral' 1918 (Moscow, 1958), 122–3 (hereafter *Protokoly TsK*)

2.2
[On Negotiations for a Coalition Government]   14 November 1917

On 14 November the Central Committee met again, this time with Lenin and Trotsky, who may have been responsible for inviting various non-members of the committee (e.g., representatives of the Petrograd city party organization). In any case they wished to stiffen the resistance of the Central Committee to the idea of a coalition government, and argued against the position of Kamenev, who had been representing the party in negotiations for a coalition (by a vote of 10 to 4, which implies a number of abstentions, the total meeting consisting of twelve Central Committee members and eleven others). However, an alternative resolution, expressing hostility to the negotiations, drafted by Trotsky, was passed (paragraph 1 by 8–4; paragraph 2 by 9–4; one abstention was recorded in each vote, which is hard to square with the recorded figures on attendance).

The meeting also approved a rough outline of an ultimatum, to be accepted in two hours by the negotiators from the other side, which was significantly less conciliatory than the position adopted on 11 November.

Considering, on the basis of the experience of previous negotiations, that the conciliatory parties are conducting these negotiations not to create a unified Soviet government [a coalition of socialist parties] but to sow dissent among the workers and soldiers, to undermine the Soviet government and finally to bind the Left Socialist Revolutionaries to a policy of compromise with the bourgeoisie, the Central Committee resolves: to allow our party members, in view of the previous decision on the [Soviet] Central Executive Committee, to participate today in the latest attempt of the Left Socialist Revolutionaries to form a so-called united government in

order to expose once and for all the failure of these efforts and to terminate
decisively further negotiations concerning a coalition government.

Protokoly TsK, 130   *KPSS v rezoliutsiiakh* 11, 14

2.3
[On the Question of the Opposition within the
Central Committee]   15 November 1917

Lenin carried the day at the following Central Committee meeting on 15
November. He had personally drafted a rough resolution assailing the 'vacillators' who favoured coalition. The only record of the voting is a series of
notations that Lenin scribbled on his copy of the resolution, but it appears
that he carried the final vote on resolution as a whole by 10–5. The ten were
almost certainly the ones (including Trotsky and Stalin) who signed an
'Ultimatum of the majority of the Central Committee of the RSDRP(b) to the
minority,' insisting on party discipline. The outcome of Lenin's victory was
the resignation from the Central Committee of five members including
Kamenev and Zinoviev, who argued, among other things (in an open letter to
the Central Committee of 7 November 1917), that they could not assume
responsibility for such a disastrous policy of the Central Committee.
Zinoviev, however, recanted three days later in a letter which was published
in *Pravda* on 21 November 1917, and the other dissenters followed suit
shortly afterwards.

The professed willingness of Lenin, expressed in the resolution below, to
readmit the other socialist parties into a coalition, must be properly understood. This was to be done only on his own terms: Bolshevik majority in
VTSIK, in the government, and acceptance of the Bolshevik programme (*Protokoly TsK*, 125–6).

The Central Committee recognizes this session as having historical importance. Hence it is necessary to concentrate on the two positions that have
come to light here.

1   The Central Committee states that the opposition in the Central
Committee wholly departs from all the basic positions of bolshevism and
the proletarian class in general, repeats profoundly non-marxist slogans on
the impossibility of a socialist revolution in Russia, on the need to yield to
ultimatums and threats by the notorious minority in Soviet organizations
that they will walk out, thus frustrating the will and the decisions of the
II All-Russian Congress of Soviets, thus sabotaging the nascent dictatorship of the proletariat and the poor peasantry.

2   The Central Committee places on this opposition complete responsibility for hindering revolutionary work and for the current vacillations, which are criminal in the present situation. It invites the opposition to put their arguments and their skepticism in print, and to keep away from practical work, in which they do not believe. For there is nothing in this opposition except fear of the bourgeoisie and the reflection of the mood of the weary (not the revolutionary) part of the population.

3   The Central Committee states that, without betraying the slogan of a Soviet government, one cannot renounce a purely bolshevik government, if the majority of the II All-Russian Congress of Soviets, which excluded nobody from the congress, reposed power in this government.

4   The Central Committee states that, without betraying the slogan of the rule of Soviets of Workers', Soldiers', and Peasants' Deputies, one cannot start peddling fusion with organizations of non-Soviet type, that is, organizations that are not voluntarily united with the revolutionary vanguard of the masses, which is fighting for the overthrow of the landlords and the capitalists.

5   The Central Committee states that concessions to the ultimatum and threats of the minority in the soviets are tantamount to a complete renunciation not only of the Soviet government but of democracy, because such concessions are tantamount to the majority's fearing to use their majority, are tantamount to submission to anarchy and further ultimatums from any minority.

6   The Central Committee states that, without excluding anyone from the II All-Russian Congress of Soviets, it is now fully prepared to restore [as members of the Soviet] those who left and to recognize in the Soviet the coalition of those who left; that, consequently, talk about the Bolsheviks supposedly being unwilling to share power with anyone is absolutely false.

7   The Central Committee states that on the day this government was formed, for several hours prior to its formation, the Central Committee invited three representatives of the Left Socialist Revolutionaries to its session and formally asked them to participate in the government. The refusal of the Left Socialist Revolutionaries, although it was temporary and conditional, in every possible way places the entire responsibility for the absence of an agreement on these same Left Socialist Revolutionaries.

8   The Central Committee recalls that the Bolshevik fraction introduced in the II All-Russian Congress of Soviets a resolution expressing readiness to enlarge the Soviet with soldiers from the trenches and with peasants from the hamlets, the countryside; that, consequently, assertions about the Bolsheviks' government being against a coalition with peasants are completely false. On the contrary, the Central Committee declares that the land law of our government, which is wholly copied from the Socialist Re-

volutionary instruction [a document reflecting the ideas of peasant deputies at a meeting in the summer and dominated by the Socialist Revolutionaries], in fact proves the complete and most sincere readiness of the Bolsheviks to form a coalition with the great majority of the Russian populace.

9   The Central Committee states, finally, that, despite all difficulties, the victory of socialism in Russia and Europe is secured only by the unwavering continuation of the policies of the present government. The Central Committee expresses complete confidence in the victory of this socialist revolution and invites all skeptics and vacillators to cease their wavering and support wholeheartedly and with all their energy the activities of this government.

Protokoly TsK, 131–2   *KPSS v rezoliutsiiakh* II, 14–15

VII Special Party Congress   6–8 March 1918

This relatively small gathering of forty-seven delegates with a deciding vote and fifty-nine delegates with a consultative vote was called 'special' because it was convened in order to approve the Treaty of Brest-Litovsk, signed by the Soviet government on 3 March 1918, after prolonged negotiations and after equally prolonged opposition in the Central Committee to the signing of the peace. Throughout January and February Lenin failed to convince the majority of the Central Committee about the desirability of signing the peace with the Central Powers. It was not until 25 February, a few days after the Germans broke the armistice signed in December 1917, and threatened the existence of the Soviet regime by their advance, that the Central Committee gave Lenin a majority and agreed to accept the final German terms.

Lenin's main reason for wishing to sign the peace was his conviction that continued hostilities would sweep the Bolsheviks out of power. What Lenin felt his regime needed most was a *peredyshka* or a breathing space to consolidate its position. However, this failed to impress a relatively small but vocal group of Central Committee members, dubbed Left Communists, with Bukharin at their head, who argued that signing the peace was a betrayal of the international revolution. Lenin, in his political report on behalf of the Central Committee (V.I. Lenin, *Collected Works* XXVII, Moscow 1960–70 (45 volumes), 87–90; also 110–17; hereafter cited as *Collected Works*) hit hard at the opposition, accusing them of adopting the stance of an aristocrat who 'dying in a beautiful pose with a sword in his hand' says: 'Peace is disgrace – war is honour.' So far, the international revolution was but a fairy tale, Lenin concluded, and serious revolutionaries had no right to believe in fairy tales. The resolution 'On War and Peace' (2.4), based on Lenin's report was accepted by 30 votes against 12, with 4 abstentions (one vote not accounted for).

This does not mean that Lenin dismissed the international revolution. Just as all the other Bolsheviks, he believed that the regime could not survive without the eventual assistance from the international proletariat. The difference between him and those who opposed him was on the point of timing rather than on the point of principle. Also, he was fully determined to hold on to power until the arrival of the international revolution whereas the Left Communists argued, somewhat incomprehensibly, that the Soviet regime may have to be sacrificed for the sake of the international revolution.

On the basis of the procedural rules adopted on the first day of the Congress, which gave any group of ten delegates the right to submit their own co-reports, Bukharin presented an opposing resolution which received only 9 votes.

In an obvious desire to appease the opposition, Lenin included in his resolution several bellicose anti-capitalist statements, including the readiness to break the treaty at any time. This was deemed, however, too provocative, and as a result, it was decided to keep the resolution secret. It was not published until January 1919, after the collapse of Imperial Germany. The peace was formally and publicly approved at the IV Congress of Soviets which opened on 14 March 1918.

Bukharin and his Left Communists, although elected to the Central Committee by the Congress, refused to serve on it because (as they put it) of their unwillingness to assume responsibility for the treaty. This created a minor crisis at the Congress since nobody had ever before refused to serve on the Central Committee when elected and there was no provision in the Rules covering such an eventuality. The Congress appealed, in a resolution drafted by Lenin, to the Left Communists to reconsider (2.6) but Bukharin and his followers boycotted the Central Committee meetings until the summer of 1918.

Sverdlov, who delivered the organizational report on behalf of the Central Committee, suggested a reduction in the Central Committee's membership from twenty-one to fifteen, justifying the proposal by the argument that the meetings were seldom attended by more than fifteen or sixteen members, because those who worked in the localities rarely had the time to attend. The proposal was accepted and a Central Committee with only fifteen members and eight candidates was elected. It is interesting to speculate to what extent this decision was influenced by Lenin's difficulties with the Central Committee on the question of the peace treaty.

The Congress also passed a resolution, drafted by Lenin, changing the name of the party from 'Social Democratic' to 'Communist' (2.5) and a resolution to prepare a new party Programme. Both these steps had been advocated by Lenin before the revolution because he regarded them as a symbol of the Bolsheviks' break with the old 'compromising' social democracy.

2.4
On War and Peace   8 March 1918

The Congress considers it necessary to confirm the highly distressing, degrading peace treaty with Germany, which the Soviet government signed because of our lack of an army, the extremely unhealthy condition of the demoralized front-line units, the necessity of utilizing any, however small, opportunity for a breathing space before the onslaught of imperialism on the Soviet socialist republic.

In the present period repeated military attacks by the imperialist states on Soviet Russia (in the west and south) are historically inevitable. The historical inevitability of such attacks, given the present extreme aggravation of all intra-state, class and, equally, international relations, may at any moment now, even in a few days, lead to new imperialist offensive wars against the socialist movement in general, against the Russian Socialist Soviet Republic in particular.

The Congress therefore declares that it recognizes as the primary and fundamental tasks of our party, of the entire vanguard of the conscious proletariat and of the Soviet government, the adoption of the most energetic, mercilessly resolute, and draconian measures for the heightening of self-discipline and the discipline of the workers and peasants of Russia; the explanation of the inevitability of the historic approach of Russia to the liberating, fatherland, socialist war; the creation everywhere of strongly united and iron-willed organizations of the masses, organizations capable of cohesive and selfless action in everyday life and especially at critical moments in the life of the people; finally, the thorough, systematic, universal training of the adult populace, regardless of sex, in military knowledge and military operations.

The Congress finds the most reliable guarantee of the strengthening of the socialist revolution, which was victorious in Russia, only in its transformation into an international workers' revolution.

The Congress is certain that, from the standpoint of the interests of the international revolution, the step that Soviet power has taken in signing the Treaty of Brest-Litovsk, given the prevailing alignment of forces in the international arena, was unavoidable and necessary.

In the belief that the workers' revolution is maturing in all belligerent countries, preparing the inevitable and complete defeat of imperialism, the Congress declares that the socialist proletariat of Russia, with all its strength and all the means at its disposal, will support the fraternal revolutionary movement of the proletarians of all countries.

SUPPLEMENT TO THE RESOLUTION ON WAR AND PEACE

The Congress considers it necessary not to publish the resolution that it has adopted and obliges all party members to keep this resolution secret. Only a report that the Congress favours confirmation of the treaty will appear in print – not today but when the Central Committee authorizes it.

Moreover, the Congress especially emphasizes that the Central Committee is given plenipotentiary power to break at any time all peace treaties with imperialist powers and bourgeois states and to declare war on them.

2.5
On Changing the Name of the Party and
the Party Programme   8 March 1918

The Congress resolves henceforth to call our party (the Russian Social Democratic Workers' Party of Bolsheviks) the *Russian Communist Party*, with 'of Bolsheviks' added in parentheses.

The Congress resolves to change the Programme of our party after reworking the theoretical part or supplementing it by characterizing imperialism and the opening of the era of socialist revolution.

Therefore the change in the political part of our Programme must consist in the most exact and detailed reference possible to the new type of state, the Soviet republic, as a form of dictatorship of the proletariat and as a continuation of the gains of the international workers' movement that were begun by the Paris Commune. The Programme must indicate that our party will not refrain from using even bourgeois parliamentarianism if the course of the struggle forces us backward for a time to that historic stage which our revolution has now surpassed. But in any case, the party will fight for the Soviet republic as the superior democratic type of state and as a form of the dictatorship of the proletariat, the overturning of the yoke of exploiters and the suppression of their resistance.

In the same spirit the economic, agrarian, pedagogic, and other parts of our Programme must be revised. The centre of gravity must fall on an exact description of the economic and other reforms initiated by our Soviet government and a specific statement of the next concrete tasks set by the

Soviet government, which arise from practical steps that we have taken for the expropriation of the expropriators.

The Congress instructs a special commission, if possible without delay, to write a Programme for our party based on these instructions and to approve it as the Programme of our party.

2.6
On the Refusal of the 'Left Communists' to
Serve on the Central Committee   8 March 1918

The Congress considers that refusal to serve on the Central Committee, given the present situation of the party, is especially undesirable, because, being intolerable in principle to those who desire party unity, such refusal would doubly threaten the unity of the party.

The Congress declares that each person can and should decline – by means of a declaration, not by quitting the Central Committee – responsibility for the steps of the Central Committee he does not approve of.

For this reason the Congress hopes that after taking counsel with the mass organizations, the comrades will retract their declarations and will abide by their elections to the Central Committee, regardless of these declarations.

Kommunar, 1 January 1919 (2.4)   *KPSS v rezoliutsiiakh* II, 26–8
Pravda, 9 March 1918 (2.5)
VKP(b) v rezoliutsiiakh I (4th edi-
tion), 22 (2.6)

VIII Party Congress   18–23 March 1919

The VIII Party Congress may well be regarded as the 'constitutional congress' of the post-revolutionary party. The brief VII Congress of March 1918 was preoccupied with the peace treaty with Germany and did not address itself to any of the basic organizational questions regarding the party. A year later it was difficult to postpone these questions any longer, and the leaders had to solve the problem of the party organization and attempt to take into account the fact that they were now trying to maintain a government, and not to overthrow one.

Until the VIII Congress, the party was still supposedly functioning on the basis of the internal Rules adopted in 1903 and modified in subsequent years. Clearly a thorough reconsideration of its internal structure and functions was essential, as well as the establishment of its relationship to the government organs – the soviets. The major step in this direction was the adoption of a resolution 'On the Organizational Question' (2.9), based on a report by Zinoviev. While it remained for a party conference later in 1919 to codify many of the points in the form of a new set of Rules (2.10), the main outlines of the new structure were visible in this resolution.

More specifically, the new system introduced the arrangement of supreme party bodies that has endured with minor changes for over half a century. The key centres of power were the Politburo and Secretariat, along with the Orgburo (until its merger with the Secretariat in 1952).

The establishment of these high organs was, for all practical purposes a recognition of reality. During the previous year, decision making was concentrated in the hands of a few men, possibly those of Lenin and Sverdlov alone. What no one seemed to realize fully was that the head of the Secretariat would become the most powerful authority. In practice, this position was occupied by Ia. M. Sverdlov until his death, just before the Congress. Sverdlov did not go about his work in a very methodical way and as a result, when he died, took all the party files with him into the grave, as one delegate to the Congress put it. This suggested not only the chaotic state of the party organization but also the power the office had to offer and the role Sverdlov's successors were to play. However, in 1919 the office of the 'General Secretary' had not yet been established, Lenin was still functioning as the party leader without any institutionalized position and N. N. Krestinsky was appointed as the first 'responsible secretary.' A member of the Left Communists at the time of Brest-Litovsk, and later a supporter of Trotsky, Krestinsky became also a member of the Politburo and Orgburo but did not rank, in ability or prestige, with Lenin's other senior lieutenants.

Below this central party command there was to be a strictly controlled pyramid of party bodies, penetrating and guiding every other form of public institution through the presence of party 'fractions' (the party members working in the non-party institutions), and totally ignoring the federal character of the emerging Soviet multinational state. This was a bold new conception which, as a practical matter, represents Lenin's political legacy much better than any of his theoretical writings. It is perhaps the most unique institutional innovation in twentieth century politics.

This drift towards an authoritarian, elitist rule within the party was at least partly understood and opposed by a group of members called 'Democratic Centralists,' with T. V. Sapronov and V. V. Osinsky at their head. At the Congress they charged that in the preceding year even the Central Committee ceased to exist for all practical purposes because all its members were either at the front or serving in the various commissariats (ministries). In Sapronov's view a majority of the Central Committee members should have served only on that committee and in no other capacity. Their criticism extended also to the organization of the soviets, an issue which was more thoroughly aired at the VIII Party Conference later in the year. However, the opposition did not challenge the fundamental idea of the party as a leading elite.

The organizational question, the related question of military organization, and the agricultural question were each referred by the Congress to separate 'sections' – groups of delegates which, separated from the plenary meeting, debated a proposed resolution and reported back to the plenary meeting. This device was intended to save time by having three basic questions debated concurrently. The Democratic Centralists argued for their position in the meetings of the 'Organizational Section' but in the end the leninist resolution, based on theses presented by Zinoviev, passed unanimously with one abstention.

Matters were more difficult for the party leaders in the sessions of 'Military Section,' which addressed itself to another kind of fundamental constitutional question: the character of the Red Army. A revealing description in a long footnote to the VIII Congress refers to "strong disagreements" at these meetings (VIII Congress, 538–40, note 58). Unlike the debates in the rest of the Congress, those on the military question have remained unpublished to this day (though a stenographic record was kept), for reasons of political sensitivity rather than military security. Trotsky, the Commissar of War, was unable to attend, owing to the exigencies of the Civil War, but his theses, favouring a conventional, disciplined army, were presented to the Congress and defended by Sokolnikov.

They were published in the earliest edition of the proceedings of the congress: *Vos'moi s"ezd Rossisskoi Kommunisticheskoi Partii (bol'shevikov), Stenograficheskii otchet* (Saratov, 1919). Although almost all of Trotsky's draft survived in the resolution of the Congress on the military question, the attribution of this basic document to him was suppressed in some later editions of the records of this meeting.

The opposing position in favour of the new style army, based on democratic control and partisan warfare, was presented in theses by V. M. Smirnov, the leader of the 'Military Opposition.' Like the Democratic Centralist opposition, this group opposed the authoritarian policies of the leadership in the name of the democratic revolution as well as the employment of military specialists.

The military section was composed of eighty-five delegates, fifty-seven of whom had a 'deciding vote' (the rest having merely 'consultative votes'). After stormy discussions, Smirnov's theses were accepted by a vote of 37 to 20. Upset, the Trotsky-Sokolnikov supporters seceded and formed a rival version of the military section and as a result, alternative drafts of the resolution on the military question were reported back to the plenary session of the Congress. Here the orthodox leninists had the upper hand. Lenin and Stalin spoke in favour of Sokolnikov's (Trotsky's) theses, although Stalin's supporter, Voroshilov, possibly at Stalin's instigation, spoke against them, and Sokolnikov's theses ultimately prevailed in a vote of 174 to 95. This is, by bolshevik standards, a very sizeable minority, especially if one notes that it implies quite a few abstentions, which in this context implies an unwillingness to toe the party line.

The exact number of abstentions is uncertain. The 1919 edition of the stenographic account of the Congress lists 286 delegates with a deciding vote plus 118 with a consultative vote. The 1959 edition, 286 to 100, but the eighth edition of *KPSS v rezoliutsiiakh* (II, 35) states that the figure is 301 with a deciding vote and 102 consultative. It appears that the original records of the Congress were confused, overlooking the names of various delegates. If indeed there were 301 delegates with a deciding vote, then it might mean that thirty-two delegates abstained from voting in favour of the orthodox party resolution on the military question.

Because of the strength of the opposition, even Lenin felt obliged to accept a compromise. A new drafting commission was appointed, with Stalin, Pozner, and Zinoviev representing the majority, and Iaroslavsky and Safarov the military opposition. In their compromise resolution (2.8) they retained almost all of Trotsky's draft, but added a section on 'Practical Measures.' This seems to have mollified the opposition, for the new document passed unanimously, with one abstention, according to the official record.

Two other important documents also emerged from the Congress: the first post-revolutionary party Programme, a rough draft of which was prepared by Lenin, and a resolution on the Communist International. The former was a rather verbose statement of long-term goals, parts of which were incorporated later in other resolutions (2.7). The latter was a short statement on the Russian Communists' foregone decision to join the International that Lenin had founded in January 1919.

The Congress also passed resolutions on relations with the middle peasantry, political propaganda and cultural-educational work in the countryside, work among proletarian women, work among the youth, and the party-Soviet press.

The increase of the Central Committee membership to nineteen members and eight candidates may well have been the result of the Democratic Centralists' criticism at the Congress. While this body was still small enough to meet as a kind of executive council, its function was overshadowed by the still smaller Politburo, which was elected following the Congress and was composed of Lenin, Trotsky, Stalin, Kamenev, and Krestinsky, with Bukharin, Zinoviev, and Kalinin as candidate members.

The Congress debates were conducted on the basis of procedural rules adopted at the first session which gave any group of 40 delegates the right to submit co-reports. As was the case at the VII Congress, none of the Central Committee members had a deciding vote.

2.7

Programme of the RKP(b)   22 March 1919

The October Revolution of 25 October (7 November) 1917, in Russia, established the dictatorship of the proletariat, which, assisted by poor peasantry and semi-proletariat, began to lay the foundations of a communist society. The course of development of revolutions in Germany and Austria-Hungary, the growth of the revolutionary movement of the proletariat in all advanced countries, the spreading of the Soviet form of this movement, that is, a form that is directed to the immediate establishment of the dictatorship of the proletariat – all this proved that there had begun the era of a world-wide proletarian communist revolution.

This revolution was the inevitable result of the development of capitalism which still rules in the majority of civilized countries. Our old Programme, except for the incorrect designation of the party as the Social Democratic Party, quite correctly characterizes the nature of capitalism and of bourgeois society in the following tenets:

'The chief characteristic of such a society is the production of goods on the basis of capital, where the most important and the greatest part of the means of production and exchange belong to a numerically small class of individuals, while the rest of the population consists of proletarians and semi-proletarians whose economic position compels them permanently or periodically to sell their labour power, i.e., to work as hirelings of the capitalists and to create by their labour the income of the upper classes of society.

The sphere of domination of the capitalist relations of production extends more and more with the development of technical improvements which, increasing the economic importance of large enterprises, leads to the abolition of small independent manufacturers. Some of these are reduced to the state of proletarians; the part played by the remainder in social and economic life is greatly narrowed, and in some cases the small manufacturers are put into a more or less complete, more or less obvious and more or less heavy dependence upon capital.

In addition, the same technological progress, gives the employers the opportunity to apply on a large scale woman and child labour in the production and circulation of goods. On the other hand, the development of technical improvements leads to a relative decrease in the demand for human labour on the part of the employers, and the supply of labour power exceeds the demand, which results in increased dependence of hired labour upon capital, and in an increased degree of exploitation.

Such a state of affairs within bourgeois countries, together with the continual sharpening of their mutual rivalries on the world market, makes the sale of goods, the production of which continually increases, more and more difficult. Over-production which results in more or less sharp industrial crises, followed by more or less lasting periods of industrial stagnation, is the inevitable outcome of the development of productive power in bourgeois society. Crises and periods of industrial stagnation in their turn ruin the small manufacturers still more, increase the dependence of hired labour upon capital, lead more quickly to a relative and sometimes to an absolute deterioration of the conditions of the working class.

Thus the improvement of technique, which means an increase in the productivity of labour and the growth of social wealth, in bourgeois society leads to the increase of social inequality, widens the gap between the wealthy and the poor, and leads to increased insecurity of existence, unemployment, and all sorts of deprivations for broader and broader strata of the working masses.

Just as all these contradictions which are inherent in bourgeois society, grow and develop, so also grows the discontent of the working and exploited masses with the existing state of affairs, and the number and the solidarity of the proletariat increases and its struggle with the exploiters becomes sharper. At the same time, the development of technique, as a result of which means of production and exchange are concentrated in a few hands and the process of labour in capitalist enterprises becomes more collective, more and more rapidly creates the opportunity for replacing the capitalist relations of production by communist relations, i.e. for bringing about that social revolution, which is the final aim of the international communist party, as the conscious expression of the class movement.

Social revolution, replacing private property by social production and exchange, and introducing the systematic organization of production to secure the welfare and the development of all the members of society, will abolish the division of society into classes and liberate all oppressed mankind, just as it will put an end to all kinds of exploitation of one section of society by the other.

The necessary condition for this social revolution is the dictatorship of the proletariat, i.e., the proletariat must seize political power which will enable it to crush all resistance of the exploiters.

The international communist party, the aim of which is to make the proletariat capable of fulfilling its great historic mission, organizes the proletariat into an independent political party which opposes all the bourgeois parties, leads it in all stages of the class struggle, reveals to the proletariat the irreconcilable difference of interests between exploiters and exploited, and explains to the proletariat the historic significance and the essential conditions of the approaching social revolution. At the same time, the international communist party reveals to all the rest of the toiling and exploited masses the hopelessness of their condition in capitalist society and the necessity for a social revolution in the interest of their own liberation from the yoke of capital. The party of the working class, the Communist Party, calls to its ranks all the toiling and exploited masses who share its proletarian point of view.'

At the beginning of the twentieth century, the process of concentration and centralization of capital, destroying free competition, led to the creation of great capitalist monopolies, syndicates, cartels, trusts – which dominated all economic life. The same process led to the amalgamation of bank capital with highly concentrated industrial capital, and to increased export of capital abroad. The trusts, embracing whole groups of capitalist states, began the economic partition of the world, the territories of which had already been divided among the richest countries. This epoch of financial capital, in which the struggle between the capitalist countries inevitably grows sharper, is the epoch of imperialism.

Imperialist wars therefore become inevitable, wars for markets for the sale of goods, for spheres for investing capital, for raw material and for a labour force, i.e., for world domination and for power over small and weak nations. The first great imperialist war of 1914–18 was precisely such a war.

The exceedingly high stage of development of world capitalism, the replacement of free competition by state-monopoly capitalism, the establishment by banks and also by groups of capitalists of an apparatus for the regulation of production and distribution, the resulting rise in cost of living, the yoke of the syndicates over the working class and the oppression of the working class by the imperialist state, the tremendous difficulties of the economic and political struggle of the proletariat, and all the horrors, misery, and destruction which an imperialist war brings – all this made the collapse of capitalism and the transition to the higher type of public economy inevitable.

The bourgeois governments could end the imperialist war neither by a just peace nor by any kind of stable peace. Capitalism has reached the point where an imperialist war must inevitably become transformed, and is becoming transformed, into a civil war of the exploited toiling masses, headed by the proletariat, against the bourgeoisie.

The increasing pressure of the proletariat, particularly its victories in individual countries, strengthens the resistance of the exploiters and compels them to create new forms of international capitalist unity (League of Nations, etc.), which by organizing the systematic exploitation of all peoples on a world scale, direct all their efforts to the immediate suppression of the revolutionary movement of the proletariat of all countries.

All this inevitably leads to the merging of the civil war within individual countries with the defensive wars of revolutionary countries, and the struggles of oppressed nations against the yoke of imperialist powers.

Under such conditions, the slogans of pacifism, international disarmament under capitalism, courts of arbitration, etc., are not only reactionary utopias, but an outright deception of the toiling classes, directed to the disarming of the proletariat and to diverting it from the task of disarming the exploiters.

Only the proletarian communist revolution is able to lead mankind out of the blind alley which was created by imperialism and imperialist wars. In spite of all the difficulties the revolution will have to face, temporary failures, waves of counter-revolution – the final victory of the proletariat is inevitable.

To attain the victory of the world proletarian revolution, the fullest confidence, the closest brotherly unity and co-ordination of all revolutionary activities of the working class in all advanced countries are necessary.

These conditions cannot be realized without a complete break with and bitter opposition to that bourgeois perversion of socialism which has obtained the upper hand in the higher circles of the official social democratic and socialist parties.

One form of this perversion is the current of opportunism and social chauvinism – socialism in name but chauvinism in fact, disguising the defence of the predatory interests of the national bourgeoisie under the false slogans of defence of the fatherland in general and, particularly during the imperialist war of 1914–18. This current of opportunism is due to the opportunities created by the robbery of colonial and weak nations by advanced capitalist states; the surplus profits acquired from these by the bourgeoisie enables it to bribe the upper strata of the working class by placing them in a privileged position and guaranteeing them in time of peace a tolerable existence and taking their leaders into its service. The opportunists and the social chauvinists are the servants of the bourgeoisie and the direct enemies of the proletariat, especially now, when together with the capitalists they are suppressing by armed force the revolutionary movement of the proletariat in their own as well as in foreign countries.

The other form of perversion is the so-called 'centre,' which is also a bourgeois perversion of socialism. This current is observed in equal degrees in all capitalist countries, and fluctuates between social chauvinists and communists, striving to preserve unity with the former and trying to revive the bankrupt II International. The new III Communist International alone conducts the struggle of the proletariat for its emancipation, and the All-Russian Communist Party is one of its sections. This International was in fact created when the real proletarian elements of former socialist parties in different countries, particularly in Germany, formed communist parties, and was formally established in March 1919 at the I Congress in Moscow. The Communist International, which is more and more gaining the sympathies of the masses of the proletariat of all countries, not only in words but in deeds, by its political content and ideology, returns to marxism and realizes the revolutionary teaching of Marx, now cleansed of all bourgeois-opportunistic perversions.

The All-Russian Communist Party, developing the concrete aims of dictatorship of the proletariat with reference to Russia, the chief characteristic of which is that the majority of the population consists of petty bourgeois strata, defines these aims as follows:

THE GENERAL POLITICAL SPHERE

1   A bourgeois republic, even the most democratic, sanctified by such slogans as 'will of the people,' 'will of the nation,' 'no class privilege,' remains in fact, because of the existence of private property in land and other means of production, the dictatorship of the bourgeoisie, an instrument for exploitation and oppression of the broad masses of workers by a small group of capitalists. In opposition to this, proletarian or Soviet democracy transformed mass organizations precisely of the classes oppressed by capitalism, of proletarians and poorest peasantry or semi-proletarians, i.e., the vast majority of the population, into a single and permanent basis of the state apparatus, local and central, from top to bottom. By this act, the Soviet state realized among other things local and regional autonomy without the appointment of authorities from above, on a much wider scale than is practised anywhere. The task of the party is to exert the greatest efforts in order to realize fully this higher type of democratism, which to function properly requires a continually rising standard of culture, organization, and independent activity on the part of the masses.

2   In contrast to bourgeois democracy, which concealed the class character of the state, the Soviet government openly acknowledges that every state must inevitably bear a class character until the division of society into classes has been abolished and all government authority had disappeared. By its very nature, the Soviet state directs itself to the suppression of the resistance of the exploiters, and the Soviet constitution does not shirk from depriving the exploiters of their political rights, bearing in mind that any kind of freedom is a deception if it is opposed to the emancipation of labour from the yoke of capital. The task of the party of the proletariat consists in carrying on a determined suppression of the resistance of the exploiters, in struggling against the deeply rooted prejudices concerning the absolute character of bourgeois rights and freedom, and at

the same time explaining that deprivation of political rights and any kind of limitation of freedom are necessary as temporary measures in order to defeat the attempts of the exploiters to retain or to re-establish their privileges. On the basis of the disappearance of the objective possibility of the exploitation of one human being by another, the necessity for these measures will also gradually disappear and the party will strive to reduce and completely abolish them.

3   Bourgeois democracy has limited itself to formally extending political rights and freedoms, such as the right of assembly, right of union, right of press, equally to all citizens. In practice, however, particularly in view of the economic slavery of the working masses, it was impossible for the workers to enjoy widely these rights and freedoms under bourgeois democracy. In contrast, proletarian democracy instead of formally proclaiming these rights and freedoms, actually grants them first of all to those classes which have been oppressed by capitalism, i.e., to the proletariat and to the peasantry. For that purpose, the Soviet state expropriates premises, printing offices, supplies of paper, etc., from the bourgeoisie, placing these at the disposal of the workers and their organizations.

The task of the RKP [the omission or inclusion of (b) follows the original Russian text throughout] is to encourage the broad working masses of the population to avail themselves of these democratic rights and freedoms, and to raise the material possibility for them to do so.

4   Bourgeois democracy through the ages proclaimed equality of persons, irrespective of sex, religion, race, or nationality, but capitalism did not allow the realization of this equality and in its imperialist stage intensified race and national oppression. The Soviet government, by being the government of the toilers, for the first time in history could realize this equality in all spheres of life, destroying the last traces of women's inequality in the sphere of marriage and the family. At the present moment the task of the party is principally intellectual and educational with the aim of abolishing the last traces of former inequality and prejudices, especially among the backward sections of the proletariat and peasantry.

The party's task is not to limit itself to the formal proclamation of women's equality, but to liberate women from all the material burdens of antiquated methods of housekeeping, replacing these by house-communes, public kitchens, central laundries, nurseries, etc.

5   The Soviet government, securing for the working masses an incomparably greater opportunity to vote and to recall their delegates in an easier and more accessible manner than they possessed under bourgeois democracy and parliamentarism, at the same time abolishes all the negative features of parliamentarism, especially the separation of legislative and executive powers, the isolation of the representative institutions from the masses, etc.

The Soviet state brings the state appratus close to the masses also by the fact that the electoral unit and the fundamental cell of the state is based not on a territorial district but on a productive unit (plant, factory).

The task of the party consists in conducting its work in such a way as to bring the government organs into still closer contact with the toiling masses, for the purpose of realizing democratism more fully and strictly in practice, in particular by making government officials responsible and accountable to the masses.

6   At the same time, whereas bourgeois democracy, in spite of all its declarations, transformed the army into an instrument of the wealthy classes, separated it from the working masses, and set it against them, depriving the soldiers of any opportunity of exercising their political rights, the Soviet state fuses in its organs – in the soviets of workers and soldiers, on the basis of full equality, their rights and the unity of their interests. The task of the party is to defend and develop this unity of the workers and soldiers in the soviets and to strengthen the unbreakable ties between the armed forces and the organizations of the proletariat and semi-proletariat.

7   The urban industrial proletariat, being the more concentrated, united, and educated section of the toiling masses, hardened in battle, played the part of leader in the whole revolution. This was evidenced in the establishment of the soviets, as well as in their course of development into organs of authority. Our Soviet constitution reflects this by the retention of certain privileges for the industrial proletariat, in comparison with the more scattered petty bourgeois masses in the countryside.

The RKP, explaining the temporary character of these privileges, which are historically connected with difficulties of socialist organization of the village, must try undeviatingly and systematically to use this position of the industrial proletariat in order closer to unite the backward and the scattered masses of the village proletarians and semi-proletarians, as well as the middle peasants, as a counterbalance to the narrow craft and professional interests, which were fostered by capitalism among the workers.

8   The proletarian revolution, thanks only to the Soviet organization of the state, was able at one stroke completely to destroy the old bourgeois, official, and judicial state apparatus. However, the low standard of culture of the masses, the absence of necessary experience in state administration on the part of responsible workers who are elected by the masses, the pressing necessity, due to the critical situation, of engaging specialists of the old school, and the drafting into military service of the most advanced section of urban workers, all led to the partial revival of bureaucratism within the Soviet system.

The RKP, carrying on the most resolute struggle with bureaucratism, suggests, in order completely to overcome this evil, the following measures:

1 Every member of the Soviet is obliged to perform a certain duty in state administration.

2 These duties must change in rotation, so as gradually to embrace all the branches of administration.

3 All the working masses without exception must be gradually induced to take part in the work of state administration.

The complete and all-round realization of all these measures, which represents a further step along the road stated by the Paris Commune, and the simplification of the work of administration, together with the rising of the cultural level of the workers lead to the abolition of state authority.

IN THE SPHERE OF RELATIONS OF NATIONALITIES

9   With reference to the nationality question the RKP is guided by the following tenets:

1 The principal aim is the policy of bringing about closer relations between the proletarians and semi-proletarians of different nationalities, in order to carry on a general revolutionary struggle for the overthrow of the landlords and the bourgeoisie.

2 In order to remove mistrust on the part of the working masses of the oppressed countries toward the proletariat of those states which oppressed them, it is necessary to abolish all privileges of any national group, to proclaim the full equality of nations and to recognize the rights of colonies and dependent nations to state separation.

3 For the same purpose, as a temporary measure toward achieving full unity, the party suggests a federative union of all states organized on the Soviet basis.

4 The All-Russian Communist Party regards the question as to who expresses the desire of a nation for separation, from a historical-class point of view, taking into consideration the level of historical development of any given nation: whether the nation is passing from medievalism toward bourgeois democracy or from bourgeois democracy toward soviet or proletarian democracy, etc.

In any case, particular care and attention must be exercised by the proletariat of those nations which were oppressing nations, toward the remnants of national feelings of the working masses of the oppressed or dependant nations. Only by such a policy is it possible to create favourable conditions for a voluntary and real unity of different national elements of the international proletariat, as has been proved by the experiment of the union of several national Soviet republics around Soviet Russia.

IN THE SPHERE OF MILITARY AFFAIRS

10   The tasks of the party with reference to military matters are defined by the following fundamental tenets:

1 In the period when imperialism is decaying and civil war is spreading, it is possible neither to retain the old army nor to construct a new one on a so-called common-national or non-class basis. The Red Army, as the instrument of the proletarian dictatorship, must necessarily have an open class character, i.e., it must be composed exclusively of the proletariat and of the related semi-proletarian strata of the peasantry. Only with the abolition of classes will this class army be transformed into an all people's socialist militia.

2 All proletarians and semi-proletarians must undergo thorough military training and introduction of corresponding subjects must be introduced in schools.

3 The work of military training and of education of the Red Army is conducted on the basis of class solidarity and socialist enlightenment. Therefore, political commissars chosen from devoted and trustworthy Communists are as necessary as military chiefs, and communist cells must be organized in all sections of the army, in order to establish internal ideological bond and conscious discipline.

4 As a counterbalance to the old army, the following changes are necessary: as short as possible periods of barracks training, barracks to approximate the type of military and military-political schools, as close a bond as possible between military formations and plants, factories, trade unions, and organizations of the village poor.

5 The necessary organization and stability of the young revolutionary army can be accomplished only with the help of the commanding staff of which at first at least the lower ranks are drawn from among class-conscious workers and peasants. Therefore, one of the principal tasks in the construction of the army is the training of the most energetic and capable soldiers devoted to the cause of socialism, for the duties of commanders.

6 It is necessary to make use of, and adopt on a wide scale, the operational and technical experience of the last world war. In connection with this it is necessary widely to attract military specialists, who have gone through the training of the old army, in order to organize the army and its operational leadership. At the same time the necessary condition of such employment of military specialists is that political guidance and full control over military officials remains concentrated in the hands of the working class.

7 The demand that the commanding staff should be elected had enormous significance with reference to the bourgeois army where the military commanders were selected and trained to become an instrument of class oppression of soldiers, and through them of the working masses. This demand has no significance with reference to the workers and peasants class Red Army. The possibility of combining the election and appointment of the commanders of the revolutionary class army is dictated exclusively by practical considerations, and depends upon the standard of organization reached, the degree of solidarity of the parts of the army, the effective supply of commanders, etc.

IN THE SPHERE OF JURISPRUDENCE

11   Proletarian democracy, taking power into its own hands and finally abolishing the organs of supremacy of the bourgeoisie – the former courts of justice – has replaced the formula of bourgeois democracy: "judges elected by the people" by the class slogan: "judges elected from the workers and only by the workers" and has applied the latter in the organization of law courts, having extended equal rights to both sexes, both in the election of judges and in the exercise of the functions of judges.

In order to attract the broadest masses of the proletariat and the poor peasantry to take part in the administration of justice, a system of constantly changing, temporary judges-jurors is introduced in the law courts and the mass workers' organizations, the trade unions, etc., must be attracted to compile lists of such prospective judges-jurors.

The Soviet government has replaced the former endless series of courts of justice with their various divisions, by a very simplified, uniform system of people's courts, accessible to the population, and free of all red tape.

The Soviet power, abolishing all the laws of the overthrown governments, ordered the judges elected by the soviets to carry out the will of the proletariat in compliance with its decrees, and in cases of absence or incompleteness of such decrees, to be guided by socialist conscience.

Constructed on such a basis, the courts of justice have already led to a fundamental alteration of the character of punishment, introducing suspended sentences on a wide scale, applying public censure as a form of punishment by obligatory labour with the retention of freedom, turning prisons into institutions for training, and applying the principle of comradely tribunals.

The RKP, in order to assist the further development of the courts of justice along these lines, must strive to induce all workers without exception to perform judicial duties and finally replace the system of punishment by measures of an educational character.

IN THE SPHERE OF PUBLIC EDUCATION

12   In the field of education, the RKP sets itself the task of bringing to conclusion the work begun by the October Revolution of 1917, of transforming the school from an instrument of class rule of the bourgeoisie into an instrument for the abolition of the class divisions of society, into an instrument for a communist regeneration of society.

In the period of dictatorship of the proletariat, i.e., in the period of preparation of conditions suitable for the realization of communism, the school must be not only the bearer of communist principles in general but it must also become the bearer of the intellectual, organizational, and educational influences of the proletariat on the semi-proletariat and the non-proletarian sections of the toiling masses, in order to educate a generation definitely capable of establishing communism. The immediate task in this direction is at the present time the further development of the following principles of school and educational work, already established by the Soviet government:

_1_   The introduction of free and compulsory general and polytechnical education (instruction in the theory and practice of the principle branches of production) for all children of both sexes up to the age of 17.

_2_   The establishment of a system of pre-school institutions: nurseries, kindergartens, homes, etc., to improve the social development of women and assist in their emancipation.

_3_   Full realization of the principle of a uniform industrial school with instruction in the native language, with co-education for children of both sexes, unconditionally secular, i.e., free of any religious influence, a school where instruction is closely connected with socially useful labour and which turns out all-round mature members of the communist society.

_4_   To provide all pupils with food, clothes, boots, and school supplies at the cost of the state.

_5_   The preparation of new cadres of educational workers who are imbued with the ideas of communism.

_6_   To draw the toiling population into taking an active part in educational work (the development of 'councils of public education,' mobilization of literate people, etc.)

_7_   General state assistance to self-education and the intellectual development of workers and peasants (creation of a system of institutions for education outside of the schools, such as libraries, schools for adults, people's clubs and universities, courses of lectures, cinemas, studios, etc.)

_8_   Large-scale development of professional education for persons from the age of 17, in connection with general polytechnical knowledge.

_9_   Making all institutions of higher learning accessible to all who desire to study, in the first place to workers; attracting all people able to lecture to become instructors in these universities; abolishing all artificial barriers standing in the way of young scientists reaching professional chairs; material support of students in order to offer the proletarians and the peasants a concrete opportunity to take advantage of the institutions of higher learning.

_10_ Equally necessary is opening and making accessible to the workers of all the art treasures which were created by the exploitation of their labour, and which have been so far only at the exclusive disposal of the exploiters.

11 Large-scale development of propaganda of communist ideas and employment of state resources and apparatus for that purpose.

IN THE SPHERE OF RELIGIOUS RELATIONS

13   With reference to religion, the RKP does not content itself with the already decreed separation of church from state, and separation of schools from church, i.e., measures which bourgeois democracy includes in its programmes but which it has never implemented because of the numerous ties binding capital with religious propaganda.

The RKP is guided by the conviction that only the realization of conscious and systematic social and economic activity of the masses will lead to the complete disappearance of religious prejudices. The aim of the party is the complete destruction of the ties between the exploiting classes and the organization of religious propaganda, at the same time helping the toiling masses actually to liberate their minds from religious prejudices and organizing on a wide scale scientific-educational and anti-religious propaganda. It is however, necessary carefully to avoid offending the religious susceptibilities of believers, which leads only to the hardening of religious fanaticism.

IN THE SPHERE OF ECONOMICS

1   Undeviatingly to continue and complete the expropriation of the bourgeoisie which was begun and which has already been fundamentally accomplished, and also to turn all means or production and exchange into the property of the Soviet republic, i.e., the common property of all workers.

2   All possible increase of the productive forces of the country must be considered the fundamental and principal point upon which the whole economic policy of the Soviet government is based. In view of the serious disorganization of the country, everything else must be subordinated to the practical aim of immediately and at all costs to increase the quantity of the most indispensible products required by the population. The successful functioning of every Soviet institution connected with economy must be measured by the practical results in this direction.

At the same time it is necessary, first of all, to pay attention to the following:

3   The collapse of imperialist economy left the Soviet state, during the first period, a legacy of chaos in the organization and management of production. It is therefore the more pressing to advance, as one of the most fundamental tasks, the consolidation of all economic activity in the country according to a general state plan: the greatest centralization of production in the sense of amalgamating it into various branches and groups of branches, and concentrating it in the most productive units, and in the

sense of rapidity in fulfilling economic targets; the most efficient arrangement of the productive apparatus, and a rational and economical utilization of all material resources of the country.

It is also necessary to extend economic co-operation and political ties with other nations, and try at the same time to establish a single economic plan with those among them which have already come over to the Soviet system.

4 It is necessary to use small-scale and handicraft industry to the widest extent by placing government orders with handicraftsmen; to include handicraft and small-scale industry in the general plan of supplying raw materials and fuel, and to support them financially, on condition that individual handicraftsmen, handicraft associations, productive co-operatives, and small enterprises amalgamate into large productive and industrial units; to encourage such amalgamations by offers of economic privileges, which together with other measures are aimed at paralyzing the aspirations of the handicraftsmen to become small manufacturers, and in this way bring about a painless transition from the backward forms of production to the higher form of large-scale mechanized industry.

5 The organizing apparatus of socialized industry must first of all rest upon the trade unions. The latter must free themselves from their narrow guild outlook and transform themselves into large productive combinations comprising the majority, and gradually all the workers of a given branch of production.

Trade unions, which are already according to the laws of the Soviet republic and established practice participants in all local and central organs for the administration of industry, must actually concentrate in their hands the entire administration of the whole public economy as a single economic unit. The trade unions, thus securing an unbreakable union among the central state administration, the economy and the broad masses of workers, must attract the last on a large scale to the direct management of the economy. The participation of trade unions in the management of the economy and the attraction by them of the broad masses to this task are, moreover, the principal means of the struggle against bureaucratization in the economic apparatus of the Soviet government, and afford the opportunity of establishing a truly popular control over the results of production.

6 A maximum utilization of all available labour power in the state, its regular distribution and redistribution among various territorial regions as well as among various branches of the economy, is necessary for its systematic development, and must be the immediate task of the economic policy of the Soviet government. This task can be accomplished only through close unity with the trade unions. In order to fulfil certain social duties, the Soviet government must carry out a general mobilization of all those capable of work among the population, with the participation of the

trade unions, and on a much wider scale and more systematically than has been done so far.

7 Under the conditions of the disintegration of the capitalist organization of labour, the productive forces of the country can be restored and developed, and a socialist system of production strengthened, only on the basis of the comradely discipline of the workers, maximal independent action on their part, consciousness of responsibility and the strictest mutual control over the productivity of labour.

Persistent systematic work directed to the re-education of the masses is needed to reach this aim. This work is now made easier as the masses actually see the elimination of the capitalists, landowners, and merchants, and from their own practical experience come to the conclusion that the level of their prosperity depends entirely upon the disciplining of their own labour.

The trade unions play a major role in the creation of the new socialist discipline. Breaking with the old pattern, they must put into practice and experiment with various measures, such as the establishment of accountability, production norms, the introduction of responsibility before special comradely workers' tribunals, etc., for the realization of this aim.

8 The same development of the productive forces requires the immediate wide and full utilization of all specialists in science and technology left to us as a legacy of capitalism, in spite of the fact that the majority of them are inevitably imbued with bourgeois world outlook and habits. The party considers that the period of sharp struggle with this stratum, due to organized sabotage on their part, is ended as the sabotage is in general broken. The party, in closest union with the trade unions, must follow its former line of action, i.e., on the one hand it will make no political concessions to this bourgeois stratum and will mercilessly suppress any counter-revolutionary moves on its part, and on the other hand it will carry on a merciless struggle against the seemingly radical, but also, ignorant and conceited opinion that the working class can overcome capitalism and the bourgeois order without the aid of bourgeois specialists or taking advantage of their knowledge, without going with them through a long schooling of work.

While striving toward equal remuneration of labour and toward full communism, the Soviet government cannot set itself the task of immediate realization of such equality at the moment, when only the first steps are being taken on the road to transition from capitalism to communism. It is therefore necessary to maintain for a certain time higher remuneration for specialists so that they could work not worse but better than before, and for that purpose it is not possible to abandon the system of bonuses for the most successful, and especially organizational work.

It is equally necessary to place the bourgeois experts in an environment of comradely common work, side by side with the mass of ordinary workers, led by class-conscious Communists, and thus to assist the mutual understanding and closer relations between manual and intellectual workers formerly separated by capitalism.

9   The Soviet government has already adopted a number of measures directed to the development of science and its closer contact with production: the establishment of a number of new scientific institutions, laboratories, research institutes, and experimental production to verify new technical methods, improvements and inventions, registration, and organization of all scientific forces and means. The RKP, supporting all these measures, strives for their further development and for the establishment of more favourable conditions for scientific work in connection with the increase of the productive forces of the country.

IN THE SPHERE OF AGRICULTURAL ECONOMY

10   The Soviet government, having carried out complete abolition of private property in land, has already started to put into effect a series of measures directed to the organization of large-scale socialist agriculture. The more important among these measures are: 1) the establishment of Soviet farms, i.e., large socialist economic enterprises; 2) support of societies as well as associations for common land cultivation; 3) organization by the state of the cultivation of all and every uncultivated land; 4) state mobilization of all agricultural forces to take the most energetic measures to increase agricultural productivity; 5) the support of agricultural communes as absolutely voluntary unions of agricultural labourers for the purpose of engaging in large-scale agricultural production.

The RKP, regarding all these measures as the only way toward the absolutely necessary increase in productivity of agricultural labour, strives for the highest possible realization of these measures, for their extension to the more backward regions of the country, and for further steps in that direction. In particular the RKP advocates:

1   All possible state encouragement of agricultural co-operatives engaged in the processing of agricultural products.

2   Large-scale execution of land improvement.

3   Large-scale and systematic supply of agricultural implements, through special establishments, to the poor and middle peasantry.

The RKP, taking into consideration that the small-scale system of agriculture will continue for a long time, strives to carry out a series of measures directed to the increase of productivity of agriculture. The measures are: 1) the regulation of peasant exploitation of land (abolition of scattered fields, etc.); 2) to supply the peasantry with improved seeds and artificial fertilizer; 3) improvement in livestock breeding; 4) spreading of agricultural knowledge; 5) agricultural aid to the peasantry; 6) the repair of

peasants' agricultural implements in soviet workshops; 7) the establishment of loan centres, experimental stations, exhibition fields, etc.; 8)
improvement of agricultural lands.

11 In view of the fact that the opposition between the town and the
village is one of the chief causes of the economic and cultural backwardness of the village, and that, in periods of serious crises, such as the
present, this opposition places the town as well as the village in immediate
danger of degeneration and destruction, the RKP sees in the abolition of this
opposition one of the principal tasks of communist construction, and
together with other measures considers essential the systematic attraction
of industrial workers to communist construction in agriculture, and the
development of activity on the part of the 'Workers' Committee of Assistance,' already established by the Soviet government, etc.

12 The RKP in all its work in the village, as before, looks for support to
the proletarian and semi-proletarian strata in it, and above all organizes
these into an independent force, creating party cells in the village, organizations of the poor, special types of trade unions of village proletarians and
semi-proletarians, and so on, bringing them in every possible way into
closer contact with the urban proletariat, freeing them from the influence of
the rural bourgeoisie and the interests of small property-holders.

The policy of the RKP in relation to the kulaks, the rural bourgeoisie,
is one of carrying on a resolute struggle against their attempts at exploitation, and suppressing their resistance to Soviet policy.

The policy of the RKP with reference to the middle peasantry consists
in gradually and systematically attracting it to the work on socialist construction. The party sets itself the task of separating this section from the
kulaks and drawing it to the side of the working class by giving consideration to its needs, by struggling against its backwardness with ideological
influence and not with means of suppression, by striving in all cases where
the vital interests of this section are involved to come to practical agreements with it, making concessions to it on the ways and means of realizing
socialist transformation.

IN THE SPHERE OF DISTRIBUTION

13 In the sphere of distribution, the task of the Soviet government at the
present time is undeviatingly to continue to replace private trade by a
systematic distribution of products on an organized national scale. The aim
is to organize the population into a single network of consumers' communes, which will be able with the greatest rapidity, systematically,
economically and with the smallest expenditure of labour, to distribute all
necessary products, strictly centralizing the whole distribution apparatus.

The general and workers' co-operatives which are the largest organizations of consumers and which the history of capitalism turned into a most

efficient apparatus for large-scale distribution, will become the basis of the consumers' communes and their unions.

The RKP, considering this kind of further communist development of the co-operative apparatus, and not its abolition, the only principally correct one, must systematically continue its policy: to make the work in co-operatives compulsory for all party members, to direct them, also with the help of trade unions, in the communist spirit, to develop among the working population in co-operatives initiative and discipline, to strive towards the inclusion of the whole population in the co-operatives, combined into one co-operative embracing the whole Soviet republic and finally – and most essentially – to see that the influence of the proletariat on the other strata of toilers is constantly assured, and to introduce various practical measures facilitating and realizing the transformation of petty bourgeois co-operatives of the old capitalist type into consumers' communes led by the proletariat and semi-proletariat.

IN THE SPHERE OF MONEY AND BANKING

14   The Soviet government in Russia, avoiding the mistakes of the Paris Commune, immediately expropriated the State Bank, then proceeded to the nationalization of private commercial banks and combined the nationalized banks and saving banks with the State Bank, laying in this fashion the foundation of a single national bank of the Soviet republic and transforming the banks from an instrument of economic domination of financial capital, and of the political domination of exploiters, into an instrument of workers' power and a lever of economic revolution. The RKP setting itself the aim of bringing to a consistent conclusion the work begun by the Soviet government, regards the following principles as paramount:

1   Soviet government monopoly over all banking.

2   A complete alteration and simplification of bank transactions by transforming the banks into an apparatus for uniform accounting and general bookkeeping of the Soviet republic. The organization of a systematic public economy will lead to the abolition of the bank and to its transformation into central bookkeeping of communist society.

15   In the initial stage of transition from capitalism to communism, while communist production and distribution of products is not yet fully organized, it is impossible to abolish money. Under such conditions the bourgeois elements of society continue to use money, which still remains private property, for speculation, profiteering, and robbery of the workers. The RKP, assisted by the nationalization of banks, strives toward the adoption of a series of measures which will extend the sphere of non-monetary calculations and which will prepare the ground for the abolition of money, such as compulsory holding of money in the national bank; the introduction of budget books; the replacing of money by checks, short-term tickets for obtaining goods, and so on.

IN THE SPHERE OF FINANCE

16   In the epoch of the beginning of the socialization of the means of production expropriated from the capitalists, the state ceases to be a parasitic apparatus over the process of production: it begins to transform into an organization immediately fulfilling the function of administration of the economy of the country, and to that extent the state budget becomes the budget of the whole economy.

Under such conditions the balancing of state revenues and expenditures can be realized only by correct performance in the sphere of state production and distribution of products. The RKP, with reference to meeting immediate state expenditures in the transitional period, defends the transition from the system of levies imposed on the capitalists which was historically necessary and legal in the first stage of the socialist revolution, to the progressive income and property tax. As this tax becomes obsolete, due to the large scale expropriation of the propertied classes, state expenditure must be met by the direct conversion of a part of the income derived from the various state monopolies, into state revenue.

IN THE SPHERE OF HOUSING

17   The Soviet government, in trying to solve the housing problem which was particularly sharpened during the war, has expropriated completely all the houses of capitalist landlords, and handed them over to the city soviets; has moved, in mass, workers from the suburbs into bourgeois homes; has handed over the best houses to the workers' organizations undertaking the maintenance of these at state's expense; and has arranged for the supply of furniture to workers' families.

The task of the RKP consists in following the above indicated course by exerting the greatest effort for the improvement of the housing conditions of the toiling masses without infringing on the interests of non-capitalist home-ownership; by abolishing overcrowding and unsanitary conditions in old housing quarters; by abolishing inadequate housing, by rebuilding old and constructing new houses corresponding to the new life conditions of the working masses, and by rational resettlement of the working masses.

IN THE SPHERE OF LABOUR PROTECTION AND SOCIAL SECURITY

The establishment of the dictatorship of the proletariat made it possible for the first time to realize fully the minimum programme of socialist parties in the sphere of labour protection.

The Soviet government has introduced by legislative enactment and codified in the 'Code of Labour Laws' a maximum eight-hour day for all workers and a six-hour day for persons under eighteen years of age and those working in unhealthy branches of production, and for miners working underground; a forty-two-hour uninterrupted rest every week for all toilers; prohibition of overtime as a general practice; prohibition of employment of children and youngsters under the age of sixteen; the prohibition of night work, and work in unhealthy branches of production, for all women and for men under eighteen; the exemption from work of pregnant women eight weeks before and eight weeks after confinement, with full wages during all this time together with free medical assistance and free drugs; granting working women not less than half an hour every three hours for nursing their babies, and supplementary subsidies to all nursing mothers; factory and sanitary inspection teams elected by the trade union councils.

The Soviet government has introduced by legislative enactment complete social maintenance of all toilers not exploiting the labour of others in all cases of loss of ability to work, and for the first time in the world has introduced unemployment insurance of workers at the expense of employers and of the state, granting complete self-administration to the insured and with wide participation of trade unions.

Furthermore, the Soviet government in some ways has gone further than the minimum programme and provided in the same 'Code of Labour Laws' for the participation of workers' organizations in decisions of questions on hiring and discharging of workers; one month's paid holiday for all workers who have worked continually for not less than a year; state regulation of wages based on rates worked out by trade unions; departments for the distribution and regulation of the labour force attached to the soviets and the trade unions, to provide work for the unemployed.

The extreme destruction caused by the war and the pressure of world imperialism have forced the Soviet government into the following retreats: to allow overtime in exceptional cases, with a limit of fifty days in one year; to permit youths between fourteen and sixteen to work, limiting their working day to four hours; temporarily to reduce holidays from one month to two weeks; to increase night work to seven hours.

The RKP must carry on an extensive propaganda for active participation of all workers in the energetic fulfilment of all measures for the protection of labour, for which purpose it is necessary:

1 To strengthen the work of organization and extension of labour inspection by choosing and preparing for that purpose active workers from the ranks of workmen and to extend that inspection to small and cottage industry.

2 To spread labour protection to all aspects of work (machine workers, land and water transport, servants, and agriculture workers);

3 To abolish completely child labour and further to decrease the working hours for youngsters.

In addition the RKP must set itself the task of establishing:

1 Further, with the general increase of labour productivity, a maximum six-hour working day without reduction of wages, but on condition that all workers will devote additional two hours' overtime without pay to the study of the theory of trade and industry, to practical military and state administration training.

2 The introduction of the system of premiums for the increase of labour productivity.

The RKP in the sphere of social security strives to organize on a large scale state support not only for war victims and victims of various catastrophes, but also for the victims of abnormal social relations. The party also conducts resolute struggle against parasitism of any kind and against idleness and sets itself the task of returning to a life of work anyone who has been dislodged from it.

IN THE SPHERE OF PROTECTION OF PUBLIC HEALTH

The RKP proposes as the basis for its work of protection of public health above all the fulfilment of large-scale sanitary and health measures to prevent the spreading of disease. The dictatorship of the proletariat has already made it possible to carry out a whole series of health and medical measures, the realization of which was impossible within the framework of bourgeois society: the nationalization of drugstores, of large private medical institutions, of health resorts, compulsory work for all medical staff, and so on.

In conformity with the above the RKP sets as its immediate task:

1 Resolute fulfilment of large-scale sanitary measures in the interest of workers, such as:

a Sanitation of population centres (protection of soil, water, and air).

b Establishment of communal meals on a scientific-hygienic basis.

c The organization of measures for the prevention of development and spreading of infectious diseases.

d Introduction of sanitary legislation.

2 The struggle with social diseases (consumption, venereal diseases, alcoholism, etc.).

3 Free, qualified assistance and medical drugs available to all.

2.8
On the Military Question 20 March 1919

A GENERAL PREMISES

I

The old social democratic programme called for the establishment of a people's militia made up of all citizens capable of bearing arms, whose military training would be conducted, in so far as possible, outside military camps. This programmatic demand, advanced at the time of the II International as a counter to imperialist standing armies with their army camp training, long terms of service and officer castes, had the same historic importance as the other demands of social democracy, such as those for universal, equal voting rights, for a unicameral system, etc. In conditions of 'peaceful' capitalist development and the need to adapt the proletarian class struggle from time to time to the context of bourgeois legality, one of the tasks of social democracy was, naturally, to demand the most democratic forms for the organization of the capitalist state and army. The struggle waged on this basis unquestionably had educational value, but as the great experience of the last war showed, the struggle to democratize bourgeois militarism yielded even fewer results than the struggle to democratize bourgeois parliamentarism. The reason is that in the military sphere the bourgeoisie, without being untrue to its very nature, can only permit the kind of 'democratism' that leaves its class rule untouched, i.e., an illusory and imaginary democratism. When the basic interests of the bourgeoisie were affected in the international sphere or in domestic affairs, bourgeois militarism in Germany, France, Switzerland, Britain and America, despite all the differences in the forms of government and in the military structures of these countries, displayed the very same traits of pitiless class brutality.

II

When the class struggle is transformed into open civil war, tearing away the cover of bourgeois law and bourgeois-democratic institutions, the slogan 'people's militia' is deprived of its meaning in precisely the same way as the slogan of democratic parliamentarism, and consequently becomes a weapon of the reaction. Just as the slogan 'Constituent Assembly' became a cover-up for efforts to restore the power of the landowners and capitalists, so today the slogan of a 'people's' army or army 'of all the people' has become a means for building the army of Krasnov and Kolchak.

After the experience of the Russian revolution, it takes the truly contemptible petty bourgeois blindness of a Kautsky to preach formal democracy in the organization of state power and the army at a time when the German Constituent Assembly has fled from Berlin to Weimar and placed itself under the protection of 'White Guard' regiments, when General Hoffmann is recruiting his iron battalions from the sons of Junkers, kulaks, and the bourgeoisie, while the Spartacists are arming the revolutionary workers. The era of proletarian revolution that has dawned is an era of open civil war by the proletariat against any and all bourgeois states and armies, regardless of whether they are cloaked in the forms of democracy. The victory of the proletariat in this civil war leads irrevocably to the establishment of a class proletarian state and a class army.

III

In rejecting for the historical period immediately ahead the idea of a so-called militia *of all the people*, as it is designated in our old Programme, we are by no means discarding the notion of a militia per se. We place political democracy on a class basis and convert it to Soviet democracy. We transpose the militia to class principles and convert it to a Soviet militia. Consequently, our next task is one of creating an army of workers and poor peasants on the basis of obligatory military training outside military installations, where possible, i.e., in those circumstances where this can be done close to their places of work.

IV

The actual course of development of our Red Army contradicts, as it were, the demands (of the old Programme) which were noted above. Originally, we created an army on the basis of volunteer service. Moreover, at the same time we began introducing obligatory military training for workers and peasants who do not exploit the labour of others, we also started the conscription of several age groups of the labouring classes. These contradictions were not gratuitous blunders, but grew out of the situation and represented completely unavoidable transitional forms in the creation of an army in the concrete conditions bequeathed us by the imperialist war and bourgeois (February) revolution.

The *voluntary principle* is the only possible means for creating units of any appreciable combat readiness in conditions of a catastrophic collapse of the old army and of all the agencies for forming and directing it. The best proof of this statement is the fact that the counter-revolutionary generals in present-day Germany are being forced, to the same extent as the Spartacists, to resort to the formation of voluntary battalions. The transition from the voluntary to the compulsory principle became possible from the moment the principal masses of the old army had been absorbed into the towns and villages and when success had been achieved in setting up agencies of military command locally: registration, formation and supply (volost, uezd, guberniia, and okrug commissariats).

V

To oppose the idea of guerrilla units to that of a centralized army organized in a planned fashion (as preached by the 'left' Social Revolutionaries and their ilk) is to ape the political thought – or inanity – of the petty bourgeois intelligentsia. Guerrilla methods of struggle were imposed on the proletariat in the early period because of its oppressed position in the state, just as the use of primitive underground printing presses and secret meetings were imposed upon it. The conquest of political power has enabled the proletariat to use the state apparatus for the planned construction of a centralized army, whose unity of organization and unity of command alone can assure achievement of the greatest results with the smallest losses. To preach the doctrine of guerrilla forces as a military programme is tantamount to recommending a return from large-scale to cottage industry. This doctrine is fully in keeping with the nature of intellectual groups incapable of exercising state power, incapable even of seriously envisaging the exercise of this power and excelling in partisan (polemical or terrorist) attacks on the workers' system.

VI

It can be considered theoretically irrefutable that we would obtain the very best army by building it on the basis of obligatory training for workers and working peasants *in conditions close to those of their daily work*. To improve industry and to increase collectivism and productivity of agricultural labour would create the soundest basis for an army, company, battalion, regiment, brigade, or division, which would, in turn, coincide with plant shops, plants, villages, volosts, uezds, guberniias, etc. This sort of army, whose formation would proceed step by step with the country's economic progress, with parallel training of the command staff, would become the most invincible army in the world. It is precisely this sort of army we are aiming for, and sooner or later we shall accomplish it.

VII

The necessity for a direct, immediate rebuff to our internal and external class enemies did not permit us, however, to proceed by such an 'organic' route to a workers' and peasants' militia, a transition that would have taken several years, or in any case many months. Just as we were obliged immediately after the October Revolution to resort to voluntary formations, so were we forced in the following stage – in the summer of last year – when the ring of imperialism had closed particularly tightly around Soviet Russia – to step up our military work and – unable to wait for militia formations (i.e., for formations of a territorial type not billeted in barracks) – to resort to compulsory, universal mobilization of specific age groups, to give them intensive training, and to keep them together in barracks. At the same time, all the efforts of the military sector are aimed at turning the barracks, as much as possible, into military schools and transforming them not only into centres of purely military training but also into centres of general and political education.

VIII

Our present active army, i.e., our army in the field or preparing directly for the field, is precisely an army of the above-described, transitional type.

While a class army in its social make-up, it is not a militia but a 'standing' or 'regular' army according to the methods by which it was formed and trained. While the latter circumstance is the source of many internal difficulties, particularly in conditions of the country's exceptional exhaustion, at the same time we can state with satisfaction that this army of a transitional type, created in the most disadvantageous conditions, has also proved capable of defeating its enemies.

IX

Concurrently with the formation of units in the barracks and directly in the field – i.e., under battle conditions – there is in progress a widespread effort to provide training locally to all workers and labouring peasants. In its relationship to our regular formations, this work of universal training was viewed, in its early stages, as a rudimentary training, as a way to equip the individual soldier with certain skills in order to speed up his subsequent training in the combat unit to which he is assigned. Unquestionably, from this limited point of view as well, universal training is already rendering valuable service in the creation of an army.

X

But in no case must the task of universal military training be limited to the above-indicated auxiliary service role. Universal training must lead – over the course of a number of stages co-ordinated with the more indispensible and urgent work of forming the regular units – to the creation of a genuine militia army.

XI

The stated goal requires that universal training not limit itself to the tasks of individual military training, but make the transition to the formation of troop units – all being of the smallest sort in the initial period – without, in so far as possible, removing their component elements, i.e., the workers and peasants, from their normal work surroundings. Universal training must switch to the formation of individual platoons and companies, and subsequently of battalions and regiments, with longer-range plans for the formation of entire divisions from local workers and peasants – units with a local command structure, and local supplies of armaments and equipment.

XII

On the assumption of a continued, unbroken, and prolonged struggle with imperialist troops, the gradual transition to a militia army is possible only if we set up a new method of replacing losses in the active forces. At present, reserve units are formed according to the same pattern as basic units, through the so-called reserve battalions. In the future, and in the very near future, reserves should be formed during the process and on the basis of comprehensive training, and should be sent into existing regiments of the same territorial origin so that after demobilization the regiment's component elements are not scattered over the whole country but, as natives, retain their local working ties. The appropriate organs of the military department are to work out a series of measures for a gradual transition from our present transitional army to one of the territorial militia type, and they have already taken the first decisive steps in this direction.

XIII

The class militia army toward which we are proceeding does not signify, as is clear from the preceding discussion, an improvised, slapdash, poorly trained army with fortuitous selection of weapons and a half-prepared command personnel. On the contrary, its preparation through comprehensive training should be such that, in association with manoeuvers, rifle drills, and military ceremonies, the result is a more highly skilled individual soldier and a more highly skilled unit. A militia army must be an army trained, armed, and organized according to the last word in military science.

XIV

The commissars in the army are not only direct and immediate representatives of the Soviet power but are, above all, carriers of the spirit of our party, its discipline, its steadfastness and manliness in the struggle to implement the goal which has been set. The party can take perfect satisfaction in the heroic work of its commissars who, shoulder to shoulder with the best elements of the command staff, in a short space of time created a battle-worthy army. At the same time, the army's political sections, under the direct leadership of the Central Committee, must in the future be selective with respect to the commissars, eliminating any who were appointed by accident, who are unstable careerist elements.

The work of the commissars can yield its full results only if in each unit it has the direct support of the cell of soldier-communists. The rapid numerical growth of communist cells is an extremely important guarantee that the army will be increasingly permeated by communist ideas and discipline. But precisely because of the enormous role of the communist cells, the commissars, and all the most mature party workers in the army generally, must take steps to ensure that unstable elements not find their way into the cells in the chase after imaginary rights and privileges. Respect for the communist cells will be higher and more unwavering the more clearly each soldier understands, and is convinced by experience, that membership in a communist cell does not give the soldier any special rights but only imposes on him the obligation to be the most selfless and heroic fighter possible.

While on the whole approving the Central Committee's regulation on the rights and obligations of the communist cells, commissars, and political sections, the Congress hereby places all comrades working in the army under the obligation of complying undeviatingly with this resolution.

XV

The requirement that the command staff be elected, a principle of enormous significance in a bourgeois army where the command staff was selected and trained as an apparatus of the class subjection of the soldiers and – through the soldiers – of the labouring masses, entirely loses its significance as a principle in the class-based workers' and peasants' Red Army. A possible combination of election and appointment is imposed on the revolutionary class army exclusively by practical considerations and depends upon the level of training achieved, the degree of cohesiveness of the army's units, the availability of command cadres. It may generally be asserted that the less seasoned the army units, the more fortuitous and transitional their composition, the less practical testing the young command staff have undergone, the less advisable it is to apply the principle of electing commanding officers, and, on the contrary, the growth in the unit's internal cohesion, the soldier's development of a critical attitude toward himself and his commanding officers, the creation of sizable cadres of battle-trained officers at lower and higher levels who have manifested their qualities in the conditions of the new war, create favourable conditions for the increasingly broad application of the principle of election of the command staff.

XVI

The problem of the command staff, while offering great practical difficulties contains, in substance, no grounds for disputes on matters of *principle*.

Even if our army had had several years in which to shape itself according to plan and simultaneously to prepare itself new command staff – we still would not have had any reasons of principle for rejecting those elements of the former command staff who had either internally adopted the viewpoint of the Soviet power or by the force of circumstances saw themselves compelled to serve it in good faith. The revolutionary character of the army is determined primarily by the character of the Soviet regime which creates this army, which assigns its mission, and thus converts it into its own instrument. On the other hand, this instrument is brought into conformity with the Soviet regime through the class make-up of the main body of the soldiers, through the organization of commissars and communist cells, and finally through the overall party and Soviet guidance of the army's life and activity.

One of the principal tasks involved in creating an army is the training and education of the new officers, who are primarily of working-class or progressive peasant origin. The steady growth in the number of instructors' courses and of their graduates is evidence that the military department is devoting to this subject all the attention which it deserves. Together with the higher military academy (of the general staff) five intermediate schools are being organized – between the instructors' courses and the higher military academy. Even so, the ranks of the present Red Army contain a great many commanding officers from the old army who are carrying out their responsible work with great benefit for the cause. The necessity of removing traitors and provocateurs, and blocking them, goes without saying and – as far as experience indicates – is being implemented in practice more or less successfully by our military organization. In this connection, the party cannot have any grounds at all for revising our military policy.

XVII

The regulations issued to date (for domestic service, field and garrison duty) represent a major step forward in that they introduce firmness and stability into the army's internal relationships and into the rights and obligations of its component elements, but they nonetheless reflect a transitional period in the formation of our army and will be subsequently revised as the old 'barracks' characteristics in the formation of the army are overcome and it is increasingly transformed into a class army, a militia.

XVIII

The agitation in the camp of bourgeois democracy (the Socialist Revolutionaries, Mensheviks) against the Red Army – both against the manifestation of 'militarism' and against the foundations of incipient bonapartism – reflect only political ignorance or charlatanism or a combination of the two. Bonapartism is not the product of military organization as such, but is the product of specific social relations. The political domination of the petty bourgeoisie, standing between the reactionary big bourgeois elements and the revolutionary proletarian depths still incapable of an independent political role and of political rule, created the necessary preconditions for the appearance of bonapartism which found support in the prosperous peasantry and rose above the class contradictions which did not find a resolution in the revolutionary programme of the petty bourgeois (Jacobin) democracy. In so far as the kulak peasant is the basis of bonapartism, the very social composition of our army, which does not admit kulaks and drives them out, is a serious guarantee against bonapartist tendencies. The Russian parodies of bonapartism, in the form of Krasnov, Kolchak, etc., did not arise out of the Red Army but in direct and open struggle against it. Skoropadsky – a Ukrainian Bonaparte with Hohenzollern assistance – formed his army on the basis of qualifications which were in direct contradiction to those of the Red Army, recruiting rich kulaks into his regiments. Under these conditions, those who view an army of proletarians and village poor as a bastion of bonapartism can only be persons who just yesterday were giving direct and indirect support to Ukrainian, Don, Archangel, and Siberian candidates for Bonaparte.

Since the Red Army itself is only the instrument of a particular regime, the fundamental guarantee against bonapartism, as against any other varieties of counter-revolution, must be sought in the regime itself. In no sense can counter-revolution develop out of a proletarian dictatorship – it can only become established in consequence of a direct and open, bloody victory over this regime. The Red Army must be developed and strengthened precisely in order to make such a victory impossible. Thus the existence of the Red Army has historic meaning as a weapon of socialist self-defence of the proletariat and the village poor, protecting them against the dangers of kulak-bourgeois bonapartism supported by foreign imperialism.

XIX

A class militia is not the last word in communist construction since the goal of the latter is to eliminate the class struggle by annihilating the classes themselves, and consequently the class army as well. With progressive organization of the socialist economy the Soviet class state will increasingly be dissolved in the guiding apparatus of production and distribution and in the cultural and administrative organs. Relieved of its class character, the state will cease being a state and will become the organ of economic and cultural self-government. At the same time the army will lose its class character. It will become an army *of the whole people* in the true meaning of the expression because no parasitic, exploitative, kulak elements will remain in the socialist community. This army will be made up directly from mighty labour groupings of citizens of the socialist republic just as it will be supplied directly by the expanded and mighty socialist production. Such an army, i.e., the well-trained and armed, socialistically organized people, will be the mightiest army the world has ever known. Not only will it be a weapon to defend the socialist community against possible attack from the remaining imperialist states, but it will make possible the granting of decisive assistance to the proletariat of these states in its struggle against imperialism.

B PRACTICAL MEASURES

In the light of these fundamental provisions, the VIII Congress of the RKP considers it essential to carry out the following regular practical measures:

I   Undeviating implementation of the principle of class mobilization of working-class elements only, with careful isolation of kulak and parasitic elements into special labour battalions (companies), a principle which at present is not being implemented despite official decrees.

2   While the recruitment of military specialists [former tsarist officers] to commanding positions and administrative positions is to continue, with selection of the reliable elements, an unwavering centralized party-political supervision is to be established over them by means of the commissars, with those who prove politically and technically unsuitable being eliminated.

3   A system of certification of the command staff is to be organized, with the commissars compiling these certifications on a periodic basis.

4   The training of proletarians and semi-proletarians for command positions is to be intensified, and both its political and its military aspects improved, for which purpose competent certifying commissions are to be set up at the front and in the rear, with party members in the majority, for the systematic recruitment to Red Officers' schools of those Red Army men who have been best prepared by combat experience for the role of Red Officer.

The course programmes are to be revised in conformity with the spirit of the Red Army and the Civil War situation.

Local party organizations are to devote particular attention to the proper organization of political training in the courses.

5   Local party organizations are assigned the job – as part of their regular responsibilities – of conducting regular and intensive training in communism for the soldiers of the Red Army in units stationed in the rear, by means of assigning special people to this work.

6   The Central Committee is instructed to organize a planned distribution of Communists throughout the units of the army and navy.

7   The centre of gravity of communist work at the front is to be transferred from the politotdels of fronts to the politotdels of armies and divisions, in order to enliven this work and bring it closer to the active units at the front. Agreed upon and precise regulations governing the authority and duties of political commissars, politotdels, and communist cells are to be published.

8   The All-Russian Bureau of the Military Commissariat is dissolved. A politotdel of the republic's Revolutionary Military Council is created and all the functions of the All-Russian Bureau of the Military Commissariat are to be transferred to this politotdel; the politotdel is to be headed by a member of the RKP Central Committee, who is to enjoy the status of a member of the republic's Revolutionary Military Council.

9   Military regulations are to be reworked and shortened as much as possible; all archaisms and rulings that establish excessive privileges for the command staff are to be eliminated, and suitable space is to be devoted to questions of political training in the regulations on training.

10   The regulations concerning the commissars and the revolutionary military councils are to be quickly reworked in the sense of spelling out exactly the rights and duties of commissars and commanders; in so doing, provision is to be made for the solution of economic and administrative matters by commanders jointly with commissars, and commissars are to be given authority to take disciplinary action (including the right of arrest) and authority to take a case before the courts.

11   It is considered necessary to subordinate the 'special departments' [security – the Cheka] of armies and fronts to the respective commissars of the armies and fronts, while reserving to the republic 'special department' the functions of overall direction and supervision of their work.

12   It is considered necessary when working out generally applicable rules, regulations, and instructions to arrange, in so far as possible, for preliminary discussion of them by the political personnel of the armies.

The VIII Congress of the RKP instructs the Central Committee to take steps immediately:

1   to reorganize the Field Headquarters and, in so doing, to establish closer contact with the fronts and immediate direction of them;

2   to regulate the work of the republic's Revolutionary Military Council;

3   to put in order the work of the All-Russian General Staff Headquarters in connection with the defects in its activity (formation of units, publication of regulations, etc.) and, because of the necessity to strengthen party representation in the All-Russian General Staff Headquarters:

4   to call periodic meetings of party workers at the front who hold positions of responsibility;

5   to poll party workers at the front on the extent to which the question of insignia to differentiate the command staff has been satisfactorily solved.

2.9
On the Organizational Question   22 March 1919

A   PARTY CONSTRUCTION
1   *Growth of the party*
Numerical growth of the party is progressive only to the extent that healthy proletarian elements of town and countryside are brought into the party. The party's door should be opened wide to workers and to worker and peasant youth. But the party must constantly follow with care the changes occurring in its social composition. All party organizations are under orders to keep careful track of their composition and to report on it periodically to the Central Committee. Expansion of the numerical base of party organizations must in no case be conducted at the cost of worsening

their qualitative composition. Great care must be exercised in admitting non-worker and non-peasant elements to the party.

The Congress resolves to conduct a general registration of all party members throughout the whole of Russia by 1 May. The Central Committee is instructed to publish not later than 10 April, detailed instructions on the implementation of the re-registration in such a way that particular control measures are applied to those party members who joined the party ranks after October 1917.

2 *Ties with the masses*

It is natural for the Russian Communist Party, as the party that is in power and that holds the entire Soviet apparatus in its hands, to have assigned tens of thousands of its members to the task of running the country. A most important task of the party at the present moment is to enlist new thousands of its best people in the network of state management (the railroads, food, supervision, the army, the courts, etc.).

However, in connection with the carrying out of this urgent task there arose a serious danger. Many of the party members assigned to these state tasks are becoming cut off from the masses to a considerable extent and are becoming infected with bureaucratism; very often the same is true of many of the staff and members of the soviets. Immediate steps must be taken to wage a most resolute struggle against this abuse. Communists who are members of soviets must be ordered to report back to their constituents not less than once every two weeks, without fail. Workers who have been engaged exclusively in the work of the soviets for more than three months running are to be returned to the factories for at least one month. All staff workers of the soviets who are party members are obliged to conduct some sort of party work in their district. All Communists are ordered to become members of trade unions and to attend their general meetings.

3 *The Central Committee and the local organizations*

The Central Committee is made up of nineteen members (eight candidate members). Not less than once every three months the Central Committee convenes a party conference of representatives of guberniia and capital [Moscow and Petrograd] committees. These conferences discuss the most important current questions confronting the party.

Not less than once a month the Central Committee is to distribute to the guberniia and capital party committees a written report on its work. Matters that require widespread dissemination are to be printed in the newspapers every two weeks, conditions permitting.

A special travelling collegium of party instructors made up of party workers who hold responsible positions is to be set up under the Central Committee.

Local organizations are ordered to submit written reports on their activities not less than once every two months – the uezd committees reporting to the guberniia committees, and the guberniia committees reporting to the Central Committee.

All party and soviet press organs must include a section entitled, 'From Party Life.'

The Central Committee is instructed to take energetic measures to assure that all party organizations are provided sufficient financial resources for necessary party work.

4 The internal structure of the Central Committee

The Central Committee holds no less than two plenums a month on days determined in advance. All of the more important political and organizational questions that do not require extremely urgent handling are to be discussed at these plenary meetings of the Central Committee.

The Central Committee is to set up, first, a *Political Bureau* [Politburo]; second, an *Organizational Bureau* [Orgburo], and third, a *Secretariat*.

The Politburo is composed of five members of the Central Committee. All other members of the Central Committee who have the opportunity to participate in one or another meeting of the Politburo enjoy the right of a consultative vote in the Politburo. The Politburo adopts decisions on questions requiring immediate action, and reports on all its work for the two-week period in question to the regular, periodic plenary session of the Central Committee.

The Orgburo is composed of five members of the Central Committee. Each member of the Orgburo heads up a corresponding segment of the work. The Orgburo meets not less than three times a week. The Orgburo directs all the party's organizational work. The Orgburo reports on its work to the Central Committee plenum every two weeks.

The Secretariat of the Central Committee is composed of one responsible secretary, who is a member of the Central Committee's Orgburo, and of five technical secretaries from among experienced party workers. The Secretariat organizes a number of departments. The Secretariat reports on its work to the Central Committee plenum every two weeks.

5 National organizations

At the present time, the Ukraine, Latvia, Lithuania, and Belorussia exist as separate Soviet republics. That is the present solution to the question of the forms of the *state's* existence.

But this in no sense means that the RKP(b) must, in turn, organize itself as a federation of independent communist parties.

The VIII Congress of the RKP resolves that it is necessary that there exist a *single*, centralized Communist Party with a single Central Committee that directs all the party's work in all parts of the Russian republic. All decisions of the RKP and of its directing institutions are unconditionally binding for all elements of the party, regardless of their national composition. The central committees of the Ukrainian, Latvian, and Lithuanian communists enjoy the rights of oblast party committees and are entirely subordinated to the Central Committee of the RKP.

6 *The existence of special organizations*
The existence of special party organizations for the railroads, post and telegraph, the military, etc., is superfluous, and therefore the Central Committee, in co-ordination with local organizations, is to liquidate gradually such organizations, dissolving them in the general communist organization.

7 *Centralism and discipline*
The situation of the party is such that the strictest centralism and the most severe discipline are an absolute necessity. All decisions of higher echelons are absolutely binding for those below. Every resolution must first be carried out, and only then is it permissible to appeal the resolution to the appropriate party body. In this sense regular military discipline is necessary for the party in the present era. All party undertakings susceptible of centralization (publishing, propaganda, etc.) must be centralized for effectiveness.

All conflicts are resolved by the appropriate higher party echelon.

8 *Distribution of party forces*
The correct distribution of party forces at the present time is a major guarantee of success and one of our most important tasks. The entire question of the distribution of party workers is in the hands of the party Central Committee. The Central Committee's decisions are binding for all. In each guberniia the guberniia party forces are assigned by the guberniia party committee, and in the capital cities, by the city party committees under the overall direction of the Central Committee. The Central Committee is instructed to conduct a most resolute struggle against all manner of localist sentiment and separatism in these matters.

The Central Committee is instructed to regularly re-assign party workers from one sphere of work to another and from one area to another for maximum efficiency.

9 *The training of party workers*
The Central Committee is instructed: 1) to organize a higher party school attached to the Central Committee; 2) to work out a general program and

plan of studies at local party schools; 3) to assist local party schools by supplying them with lecturers, as appropriate.

10 *Izvestiia of the Central Committee*
The Central Committee is instructed to arrange for the weekly publication of *Izvestiia tsentral'nogo komiteta* devoted entirely to party life. [This *Izvestiia* should not be confused with the newspaper usually called *Izvestiia*, the organ of the soviets, which has existed from 1917 to the present.]

11 *Party Rules*
The Congress instructs the Central Committee to indicate, on the basis of materials received from various localities, a number of necessary changes in the Rules. These changes are to be confirmed by the next party conference to be called by the Central Committee.

All materials of an organizational nature that have been received by the organizational section are also to be given to the Central Committee for processing.

B SOVIET CONSTRUCTION
1 *Composition of the All-Russian Central Executive Committee*
The Congress considers that the make-up of the All-Russian Central Executive Committee should be changed in the sense that members of the All-Russian Central Executive Committee should be recruited primarily from among local officials engaged in regular work among the masses of peasants and workers.

2 *The Presidium of the All-Russian Central Executive Committee*
The functions of the presidium of the All-Russian Central Executive Committee are not elaborated in the Soviet constitution. At the next congress of soviets it is necessary, on an urgent basis and on the basis of all practical experience, to formulate the rights and responsibilities of the presidium of the All-Russian Central Executive Committee and to delimit the sphere of its functions from those of the Sovnarkom.

3 *The soviets and executive committees*
All fundamental problems of local life and of the life of the country in general should, as far as possible, be posed and solved at the general meetings of the soviets. It is necessary to combat the tendency to transfer the resolution of all questions to the executive committees exclusively. The soviets must function not merely as an apparatus for agitation and information, but also as a well-regulated mechanism for dealing with substantive issues.

4   *The enlistment of all workers in the soviets*

Not just the représentatives of the industrial proletariat, but representatives of toilers in general (see the Constitution of the Soviet regime) should be enlisted in the soviets in towns. In this sense, electoral rights with respect to the soviets should gradually be expanded in accordance with local conditions. Initiative in this matter must lie with the RKP.

5   *Socialist supervision*

The matter of supervision in the Soviet republic must be radically reorganized in order to create genuine and actual supervision of a socialist character. The leading role in carrying out socialist supervision must fall to the party organizations and trade unions. To this end, in the immediate future the very best people must be assigned to learn not just to supervise the work of the soviets, but also to organize it themselves.

C   RELATIONS BETWEEN THE PARTY AND THE SOVIETS

The soviets are the state organizations of the working class and the poorest peasantry that are carrying out a dictatorship of the proletariat during the period until all state power of whatever sort withers away.

The soviets unite in their ranks tens of millions of working people and must strive to unite within those ranks the entire working class and all poor and middle peasants.

The Communist Party is an organization that unites in its ranks only the vanguard of the proletariat and the poorer peasantry, i.e., the portion of these classes that is consciously striving to make a communist programme a reality.

The Communist Party sets itself the task of winning decisive influence and complete control in all organizations of the working people: in trade unions, co-operatives, rural communes, etc. The Communist Party particularly strives to carry out its Programme and establish its complete control in the contemporary stage organizations that are the soviets.

It is absolutely necessary that a party fraction be set up in all soviet organizations, and that such fractions be strictly subordinated to party discipline. Such party fractions are to include all members of the Russian Communist Party who work in the given Soviet organization.

Through its practical, day-to-day, selfless work in the soviets, the RKP must win for itself a position of undivided political supremacy in the soviets and of actual control over all their work.

In no case would it do to confuse the functions of party collectives with the functions of state bodies such as the soviets. Such a confusion would yield fatal results, particularly in military matters. The party must implement its decisions through the soviet bodies, *within the framework of the Soviet Constitution*. The party strives to *direct* the work of the soviets, not to replace them.

Many alien elements have made their way into the soviet organization. The soviets have to fight bureaucratism, red tape, slipshod work, organizational diffuseness and narrow-minded local 'patriotism,' etc.

But unhealthy symptoms are observable within party organizations as well. On the one hand, the party's best forces pour out of the party and into the soviet organizations and devote all their energies and all their time to soviet state work. On the other hand, there is an extensive influx into the party of elements that are insufficiently communist and even of outright hangers-on. The RKP is in power, and this inevitably attracts not just the best elements, but also careerist elements, to its ranks. And this is the reason for the quite correct limitations placed on party members' voting rights as concerns the all-Russian party congress.

A thorough-going *purge* of both soviet and party organizations is necessary. The strictest discipline is required of every last party member. All party members, however important the state positions they might hold, are unconditionally subject to party control. But at the same time, party organizations must never have recourse to petty tutelage over the soviets and must give their members to understand that membership in the RKP accords no privileges whatsoever, but merely puts heavier responsibilities on them.

Spravochnik partiinogo rabot-   *KPSS v rezoliutsiiakh* II, 36–86
nika I, 1–13, 17–26

VIII Party Conference   2–4 December 1919

The VIII Party Conference was the first one to take place after the bolshevik seizure of power. It was attended by forty-five delegates with a deciding vote and seventy-three delegates with a consultative vote. As in the case of the VII and VIII congresses, all Central Committee members and candidates had only a consultative vote. The Conference adopted the procedural rules of the VIII Congress which stipulated that any group of forty delegates could put forward its own co-reporter.

In addition to the party Rules (2.10), the Conference also passed resolutions on the international situation, on Soviet policy in the Ukraine, on Soviet power in the Ukraine (this was a resolution passed previously by the Central Committee and confirmed by the Conference), and a resolution on soviet construction. The last was the result of the continued efforts of Sapronov, one of the leaders of the Democratic Centralists. Sapronov's resolution won over the official one defended by Vladimirsky. Since Sapronov spoke as a co-reporter against the official resolution and since the procedural rules of the Conference stipulated that a co-report had to have a support of forty delegates, it may indicate that as many as forty of the forty-five delegates with a deciding vote were in favour of it. Sapronov's main target was first, the unrepresentative character of vTSIK, a legislative governmental body elected by the All-Russian Congress of Soviets; and, secondly, the lack of power of the executive committees of the local soviets. Sapronov was attacking not only the practice but even the theory of the Soviet Constitution of 1918. He did succeed in bringing about a change in the composition of vTSIK which in the future was to draw representatives from the various guberniias, on the basis of population, in addition to eighty delegates elected by the Soviet Congress.

Sapronov's recommendations were discussed at the VII Congress of Soviets which opened a day after the Conference concluded and were for the most part accepted. However, as was the case in similar instances in the future, they were never put into effect.

2.10
Rules of the RKP(b)   4 December 1919
[Replaces Rules adopted in 1917; see 1.174]

I   ON PARTY MEMBERS
1   [As in 1.174, art. 1 with minor changes of wording]   A party member is anyone who accepts the party Programme, works in one of its organizations, obeys party decisions, and pays membership dues.
2   [Revises 1.174, art. 2]   New members are accepted by local party committees from among candidates and are approved by the next general meeting of the organization.
Note In exceptional cases, upon the recommendation of two party members from before October 1917, persons who are not candidates may be brought into the party. The same exception is permitted during party week, according to Central Committee instructions.
3   [New]   Any member of one [party] organization who is transferred to the area of work of another organization, is registered in the latter with the agreement of the first organization.
4   [Revises 1.174, art. 4]   The question of expelling anyone from the party is decided by the general meeting of that person's organization. The resolution on expulsion takes effect only when approved by the guberñia committee, with the person being removed from party work until approval of his expulsion. The party press will publish the names of those expelled, together with the reasons for the expulsion.

II   ON CANDIDATE MEMBERS OF THE PARTY
5   [New]   All persons who wish to join as party members pass through

a period of candidacy, which is intended to acquaint them with the Programme and tactics of the party and to verify their personal qualities.

6   [New]   New persons are accepted as candidates upon recommendation by two party members of six months' standing after the recommendations have been verified by the local party committee.

7   [New]   Workers and peasants must remain candidates for at least two months, others at least six months.

8   [New]   Candidates may attend open general meetings of the party organization with a consultative vote.

9   [New]   Candidates pay the customary membership dues to the treasury of the local party committee.

[Articles 7 and 8 of the 1917 Rules deleted (on units of party organization and confirmation of new party organizations)].

III   ON THE ORGANIZATIONAL STRUCTURE OF THE PARTY

10   [As in 1.174, art. 5, with minor word changes]   The guiding principle of the organizational structure of the party is democratic centralism.

11   [New]   The party is built on the basis of democratic centralism on territorial lines: the organization serving a given district is considered to be higher than all the organizations serving parts of this district.

12   [Revises 1.174, art. 6]   All party organizations are autonomous in resolving local problems.

13   [New]   The highest leading organ of each organization is the general meeting, conference, or congress.

14   [New]   The general meeting, conference, or congress elect a committee which is their executive organ and directs all current work of the local organization.

15   [New]   The party's organizational structure is as follows:

   a   territory of the RSFSR – the All-Russian congress, the Central Committee;

   b   oblasts and Soviet republics within the RSFSR – oblast conferences, oblast committees;

   c   guberniias – guberniia conferences, guberniia committees;

   d   uezds – uezd conferences, uezd committees;

   e   volosts – volost meetings, volost committees;

   f   enterprises, villages, Red Army units, institutions – general cell meetings, cell bureaus.

16   [New]   The order of subordination and accountability, as well as of adoption or questioning of all party decisions (from the highest authority to the lowest), is as follows: All-Russian congress, Central Committee, oblast conference, oblast committee, guberniia conference, etc.

17   [New]   For special forms of party work special sections are formed (national sections, sections for work among women, among youth, etc.). Sections are attached to committees and are directly subordinate to them.

The procedure for organizing sections is set out in special instructions approved by the Central Committee.

18   [New]   Membership of all lower organizations up to the uezd is approved by the uezd committee with the sanction of the guberniia committee; at the uezd level – by the guberniia committee with the sanction of the oblast committee, and in the absence of the latter – by the Central Committee; at the guberniia level – by the oblast committee with the sanction of the Central Committee, and in the absence of the oblast committee – by the Central Committee directly.

19   [Revises 1.174, art. 6]   Following its definite approval, every party organization has the right to acquire its press, but only with the sanction of the next higher party organization.

IV   ON THE CENTRAL INSTITUTIONS OF THE PARTY

20   [Revises 1.174, art. 10]   The party congress is the highest organ of the party. Regular congresses are convened annually. Extraordinary congresses are convened by the Central Committee on its own initiative or at the request of at least one-third of the party members represented at the preceding party congress. The convocation of a party congress and its agenda are announced at least a month and a half before the congress. Extraordinary congresses are convened on two months' notice. A congress has a quorum if at least half the party members who were represented at the previous congress are represented at it.

Standards of representation at a congress are set by the Central Committee and the regular pre-congress conference.

21   [As in 1.174, art. 11]   If the Central Committee does not convene an extraordinary congress as set forth in paragraph 1 [sic; should read '20'] above, the organizations demanding it have the right to form an organizational committee possessing the rights of the Central Committee with respect to the convening of the congress.

22   [As in 1.174, art. 12]   The congress:

a   hears and approves the reports of the Central Committee, the Revision Commission, and other central institutions;

b   revises and alters the party Programme;

c   defines the tactical line of the party on current problems;

d   elects the Central Committee and the Revision Commission, etc.

23   [Revises 1.174, art. 13]   The Central Committee is elected with a membership of nineteen (twelve candidate members). If the Central Committee loses members, they are replaced from among the candidate members elected by the congress, in the order determined by the congress.

24   [As in 1.174, art. 13 with minor rewording and additions]   The Central Committee represents the party in its relations with other parties and institutions, organizes the various party institutions and directs their activities, appoints the editors of the central organs working under its

supervision, organizes and directs enterprises of general significance for the party, allocates party funds and personnel, and controls the central treasury.

The Central Committee directs the work of the central soviet and social organizations through the party fractions.

The Central Committee holds at least two plenums monthly, with the meeting day being set in advance.

25   [New]   The Central Committee organizes: for political work – a Political Bureau; for organizational work – an Organizational Bureau and a Secretariat, headed by a secretary who is a member of the Organizational Bureau of the Central Committee.

26   [New]   Once every three months the Central Committee convenes a party conference of the representatives of the guberniia and capital [Moscow and Petrograd] committees of the party.

27   [New]   Once a month the Central Committee circulates to the guberniia and capital [Moscow and Petrograd] committees of the party a written report on its activities.

28   [Revises 1.174, art. 14]   The Revision Commission consists of three persons, periodically reviews the state of the treasury and of all Central Committee enterprises, and reports to the next party congress.

V   ON OBLAST ORGANIZATIONS

29   [New]   With the permission of the Central Committee the party organizations of an oblast may unite. The oblast committee is elected at the oblast conference. The oblast boundaries are determined by the oblast conference and are approved by the Central Committee.

30   [New]   Party organizations serving the territory of a federative part of the RSFSR are in all respects equivalent to oblast organizations of the party, i.e., they are wholly subordinate to the Central Committee of the RKP(b).

31   [New]   An ordinary oblast conference is convened by the oblast committee every six months; an extraordinary conference is convoked by decision of the oblast committee or of one-half of the total membership of the organizations in the oblast.

The norm of representation at the oblast conference is set by the oblast committee by agreement with the guberniia committees within the oblast.

The oblast conference hears and approves the reports of the oblast committees, of the revision commission, and of other oblast institutions, elects the oblast committee and the revision commission.

32   [New]   The oblast committee is elected at an ordinary conference.

For the conduct of current work the oblast committee elects a presidium of not less than three persons.

The oblast committee organizes the various party institutions within the oblast; directs their activities, appoints the editors of the oblast party organ which operates under its supervision; organizes and directs enterprises of general significance for the oblast; allocates party funds and personnel within the oblast; and controls the oblast treasury. The oblast committee directs the activities of soviet executive organs through the party fractions and reports in detail to the RKP(b) Central Committee every three months on its activities.

The oblast committee meets twice a month, with the meeting day being set in advance.

VI   ON GUBERNIIA ORGANIZATIONS

33   [New]   The regular guberniia party conference is convened by the guberniia committee once every three months, the special conference by decision of the guberniia committee or one-third of the total membership of the organizations in the guberniia.

The guberniia conference hears and approves the reports of the guberniia committee, the revision commission, and the other guberniia institutions, elects the committee and the revision commission.

34   [New]   The guberniia committee is elected by the conference and must include party workers of the guberniia centre and of the other major working-class centres of the guberniia.

The guberniia committee meets twice a month, with the meeting day being set in advance.

For the conduct of current work the guberniia committee appoints a presidium of not less than five of its members.

35   [New]   The guberniia committee approves the membership of the uezd or raion organizations of the guberniia with the sanction of the oblast committees or of the Central Committee; organizes the various party institutions within the guberniia and directs their activities; appoints the editors of the guberniia party organ, which operates under its supervision; organizes all enterprises of significance of the guberniia, allocates party funds and personnel within the guberniia; and controls the guberniia treasury. The guberniia committee directs the activities of the soviet, the trade unions, and the co-operatives through the corresponding party fractions. The guberniia committee submits a detailed monthly report to the Central Committee on its activities and on the activities of the uezd committees.

36   [New]   During the intervals between conferences the guberniia committee makes periodic informational reports to the general meeting or conference of the city organization; furthermore, every month the guberniia committee convenes a guberniia conference of the representatives of uezd and city organizations.

37   [New]   City committees, subordinated to guberniia committees, may be formed in guberniia cities only with the permission of the guberniia committees and with the sanction of the Central Committee.

Note The city committees in Petrograd and Moscow are in all respects equivalent to guberniia committees.

VII ON UEZD ORGANIZATIONS

38 [New] The uezd conference hears and approves the report of the uezd committee and elects a committee and a revision commission. The conference meets at least once every three months.

39 [New] The uezd committee is elected by the uezd conference and has a membership of five to nine persons.

The uezd committee appoints a presidium of three of its members, of whom the secretary must be released from all except party work.

40 [New] The uezd committee approves the membership of the volost organizations and cells within the uezd with the sanction of the guberniia committee, organizes the various party institutions within the uezd and directs their activities, organizes all enterprises that have significance for the uezd, arranges conferences of volost cells, and controls the uezd party treasury.

Note Only the uezd committee may issue a party organ and party literature within the uezd.

41 [New] Through party fractions the uezd committee directs the work of the uezd executive committee, the soviet, and all volost soviets, as well as of trade unions, co-operative and other associations in the uezd.

VIII ON VOLOST ORGANIZATIONS

42 [New] The highest organ of the volost is the general meeting of the party members of the volost.

Note In large volosts where it is difficult to convene a general meeting, a volost conference may be substituted for the general meeting.

43 [New] The volost general meeting is convened at least once a month. The general meeting: a) accepts and expels party members; b) elects the volost committee and revision commission; c) discusses and approves the reports of the volost committee and the revision commission; d) elects the delegates to the guberniia, uezd, and other conferences; e) discusses and approves the report of the volost executive committee fraction.

44 [New] The volost committee of three to five members serving for three months is elected at the general meeting (or conference).

45 [New] The volost committee guides and directs the work of all organizations within the volost, registers all party members, organizes the distribution of literature, holds public rallies, lectures, etc., organizes new cells and submits them to the uezd committee for approval, controls the volost party treasury, reports on its activities once a month to the uezd, guberniia, oblast committees and to the Central Committee, directs the work of the volost soviet and of its executive committee through the party fraction.

46   [New]   The revision commission reviews the state of the volost treasury once a month.

IX   ON PARTY CELLS

47   [New]   The basis of the party organization is the party cell. The cell is approved by the uezd, city, or raion committee and has at least three members.

Note   The cell which has grown to large dimensions may, with the permission of the appropriate committee, be subdivided into several cells, constituting one subraion.

48   [New]   The cell is the organization which binds the worker and peasant masses to the guiding organ of the party in the given locality. The cell has the task: 1) of bringing the party's slogans and decisions to the masses; 2) of attracting new members; 3) of helping the local committee in its organizational and agitational work; 4) of participating actively as a party organ in the economic and political life of the country.

49   [New]   For the conduct of current work the cell elects a bureau of three members serving for one month.

X   ON PARTY DISCIPLINE

50   [New]   The strictest party discipline is the primary duty of all party members and all party organizations. Resolutions of party centres must be implemented rapidly and accurately. At the same time, within the party there is entirely free discussion of all disputed issues of party life until a decision is taken.

51   [New]   Failure to implement resolutions of higher organizations and other offences recognized as criminal by party opinion are punished as follows: in the case of the organization, by censure, appointment of a provisional committee from above, and general re-registration (dissolution of the organization); in the case of the individual party members, by party censure, public censure, temporary removal from responsible party and soviet work, temporary removal from any party or soviet work, expulsion from the party, expulsion from the party with a report of the offence to the administrative and judicial authorities.

52   [New]   For the examination of various disciplinary offences each committee has the right to set special meeting days and to form special commissions, but the latter may not, in any sense, be transformed into permanent party courts.

53   [New]   Disciplinary offences are examined by committees and general meetings in the usual order up through the established authorities.

XI   ON PARTY FINANCES

54   [New]   The sources of funds of the organization are membership dues, subsidies from higher party organizations, and other receipts.

55   [Revises 1.174, art. 3]   Membership dues are set at not less than one-half of one per cent of wages. There are four categories of membership dues, depending upon the amount earned. The first category pays one-half of one per cent, the second – one per cent, the third – two per cent, and the fourth – three per cent. Precise figures for assessable wage levels are set by instructions.

56   [New]   New members pay initiation dues of five rubles.

57   [New]   In the case of persons, such as peasants, whose wages are indeterminate, membership dues are established by the local guberniia committee on the basis of general norms.

58   [As in 1.174, note to art. 3]   Party members are considered to have left the organization if they have failed to pay dues for three months without an acceptable excuse; this is brought to the notice of the general meeting.

59   [Revises 1.174, art. 9]   All local organizations must forward to the Central Committee ten per cent of all membership dues and other unassigned monetary receipts. Volost organizations forward sixty per cent to the treasury of the uezd committee, this including ten per cent for the Central Committee; the uezd committee forwards thirty per cent to the treasury of the guberniia committee.

Ten per cent of all the guberniia committee's receipts are forwarded to the treasury of the Central Committee.

XII   ON FRACTIONS IN NON-PARTY INSTITUTIONS AND ORGANIZATIONS

60   [New]   In all non-party congresses, meetings, institutions, and organizations (soviets, executive committees, trade unions, communes, etc.) which have at least three party members, fractions are organized. Their task is the comprehensive strengthening of party influence, implementation of its policy in the non-party environment, and the establishment of party supervision over the work of all of these institutions and organizations.

61   [New]   When matters affecting any fraction are being discussed in a committee, the fraction will send its representatives to the plenum of the committee with a consultative vote. For the conduct of current work the fraction may elect a bureau.

62   [New]   Fractions, regardless of their importance are entirely subordinate to the party. In all matters with respect to which there exists a legal decision of the appropriate party organization, the fraction must adhere to this decision strictly and undeviatingly. The committee has the right to introduce any member into the fraction or recall him from it but must inform the fraction of the reasons for such a step. The fraction is autonomous in matters of its internal life and current work. If there is a substantial disagreement between the party committee and the fraction on any matter within the latter's competence, the committee must examine the matter

a second time with representatives of the fraction and adopt a final decision which is immediately to be carried out by the fraction.

63   [New]   The fraction, together with the appropriate party organization, proposes candidates for all the major positions in the institution or organization in which the fraction is working. Transfers from one position to another are handled in exactly the same way.

64   [New]   All matters of political significance subject to discussion in the fraction must be discussed in the presence of representatives of the committee. Committees must delegate their representatives as soon as the fraction so requests.

65   [New]   Any matter subject to decision by the non-party organization in which the fraction works must first be discussed in the fraction's general meeting or its bureau.

66   [New]   At the general meeting of the non-party organization in which the fraction is working all fraction members must vote unanimously on any matters which have been decided within the fraction. Persons violating this rule are subject to the usual disciplinary procedures.

<table>
<tr><td>Izvestiia tsentral'nogo komiteta,
14 January 1920</td><td>KPSS v rezoliutsiiakh II, 122–142</td></tr>
</table>

IX Party Congress   29 March–5 April 1920

The reorganization of the party which took place in the preceding year did not as such preclude a degree of intra-party political pluralism. The supposedly elective form of the party congress, the highest party body, did not rule out the possibility that differences of opinion and opposition to the party leadership which had emerged at each congress or conference since the seizure of power, would not continue. As a result, in the absence of any serious effort on the part of Lenin to prevent it, opposition arose once again at the IX Party Congress. The criticism centred on the character of party leadership and on economic policy, especially questions concerning industry and labour.

The 554 delegates with a deciding vote this time included also members of the Central Committee. There were also 162 delegates with a consultative vote.

Lenin (*Collected Works* XXX, 443–62, 463–71) and Krestinsky, respectively, reported on the political and organizational activities of the Central Committee and were answered by the Democratic Centralists with a barrage of criticism in the debate which followed. The debate was essentially a continuation from the VIII Congress. Lenin was attacked for the centralizing tendencies apparent at every step taken by the leadership. Lenin did not strike a responsive chord when he told the Congress that 'Phrases about minority and majority, about democracy and freedom, do not solve anything.' He was criticized for his personal style of leadership and his Central Committee report was bitterly termed 'a condescending lecture.' Sapronov attacked the leaders as a small clique ruling by 'vertical centralism' rather then by democratic centralism which the party was supposed to practice and which the Democratic Centralists adopted as their slogan. Lenin attempted to resist them but they were not to be silenced by his prestige. When a short, rather vague resolution approving the Central Committee report was introduced, Sapronov countered by submitting an alternative resolution. It, too, approved the report but reproached the leadership for neglecting 'to raise to the necessary level the organizational work of the party in all its branches.' In the end Lenin's resolution was accepted by a majority; no record of the actual count was given.

Still more criticism was evoked by Trotsky's report on the economic problems of the day, which he proposed to attack by introducing military conscription and discipline with respect to the labour force. Among the points of view aired on this issue was a co-report of V.V. Osinsky, who criticized both Trotsky and Lenin. When it came to draft a resolution on this matter a compromise was needed. Osinsky was given a place on the Presidium of the Congress when it met to prepare an acceptable version of the resolution on Trotsky's report; the resulting resolution was accepted without any recorded vote.

The question of trade union organization, on which Bukharin reported, also evoked debate from several sides. Another critical group, later known as the 'Workers' Opposition' appeared and submitted a co-report through their spokesman, Lutovinov, which emphasized the autonomy of the trade unions more than did Bukharin's report.

Still another position was represented by the Bolshevik trade union leader M.P. Tomsky. The official resolution based on Bukharin's report did not, however, prove as controversial as the report itself, and it was adopted unanimously (2.11).

As at the VIII Congress, two separate 'sections' of the body met to attempt to expedite the work at hand: one on co-operation in the countryside and one on party organization. The former was not an area, as yet, in which any definite group took a keen interest, but four different resolutions were introduced during the deliberations. The discussion was more factional at the organizational section, to which Kamenev delivered the official report. Again the Democratic Centralists took the floor and offered their own resolution on party organization, but it apparently did not gain much support.

Lenin won one important victory at the Congress on the issue of one-man management of industrial plants as opposed to a trade union collective management (*Collected Works* xxx, 472–9). This problem had plagued Lenin since shortly after the revolution, when the workers took over factories and attempted to run them, with a notable lack of success. Lenin's solution was centralization and employment of specialists as managers. In this effort he was repeatedly criticized by the Democratic Centralists, the Workers' Opposition, and the trade union leaders such as Tomsky, who summed up the difference between the two groups as: 'We say: collective of three; no, they say, one specialist and two commissars.' Lenin curtly dismissed their arguments as a 'theoretical muddle' with which the Central Committee could never get reconciled.

The lesson of the Congress seems to be not that Lenin's leadership was in danger but that the party would produce divergent factions if something was not done to curtail them. Surprisingly, Lenin did not seem to have anticipated that problem, and did not act decisively to dispose of it. It may well be that he believed the opposition would come over, as they did in 1918, once they realized that he held the magic key to the truth.

Other resolutions of the IX Congress dealt with liaison between economic commissariats, the relations between regular party organizations and special 'political sections' (politotdel) that existed in some institutions, work among proletarian women, the transport problem, and the establishment of the militia.

The Congress elected a Central Committee of nineteen members and twelve candidates. This body met at the end of the Congress and re-elected the same Politburo that had been chosen the previous year following the VIII Party Congress.

2.11
On the Question of the Trade Unions
and their Organization   1 April 1920

I   THE TRADE UNIONS AND THEIR ORGANIZATION

1   *The general situation and the general tasks of the trade unions in the epoch of the proletarian dictatorship*

Under the dictatorship of the proletariat the trade unions cease being organs which struggle against the capitalist ruling class as sellers of labour and are converted into the apparatus of working-class rulers. The tasks of the trade unions are principally organizational-economic and educational.

The trade unions must carry out these tasks not as a self-contained and organizationally isolated force but as one of the fundamental apparatuses of the Soviet state, guided by the Communist Party. Only this condition will ensure the maximum stability of the whole system of the proletarian dictatorship as well as maximum productivity.

II   THE TRADE UNIONS AND THE SOVIET STATE

1   The Soviet state is an extremely variegated and all-encompassing form of workers' organization which is in practice building communism and involving ever-broader masses of the peasantry in this work. On the other hand, the Soviet state is a workers' organization which has at its disposal all the material instruments of compulsion. Being a proletarian dictatorship, the Soviet state is a lever of economic revolution. Therefore, there can be no possibility of any opposition between the trade unions and the organs of Soviet power.

2   Politics is the most concentrated expression of economics, its generalization, and its culmination. Therefore, any opposition between the trade unions, as the economic organization of the working class, and the soviets, as its political organization, is completely absurd and is a deviation from marxism in the direction of bourgeois – specifically, bourgeois trade-unionist – prejudices. Such an opposition is especially absurd and harmful in the epoch of the proletarian dictatorship when its whole struggle, its whole activity – both economic and political – must be unified more than ever before, must be concentrated and directed by a single will, bound together in an iron unity.

3   As a school of communism and a link between the vanguard of the proletariat, the Communist Party, and the most backward masses of the proletariat, those who are not yet entirely free of the old shop and trade union narrow-mindedness, the trade unions must educate, organize culturally, politically, and administratively, must raise these masses to the communist level and train them for the role of creators of the communist order which the Soviet state is bringing into being. In this the trade unions act as the historically determined form of the proletarian dictatorship.

4   Therefore, the first requirement is for a closer tie between the Soviet apparatus and the trade union apparatus. Since the Soviet power is the broadest possible organization and one which concentrates the whole social power of the proletariat, it is clear that with the expansion of communist consciousness and of the creative role of the masses, the trade unions must be gradually converted into auxiliary organs of the proletarian state, and not the other way around.

5   By adopting this course the trade unions will fulfil their most impor-

tant function, the economic-administrative function, entering the Soviet organizations and saturating them, in this way becoming increasingly the foundation of Soviet economic apparatuses.

III THE TRADE UNIONS AND THE COMMUNIST PARTY

1   The Communist Party is the organization of the vanguard of the working class, the leader of the proletarian movement and of the struggle for a communist order.

2   The party exerts its influence on the broad non-party strata of toilers through the communist fractions and cells in all other worker organizations, especially in the trade unions. The dictatorship of the proletariat and the building of socialism are ensured only to the extent that the trade unions, while formally remaining non-party, become communist in their essence and carry out Communist Party policy.

3   Therefore, each trade union must contain a disciplined and organized communist fraction. Each party fraction is a part of a local organization and subordinated to a party committee, while the fraction in the All-Russian Central Council of Trade Unions is subordinated to the Central Committee of the RKP. All decrees of the All-Russian Central Trade Union Council relating to the conditions and organization of work are binding on all trade union organizations and on party members working in them and may not be repealed by any party organs other than the party Central Committee. The local committees, while entirely responsible for directing the ideological work of the trade unions, must in no way resort to petty tutelage over them. The relations between local party committees and trade union fractions are regulated precisely by the appropriate paragraphs of the party Rules.

IV THE FORMS OF TRADE UNION PARTICIPATION IN THE ECONOMIC APPARATUS OF THE PROLETARIAN STATE

1   Since the trade unions organize the workers according to major production branches, and are thereby directly connected with production, and therefore extremely competent organizations in each production branch, they form the underlying foundation of the economic organizations which direct industry.

2   This is manifested in the fact that the trade unions, without being an isolated organization and in no way being the complete and exclusive directors of the economy of the Soviet republic, none the less participate from top to bottom in the organization of production. However, no trade union organization interferes directly in the functioning of enterprises.

3   The lowest-level trade union cell is the factory committee. Without interfering in the administration of the enterprise, the factory committee fulfils the following functions: it helps to improve labour discipline and to this end uses all measures up to comradely courts of discipline; in addition

to general propaganda, it conducts propaganda for productive labour; it involves the workers in workers' inspection; it trains the workers and interests them in understanding the role of the factory (through reports and speeches, etc.); it helps in the selection of worker administrators, watches over the activities of rates and conflicts commissions, etc.

4   The trade unions participate in the factory administration by forming such administrations by agreement with the appropriate organs of the Supreme Council of the National Economy. In this the electoral principle yields to that of selection on the basis of the candidate's practical experience, technical competence, firmness, organizational capacity, and business sense.

5   The raion administrations and factory administrations consist of persons appointed by agreement between the central committee of the corresponding union, on the one hand, and the board of the glavk [central board] and the centre on the other, or (in the case of direct subordination to the Supreme Council of the National Economy) by agreement with the latter's presidium and with its final sanction.

6   The boards (presidiums) of guberniia councils on the economy are appointed by agreement between the guberniia trade union council and the guberniia executive committee; the glavks and centres are appointed by agreement between the trade union central committee and the corresponding section of the Supreme Council of the National Economy. Finally, the latter itself, inasmuch as candidates to its presidium are appointed by the congress of economic councils, is formed with the very intimate participation of the trade unions.

7   Other leading economic organizations such as, for example, those in charge of the mobilization, distribution, registration, and protection of labour (Labour glavk and others) are formed in a similar way.

Thus, in all links of the industrial administration and in the national economic administration generally, the trade unions have a particularly important role, one which will steadily increase with the rising level of the working class as a whole.

V   CURRENT TASKS OF THE TRADE UNIONS

1   The defeat of the white armies and the peaceful construction efforts required by the unbelievably catastrophic condition of the economy demand an entirely unprecedented concentration of the forces of the proletariat and the involvement of the broad peasant masses in social labour. Therefore, all apparatuses of the trade unions must take part in this intense and excessively difficult struggle for economic regeneration.

2   Accordingly, the methods and themes of trade union work must be radically changed. If the proletariat, as a class, is being confronted with the task of adopting the system of 'war work,' i.e., one of maximum accu-

racy, effectiveness, responsibility, rapidity, and intensity, together with selflessness and self-sacrifice on the part of the workers, then this must above all apply to the organs of industrial administration in general and, consequently, of the trade unions.

3   Like the guiding proletarian party, the trade unions must reorganize their own apparatus, first of all eliminating all remnants of slovenliness and introducing discipline and the strictest business spirit as well as complete accountability for the fulfilment of every assignment.

4   The trade unions must assume the task of explaining to broad working-class circles the full necessity of restructuring the apparatus of industrial administration, making it more elastic and businesslike; this can be attained only by a maximum reduction in the numbers of boards of administration and by the gradual introduction of direct one-man administration of production units.

In this agitation it is necessary to give special prominence to the following points:

a   one-man management cannot be counterposed to worker management; on the contrary, the most economic and widespread exercise of worker management requires one-man management, since a given number of worker-administrators is spread, in this case, over a large number of factories;

b   one-man management in no way violates or limits either the rights of class or the 'rights' of the trade unions, for a class can rule in any suitable form whatever, and the form is determined by technical expediency; in each case, the ruling class as a whole 'appoints' the people who direct and administer;

c   one-man management presupposes selection of competent people and assures a maximum of businesslike and responsible arrangements;

d   one-man management, even in cases where a specialist is in charge, is in the final analysis a manifestation of the proletarian dictatorship, which not only sees to it that work proceeds along specific lines, but also exercises supervision in the form of worker commissars;

e   one-man management does not rule out the enlistment of the broad worker masses in the concerns of management; it simply distinguishes the functions of immediate management from those of training, which latter should comprise an entirely separate branch of activity and a separate task. This distinction has become an absolute necessity at the present moment. On the other hand, it is completely incorrect to enlist the masses in management in the form of joint management bodies composed of three or five persons.

5   One of the particularly important tasks of the trade unions is to train the officers' corps of our industry from among the workers, i.e., the question of technical vocational training. Enlisting the broad working masses in

this effort, training them, labour propaganda, etc., remain in the forefront, for without a solution of these tasks labour can not move forward, and without such an advance a rebirth of our country's economic life on socialist principles is impossible.

6   The Congress believes that today, more than ever before, the party must devote the most serious attention to strengthening trade unions, and above all to reinforcing their staffs with infusions of the most devoted and steadfast Communists, and preferably those who have been through the stern school of the Civil War. The party must give a resolute rebuff to all attempts whatsoever to reduce to nothing the role and importance of the trade unions.

Spravochnik partiinogo rabot-   *KPSS v rezoliutsiiakh* II, 150–179
nika I, 38–40

IX Party Conference   22–25 September 1920

The IX Party Conference was a relatively small gathering, attended by 116 delegates with a deciding vote and 125 delegates with a consultative vote. However, the attendance figures of all the congresses and conferences through the early twenties must be taken with a grain of salt. The breakdown of the organizations represented at the Conference, given by Lisitsyn on behalf of the mandate commission, left something to be desired. From local organizations (guberniia, oblast, army, navy, etc.) there were ninety-four delegates with a deciding vote and sixty-three with a consultative vote. In addition there were fifty-eight delegates with a consultative vote consisting of 'leaders of the Central Committee sections, members of the vTSIK presidium and others.' Unaccounted for are twenty-two delegates with a deciding vote and four with a consultative vote.

The Conference saw a continuing drift towards factionalism already evident in previous years. Lenin still had not taken any steps to counter this trend and this time it may well have been because of his preoccupation with the Polish war which broke out in May 1920. The crisis, though past its peak, occupied Lenin's attention in his Central Committee report (*Collected Works* XXXV, 275–9) as well as Trotsky's report on the military situation. In fact, considerable time at the Conference was spent on the discussion of the Polish war with charges and counter-charges as to who bore the responsibility for the fiasco of the Soviet counter-offensive which aimed at the capture of Warsaw. It appears that the man most responsible for the failure was Lenin himself. Against the advice of Trotsky, Radek, and others, he pressed for the counter-offensive believing the revolution in Poland and even Germany to be imminent. With the exception of the seizure of power, when he counted on the ultimate outbreak of the international revolution to save the Soviet regime, this was the only instance when Lenin became truly carried away and placed his faith in the international proletariat.

Karl Radek, the enfant terrible of the party, astonished the delegates by giving a reasoned and objective analysis, in which he argued that, if a military mistake was made, it followed in the wake of a political one. The army simply followed a political order from the Politburo to take Warsaw. At the bottom of the mistake was, Radek concluded, an over-estimation of the maturity of the revolution in Central Europe. The debate on the war is also significant because it produced the first public clash between Trotsky and Stalin.

In dealing with the intra-party critics, Lenin found it expedient to retreat at this juncture. The Conference was preceded by a commission to consider 'bureaucratism' and the advocates of trade union autonomy, the Workers' Opposition (which, as such, emerged for the first time), and the Democratic Centralists were all represented. The arguments of the critics apparently could not have gone unheeded, although they were unsuccessful in their attempts to pass their own resolutions on organization or to defeat the official resolution. They freely voiced their opinions about 'bureaucratic centralism' on the floor and the main orthodox speaker, Zinoviev, presented a resolution 'On Current Tasks of Party Construction' (2.12), based partly on Lenin's guidelines, which must be regarded as a retreat or concession. The opposition charges were devastating. The attack was aimed not only at the excessive bureaucratism but also at the lack of proper organization and the complete neglect of both the local party organizations as well as the whole government apparatus of the soviets. Far from castigating the critics, the Zinoviev resolution attempted to establish specific measures for checking up on officials, for involving more ordinary party members in decision making, and for levelling privilege in the party hierarchy.

The resolution also included the decision to establish the so-called Central Control Commission to serve as a watchdog against the excesses of the party apparatus as well as to implement strict party control. The establishment of this commission may well have been a concession to the opposition at the time, but paradoxically it was later turned against them.

To some extent this coincided with Lenin's own ideas about the proper evolution of the apparatus, especially with his desire to attract genuine proletarians into its work, but the implications in the resolution concerning the rights of the rank and file against the leaders were another matter. Still more serious was the future of organized opposition factions, such as those which had helped push through the resolution. In September 1920 it may have appeared that they had some future, since the resolution generally supported their position (and it must be assumed that they voted for it, accepting the concessions that it represented). More importantly, however, while Zinoviev promised there would be no repression of dissenters and, 'above all a great freedom of criticism' (this to the accompaniment of applause from the delegates), no resolution was voted to secure the rights of critics to organize. While such a resolution had a little chance of success it appears naive that the opposition did not at least attempt to take advantage of their temporary strength to secure their own existence.

On the other hand, it seems also clear that the oppositionists were highly sceptical about the professed concessions and wondered aloud with Alexandra Kollontai whether the freedom was not going to be one 'of eating peaches in nice warm climates.' They all thoroughly despised and mistrusted Zinoviev and when Lenin, who took a surprisingly small part in this particular discussion, dismissed Kollontai and the rest of the oppositionists with his stock argument (in complete contradiction to the previous assurances of Zinoviev) that when the country was in danger there could be no freedom, they must have wondered what sort of concessions they had actually won. It comes hardly as a surprise that the resolution remained a dead letter.

The Conference also passed short resolutions on Lenin's Central Committee report, on the Polish question, and on the Comintern. With regard to the last resolution it is of some interest that at the II Comintern Congress in the summer of 1920, the Bolsheviks, through the so-called twenty-one conditions imposed the organization of the Russian Communist Party on the Comintern and also established their ideological predominance. The Comintern resolution was distributed to all the delegates of the Conference, yet none of the opposition members spoke against it.

2.12

On Current Tasks of Party Construction   24 September 1920

The unprecedented difficulty of the situation of the Soviet republic in the first years of its existence, the extreme devastation and the very great military danger, made it imperative to put forward 'shock' (and therefore, in fact, privileged) departments and groups of staff workers. It was imperative because it would have been impossible to save the devastated country without concentrating our forces and our means in the kinds of departments and groups of staff workers, without which the united imperialists of the entire world would doubtless have crushed us and not permitted our Soviet republic to so much as make a start on economic construction. This state of affairs, together with the difficulties in overcoming the habits and attitudes that were the legacy of capitalism and private ownership, explains the necessity for directing the attention of the entire party again and again to the struggle to make greater equality a reality – first, within the party; second, within the proletariat and, subsequently, within the entire mass of the working people; and finally, third, among the various departments and groups of staff workers, and particularly between 'specialists' and executives on the one hand, and the masses on the other. The party, which differentiates between party members only with respect to their degree of political consciousness, devotion, steadfastness, political maturity, revolutionary experience, and readiness to sacrifice themselves, combats all manner of attempts to make distinctions between party members on any other basis whatsoever, be it between higher-ups and subordinates, between the intelligentsia and workers, on the basis of national distinctions, etc. Affirming the Central Committee letter of 4 September 1920, the Conference considers it necessary to carry out the following measures:

I   To convene, as often as possible, general meetings of party members, making attendance at these meetings obligatory for all staff workers in positions of responsibility. At these meetings, it is necessary to discuss all important questions of general party and political life and of local conditions. At these same meetings, raion, city, and guberniia party committees are to give reports on the work; it is desirable that these reports be followed by discussions. Apart from the raion meetings, which are to be held not less than once a month, meetings of delegates are to be convened to discuss questions of party and Soviet construction (reports by committees and executive committees, by heads of party and soviet departments, etc.).

At the volost level, general volost meetings are to be held once a month. At the volost meetings, reports are to be given by the volost party committees and by representatives of the uezd party committees and also, where possible, of guberniia party committees, as well as by department heads of the soviets. Between conferences, the uezd committees call monthly meetings of volost delegates (from one to three delegates from each volost). Between guberniia conferences the guberniia committees convene meetings of delegates representing the uezds on the basis of two to three representatives per uezd and a corresponding number representing the city raions.

These meetings should not be haphazard in nature, but must be conducted in accordance with a strict plan.

Questions on which decisions have already been taken by the Central Committee and central soviet bodies must none the less be placed on the agenda of all party meetings with a view toward explaining to all party members the motives behind the decisions adopted. In Moscow a system is being set up whereby people's commissars will deliver regular reports at general meetings of party members and at meetings of workers. Closer association and closer ties with the non-party masses require that non-party members be admitted to open meetings of party cells at all enterprises and factories.

2   In order to draw rank-and-file party members into party life, it is desirable that not only guberniia conferences, but also plenums of guberniia and local party committees dealing with questions that do not require closed sessions, be made public for all party members. It is necessary that further appropriate steps be taken to ensure success in bringing rank-and-file party members into meetings of conferences and plenums.

3   It is absolutely necessary to modify the character of the revision commissions. They must be given the authority to inspect organizations' work in substantive fashion – to inspect the fulfilment of Central Committee circulars and the resolutions of conferences, the speed with which business is handled in party committees, the efficiency of the office staff, etc. It is the duty of the revision commissions to report all short-comings not only to the elected bodies, but also directly to the party central committees. In accordance therewith, it is essential that sufficiently high-level and energetic comrades be elected to the revision commissions. Not less than twice a year the Central Committee is to make a comprehensive study of the work of the guberniia party committees, for which purpose committees are set up composed of one representative of the Central Committee and two representatives of the local party organizations chosen by the guberniia conferences. On the same timetable the guberniia party committees, in turn, make a study of the work of the uezd party committees.

4   It is essential that particularly earnest attention be devoted to organizing the re-registering of party members. In practice, these re-registrations have more than once been characterized by an excessively formalistic approach. If a questionable communist in pursuit of careerist aims brings two or three recommendations, he is made a party member without further ado, while at the same time workers who for some reason did not find the time, did not want to, or were unable to bring the appropriate recommendations, remain outside party organizations. Re-registration must be organized in such a way as to reduce to a minimum all formalities for workers and for proletarian elements of the peasantry, and to raise a maximum of obstacles to admission to the party of non-proletarian elements. The examinations being used by certain organizations during re-registration are considered to be unsuitable.

5   Serious attention is to be devoted to organizing truly mass propaganda that systematically raises the level of the basic mass of party members. All necessary measures are to be taken to bring good order into the party school network. Special crash courses – for instance on food supply – are to be created in proper time and provided with the appropriate

literature. Regular conferences are to be convened of those in charge of the agitation and propaganda departments of the guberniia party committees – where possible in conjunction with representatives of the party press.

6   The appropriate central bodies are to exercise strict supervision over the organization of special 'weeks' and 'days,' permitting such events on an all-Russian scale only in exceptional cases and by resolution of the Central Committee.

7   In order to avoid the splintering of party work that occurs in places due to the existence of special organizations (political departments, etc.) and to truly unify all party work in a given territory under the guberniia party committees, the Central Committee is instructed to work out by the time of the next conference or congress, a plan to achieve the above-mentioned unity of party work

8   With a view to strengthening and deepening party work, a two-week-long campaign will be conducted on an all-Russian scale to strengthen the party, for which purpose the Central Committee is advised to work out the appropriate instructions. The Central Committee is advised to carry out a 'Party Week' throughout the entire republic at an appropriate moment after completion of the campaign to strengthen party work.

9   It is necessary in intra-party life to carry out more extensive criticism of both local and central party institutions. The Central Committee is assigned to point out in a circular the ways for broadening intra-party criticism at general meetings. Literary organs are to be created capable of carrying out a more regular and extensive criticism of party mistakes and, in general, criticism within the party (discussion sheets, etc.), to which end a special discussion sheet is to be created as part of *Izvestiia tsentral'nogo komiteta*. It is desirable that the same sort of discussion sheets be created as part of the *Izvestiias* published by the guberniia party committees.

10   While it is admitted in principle that it is necessary in exceptional cases to appoint people to elective positions, the Central Committee is none the less advised, as a general rule, to use recommendations instead of appointments.

11   Attention is drawn to the fact that it is impermissible that party bodies and individual comrades, in mobilizing comrades, be guided by considerations other than those deriving from the job at hand. Repressions of any sort whatsoever against comrades for the fact that they hold divergent views on certain questions resolved by the party, are impermissible.

12   All members of the soviets, executive committees, and presidiums are ordered to report on their work to their electors at general meetings at least once a month; they are also ordered to give individual talks, explanations, instructions, etc.

In order to achieve the closest of ties with the population, the guberniia executive committees, under the leadership of the communist fraction, are to work out a plan to provide systematic information to the public on all branches of the economy and on the political activity of the agencies of Soviet power, and are to send responsible officials throughout the guberniias to give reports at factory, village, volost, and other meetings in accordance with this plan.

It is essential to stimulate the activities of the plenums and congresses of the Soviets by preparing them in a meticulous fashion and by placing on their agendas a comprehensive discussion of the most important economic and political questions. It is particularly essential to prepare the uezd and guberniia congresses of the soviets and to draw the attention of the entire local populace to them (through widespread pre-congress and written agitation).

In the interval between guberniia and uezd congresses of soviets, meetings of representatives of the uezds and raions are convened in the guberniias, and of representatives of the volosts in the uezds, at which questions of Soviet construction are discussed in detail.

13   In the centre and in outlying areas as well it is necessary regularly to transfer responsible officials from place to place in order to enable them to make a broader study of the soviet and party apparatus and to ease their task of combatting routine. At the same time it is necessary that an immediate start be made on carrying out the resolutions of our party's IX Congress on measures for the systematic and massive appointment of party members who have come up through the ranks ...

14   With respect to staff workers at the centre, the conference finds it necessary to carry out the following measures:

a   to order every people's commissar and every member of the collegium to outlying areas at least twice a year;

b   to change more frequently the composition of the collegium by means of calling on staff workers who have come up through the ranks.

In so doing, it is necessary to see to it that current work does not suffer and that there is no loss of accumulated experience.

Special attention is to be given to the situation of the Moscow party organization. In view of the existence in Moscow of a large number of responsible officials of both the soviets and the party, the Central Committee is instructed, together with the Moscow party committee, to effect a transfer of these staff workers to the provinces, while striving to enlist for party and soviet work in Moscow the middle-level staff workers who have come up through the ranks and, above all, men and women workers in the Moscow party organization.

15   In the army, the members of the revolutionary military councils, the commissars, and other responsible officials are steadfastly implementing revolutionary discipline and at the same time are under orders to wage a resolute struggle against the routine of the old military system and against

all manner of bureaucratism. It is their duty to spend time as often as possible – without excusing themselves on the grounds that they are too busy – in the very midst of the Red Army men and the working masses, to hold discussions with them, to provide explanations and to give information about the situation on the fronts and in the rear. It is mandatory that comrades who hold positions of responsibility participate in the life of the collectives. It is mandatory that the command staff and the political commissar of a given unit as well as members of the revolutionary council, who are to substitute for one another in their work – be present at subbotniks [voluntary extra working days] organized by the units.

16   It is necessary to commit all Communists who hold positions of responsibility without exception, to perform regular party work, particularly among the lower strata of the proletariat, peasantry, and Red Army, to which end all party staff workers in positions of responsibility – regardless of the positions they hold – are to be permanently attached to factory, plant, Red Army, or village party cells. It is their duty to attend all general meetings and to report to them on their work. For reporting purposes, they are registered with the raion party committees and bear party responsibilities on an equal footing with all members of the party. Participation in subbotniks must be made absolutely mandatory for all party members, as is stipulated in the regulations on subbotniks. Time spent on subbotniks must be viewed not merely from the standpoint of the immediate economic results, but above all from the point of view of strengthening party unity on the basis of the fulfilment of all party obligations by all Communists without exception. Staff workers who hold positions of responsibility may be relieved from one or another party obligation for compelling reasons only by resolution of the raion party committee. The established disciplinary penalties are to be applied consistently for careless attitudes toward one's obligations, and these penalties are to be extended without exception to all party members, beginning, in particular, with staff workers who hold positions of responsibility and instilling in them through acts, not words, an understanding of the equal responsibility of all before the party and the proletarian state.

17   Communists who hold responsible party staff positions are not authorized to be paid at special, individual rates or to receive either bonuses or overtime pay.

18   Fully effective practical measures are to be worked out to do away with the inequality (in living conditions, size, or earnings, etc.) between the 'specialists' and staff workers in positions of responsibility on the one hand, and the working masses, on the other. In view of the fact that this inequality violates democratism, is a source of demoralization in the party, and lowers the authority of Communists, a commission is to be set up for

the above purpose composed of one representative from the Moscow party organization, one from the Petrograd party organization, one from the People's Commissariat of Food Supply, one from the All-Russian Central Executive Committee and one from the All-Russian Central Council of Trade Unions.

19 It is deemed necessary to create, alongside the Central Committee, a Control Commission composed of the comrades with the greatest background in party affairs, the most experienced, the most impartial, and those best able to implement strict party control. The Control Commission, which is to be elected by the party congress, must have authority to receive all manner of complaints and reach conclusions on them, arriving at agreement with the Central Committee and, where necessary, holding joint meetings with the Central Committee or referring questions to the party congress. On a temporary basis, pending the next party congress, the composition of the Control Commission is confirmed as follows: Comrades Dzerzhinsky, Muranov, and Preobrazhensky and one representative each from the Moscow, Petrograd, Ivanovo-Voznesensk, and Nizhegorod party organizations, who are to be elected at the guberniia conferences (pending the convening of these conferences, the representatives are to be chosen by the guberniia party committees together with the aktiv of staff workers). Special party commissions are to be formed at all guberniia party committees to receive corresponding complaints; these commissions are to be formed from the most impartial comrades, those who enjoy the unanimous trust of the party organization. Not a single complaint, if it is signed by so much as a small group of party members, is to go without a well-reasoned reply from the commission or a resolution by the guberniia party committee.

20 The bureaucratism that holds sway in many of our chief administrations and centres often causes serious damage to the legitimate interests of the popular masses and serves as a most important source of grievances against the party, which is held responsible for the sins of the chief administrations and the centres.

The Central Committee must take very serious measures to combat this. The local organizations must help the Central Committee in this struggle, above all by providing it with the requisite information.

Therefore the conference advises the local organs of the military department to do everything possible in the sphere of billetting etc., to take only the most necessary facilities in order to avoid criticism on the part of the working people.

In numerous areas the military is showing a tendency to excessive expansion, without regard for the extremely difficult conditions in which workers are living. At the local level it is necessary to create, attached to the guberniia party committees, special commissions to review the list of houses occupied by the military in order to reach agreement with the military on vacating, in favour of workers, those buildings that can be released.

In publishing the resolution of the All-Russian Conference – confirmed by the plenum of the Central Committee – on the question of the composition of the Control Commission the Central Committee holds: that Comrades Preobrazhensky and Dzerzhinsky, who are members of the Central Committee, are named to serve on the first Control Commission only by decision of the party conference, and that, in general, members of the Central Committee are not to be elected members of the Control Commission.

In their work on the Control Commission, these members of the Central Committee are not bound by the decisions of the Central Committee. They do not vote in the Control Commission if the question concerns their sphere of work.

Izvestiia tsentral'nogo   *KPSS v rezoliutsiiakh* II, 189–96
komiteta, 12 October 1920

X Party Congress   8–16 March 1921

The X Party Congress was probably the most important post-1917 gathering of Lenin's career. The party and his leadership faced three serious, overlapping crises: the intra-party opposition centreing around the question of the trade unions, the Kronstadt revolt against bolshevik rule, and the necessity to change economic policy in order to save the country from total collapse. In contrast to his role at the previous congress, Lenin rose aggressively to the occasion with four major addresses: the Central Committee political report (*Collected Works* XXXII, 170–91, 192–207), on party unity, on the introduction of a new agrarian tax policy (the foundation of the New Economic Policy), and on trade unions. By the time the Congress was over, the Kronstadt revolt was suppressed, the regime made a first step on the road to economic recovery, and all opposition groups were outlawed. Lenin reconfirmed his position, while Stalin and Zinoviev established themselves as potential successors to that position.

The Democratic Centralists and the Workers' Opposition, the two principal opposition groups, as well as the leninists and the coalition on the trade union issue formed by Trotsky and Bukharin, campaigned in the elections of delegates to the Congress in the regional party conferences on the bases of platforms on the trade union issue. This arrangement, of course, turned the whole debate into the first and last, officially sanctioned, factional power struggle. It was evidently suggested by Zinoviev, and approved by Lenin, although their reasons were different. Zinoviev was primarily motivated by his undisguised hatred of Trotsky and by his desire to weaken him, in which he was successful, while Lenin was more concerned with the advantages of forcing the opposition into the open and show their true strength.

It was a foregone conclusion, of course, that the leninists, the so-called Platform of Ten, with their leader's prestige and with their control (thanks to Stalin) over the party apparatus, were going to win a decisive majority among the delegates. The Workers' Opposition and the Democratic Centralists mustered only about ninety delegates out of around 700 with a deciding vote, judging by the voting on the alternative resolutions on the political report (exact figures are difficult to determine; there were also some 296 delegates with a consultative vote but no factional breakdown is available). It is open to question, too, how the delegates were actually elected. Many of them were new to the Congress and many of the old members came only with a consultative vote, as was charged by Riazanov. The Democratic Centralist, R.B. Rafail, went further and accused the Central Committee and the Orgburo of invalidating elections of certain party members into various committees and imposing on them candidates of their own – a practice started at the centre but extended to the localities as well. This development was made possible by 'Lenin's supporter Stalin,' who tightened his grip on the party apparatus. As Rafail concluded, the party organs in Petrograd and in Moscow were given communiqués from the party front instead of from the military front, edited under the supervision of 'that military strategist and arch-democrat Stalin.'

However, apart from this organizational insurance, the key to Lenin's success at the Congress was his skill in exploiting the Kronstadt revolt and the desperate state of the country. Far from showing any embarrassment that his regime was under attack from proletarian and peasant revolutionary sailors, he maintained that the uprising constituted a reactionary coalition of all the foes of the Soviet state from White generals to anarchists. The crisis atmosphere at the Congress reached its height when the dramatic decision was made to dispatch almost 300 delegates (close to 200 with a deciding vote) to Kronstadt to strengthen the leadership's forces there. The subsequent voting results indicate that, ironically, more than one half of the Workers' Opposition and the Democratic Centralists were among them, apparently fully associating themselves with the leninist position on this question. While the voting on the Central Committee report produced ninety-two votes for the opposition resolutions, the voting on the equally divisive resolution on the organizational report, which took place after the departure of the delegates for Kronstadt, showed only thirty-two votes for the alternative resolution of the opposition. It is unlikely that they would have changed their votes on this deeply felt issue.

In addition to Kronstadt, Lenin also exploited to the full the situation in the country as a whole. When there is an enormous predominance of peasantry in the country, Lenin argued, when their discontent with the proletarian dictatorship grows, when the crisis in the peasant economy reaches its limits, when the demobilization of the peasant army releases hundreds and thousands of people who know war as their only trade and give rise to banditry – that is no time to argue about theoretical deviations: '... we shall not tolerate any arguments about deviations ... the argument ... is becoming a direct threat to the dictatorship of the proletariat.'

With this atmosphere of crisis Lenin was able to secure on the last day of the Congress, the passage of resolutions 'On Party Unity' (2.13) and 'On the Syndicalist and Anarchist Deviation in Our Party' (2.14), which were not on the original agenda and which suppressed factions in general and the two major opposition groups in particular. Although not on the Congress agenda, these questions were discussed at one of several, evidently secret, meetings of the delegates supporting the Platform of Ten, just before or at the beginning of the Congress (Lenin 5, XLIII, 378, 461, notes 127, 128). These were the most important of the few resolutions of the post-revolutionary congresses that Lenin drafted personally, and these, more than the ineffectual 'Testament' that he dictated during his final illness, constituted his durable legacy to the party. The voting gave Lenin an overwhelming mandate to impose his kind of unity, 400 to 25 for the resolution 'On Party Unity' and 368 to 30 'On the Syndicalist and Anarchist Deviation.'

The members of the opposition now stood under threat of expulsion from the party, and according to point 7 of the resolution 'On Party Unity,' the power of expulsion was vested in the Central Committee. So as not to alarm the rest of the party, this point was kept secret at the time and was published only in 1924 after the XIII Conference. A short, separate resolution specifically appealed to the Workers' Opposition to obey party discipline.

Lenin achieved another important victory in securing the passage of the resolution 'On the Role and Tasks of Trade Unions' (2.16). Here his competition included not only the Workers' Opposition, which submitted their alternative resolution, but also the Trotsky-Bukharin group, which submitted their own. Initially, Lenin's resolution won by 336 votes to 50 and 18, with 4 abstentions. A commission which included Trotsky, Bukharin, and Shliapnikov was appointed to prepare the final draft which was then approved by a majority, against 6, with 4 abstentions. The final Lenin resolution neither gave these institutions the kind of independence which the Workers' Opposition desired, nor openly annexed them to the state, as the Trotsky-Bukharin group wanted. The point here was not a reversal of the IX Party Congress resolution that subordinated the unions to the party-state regime (2.11), but rather the recognition that the symbol of autonomous trade unions should not be treated scornfully, at least in the initial stages of development.

The other major victory that Lenin achieved was the passage of the resolution that replaced the arbitrary, forcible requisitioning of food from peasants with a regulated tax in kind. Peasant anger at the requisitions had contributed to widespread unrest, and the programme was economically self-defeating because the peasant had little incentive to produce any surplus. While Lenin could be criticized by left communists for yielding to petty bourgeois peasant interests, the crisis atmosphere of the X Party Congress again assisted him in getting his way. His resolution (2.17) was opposed by an alternative one, but passed easily. Other elements in the New Economic Policy which enabled Russia to recover from the war, revolution, and Civil War, emerged following the Congress. A resolution on control commissions was also passed providing for their organization at local levels (2.15).

The Congress passed additional resolutions, dealing with the Main Administration of Political Education, party construction, the organization of courses on marxism, the nationality question, co-operatives, financial policy, relief for needy workers and peasants, capitalist encirclement, the Comintern, the threat of imperialist war, and the military situation. The last resolution rejected any suggestion of local party organizations' control over the army's political work as dangerous and contributing to the disintegration of the Red Army. The resolution was classified as 'top secret' and 'not for publication' and did not appear in the first edition of the stenographic report of the Congress. It was released only in 1933.

A new larger Central Committee of twenty-five members and fifteen candidates was elected with notable changes in the composition. The three former secretaries Krestinsky, Preobrazhensky, and Serebriakov and several others were dropped. Of the new members, nine, including Molotov, Voroshilov, and Frunze could be counted upon to support Stalin. Of the new candidates four were followers of Stalin. The elections to the Central Committee were conducted in a closed session, and delegates with a consultative vote apparently were not to participate. It was only on the intervention of Riazanov that Zinoviev announced on behalf of the Congress presidium that the session did not include any special secrets and these delegates were permitted to participate although not to vote. The session still remained a closed one and only the results but not the debate were published. The total number of votes cast in the Central Committee election was given as 479 which is appreciably higher than any total cast for the various resolutions, after the departure of the delegates for Kronstadt. No explanation was given for this discrepancy.

There is some indication that Lenin was concerned, in spite of his majority at the Congress, about the Central Committee elections. In the 5th edition of his works there appears a note with the following set of figures:

$$25 - 9 \qquad 2/3$$
$$15 - 2(3) \qquad \Sigma = 47 \qquad 11(12)$$
$$7 - 0$$

This is explained by the editors of his works as Lenin's attempt to secure for the joint plenum of the Central Committee and Central Control Commission two-thirds of votes for the partisans of the Congress majority, so that they could be relied upon to carry out the Congress resolutions. Lenin, so the editors say, felt it necessary to submit a proposal on behalf of the Platform of Ten to elect twenty-five Central Committee members and fifteen candidates as well as seven Central Control Commission members. Those delegates not subscribing to the Platform of Ten were to be given nine places among the full members and two to three places among the candidates. A glance at the composition of the new Central Committee indicates that the opposition did not get anything like nine places on the new Central Committee (Lenin 5, XLIII, 376, 460, note 125). During the session Lenin submitted his own list of candidates, which, interestingly enough, included Shliapnikov, one of the most outspoken members of the Workers' Opposition. However, since there were ninety-three delegates competing for the Central Committee membership and ninety-one delegates for the candidate membership, and twenty-nine and fourteen for the Central Control Commission membership and candidate membership respectively, Lenin had to make certain that nothing went wrong. The problem was discussed at one of the secret meetings of the delegates supporting the Platform of Ten. Lenin apparently made certain that his followers understood what was expected of them and later also canvassed followers of the other platforms to gather support for his list (cf. A.I. Mikoyan, *Mysli i vospominaniia o Lenine*, Moscow, 1970, 135–45). As final assurance, in an obvious desire to intimidate the delegates during the Central Committee elections, Lenin insisted that the members be elected by a roll-call. Lenin also hoped that he could get rid of the intellectuals on the Central Committee, whom he for the most part despised, and replace them by 'genuinely proletarian elements' (Lenin 5, XLIII, 378). These steps were an integral part of the general purge announced at the Congress. Lenin's strategy was also partly designated to facilitate, when needed, the application of point 7 of the 'On Party Unity' resolution, a hope which was not fulfilled a few months later when the Central Committee refused by one vote Lenin's demand for the expulsion of Shliapnikov (2.30).

As Lenin planned, a new Central Control Commission of seven members and four candidates was also elected. Solts, a follower of Stalin, was obviously its leading member even before the Congress, as was apparent from his assignment to deliver the Central Control Commission report. His re-election confirmed him in that position. Following the Congress the Central Committee elected a new Politburo, dropping Trotsky's supporter Krestinisky, elevating Zinoviev to full membership, and adding Molotov as a candidate member.

2.13
On Party Unity   16 March 1921

1   The Congress draws the attention of all party members to the fact that the unity and cohesion of their ranks, and the achievement of full trust among party members and of truly friendly work that truly embodies the unity of will of the proletarian vanguard, are particularly necessary at the present moment, when a number of circumstances are intensifying the waverings of the petty bourgeois population in the country.

2   However, even before the general party discussion on the trade unions, there had come to light within the party certain signs of factionalism, i.e., of the appearance of groups with platforms of their own and with a will to close ranks to a certain extent and create their own group discipline.

It is essential that all class-conscious workers clearly realize the harmfulness and inadmissibility of any factionalism whatsoever which inevitably leads, in practice, to less friendly work and to repeated and intensified attempts by enemies of the ruling party who have attached themselves to it under false pretenses, to deepen the divisions and use them for purposes of counter-revolution.

The fact that the enemies of the proletariat take advantage of all deviations from a strictly consistent communist line was seen most clearly in the example of the Kronstadt uprising, when the bourgeois counter-revolution and White Guards in all the world's countries immediately manifested their readiness to accept even slogans favouring a Soviet system, if only the dictatorship of the proletariat could be overthrown in Russia; when the Socialist Revolutionaries and the bourgeois counter-revolution in general made use, in Kronstadt, of slogans allegedly favouring an uprising in favour of a Soviet system but opposed to the Soviet government in Russia. Such instances fully prove that the White Guardists are striving – and are able – to assume the guise of communists and even to assume positions to the 'left' of communism, if only they can weaken and overthrow the bulwark of the proletarian revolution in Russia. The Menshevik leaflets in Petrograd on the eve of the Kronstadt uprising show in the same way how the Mensheviks were using differences within the RKP in order, by deeds, to incite and support the Kronstadt rebels, Socialist Revolutionaries, and White Guardists, while presenting themselves – in words – as opponents of uprisings and champions of the Soviet system with, allegedly, only minor modifications.

3   Propaganda on this matter takes the form on the one hand, of detailed explanations of the harm and danger of factionalism from the standpoint of party unity and of achieving unity of will of the proletarian vanguard as a basic condition for the success of the dictatorship of the proletariat and, on the other hand, of an explanation of the elements peculiar to the latest tactical devices of the enemies of the Soviet system. These enemies, who have become convinced of the fact that counter-revolution under an openly White Guardist flag is hopeless, are bending every effort today to use differences within the RKP to advance the cause of counter-revolution in one sense or another by a transfer of power to the political groups which come closest, externally, to recognizing the Soviet system.

Propaganda should also explain the experience of previous revolutions, in which the counter-revolution supported the petty bourgeois groups that were closest to the extreme revolutionary party, in order to shake and then overthrow the revolutionary dictatorship, thus opening the way for the subsequent complete victory of counter-revolution, the capitalists, and the landowners.

4   It is essential that every party organization be very strict in seeing to it that the unquestionably necessary criticism of party short-comings, that all analyses of the general party line, or stocktaking of practical experience results, that verification of the fulfilment of party decisions and of ways for correcting mistakes, etc., not be submitted for discussion by groups formed on the basis of some 'platform' or other, but that they be submitted for discussion by all party members. For this purpose, the Congress directs that 'Discussion Pamphlets' and special anthologies be published on a more regular basis. Every person who voices criticism must be mindful of the party's situation, in the midst of enemy encirclement, and must also, through direct participation in Soviet and party work, strive in practice to correct the party's mistakes.

5   While instructing the Central Committee to carry out the complete destruction of all manner of factionalism, the Congress at the same time states that where questions are involved which command particular attention of party members – questions of purging the party of non-proletarian and unreliable elements, of combatting bureaucratism, of developing democratism and initiative among the workers, etc. – all businesslike proposals whatsoever are to be considered with the greatest of attention and are to be tested in practice. All members of the party should know that on these questions the party is not taking all necessary measures, meeting, as it is, with a number of obstacles of various types, and that while resolutely refusing unbusinesslike and factional criticism, the party will continue tirelessly – constantly testing new methods – to use every means

to combat bureaucratism, to expand democratism and initiative, and to seek out, expose, and expel those who have adhered to the party under false pretenses.

6   The Congress orders the immediate dissolution, without exception, of all groups that have been formed on the basis of some platform or other, and instructs all organizations to be very strict in ensuring that no manifestations of factionalism of any sort be tolerated. Failure to comply with this resolution of the Congress is to entail unconditional and immediate expulsion from the party.

7   In order to ensure strict discipline within the party and in all Soviet work, and to achieve maximum unity while eliminating all factionalism, the Congress gives the Central Committee full powers to apply all measures of party punishment up to and including expulsion from the party in cases of violation of discipline or of a revival or toleration of factionalism, and where members of the Central Committee are involved, to go as far as to reduce them to candidate members and even – as an extreme measure – to expel them from the party. The condition for the application of such an extreme measure to Central Committee members and candidate members and to members of the Control Commission is the convening of a Central Committee plenum, to which all candidate members of the Central Committee and all members of the Control Commission are to be invited. If such a general meeting of the most responsible party officials decides by a two-thirds majority that it is necessary to demote a Central Committee member to the status of candidate member or to expel him from the party, then such action must be taken immediately.

2.14
On the Syndicalist and Anarchist Deviation in Our Party   16 March 1921

1   In recent months a syndicalist and anarchist deviation has emerged in party ranks. This deviation requires the most resolute measures of ideological struggle, as well as a purge of the party and restoration of it to a condition of soundness.

2   The deviation in question has been caused in part by the entrance into the party of elements that have not yet fully assimilated the communist world view, but in major part this deviation has been caused by the influence on the proletariat and on the RKP of the petty bourgeois elements that are exceptionally strong in our country and that inevitably cause waverings in the direction of anarchism, particularly at moments when the situation of the masses has taken a sharp turn for the worse as a result of a poor harvest and the extremely destructive consequences of war, and when demobilization of a millions-strong army turns loose hundreds and

hundreds of thousands of peasants and workers who are unable to find work and the means to support themselves.

3   One of the most complete and best-formulated expressions of this deviation are the theses and other printed works of the group known as the so-called 'Workers' Opposition.' The following thesis, for example, is rather indicative: 'Organization of the management of the economy belongs to an all-Russian congress of producers, who are organized in production trade unions that elect the central agency that directs the republic's entire economy.'

The ideas behind this and other, similar statements are fundamentally incorrect in theory and represent a complete break with marxism and communism, as well as with the results of the practical experience of all semi-proletarian revolutions and of the present proletarian revolution.

In the first place, the concept of 'producer' lumps together the proletarian with the semi-proletarian and with the small commodity producer, thus deviating in a fundamental fashion from the basic concept of class struggle and from the basic requirement that a clear distinction be made between the classes.

In the second place, the incorrect formulation of the question of relations between the party and the broad non-party masses – a formulation that results in subordination of the party to non-party elements – as contained in the thesis in question, is not any less a fundamental divergence from marxism.

Marxism teaches – and these teachings are not only formally confirmed by the entire Comintern in a decision of the II Comintern Congress on the role of the political party of the proletariat, but also proven in practice by the entire experience of our revolution – that only the political party of the working class, i.e., the Communist Party, is capable of unifying, teaching, and organizing a vanguard of the proletariat and of the entire mass of working people, a vanguard capable of countering the inevitable petty bourgeois waverings of this mass, of countering the traditions of, and inevitable backsliding to, a narrow trade-unionism or trade union prejudices among the proletariat, and of guiding all aspects of the proletarian movement or, in other words, all the labouring masses. Without this, the dictatorship of the proletariat is unthinkable. The incorrect understanding of the role of the Communist Party in its relations to the non-party working masses, on the one hand, and the equally incorrect understanding of the role of the working class in its relationship to the entire mass of working people, on the other hand, are a fundamental theoretical divergence from communism and a deviation in the direction of syndicalism and anarchism, a deviation that pervades all the views of the 'Workers' Opposition.'

4   The X Congress of the RKP declares that it also considers fundamen-

tally incorrect all attempts by the group in question and by individuals to defend their mistaken views by citing paragraph 5 of the economic section of the RKP Programme, which is devoted to the role of the trade unions. This paragraph states that the trade unions 'must actually concentrate in their hands the entire administration of the whole economy as a single economic unit,' and that in this way they provide an unbroken link between central state management, the economy, and the broad masses of the working people, 'attract' these masses 'to the direct management of the economy.'.

In the very same paragraph the RKP Programme considers a preliminary condition for the situation at which the trade unions 'are to arrive,' to be the process of 'freeing themselves from a narrow guild outlook' and the enlistment in their ranks of the majority of workers, 'and gradually all workers.'

Finally, in the very same paragraph the RKP Programme stresses the fact that the trade unions are already, 'according to the laws of the Soviet republic and established practice, participants in all local and central organs for the administration of industry.'

Instead of taking account of precisely this practical experience of participation in administration, instead of developing this experience further, in strict accord with achieved successes and corrected mistakes, the syndicalists and anarchists declare outright the slogan of 'congresses or a congress of producers,' who 'are to elect' the bodies which manage the economy. The leading educational and organizing role of the party with respect to the trade unions of the proletariat, and of the latter with respect to the semi-Philistine and outright petty bourgeois masses of the working people, is, consequently, completely by-passed and eliminated, and instead of a continuation and correction of the practical work of building new economic forms – work which was already begun by the Soviet system – we find a petty bourgeois and anarchist destruction of this work, a destruction that can only lead to a triumph of the bourgeois counter-revolution.

5   Apart from their incorrectness from a theoretical point of view and their fundamentally erroneous approach to the practical experience of the economic construction already launched by the Soviet system, the views of the group in question and of similar groups and persons are, in the view of the RKP Congress, an immense political error and an immediate political danger to the maintenance of power in the hands of the proletariat.

In a country like Russia, the immense preponderance of petty bourgeois elements and the inevitable destruction, impoverishment, epidemics, poor harvest, and extreme cases of need and human calamity that resulted from the war, give rise to particularly grave manifestations of waverings in the state of mind of the petty bourgeois and semi-proletarian masses. These waverings lean now to the side of strengthening the union of these masses with the proletariat, now to the side of a bourgeois restoration. The entire experience of all revolutions of the eighteenth, nineteenth, and twentieth centuries shows with the most categorical clarity and conviction that these waverings – given the slightest weakening in the unity, strength, and influence of the revolutionary vanguard of the proletariat – can only lead to a restoration of the power and property of the capitalists and landowners.

Therefore, the views of the 'Workers' Opposition' and similar elements are not only theoretically false, but serve in practice as the expression of petty bourgeois and anarchist vacillations; in practice, they weaken the steadfast guiding line of the Communist Party and in fact aid the class enemies of the proletarian revolution.

6   On the basis of all the foregoing, the RKP Congress – resolutely rejecting the above-mentioned ideas, expressive of the syndicalist and anarchist deviation – resolves:

1   to recognize the necessity for a determined and systematic struggle against these ideas;

2   to consider propagation of these ideas as incompatible with membership in the Russian Communist Party.

While instructing the Central Committee to implement these decisions in the strictest fashion, the Congress also points out that space can and must be made in special editions, anthologies, etc., for a more detailed exchange of opinions among party members on all the above questions.

2.15
On the Control Commissions   16 March 1921

1   Control commissions are being created to strengthen the unity and authority of the party; their tasks include combatting the bureaucratism and careerism that have crept into the party, combatting misuse of party and soviet positions by party members, violations of comradely relations within the party, dissemination of unfounded and unsubstantiated rumours and insinuations that bring disgrace to the party or to individual party members, and the dissemination of other information of this type which violates the unity and authority of the party.

2   The control commissions must not merely explain carefully the statements that they release, but must also take the initiative in removing the causes that give rise to, or facilitate the appearance of, the impermissible phenomena alluded to in point 1, above. At the same time, the control commissions are to supervise the process whereby, and see to it that, all complaints and statements about crimes and misdemeanors by party members receive appropriate handling and decision.

Note Complaints and statements by both groups and individual persons are accepted not only from party members, but also from non-party members about party members.

3 The control commissions are organized at the centre, in oblasts, and in guberniias by means of elections at the party congress and at oblast and guberniia party conferences. At the centre, the commission is elected with a membership of seven full members and three candidate members.

In the oblast ... of from three to five members.

In the oblast ... of from two to three candidate members.

In the guberniia ... of three members and two candidate members.

Obligatory length of party membership for members and candidate members of control commissions:

For the Central Control Commission – not less than ten years' party membership.

For the oblast – not less than five years' party membership.

For the guberniias – party membership since the February 1917 Revolution.

Note A new commission membership is elected following the report of the former commission.

4 Members of the control commissions cannot be members of party committees and cannot occupy administrative positions of responsibility.

Note Existing oblast and guberniia control commissions retain their staff composition until the next oblast and guberniia conferences.

5 In order to intensify their work and to enable them to investigate a matter thoroughly and obtain answers to questions, a certain portion of the members of the control commissions are to be freed from all other work: all members of the Central Control Commission, three members of the oblast control commissions, and two members of the guberniia control commissions.

6 Members of the control commissions cannot be transferred to other work prior to the conclusion of the period of their tenure.

7 The control commissions operate alongside the party committees and are accountable to the party conferences and the party congress, as appropriate.

8 Members of the control commissions have the right to attend all meetings of – and have a consultative vote in – the corresponding party and soviet committees, and all other meetings and conferences of whatever sort, of the corresponding party organizations.

9 Resolutions of the control commissions are carried out by the corresponding committees and cannot be countermanded by the latter. In cases of disagreement, a question is referred to a joint meeting. If no agreement is reached with the committee, the question is referred for decision to the party congress or appropriate conference.

Note In cases where a decision is urgently required, the matter is referred to the next highest control commission.

10   The control commissions use the apparatus of the corresponding party committee and are authorized to give assignments to all party comrades and party organizations.

11   The control commissions are to give periodic reports to the party organizations and to publish reports in the press.

2.16
On the Role and Tasks of Trade Unions   16 March 1921

I   THE ROLE OF THE TRADE UNIONS IN THE PERIOD OF THE DICTATOR-
      SHIP
1   The overall tasks and role of the trade unions in the period of the dictatorship of the proletariat are set forth with complete correctness in a number of decisions by previous congresses and conferences of both the party and the trade unions ...

These decisions retain their full force and are not in need of any sort of modification. The X Congress is confronted not with the task of finding some sort of new theoretical formulations for the role of the trade unions in the period of the dictatorship, but of determining the paths for carrying out those that have already been adopted ...

The trade unions as a support for the proletarian dictatorship
3   The Russian Communist Party has to implement a dictatorship of the proletariat in a country with an immense peasant majority. Today, when we are already past the point where the peasantry was directly threatened by a restoration of the landowners' power, the matter of implementing a proletarian dictatorship is encountering new difficulties. The successful implementation of the dictatorship is possible only with the existence of powerful trade unions imbued with unity of will and common strivings – trade unions in the form of mass organizations open to all proletarians at whatever stage of development of their class consciousness.

The trade unions as a school of communism
4   The most important role of the trade unions in Soviet Russia remains their role as *schools of communism*.

Only a trade union that shows regular concern for all aspects of the life and everyday conditions of the worker, both inside and outside of the plant, can be a primary school to provide organizational skills and political training for the broadest – and even the backward – masses of the working people.

The basic mass of trade union members (6,970,000 members, of which only about 500,000 are party members) are non-party members. Communism is being built with the human materials left us as the legacy of capitalism. The trade unions in Soviet Russia are gradually becoming organizations that embrace all workers to a man. The trade unions organize those elements of labour that under capitalism were, in the main, often strangers to the proletarian family (former workers in trade, hospital staff, those employed in the field of art, etc.). Remaking all these elements, bringing them closer to the leading strata of the proletariat, and adapting them to the task of building a communist society is one of the most important tasks of the trade unions as schools of communism.

For the successful fulfilment of these tasks, the trade unions must above all become organizations in which each individual member is a conscious and active participant in the overall life of his union. The trade unions, as schools of communism, must serve all aspects of the day-to-day life of the labouring masses, gradually enlisting the very broadest strata of the working people in the cause of state construction, constantly illuminating the way for them with the ideas of our programme, leading them from the particular to the general, and gradually lifting them from non-party status to communism.

The trade unions will in fact accomplish their roles as schools of communism in the present period to precisely the extent that they prove to be leaders of the proletarian masses in the matter of communist practice, i.e., in the practical reorganization and building of the economy on communist principles. In Soviet Russia, only that trade union is a true school of communism that is able gradually to enlist the most backward strata of the working people in the work of consciously improving Soviet economy.

The X Party Congress directs the particular attention of all party members to precisely this role of the trade unions. A communist is to win recognition and authority in the trade union movement only and exclusively through long and tireless daily work in the trade union, such that the masses themselves put him in a position of leadership. The task of the half million members of our party who are members of trade unions at the present time, is – through long, patient, and consistent educational work, through personal example, organizational ability, business acumen and concern for the material and spiritual interests of the working masses – to win over completely to the side of our party those millions of non-party workers who predominate at the present time in the trade union movement.

The question of making the trade unions state institutions
5   Rapid conversion of the trade unions to state institutions would be a major political mistake, precisely because at the present stage of development this would be a potent factor in impeding the fulfilment by the trade unions of the tasks indicated above.

The present situation of the trade unions in Soviet Russia is unusual as concerns their relations to the state. At the present moment, the trade unions are already fulfilling certain functions of purely state agencies (the working out of pay scales, the distribution of work clothing, etc.). In the Soviet state, these state functions of the trade unions will gradually be increased. But the Congress points out that any attempt whatsoever artificially to accelerate the conversion of the trade unions to state institutions, would in no sense improve the economic situation of the republic, but would merely result in making more difficult the role of the trade unions as schools of communism. The task is increasingly to win over, *in fact*, to the Soviet state these mass non-party organizations, while leaving them their character as organizations that are open to workers of various political views and attitudes, to party as well as non-party workers, to the literate and illiterate, religious and non-religious, etc....

The party and the unions
7   The Russian Communist Party in the person of its central and local organizations unquestionably directs, as before, the entire ideological side of the work of the trade unions. The communist fractions in the trade unions are completely subordinate to the party organizations, in accordance with the special regulation formulating these relationships that was confirmed by the IX Party Congress. But in addition to this, the X Party Congress insistently and categorically warns all party organizations and all individual comrades against any sort of niggling custodianship over, and excessive interference in, the current work of the trade unions. The selection of the executive personnel of the trade union movement should be made, of course, under the directing control of the party. But party organizations must exercise particular care in applying the normal methods of proletarian democracy precisely in the trade unions, which are the one place more than any other where the selection of leaders should be done by the organized masses themselves.

In this way, conditions will be created whereby the party organizations, while fully maintaining overall control in their hands, will not have to interfere directly and repeatedly in the internal activities of the trade unions, and the trade union bodies, under the leadership of the communist fractions, will be able to exercise much more planning and be much more independent and systematic in assessing and utilizing their personnel and in assigning them to one or another post in the economy with due attention to the necessary continuity in work by means of taking into consideration their work experience, by operating a system of work certification, etc., etc.

In promoting staff organizers and economic managers who are imbued with an understanding of the particular importance of production tasks, to leading positions in the trade union movement, the party must see to it that these qualities in the candidates exist in combination with a devotion to communism, with habits of discipline and, in particular, with a familiarity with working among the broad working masses and skill in dealing with them. One must not forget for a single moment that all the practical work of the trade unions demands particularly great attentiveness and sensitivity, at times to the most minor – but at the same time, urgent – questions of the everyday life of the labouring masses ...

2.17
On the Replacement of the Requisitions
with a Tax in Kind 15 March 1921

1   In order to ensure a correct and tranquil working of the land on the basis of greater freedom on the part of the farmer to dispose of his economic resources, to strengthen his peasant holdings and raise their productivity, and also in order to determine exactly the state taxes imposed on the farmers, the requisitions, as a means of state procurements of food, raw materials, and forage are replaced by a tax in kind.

2   This tax is to be lower than the amount levied by the requisitions. The amount of the tax is to be calculated in such a way as to cover the minimum needs of the army, the urban workers, and the non-agricultural population. The sum total of the tax is to be constantly reduced to the extent that the restoration of transport and industry enable the Soviet state to receive agricultural produce in the normal fashion, i.e., in exchange for the output of factories and craftsmen.

3   The tax is assessed in the form of a percentage or share of the output produced on the farm, proceeding from the size of the harvest, the number of mouths the farm has to feed, and the actual amount of livestock on the farm.

4   The tax is to be a progressive one; the percentage payable by the farms of middle peasants and those with small holdings and by the farms worked by urban workers, etc., is to be scaled down.

The farms of the poorest peasants are to be exempted from certain forms of the tax in kind, and in exceptional cases, from all forms of the tax.

Hardworking peasant proprietors who increase the sown area of their holdings or who increase the productivity of their holdings as a whole, are granted advantages in the payment of the tax in kind, either in the form of a reduction in the tax rate, or in the form of partial exemption from the tax.

5   The law on taxes is to be drawn up in such a way and published in time so that even before the beginning of the spring field work the farmers are as well informed as possible about the extent of their obligations.

6   Delivery to the state of the produce due to it under the tax law is to be completed within a definite period of time, established by law.

7   The amount of produce due for delivery under the law is calculated for the village associations (societies). Within the village association, the tax is apportioned among the proprietors as they see fit, in accordance with the general norms stipulated in point 3.

To supervise the application of the tax norms and the assessment of the same, elected organizations of local peasants are formed according to the groups of taxpayers in the various tax brackets.

8   All stocks of food, raw materials, and forage that remain in the possession of the farmers after they have paid their taxes are completely at their disposal and can be used by them to improve and strengthen their holdings, to increase personal consumption and to obtain, in exchange, products of factory and cottage industry and agricultural produce.

Exchanges are permitted within the bounds of the local economic turnover.

9   With a view to supplying the poorest of the population and for purposes of exchange against surpluses of food, forage, and raw materials voluntarily delivered to the state to cover taxes due, a special fund is to be created, a fund of farm equipment and supplies and of common consumer goods. This fund is to be created from products of domestic manufacture and from those articles being obtained abroad in part through disbursements from the state gold reserves and in part from raw materials procurements.

The Congress, in approving in general the proposals of the Central Committee to replace the requisitions with a tax in kind, instructs the Central Committee to act with all speed to co-ordinate these proposals, to work out in detail the forms for implementing the tax, and to get the appropriate law through VTSIK and Sovnarkom ...

Spravochnik partiinogo rabot-   *KPSS v rezoliutsiiakh* II, 206–66
nika II, 7–19 (2.13, 2.14, 2.15,
2.16)
Pravda, 17 March 1921 (2.17)

X Party Conference   26–28 May 1921

The resolution on the tax in kind passed by the X Party Congress (2.17) in March 1921 did not deal sufficiently with the whole question of the NEP. The policy which was formed in connection with the tax in kind, according to Lenin, remained to a large degree unclear and often even quite incomprehensible to the local authorities. In view of the importance of the policy, the leadership decided to call the 'not fully regular' (as Lenin put it) X Party Conference earlier than was originally planned. His resolution 'On Economic Policy' (2.18) made it clear that this was to be a policy of long duration and that its basis was to be trade.

Following the conference the Agitprop launched a vast campaign to popularize the principles of the NEP among the local party organizations because, as a Central Committee circular letter put it, 'only a correct understanding of the tasks confronting the RKP(b) in the sphere of economic construction can make the wide masses of toilers interested in the task of the restoration of the economy.'

The Conference also passed a resolution outlining the plan of work for the Central Committee and discussed matters relating to financial reform, light industry, co-operation, the Comintern, party organizational work, as well as the place of the Mensheviks and Socialist Revolutionaries in the contemporary situation. The last was a delicate question for the Bolsheviks. The Mensheviks had included a long time before in their programme a policy similar to the NEP, and the Socialist Revolutionaries, a peasant-based party, had argued that the peasant should be free to work his own land. (As we saw, there is evidence that the Bolsheviks favoured similar policies immediately after the revolution.)

Lenin had on several occasions stated that the only place for the Mensheviks and the Socialist Revolutionaries was prison. When the Bolsheviks adopted their programmes and thus placed their own political legitimacy into question, it was all the more important for them to suppress all open activity, or what was left of it, of the two parties. The discussion of this problem at the Conference clearly reflected this concern. As Radek concluded in his report on the Mensheviks and Socialist Revolutionaries, the tactics towards the two groups had to be 'tactics of a relentless struggle.' The Conference was attended by 239 delegates but it is not known how many had a deciding vote and how many a consultative vote.

The Conference seems to have suffered from the haste with which it was convened. The Central Committee called the Conference only on 11 May 1921 which may not have allowed sufficient time for its proper organization. As a result the published record is incomplete and, according to the 1933 edition of the protocols, the report of the mandate commission was lost. If there were other reasons for these shortcomings they are not apparent from the proceedings. Although some criticism was aired at the Conference, the published record gives the impression that the proceedings were quite orderly.

2.18
On Economic Policy

27 May 1921

1   The basic political task of the moment consists in complete adoption and exact implementation of the New Economic Policy by all party and Soviet staff workers.

The party considers that this policy has been adopted for a prolonged period of time, a period spanning a number of years, and demands of all that it be implemented with unconditional exactitude and good faith.

2   The basic lever of the New Economic Policy is considered to be trade turnover. Correct relations between the proletariat and the peasantry and the creation of a completely stable form of economic union between these two classes for the period of transition from capitalism to socialism are not possible without the establishment of a regular exchange of goods or products between industry and agriculture.

In particular, the achievement of an exchange of goods is necessary as a stimulus to the expansion of peasants' sown areas and to an improvement of peasant agriculture.

Enterprise and initiative at the local level must be comprehensively supported and developed at all costs.

The guberniias with the largest grain surpluses are to be considered top priority areas, and the exchange of goods is to be conducted first in those areas.

3   Regarding co-operatives as the basic vehicle for conducting the exchange of goods, it is deemed correct policy for agencies of the Commissariat of Food Supply to approve contracts with agencies of the co-operatives and for the former to transmit to the latter the supplies of goods for goods exchange in order to meet state targets and to meet them under state supervision.

The co-operatives are to be provided with ample opportunity for the production of procurements for the state, for all-round development of local industry and for an upswing in economic life in general.

There is to be support for the co-operatives' credit operations.

Anarchistic goods exchange (i.e., exchanges that slip through any form of state supervision and control) is to be combatted by concentrating exchanges primarily in the hands of the co-operatives; this will in no way impinge on true freedom of trade.

There is to be a study of the market.

4   Support is to be given to small and medium-sized (both private and co-operative) enterprises, chiefly to those that do not require supplying with raw materials, fuel, and foodstuffs from state stocks.

The renting of state enterprises to private persons, co-operatives, artels, and partnerships is to be permitted. Local economic agencies have the authority to conclude such contracts without permission from higher authorities. It is mandatory that the Council of Labour and Defence be informed in each such case.

5   There is to be a review (to a definite extent) of the production programmes of large-scale industry in the sense of stepping up the output of consumer goods and those goods commonly used by peasants.

There is to be an expansion of independence and initiative of every major enterprise in handling the financial means and material resources at its disposal. A corresponding, clear-cut resolution is to be introduced for approval by the Sovnarkom.

6   A system of bonuses in kind is to be set up and collective supply is to be organized on an experimental basis.

A more correct distribution of food products is to be established with a view toward increasing labour productivity.

There is to be universal adoption of the principle of individual and collective incentives for inventions, improvements, savings in labour, fuel and materials, maintenance of buildings and machinery, etc.

Stiffer punishment is to be introduced for waste and theft of state property and also for not making the most efficient use of labour.

7   It is necessary to retain and strengthen the apparatus for the rapid, complete, and universal collection of the tax in kind. The agencies that are responsible for foodstuffs are to be provided with the necessary party authority for this purpose. The centralization of the foodstuffs apparatus is to be retained and strengthened.

8   All previous measures are to be concentrated on the urgent practical task of the current year: to collect by means of the tax in kind and goods exchange, a grain fund of not less than 400,000,000 puds as a base for the restoration of large-scale industry and for carrying out the electrification plan.

9   The draft instruction of the Council of Labour and Defence is adopted in principle, and the party fraction of the All-Russian Central Executive Committee is instructed to make it into law.

It is considered an indispensible and first-priority task of the party in general to ensure the strictest observance of those instructions, and in particular to promote non-party members and enlist them in this work.

10   Procedures are to be established holding central institutions especially accountable for impeding local initiative and for failure to give it adequate support. The party fraction of the VTSIK Committee is instructed to work out a corresponding resolution and to pass it at its next session.

11   The conference instructs the Central Committee and all party organizations to carry out a systematic series of measures to strengthen agitation and propaganda, as well as to effect the appropriate shifts of party forces required to explain fully and carry out in a planned fashion, all the above-enumerated tasks.

12   The party sets itself, as an unconditionally serious task, a careful and thorough interpretation and study in the press, as well as at meetings, conferences, congresses – trade union, soviet, party, etc. – of the practical experiments in economic construction at local levels and in the centre.

Spravochnik partiinogo rabot-   *KPSS v rezoliutsiiakh* 11, 268–71
nika 11, 30–1

2.19
Instruction to RKP Cells of the Red Army
and Navy in the Rear and at the Front   27 June 1921

In addition to the resolutions passed by the Central Committee plenums, the Central Committee or the higher party organs in the name of the Committee issued resolutions, regulations, decisions, circulars, instructions, letters, etc. The two documents printed below (2.19, 2.20) are examples of an instruction and a circular issued in the name of the Central Committee. Unless otherwise indicated, the above applies to all documents in this volume not passed by a congress, conference, Central Committee plenum, or joint Central Committee and Central Control Commission plenum.

I   GENERAL PROVISIONS

1   The primary party organization in the units, institutions, and administrations of the Red Army is the company-level cell – and its equivalent – of RKP(b) members.

2   The executive organ of the company-level cell is its presidium.

3   The next higher party level in the army is the meeting of delegates and general meeting of representatives of party cells of the regimental unit. Questions of principle are decided only by the general meeting of cells of the regimental unit.

4   Overall direction of the work of the regimental bureau of RKP(b) cells in organizing political work in military units is given by the corresponding politotdels to which they are subordinate.

Note 1 Questions involving admission and expulsion of party members and dissolution of party cells are decided on the basis of representations by party cells or commissars to the party commissions attached to the politotdels of the individual brigades and divisions (see the addenda on the party commissions of the Red Army and Navy approved by the RKP(b) Central Committee and announced in the 2 July 1921 order of the Chief of the Political Administration).

Note 2 In units where party commissions have not been set up, their function is fulfilled by the Moscow Committee of the RKP(b).

6 [*sic*] Party cells of territorial units form part of the general RKP(b) organizations, reporting to the local raion or uezd party committee in the area where those units are stationed.

7 When ten or more military cells exist on the territory of a given party committee, a bureau is set up under the local party committee and is subordinate to it; the bureau is composed of three representatives: one representative of the politotdel or the commissar of the higher of the military units; one representative of the conference of delegates of the cells; and one representative of the local RKP(b) committee.

Note 1 Where there are no military cells except those united under regimental bureaus, no military bureau is set up. The functions of the military bureaus are fulfilled by the regimental bureau of cells, in which case members of the party committee of the raion in which the military unit is located serve as members of the regimental bureau.

Note 2 Cells of units that are part of a division can be part of the regimental bureau under the party committee only with the permission of the appropriate politotdel.

8 The sphere of activities of the military bureau includes the conduct of practical party work in the ranks of the Red Army and the carrying out of all directives of the politotdel and the party committee.

9 In party procedure, relations between the subordinate organizations of the RKP(b) in the Red Army are determined by analogy: the company-level cell is comparable to the factory cell and the regimental organization and its bureau to the uchastok committee.

10 The carrying out of general party duties assigned by the local party committee to members of the cells of military party organizations, is done in co-ordination with the appropriate commissars or their assistants in the politotdel.

11 Communist Party cells of transient military units and institutions register with the local party organizations.

12 Members of party cells of military units and institutions participate on an equal footing with local party cells in all party meetings of secretaries, organizers, conferences, congresses, elections to party committees, etc.

Note The politotdels of the individual brigades, divisions, and military districts may – with permission of the political bodies of the next highest level and of the local party body – convene brigade, divisional, and district conferences and meetings to discuss questions relating to the organization of political education work in the army.

2   THE ORGANIZATION OF THE PARTY CELL

13   A party cell is organized in all units of the Red Army – companies, commands, squadrons, batteries, etc. – having not less than three party members.

Note At staffs, administrations, and institutions of the military, party cells are organized on the same basis.

14   To organize a party cell, the commissar of the unit or one of the members of the RKP(b) announces, with permission of the commissar, the convening of an organizational meeting of, and the holding of elections for, a party cell, to which all party members in the unit and those who have party documents are invited.

15   The first meeting is called by the organizational bureau of the cell, which is made up of three members, of which one must be the commissar of the regiment, to check all party documents.

16   The organizational bureau of the cell checks all party documents and presents them for confirmation by the politotdel and local party committee, and upon confirmation of the setting up of the party cell, calls a second general meeting and reports to the meeting.

17   The second meeting elects a secretary to conduct the cell's affairs, if the membership of the cell does not exceed ten. If the number of members is greater than ten, a presidium of the company-level cell is elected to conduct the cell's affairs; the presidium is composed of three members, who serve for a period of two months.

Note Cells that have more than one hundred members elect a presidium composed of five persons.

18   The presidium or the secretary are subject to re-election at a general meeting when demanded by one-third of the members of the cell; application for the holding of new elections, when presented by less than the required number of members, is to be forwarded to higher authorities.

3   THE TASK AND WORK OF THE PARTY CELL

19   The cell links the Red Army masses with the directing party body in the given area and with the party organization of the next highest military unit.

The tasks of the cell are:

a   to carry party slogans and decisions to the masses,

b   to enlist new members in the party,

c   to increase the political consciousness of every party member and non-party member, *d* to unite all non-party Red Army personnel who sympathize with the RKP(b) into one compact group for joint active work to implement party slogans in the most rapid and complete fashion.

20 The cell strives to increase the combat effectiveness and political consciousness of the Red Army, for which purpose it sets itself the goal of making its unit a model unit through personal example and through increased agitation.

21 The cell gives each of its members a job to do and makes intelligent use of their abilities.

22 Far from limiting itself to the discussion of questions, the cell adopts practical decisions on each such question, decisions that indicate clearly which of the cell's members is assigned to accomplish – or see to the accomplishment of – the assigned tasks, and in what period of time.

23 In the sphere of general party duties, the cell carries out all resolutions, advice, and slogans of higher party bodies and sees that they are carried out by the members of the cell.

24 The cell sees to it that all cell members attend general meetings of the cell, uchastok and raion, that they all attend subbotniks and study sessions, and that they all perform duty in the special assignments detachment and pay their membership dues.

25 The cell elects a delegate to the regimental and general city meeting.

26 The cell informs the unit commissar, the party body of the superior military unit and the local party committee in detailed fashion about the political situation of the unit.

Note Copies of reports are also given to the local party committee in cases where a military bureau exists.

27 In the sphere of military organization, the cell sees to the correct fulfilment of all military duties by each member of the cell.

28 The cell promotes the earliest possible implementation of all orders and directives of the command staff.

29 The cell watches out for and puts an end to attempted agitation of whatever sort that weakens the combat effectiveness of the unit.

30 In combat, the cell sets a personal example with its steadfastness and courage. In cases where it is necessary to ask for volunteers for dangerous duty, the cell puts forth its members.

31 The cell contributes in every way to assist Red Army comrades in finishing their military training and conducts a permanent agitation campaign of military propaganda in its unit.

32 In the sphere of soviet construction, the cell assists in the organization of civil governing bodies in newly occupied areas.

33 Through its work, the cell popularizes all resolutions of the local soviet and augments its authority.

34 The cell gives whatever assistance it can to soviet organizations in all their undertakings.

35   In the sphere of the political education of party members, the cell strives to raise to the maximum level the political consciousness of its members.

36   Concurrently with this, the cell concerns itself with teaching the 'ABC's of Communism,' and studying the party Programme and acquaints its members with the basic principles of marxism.

37   The cell reads and discusses reports and newspaper articles on questions of economic, soviet, trade union, and military construction and on party life.

38   The cell discusses new decrees of the soviet authorities, resolutions of the trade unions, and the international and domestic situation of the federation.

39   In the sphere of political education of non-party members, the cell invites them to attend its open meetings and urges them to participate in discussion of questions of the country's economic and political life.

40   The cell arranges readings, talks, and meetings for non-party members.

41   The cell distributes newspapers, pamphlets, and brochures.

42   The cell orders all its members to conduct agitation among the masses, assigning to each member a definite group.

43   The cell takes an active part in the work of the unit's political education commissions and places its members on the commission staffs.

44   The cell's agitation must be linked to the practical slogans being implemented at the given moment.

45   In the sphere of political education of the public at large, the cell conducts intensified agitation in the area where its unit is stationed, and unites the goals and tasks of the Soviet Federation and the Red Army.

46   The cell invites the public to meetings, concerts, and discussions that it arranges; it also sets up village reading rooms.

4   GENERAL MEETINGS OF THE COMPANY-LEVEL CELL

47   All members of the cell meet once a week on a specific day established with the concurrence of the commissar, for their regular meeting.

48   When necessary, supplementary meetings are called in the same fashion.

49   Under combat conditions, the general meetings can be cancelled at the commissar's discretion.

50   No party member, regardless of his position in the armed forces, enjoys any sort of advantage at party meetings.

51   A meeting of the cell is considered legal if one-third of all the members are present. If a meeting fails to take place for lack of a sufficient number of members, it is postponed for a very brief period of time and then considered legal regardless of the number of members who attend.

52   In order to submit a petition for the admission or expulsion of members, one-half of the cell's members must be present.

53   All resolutions of the general meeting that pertain in some way to life at the front take force after they have been confirmed by the commissar of the unit of which the given company or command is a part.

54   All resolutions of the general meeting are recorded in minutes of the meeting, which are signed by the chairman of the meeting and by the secretary.

55   The carrying out of the meeting's instructions is the task of the secretary or the presidium of the cell.

5   THE TASK AND WORK OF THE CELL PRESIDIUM

56   It is the responsibility of the presidium:

a   to register members and candidate members;

b   to draw up the agenda and call general meetings;

c   to keep minutes on both general meetings and on meetings of the presidium, and to maintain the minutes in good order;

d   to submit the minutes to the commissar for confirmation and to implement the resolutions adopted;

e   to see that the activities of the cell conform to the requirements of the present instruction;

f   to render all-round assistance to the unit commissar and the company political instructor in their work;

g   to give assignments to all members of the cell and to oversee their fulfilment;

h   to promote the work of the political education agencies;

i   to maintain contact with the bureau of the regimental cell.

6   THE GENERAL MEETINGS AND MEETINGS OF DELEGATES
       OF THE REGIMENT AND THE SCOPE OF THEIR ACTIVITIES

57   The general meetings consist of all members of all cells of the regimental unit.

58   The general regimental meeting is convened twice a month.

59   The scope of the activities of the general meeting includes discussion and resolution of questions of an organizational nature and those concerning party and political education work in the units.

60   The general meeting elects the bureau of the regimental cell.

61   The general meeting elects the delegate to the party conference and meeting.

62   The general meeting hears reports on the work of the regimental bureau of the cells in its unit and approves same.

63   The general meetings discuss questions of immediate concern with regard to the Programme and tactics of the party, etc.

64   At the front the general meeting has authority – subject to the concurrence of the commissar – to expel members from the cells and to initiate petitions to the party commissions for dismissal of party members, the petitions presenting the motives behind such action. In rear areas, decisions on questions of expulsion from the party are left to the general meeting of the party organization of which the cell is a part. In the first case (i.e., at the front) such resolutions are subject to confirmation by the party commissions attached to the politotdels – the departments of brigade, division, and military district – and in the second case (i.e., in rear areas) by the guberniia party committee.

65   In cases where it is impossible, due to the combat situation or to other circumstances, to convene a general regimental meeting, its place is taken by the meeting of delegates.

66   The meeting of delegates is convened only in certain troop units (regiments, divisions) that consist of several commands at the squadron level, and the like.

67   Each company-level cell elects its representatives to the meeting of delegates at a general meeting of the cell; the delegates are chosen on the basis of one delegate for each ten members with each cell sending not fewer than two delegates.

68   Only comrades who have been members of the party for not less than three months are eligible for election to the meeting of delegates.

Note Cells that have no members who meet the qualifications for length of party membership send delegates who have only a consultative vote.

69   The meeting of delegates and the general meeting are considered to have a quorum when attended by two-thirds of all delegates elected by the cells from the entire membership of the cells. In cases where the specified number of comrades is not present, the following meeting is considered to have a quorum with one-third of all the members or delegates.

70   At conferences of delegates, members of the bureaus of the cells of the particular units for which the conferences of delegates have been convened (the regimental units, the divisions) are entitled to a deciding vote.

71   Every meeting conference of delegates and general meeting elect a presidium for the duration of the meeting.

72   Meetings of delegates and general meetings do not interfere in the dispositions and orders of the command staff of the regiment (battalion, companies, etc.).

73   All resolutions of both the general meeting and the meeting of delegates that have any bearing whatsoever on life at the front, take effect only after they have been confirmed by the regimental commissar.

74   In the units of an army in the field, the general meeting admits new party members nominated by the company-level cells, and new candidate

members, and submits their names for confirmation by the party commission attached to the politotdel of the brigade or division. In units that are not in the field, admission of new members lies with the meeting of the raion of which the given cell is a part.

7 THE BUREAU OF THE CELLS OF A REGIMENT

75 The bureau of the cells of a regiment is made up of representatives whose number is set by the general meeting, but in any case, of not more than five members and three candidate members.

Note Four of those elected have definite duties; five comrades are appointed from among the rank-and-file Communists for purely educational purposes and are not assigned any specific duties where the work of the bureau is concerned.

76 Comrades who joined the party not later than six months before the election and who have been party members ever since are eligible for election to the bureau of the cells of the regiment.

Note 1 Comrades who do not satisfy the requirement for length of party service can be members of the bureau of the cells only with the approval of the division politotdel.

Note 2 The members of the bureau of the cells divide up the responsibilities among themselves: the first performs the duties of executive secretary of the bureau, the second takes charge of political education work, the third directs party work, the fourth oversees the work of the group in assisting the RKP(b), and the fifth, who has no set duties, helps with the work of each of the rest, as required.

77 The bureau conducts a programme of political work, co-ordinating it with the overall plan for political work as laid down by the division politotdel; it maintains ties with the local party organization, working in close contact with it, and assists the organizational work of the agencies of the Soviet government at the local level.

Note The programme of political work is worked out with a view toward what can be implemented without fail in the course of the next week.

78 The bureau of the cells of the regiment helps the regimental commissar to implement the dispositions and orders of higher authorities and of the political inspections.

79 The bureau carries out the resolution of the meeting of delegates and general meeting of party cells and oversees the implementation of these resolutions by both the raion cells and by individual party members.

80 The bureau draws up agendas and prepares materials for meetings of delegates and general meetings and takes measures to ensure that they function properly and that they are convened on time.

81 In special cases the bureau adopts independent decisions on questions that are in the sphere of activities of the general meeting and meeting

of delegates, carries out the decisions, and then brings the matters to the attention of the next meeting for its confirmation.

82   The bureau organizes and conducts political education work and directs the work of the company-level cells.

83   The bureau of the regimental cell collects materials and draws up regular written reports, at least once a week, on the life of its unit, which it presents to the appropriate politotdel; it also submits reports to the newspapers on the life of its unit.

Note The bureau of the regimental cell receives members dues and other monetary receipts. For this purpose it selects a treasurer from among its members, whose job it is to keep accounts on the money that passes through the bureau's hands.

84   The regimental cell and its bureau do not have a press of their own, but use the unit press that is under the commissar.

8   RELATIONS OF THE CELLS WITH COMMISSARS AND WITH COMMAND
      STAFFS

85   The party cell of a line unit has the duty to support, and strengthen trust in, the commissar and the commander.

86   In case of treason within a unit, the party cell supports the commissar in liquidating the treason.

87   The cell does not interfere in the dispositions of the commissar, the command staff, or the administrative and quartermaster staff.

88   In cases where the local administrative and quartermaster staff deviates from the proper fulfilment of its duties, the cell immediately informs the commissar of the facts.

89   If the commissar does not take action to put a stop to the irregularities reported by the cell, the latter has the right to discuss the matter and, without making any recommendations to the command staff, to submit its decision on the matter to the politotdel.

90   Members of the cell and / or its presidium enjoy no privileges whatsoever and, with the exception of the secretary, are not excused from the military duties.

91   The company-level cell renders all possible assistance to the political instructor in his work. When any sort of conflict arises between a cell and a political instructor, the matter is resolved by the regimental commissar.

92   In the person of the commissar, the cells have a representative in higher party institutions and a director for unit party activities. In the case of a disagreement between a commissar and a party cell, the latter has the right to turn for solution of the question to the appropriate politotdel for its chain of command.

93   A commissar may not delay or forbid the forwarding to higher party authorities of a complaint against his actions by a party cell. Only under

combat conditions may such a complaint be postponed for a period of not more than seven days.

94   In cases of a deviation from the party line on the part of a party cell or individual members of the cell, the commissar has the authority to take the necessary steps on his own responsibility, up to and including dissolution of the cell, and is immediately to report such action through proper channels to the party commission attached to the division politotdel or to the political administration of the military district.

9   ADMISSION AND EXPULSION OF MEMBERS

95   Acting on the basis of the present instructions, the company-level party cells have the right to admit candidate members of the party on the basis of the party Rules and the resolution of the X Party Congress [On Party Construction], i.e., on the recommendation of two members of the cell who have been members of the party for at least one year. Candidate members are confirmed by the bureau of the cells of the regiment. The comrades who recommend candidates bear full responsibility for them. Candidate members are subject to party discipline and carry full party responsibilities.

96   Comrades who are members of the RKP(b) are confirmed as members of the party by simple registration.

97   Candidate members confirmed by the bureau of the cells can – upon completion of the term for candidate membership and by decision of a regimental general meeting or meeting of delegates – be presented to the party commission at the politotdel of the particular brigade or division, for confirmation as full members of the RKP(b); moreover, the recommendation of two party members is required in such cases.

Note 1   The required length of party service as a candidate member is up to one year for comrades who are not workers or peasants; for comrades who are workers and peasants, it is two months.

Note 2   Length of party service is calculated not from the day a comrade becomes a candidate member, but beginning on the day he is confirmed by the party commission as a full member of the RKP(b).

98   Members of cells are subject to permanent or temporary expulsion for violations of the party Rules and of party discipline as established by the Rules and by resolution of the X Party Congress [On the Military Question], as in the case of the present instruction.

99   Resolutions of general meetings and meetings of delegates on questions of the admission of candidate members to the party and expulsion of members from the party, must record exact minutes of the meetings and these minutes on admission and expulsion must be forwarded through channels within three days.

100   Persons expelled from the party have the right to appeal the expulsion

resolution to a higher party authority or to the party commission attached
to the political administration of the military district.

10   CLERICAL PROCEDURES AND REPORTS OF PARTY CELLS
101   Clerical procedures of party cells conform to the practices established by the military-political bodies.
102   The cell notes on the party cards all work done by members of the cell
and payment of membership dues.
103   At established regular intervals, the cell gives reports on its activities
to higher party and political authorities.

> *Spravochnik partiinogo rabot-*
> *nika* II, 115–20

2.20
On the Agitation and Propaganda Section
of the Central Committee   22 November 1921

1   The Agitation and Propaganda Section of the Central Committee of
the RKP(b) is organized as a part of the Secretariat of the Central Committee, and is the agency with whose help the Central Committee organizes,
unifies, and directs all verbal and printed agitation and propaganda work of
the RKP(b).
2   To carry out the above-named tasks, the Agitation and Propaganda
Section consists of four subsections: agitation, propaganda, press, and
national minorities.

THE AGITATION SUBSECTION
3   The task of the Agitation Subsection is to:
   a   provide overall direction of the political and production agitation
work of local party bodies and party supervision over the agitation work of
the appropriate soviet and trade union institutions;
   b   study, on the basis of the experience of local party organizations, the
methods, means, and forms of agitation, and to work out questions of
agitation technique.
4   The Agitation Subsection consists of three branches: political agitation (political campaigns), production agitation, and agitation techniques.
5   The Political Agitation Branch works out and prepares agitational
directives and instructions in the form of theses, slogans, and plans both for
current, planned political work, and for crash political campaigns. Apart
from regularly disseminating circularized instructions and incidental instructions, this branch works in closest co-operation with the Press Subsection in the sphere of printed agitation.

6   The Production Agitation Branch has the of organizing – through party committees and in liaison with the Cultural Department of the All-Russian Central Council of Trade Unions and central committees of the trade unions – production agitation of both a regularly planned sort and of the sort that consists in seasonal and crash campaigns.

7   The Agitation Techniques Branch collects information on the methods, forms, and apparatuses of agitation, sums up accumulated experience, and elucidates new methods for bringing agitation closer to the broad masses.

THE PROPAGANDA SUBSECTION

8   The task of the Propaganda Subsection is:

a   to organize, unify, and direct all propaganda work within the RKP(b) by means of regular instructions to the guberniia committees;

b   to take account of and systematize party propaganda experience at the local level and to work out, on this basis, new forms and methods of propaganda;

c   to elaborate questions of methodology in party propaganda;

d   to exercise party control over the work of the Propaganda Department of Main Political Education Administration by means of co-ordinating with this body decisions on questions of principle in all areas of propaganda work; by reviewing programmes for all types of propaganda work, by reviewing study curriculums, the projects of the network of cultural and educational institutions, and by reviewing guides and study aids for special political subjects;

e   to participate in the work of the Accounts and Assignments Section of the Central Committee as it relates to reporting and assignment of the RKP(b)'s propaganda forces.

9   The Propaganda Subsection consists of three branches: intra-party propaganda, schools, and methodology.

10   The Intra-party Propaganda Branch prepares theses and the summaries of reports for party meetings on various topics relevant to the present moment; it works out the plan for current propaganda work in cells, circles, and sections of party organizations and draws up the corresponding theses and summaries; it takes account of, systematizes, and studies the experience of propaganda work at the local level and draws up letters of instruction to guberniia party committees on questions of propaganda work.

11   The School Section participates in the drawing up, review, and confirmation of the curriculum and programme of the Institute of Red Professors and of the courses for the study of marxism and oversees their fulfilment; it reviews the programmes of the socio-political cycle of the higher educational institutions, the higher technical schools, and the central educational institutions subordinate to the various people's commis-

sariats, and presents its conclusions on these programmes; it works out, in conjunction with the Studies and Programme Department of the Main Political Education Administration, the programme of the soviet party schools and oversees the assignment of lecturers.

12   The Methods Branch oversees the methodological work of the Propaganda Department of the Main Political Education Administration and of other institutions of the People's Commissariat of Education in the club, library, and school areas.

THE PRESS SUBSECTION

13   It is the task of this subsection:

   a to exercise overall direction over the Russian republic provincial press and party supervision over the work of the Main Political Education Administration's Press Department;

   b to plan the current tasks of the press in the sphere of agitation and propaganda and to give direction to the work of the press in accordance with the overall political and economic tasks of the party;

   c to review and work out together with the Russian republic Main Political Education Administration the general state publishing plan for press organs;

   d to unify the publishing work of the Central Committee and to direct the publishing activities of local party organizations;

   e to participate in the work of the Accounts and Assignments Section of the Central Committee relating to reporting and assignment for Communist journalists;

   f to distribute literature for party committee libraries.

14   The Press Subsection consists of three branches: instruction, publishing, and distribution of literature.

15   The Instruction Branch gives direct instructions on editions intended for party members, jointly prepares with the Agitation Subsection the plan for regular, periodic press campaigns, and directs the work of the press in accordance with the general directives of the Central Committee.

16   The Publishing Branch unites all the publishing activities of the Central Committee and its sections, directs the work of local party organizations in the area of press activities, and establishes close ties with the State Publishing House, the Main State Paper Industry Administration, the printing section, and the editorial and publishing sections of the central institutions and organizations.

17   The Literature Distribution Branch is concerned with prompt and regular supplying of oblast, guberniia, and uezd party committee libraries with all the literature that appears on socio-political questions.

18   For the maintenance of close ties with the Press Section of the Russian republic Main Political Education Administration and for the

purpose of giving direction to its work, there are to be regular meetings of the head of the Agitation and Propaganda Section, the head of the Press Subsection, and a responsible executive of the Russian republic Main Political Education Administration.

19   The Agitation and Propaganda Section of the Central Committee directs the instructors' journal *Zhurnalist* (Journalist) and *Agit-Rost* (Main Political Education Administration Agitator), published by the Russian republic Main Political Education Administration, by appointing persons of its choice as editors of the press organs in question.

THE NATIONAL MINORITIES SUBSECTION

20   It is the task of the National Minorities Subsection:

   a   to unify and direct agitation and propaganda in the native language of the national minorities among those groups who are outside their autonomous oblast or republic or who have no such national territory within the Russian republic;

   b   to work out and place before the Central Committee, questions of party construction resulting from the particular everyday and cultural conditions in which these national minorities live;

   c   to investigate the most rational methods of party agitation and propaganda among the people of the national minorities, as well as to collect and work up the material necessary for this purpose;

   d   to participate in the work of the Accounts and Assignments Section of the Central Committee as concerns reporting and assignments for national minorities staff;

   e   to issue instructions to the guberniia national minorities subsections.

21   The National Minorities Subsection consists of the following departments: Jewish, Latvian, Lithuanian, Mari, Mordvinian, German, Polish, Finnish, Chuvash, and Estonian.

22   The Mari, Chuvash, Mordvinian, and Lithuanian departments are headed by secretaries.

23   The Jewish, Latvian, German, Polish, Finnish, and Estonian departments are headed by bureaus composed of a secretary and two members.

24   The secretaries or bureaus of the departments are appointed by the Central Committee from among the candidates recommended by a conference or meeting of staff workers of the local sections.

25   The Central Committee's National Minorities Subsection convenes regular meetings of the secretaries of the departments in order to coordinate the work of the departments and to inform the departments about the measures being taken by the Central Committee's Agitation and Propaganda Section.

26   Meetings of staff workers at the local level and conferences of com-

munists of the nationalities in question are convened only by resolution of
the Central Committee.

Izvestiia tsentral'nogo komiteta,
15 December 1921

XI Party Conference   19–22 December 1921

The XI Party Conference was attended by 241 delegates of whom 125 had a
deciding vote and 116 a consultative vote. According to the report of the
Conference's mandate commission, those with the deciding vote were representatives of guberniia and oblast party committees whereas all the members and candidates of the Central Committee, the Central Control Commission, and the Central Revision Commission had only a consultative vote.
This practice was abandoned at the IX Conference and it is not clear why it
was revived in this one instance.

Lenin could not attend, because of sickness, and the Central Committee
political report was delivered by Kamenev. A large part of the Conference
was occupied by discussion of the economy in the light of the NEP. To a point
the discussions at the Conference were similar to those at the IX Party
Conference with the difference that this time the attack was directed not so
much at the leading party organs as at the leading government organs which
were accused of 'glavkism' (central board-ism) perpetrated by 'glavkocrats'
a term which the oppositionists borrowed from Trotsky. This attack was led
once again by the former Democratic Centralists Sapronov and Osinsky. A
new opposition group briefly appeared on the stage, led by the former
Menshevik, Larin, representing the so-called 'communist reaction' to the
NEP. The official line as represented by Kamenev stood somewhere in between and was reflected in the resolution 'On Current Tasks of the Party in
Connection with the Restoration of the Economy' (2.21). The Conference
also passed a resolution on the results of the purge (2.22), and a resolution on
the Comintern.

2.21
On the Current Tasks of the Party in Connection
with the Restoration of the Economy   22 December 1921

I   Considering that the Soviet government has made the transition to
the NEP in very good time and that the correctness of this policy is fully
confirmed by the noticeable upswing in economic activity, the Conference

fully approves the NEP and, in particular, the instructions of the Sovnarkom of August of this year.

2   For the subsequent conduct of this policy, the RKP, whose responsibility it is to direct the restoration of the Soviet republic's economy, must take account in the most attentive fashion of the economic situation, whose characteristic features must be seen as: 1) the formation of an internal market as the result of the repeal of requisitions, and 2) the development of exchange based on money. Both are a direct result of the predominance of the petty bourgeois type of economy in the country. In these conditions, it would be a major mistake for the Soviet authorities to apply in the sphere of the economy the methods applied by them in the preceding period and which were an outgrowth of the conditions peculiar to an era of bitter civil war. At the present moment, the basic task of the RKP in the economic sphere is to direct the economic work of the Soviet authorities in such a way as the be able – proceeding from the existence of the market and with due regard for its law – to master it and by means of systematic, well-conceived economic measures predicated on a precise regard for market processes take into its own hands regulation of the market and of monetary circulation.

3   To make the market sound, which is a precondition for the rapid restoration of large-scale industry, a number of financial measures aimed toward the creation of a stable currency are necessary. Restoration of monetary circulation on the basis of precious metal (gold), the first step toward which is strict implementation of a plan to limit the issue of paper money, is to be the guiding principle of the Soviet government in the sphere of finance. Facilitating and developing exchange between town and countryside, the development of credit operations and systematic implementation of the tax policy and the putting of state economic services on a paying basis, are necessary steps along this road.

In so far as the development of a market inevitably creates the institutions necessary for facilitating and developing trade turnover (credit institutions, a stock market, trade partnerships, export and import societies, co-operative associations of various types, etc.), the workers' and peasants' state must assure itself an influence in those institutions that corresponds to the interests of the working masses that it represents. This influence is to be based on the economic power of the production resources concentrated in the hands of the Soviet authorities and is to be expressed in the participation of the state in the above-enumerated institutions on a basis of shareholding (participation of the Gosbank in the creation of various credit institutions, participation of the Commissariat of Foreign Trade in 'mixed' export-import companies, participation of state economic agencies in enterprises rented or given on a concession basis by the state, state orders to the co-operatives, etc.) ...

11   The basic task in carrying out all these measures is to be the all-round strengthening of large-scale industry, which remains under the direct control of the state and its agencies. The development of large-scale state industry, as the basis of the proletarian dictatorship, requires that a maximum share of general state resources – raw materials, food, fuel, and monetary resources – be concentrated on it and that these resources be distributed in planned fashion, such that enterprises that remain on the state system of supply are ensured uninterrupted production work. These enterprises are to be allocated food and money supplies that guarantee higher labour productivity by the workers employed in them. In the interests of this task it is necessary to effect a further and resolute cutback in soviet institutions and to remove from the state supply systems the enterprises whose existence cannot be provided for by available state resources.

12   Direction of large-scale state industry on the above-specified basis requires the strictest observance of the general state plan for industry based on accurate calculation of production resources and on the budget of every state enterprise separately and of all together. Economic accounting must form the basis of management of all state industry. A similar and equally strictly worked out plan is to serve as a basis for the distribution of products that become part of state stocks.

13   It is impossible under present conditions to restore large-scale industry and ensure its uninterrupted production except by means of direct ties with the internal market, where it must attempt to supplement the state resources placed at its disposal. Therefore, it is imperative that these enterprises and their associations be authorized to sell a portion of their output on the market, according to approved operational plans and according to deficiencies in deliveries to them of necessary resources by the state. At the disposal of every enterprise (or association of enterprises), there is to be an operating fund consisting of both resources of the central agencies and resources of the enterprise itself...

18   The so-called 'New-Economic Policy' whose basic principles were laid down in precise fashion as early as the first 'breathing space,' in the spring of 1918, is based on a strict stocktaking of the economic forces of Soviet Russia.

The implementation of this policy, which was broken off by the combined attack of the workers' and peasants' state by the counter-revolutionary forces of Russian landowners and bourgeoisie and European imperialism, became possible only toward the beginning of 1921, after the military liquidation of the counter-revolutionary attempts. Today the struggle between the communist and private-ownership economies has been transferred to economic ground – to the market, where nationalized industry, concentrated in the hands of the workers' state, must win decisive predominance by applying itself to market conditions and methods of competition in the market.

The more skilfully, systematically, and in a planned fashion the proletariat commands the huge centres of production concentrated – as a result of the October Revolution – in its hands the stronger the union of the proletariat and the peasantry based on the exchange of goods between the town and the village; the faster the progressive elements of the working class learn to wage the struggle on the new ground, with new methods, using the new situation and becoming leaders in the new areas of work – the more decisive will be the victory ...

2.22
On the Question of Strengthening the Party in Connection with a Study of the Experience of the Verification of Its Personnel   22 December 1921

The completion of the campaign for the verification of party personnel has removed unsuitable elements from the ranks of party organizations, and this confronts our party with the question of the need for the closest comradely cohesion among party members remaining in our ranks. However, the realization of this cohesion is often impeded by reverberations from the now-completed campaign. Therefore the Conference considers it a duty to urge all party members to destroy completely all charges and accusations reviewed by the commission during the check on party personnel. The party verification having been completed, the Conference considers that from this point on, only devotion to the interests of the working class and the proletarian revolution is to be the measure in evaluating the qualities of each party member.

The campaign to review party personnel revealed significant shortcomings in almost all spheres of party life and work. All these shortcomings, which undermine the cohesion and unity of the party, can be divided into three basic groups: a) short-comings resulting from incorrect structuring of the party apparatus or from incorrect methods of work by the apparatus; b) short-comings resulting from the weakness of ideological education and comradely cohesion occasioned primarily by the presence of a significant number of new party members of the post-revolutionary period; c) short-comings resulting from diversity in the social make-up of the party, which, in conditions of the NEP, must be the object of particular attention.

In view of the fact that the basic party line on these matters has been elaborated in decisions of both the previous Conference and the X Party Congress, the present Conference feels that the task of the present moment is not so much one of discovering new measures, as it is one of ensuring the implementation of the decisions that have already been worked out. On the basis of new experience the Conference finds it necessary to supplement past decisions with the following: ...

III IN THE SPHERE OF PARTY PERSONNEL AND COMMUNISTS' MATERIAL SITUATION.

To protect itself, on the one hand, against the threat of a repeated fouling of the party with undesirable members, and on the other hand, to create for each party member conditions that are conducive to comradely cohesion and to assist his party education, the Conference resolves:

a To retain until the XI Party Congress the procedures for admission of new party members instituted by the Central Verification Commission for the period of the purge. Exceptions are to be made only for workers and peasants who have proven their devotion to the revolution during the Civil War and who have shown a politically conscious attitude toward communism. The Conference also expresses the view that it is necessary that the XI Party Congress make changes in the party Rules concerning the conditions for the admission of new party members.

b That party duties are to be assigned to rank-and-file members so as to leave them not less than three free evenings a week, in order not to undermine their material situation and to enable them to broaden their knowledge on their own ...

Pravda, 21 December 1921 (2.21)   *KPSS v rezoliutsiiakh* II, 291–312
Izvestiia tsentral'nogo komiteta,
1 January 1922 (2.22)

XI Party Congress   27 March – 2 April 1922

This was the last Congress attended by Lenin. Already in failing health and no longer in complete control, he still delivered the political report of the Central Committee (2.23; *Collected Works* XXXIII, 263–309, 310–24) and participated in its discussions. He also delivered a short speech at the conclusion of the Congress. Possibly, because of Lenin's absence from most of the debates, this was the most unruly of all congresses or conferences up to that time. The presidium repeatedly tried to close the debate and was just as repeatedly defeated. Voices from the floor frequently interrupted the speakers and challenged the leadership.

Although the X Party Congress outlawed all factions, and although the party leadership interfered with the selection of the delegates to the Congress, the opposition still managed to turn up in sufficient force to attack vigorously the party leaders. Some delegates, Preobrazhensky among them, attacked the NEP maintaining that "state capitalism" under the NEP was all too similar to plain capitalism.

The trade union controversy continued unabated and Lenin personally drafted the theses 'On the Role and Tasks of the Trade Unions under the Conditions of the NEP,' which formed a basis for a resolution (2.24), and which for the first time explicitly stated that the trade unions, as participants in state power could not refrain from applying pressures. This was all the more important because by the time the Congress opened, the Central Committee considerably improved its hold over the trade unions by assigning its own nominees to leading positions in the party fractions of the trade unions. It was also on the basis of a decision of the Central Committee that Riazanov, one of the most intelligent and outspoken oppositionists, was banned from any future work in the trade unions.

Party organization, and especially personnel selection, were also among the issues dealt with but these did not arouse as much controversy. The resolution 'On the Strengthening of the Party and its New Tasks' (2.25) based on a report by Zinoviev supplemented and elaborated on a resolution of the XI Conference. It also changed the party Rules with regard to the admission of new members, and went against the wishes of Lenin as he had stated them before the Congress. Lenin wanted a more proletarian representation in the party than Stalin and Zinoviev, who were less opposed to peasant representation. The disregard of his wishes was an obvious manifestation of the decline of his power and the rise of Stalin and Zinoviev into even greater prominence than they had enjoyed before. However, the greatest controversy centred around the question of the control commissions. The decision to establish these bodies was made by the IX Conference and a resolution passed on them by the X Congress. It soon became clear that in practice their sole purpose was to enforce party discipline. As much was admitted, in fact, by A. A. Solts, who delivered the report on the control commissions. The short resolution on Solts' report met with stiff resistance. The presidium of the Congress tried to cut off the debate but the opposition would not be deterred. A counter-resolution, submitted by Iu. S. Myshkin, proposed the abolition of all local control commissions and an increase of Central Committee control over the Central Control Commission. When it came to the vote, by raised hands, the division was so close, that the chairman of the session, Frunze, was unable to tell the majority from the minority. A voice from the audience remarked, to the accompaniment of laughter from the delegates, that since the vote was so close some compromise between abolishing the commissions and keeping them would have to be found. Tellers were appointed for the second vote and the presidium announced the result as 223 for Solts' resolution and 89 for Myshkin's. Since the Congress was attended by 520 delegates with a deciding vote (and 154 with a consultative vote, among whom were Stalin, Solts, Rudzutak, Rykov, and Dzerzhinsky), this implied 208 abstentions and was obviously false. A piquant flavour was added to this affair at the XII Party Congress when M.F. Shkiriatov, in his Central Control Commission report, discussing the relationship between the Commission and the Central Committee, announced: 'Regardless of the fact that the XI Congress of our party showed a liquidationist tendency towards the control commissions, and their existence was saved by only a small majority (*the protocols seem to show that only 89 votes were cast against but that was not so* [italics added]), regardless of this liquidationist tendency, the Central Committee of our party, during my year of work at the Central Control Commission, not once succumbed to this liquidationist tendency.' There is no evidence to show how this manoeuvre was brought about nor is there any evidence indicating how the announced unanimous vote on the regulation on the Central Control Commission (2.26) was engineered.

The Congress defied the Central Committee in one other instance and this time successfully. In February 1922, some members of the former Workers' Opposition sent the so-called 'Declaration of 22' to the Executive Committee of the Communist International, appealing against the authoritarian methods of the Central Committee of the Russian Communist Party. The ECCI rejected their appeal to nobody's surprise, but the XI Congress, at the beginning of its session, set up a commission to investigate the matter and report back to the Congress. This report was presented on the last day of the Congress, in a secret session of which no stenographic report is available. The commission's report, however, was published and made available to the delegates. It recommended the expulsion from the party of Shliapnikov, Kollantai, and Medvedev. The majority of the delegates apparently refused to approve this recommendation because the resolution 'On Certain Members of the Former Workers' Opposition' (2.30) merely warned the three that if they did not mend their ways they would be expelled. To add weight to the warning, perhaps, two minor members, Mitin and Kuznetsov, were expelled. One other member, Miasnikov, had been expelled before the Congress.

Other resolutions of the Congress dealt with the technical administration of the purge, the Central Revision Commission (2.27) and the Communist Youth League (Komsomol), which although established in 1918 had not had its relationship to the party defined. The resolution (2.28) addressed itself to that question. A resolution on press and propaganda activities of the party (2.29) was also passed, attempting to reform and expand this important but as yet underdeveloped branch of party activity. There were also resolutions on the activity of the Comintern, the review of trade union leadership, financial policy, work in the countryside, among women, and on the strengthening of the Red Army.

During the secret session mentioned above, the Congress elected a new Central Committee of twenty-seven members and nineteen candidates, and a new Central Control Commission of five members and two candidates. After the Congress, the Central Committee elected a new Politburo to which Rykov

and Tomsky were added as full members. It was at this Central Committee
plenum (3 April 1922) that Stalin was named General Secretary.

2.23
On the Central Committee Report   28 March 1922

The XI Party Congress fully approves the political and organizational line
of the Central Committee, a line that ensures the party maximum unity and
cohesion in basic questions connected with a most difficult turning point in
the Russian and world proletarian revolution (NEP, the new tasks of the
trade unions, the struggle against the bourgeois anarcho-syndicalist deviation, the party purge, etc.)

The Congress states that the sum total of measures carried out and
adopted in the past year exhausts the concessions to private enterprise
capitalism which the party considers necessary; it acknowledges the retreat in this respect to be terminated, and considers the current task to be
that of regrouping party forces with a view toward fully ensuring the
implementation in practice of the policy adopted by the party.

The period of economic construction, that began after the phase of
acute civil war, turns the local soviets – which primarily played the role of
agitation and mobilization centres during the war – into practical directors
of economic life at the local level.

In addition, it becomes possible and necessary to relieve the party of
a number of questions that by nature properly belong to the soviets, but
which the party had to assume during the preceding period.

While retaining overall direction and management of all policies of
the Soviet state, the party must draw a much clearer delineation between
its current work and the work of soviet bodies, between its apparatus and
the apparatus of the soviets. Such a delineation, systematically adhered to,
should, on the one hand, ensure that economic questions are discussed and
decided in a more planned fashion by soviet bodies, while at the same time
increasing the responsibility of each soviet staff worker for the work
assigned him, and on the other hand, should enable the party to concentrate
to the extent necessary on the basic party work of providing overall
direction of the work of all state educational agencies and of organizing the
working masses.

Further work of economic construction on a nation-wide scale can be
based only on experience accumulated at the local level. Under these
conditions, the VTSIK, as the body that unites the local soviets, is to
participate in a more active, constant, and systematic fashion in working

out the basic principles of state and economic construction than might have been possible during the previous period.

The VTSIK is to become, in fact, the body that works out the basic questions of legislation – questions directed primarily toward the restoration of agriculture, industry, and finance – and that regularly supervises the work of both the individual people's commissariats and the work of the Sovnarkom.

In order to accomplish these tasks, VTSIK must meet regularly for prolonged sessions.

For the very same purpose of relieving the higher party bodies of matters that are properly of concern solely to the soviets, and of bringing a maximum of planning and clarity to the work of the Soviet apparatus at the centre and at the local level, it is necessary to enhance and strengthen the work of the Sovnarkom as the body that regularly directs and co-ordinates the work of all the agencies of state management.

Attaching particularly great importance to the rapid implementation in practice of the indicated changes in the system of work of soviet and party bodies, the Congress instructs the Central Committee to work out in detail the practical consequences resulting from the principles that have been adopted, and to introduce them at the next session of the VTSIK.

2.24
The Role and the Tasks of the Trade Unions under the
Conditions of NEP   2 April 1922

...

9   THE CONTRADICTION IN THE VERY SITUATION OF THE TRADE UNIONS
    UNDER THE DICTATORSHIP OF THE PROLETARIAT

From all that has been said above, there result a number of contradictions between the various tasks of the trade unions. On the one hand, their primary method of operation is to convince and educate; on the other hand, they cannot refuse – as participants in state power, to participate in coercive measures as well. On the one hand, their primary task is to protect the interests of the working masses in the most direct and immediate sense of the word. On the other hand, they cannot, as participants in state power and builders of the entire economy as a whole, refuse to exert pressure. On the one hand, they must operate in military fashion, for the dictatorship of the proletariat is the fiercest, most relentless, and most desperate war between classes; on the other hand, it is precisely to the trade unions that specifically military methods of operation are the least applicable. On the one hand, they have to adapt themselves to the masses, to their present level, and on the other hand, they must not indulge the prejudices and backwardness of the masses, but must tirelessly raise them to an ever higher level, etc., etc. There is good reason for these contradictions, and it will be impossible to eliminate them for a number of decades. For as long as there is a remnant of capitalism and small-scale production, it is inevitable that there will be contradictions in the entire social structure between these remnants and the budding institutions of socialism.

For successful trade union work, it is not enough to have a correct understanding of their tasks and it is not enough to structure them correctly – apart from these things there is a need for particular tact and for the ability to approach the masses in a particular fashion in each separate, concrete instance, achieving with a minimum of conflict the elevation of the masses to the next highest level in cultural, economic, and political matters.

The second conclusion is that the indicated contradictions will inevitably give rise to conflicts, disagreements, and friction, etc. A higher authority is needed, and one that is sufficiently authoritative to resolve these problems immediately. This authority is the Communist Party and the international association of communist parties of all countries, the Comintern ...

2.25
On the Strengthening of the Party
and its New Tasks
2 April 1922

...

5   The conditions for admission to the RKP are to be changed in such a way as to make admission more difficult for elements that are not purely proletarian. To this end, the party Rules (point 6, section II), are amended for the entire year 1922, up to the convening of the XII Party Congress, and the following regulations for admission to the party are adopted:

a   Three categories are established for admission to the party: 1) workers and Red Army men from worker and peasant backgrounds; 2) peasants (other than Red Army men) and craftsmen who do not exploit the labour of others; 3) others (office workers, etc.);

b   admission to the party for workers and Red Army men from worker and peasant backgrounds is by confirmation of uezd and raion (in guberniia centres) party committees, and then only with the recommendation of three party members with three years' party service; for peasants and craftsmen, admission to the party is by recommendation of three party members with three years' party membership, and subject to obligatory confirmation by the guberniia party committee; for others (office workers, etc.), admission to the party is exclusively by recommendation of five party members with five years' party membership, subject to obligatory confirmation by the guberniia party committee;

c   all young people up to and including the age of twenty – with the exception of Red Army men – enter the party only via the Russian Komsomol. The Congress instructs the Central Committee to work out within a month, the rules for admission to the party of Komsomol members;

d   former members of other parties are to be admitted to the party – until the XII Party Congress – on the recommendation of five party members with five years' party membership and subject to obligatory confirmation by the guberniia party committee, regardless of the social status of the person being admitted;

e   lists of those desiring admission to the party must be published ahead of time;

f   when admitting workers, it is necessary to apply the experience of the party purge as much as possible and to check up on non-party workers;

g   it is confirmed that persons who give recommendations are to be held strictly accountable for the persons they recommend, in accordance with the resolution of the Central Committee, and the Central Committee is instructed to work out additional, concrete forms of responsibility.

6   In addition, it is essential that great attention be devoted to the institution of candidate members; in connection with the fact that admission to party ranks is to be made contingent upon the satisfaction of major requirements, the role of the institution of candidate members is to assume greater importance. As an amendment to the party Rules (point 7, section II), the Congress resolves that the length of service as a candidate member before qualifying for full membership is to be set at not less than six months for workers and Red Army men of worker and peasant background, one year for peasants and craftsmen, and two years for all others. Points 8 and 9 (section II) of the party Rules concerning payment of membership dues by candidate members and concerning their right to attend open general party meetings and to exercise a consultative vote at such meetings – remain in force. Former members of other parties are admitted on condition of having completed two years' service as candidate members, regardless of the social origins of the person in question. Moreover, apart from the establishment of formal obstacles, it is essential that attention be directed to the rational utilization of the period of service as a candidate member. The transition from candidate member (a consultative vote in the party) to full member (a deciding vote) cannot be made in mechanical fashion, but must be made on the basis of the determination in each case, of the true suitability of the person in question for party membership, both from the standpoint of the candidate's revolutionary devotion and from that of his political consciousness. As a rule, it is to be established procedure that no

candidate member who has not been schooled in the rudiments of politics is eligible for the transition to full member. In addition, the Congress resolves that at the time of transition from candidate member to full member, the recommendations are to be renewed in accordance with the established categories.

7   The content and methods of the work of party cells at state enterprises must also be changed in accordance with the new conditions. Party cells are to show greater initiative and independence in defending the closest and most immediate interests of the workers. However, the cell must persistently put forward, and strive for the realization of, demands whose fulfilment is possible in the given economic situation, in so far as the interests of the group of workers being defended do not conflict with the interests of the working class as a whole. In its work the party cell is to set an example of a solicitous and assiduous attitude toward the economy. It is to cut to the absolute minimum the number of outside assignments to its members, striving to keep all members of the party cell in production work and to make greater use of non-party members for outside assignments. The cell must help the factory administration when the latter is truly defending the interests of the economy.

The NEP and the change in the wage scales are bound to alter in a fundamental way the task of the party cell in increasing labour productivity and worker discipline. The struggle against violators of the normal flow of production work and against shirkers and unsuitable elements in production is to be waged exclusively by means of exposing them before the workers of the enterprise; measures of direct influence, pressuring, and coercion are to be applied exclusively by the management bodies. In addition, the party cells are to conduct constant agitation among the masses in favour of the need for observing and strengthening work discipline.

Workers employed at private enterprises are placed in conditions of direct class struggle against the entrepreneurs. The task of the party cells is to seize the initiative in organizing the workers, enlisting them in the trade unions, and to wage their battle against the entrepreneurs through the trade unions.

8   The primary focus of party work is to be shifted to the worker sector; an end must be put at all cost to the situation whereby at large factories and major factory settlements, etc., the number of members of our party cells is insignificant. The data of the all-Russian re-registration census will give us, for the first time, a more exact picture of the situation. The Central Committee and guberniia party committees are to return a significant number of Communists from institutions, etc., to the factories. The XI Party Congress categorically orders local party organizations and the Central Committee to spare no effort to implement this policy. In the matter of

transfers to enterprises, it is essential to strive not so much for a quantitative increase in the number of Communists in production as for a qualitative improvement in the factory party cells.

9   The Congress considers it desirable that a more suitable division of labour be established among the groups of the more active party members, such that comrades are enabled to make a more careful study of one or another sphere of party, trade union, Soviet, economic, and other work. Transfers of party staff from one place to another are to be kept to a minimum. Better study and a more serious, businesslike specialization is one of the most important tasks presently confronting the party. The Congress instructs the Central Committee to make the solution of that task an object of its special concern. The all-Russian re-registration of party members that has been carried out will help to resolve this task in a relatively short period of time.

It is imperative that division of labour also be implemented among members of guberniia party committees and their presidiums, among the members of the presidiums of guberniia executive committees and in all higher party and state bodies.

10   The material situation of rank-and-file party members, and in particular of those who are active in party work, is extremely difficult. As a result of the NEP it has become desperate. The Congress instructs the Central Committee to take all possible measures to arrange satisfactory conditions of existence for this basic group of party workers, who bear the major brunt of the difficulties connected with the work. The party cannot and must not demand privileges for each of its members. But it has the right and obligation to ensure a piece of bread and bearable conditions of existence for those whose strength is totally exhausted in arduous, painstaking, but extremely valuable organizational and other work in the local party organizations – in the cities, the uezds, and the volosts.

Rational organization in the matter of mutual aid is absolutely essential.

The Congress holds that it is a most urgent matter to work out and implement the forms of mutual aid to the most needy Communists who are in particularly difficult circumstances, and also to disabled veterans, discharged servicemen, etc., who have lost their health and strength while engaged in party and revolutionary work.

In cases of unavoidable mobilizations and transfers of comrades and groups of party members, the local party organizations and the Central Committee are to see that measures are taken to ease the situation of the mobilized comrades' families that remain behind. Special attention is to be devoted to comrades who have been discharged from the army and who, upon returning from the front, often find themselves in the most desperate material situation. It is necessary to organize assistance for the families of Communists who have been killed.

Mutual assistance within the party must be carried out by special commissions attached to the party committees, commissions that create no apparatus of their own, but that make use of the apparatus of the party committee.

The commissions are dutybound to enlist in their work representatives of control commissions and of party cells, and certain of the most authoritative old party comrades. The commissions conduct all direct material assistance through the party apparatuses of the raion, uezd, and volost party committees.

The sources of material mutual aid consist of both the general party funds and of various types of deductions from members of the given party organization (obligatory, voluntary, special, etc.). Acknowledging the extreme necessity of putting a resolute end to the great disparity in the pay of various groups of Communists, the Congress instructs the Central Committee to take urgent measures to regulate the matter of excessively high earnings for party members, placing limits above which all earnings go to the party mutual aid fund.

11   The party must take clear cognizance of the dangers connected with the NEP and must display very great energy in combatting attempts to use the NEP to implant bourgeois morals in the party itself. There must be merciless prosecution of attempts to feather one's own nest on the part of 'communists' who hold executive positions in state or economic agencies. To this end the work of the guberniia and all-Russian control commissions must be improved, while the staffs of these commissions must be selected from the most proven comrades. There must be merciless prosecution of squabbles and of the 'groupings' that in places have resulted in total paralysis of party work. The Congress instructs the Central Committee not to hesitate to use expulsion from the party in the struggle against such phenomena.

12   A most important task of the times is to establish the correct division of labour between party and soviet institutions and to delineate clearly the rights and duties of the one and the other ...

Next in turn is the solution of the immense task of restoring the economy, a task that will require many years of unwearying labour. This task can only be resolved if correct and sound relations are established between party organizations and economic agencies. Just as the party stressed in 1919 that a confusion of functions would yield disastrous results in military affairs, so in 1922 the party declares that such a confusion would yield completely disastrous results in the economic sphere.

In no case are party organizations to interfere in the day-to-day, current work of the economic agencies, and they are to refrain in general from administrative orders in the sphere of soviet work. Party organizations are to direct the work of the economic agencies, but in no sense are they to attempt to replace them or take over their responsibilities. The absence of a strict delineation of functions and incompetent interference result in an absence of strict and exact responsibility on the part of each person for the work entrusted to him; they increase bureaucratism in the party organizations themselves, which end up doing everything and nothing; they impede serious specialization by staff working in the economy – the study of a question in full detail, the acquisition of truly meaningful experience – in a word, they render more difficult the correct organization of work.

The party organizations are to ensure stable direction to soviet institutions and economic agencies; they select the managerial staff and educate the entire mass of party members who work in these agencies. Party organizations explain to the working masses the significance of the NEP and, in particular, the importance and significance of trade operations, which have become – under present conditions in Soviet Russia – a method of socialist construction. Party organizations conduct all their agitation not in a way that is abstract, but above all with direct reference to the economic tasks of the given moment in the given area. In no case do party organizations limit themselves to sterotyped agitation connected with some run-of-the-mill 'week' or other, but systematically instil in their members a truly serious and profound interest in economic questions. Party organizations send their best staff members to work directly in the economic bodies. But the party organizations themselves settle economic questions only in those cases where and, to the extent that, such questions actually require a decision of principle by the party.

13   Considering, on the one hand, the extreme paucity of communist forces at the local level, and particularly in outlying areas, where it is often impossible to provide communist direction for the most responsible areas of work, and on the other hand, the relatively greater concentration of forces in the central Soviet, economic, and party institutions, the XI Party Congress approves in principle the work undertaken by the Central Committee of transferring staff from the centre – from Moscow – to the local level and advises that the transfer be firmly implemented within two months' time, in such a way that a total of not less than one thousand comrades be transferred.

2.26

Regulation on the Control Commissions   2 April 1922

I   THE CONTROL AGENCIES AT THE LOCAL LEVEL

I   Control commissions are organized at the centre, in the oblasts, and in guberniias by means of elections at the party congress and at oblast and guberniia conferences.

Note 1 Oblast control commissions are set up only in places where there are oblast party committees elected at oblast party conferences convened in accordance with the party Rules.

Control commissions are not to exist under the central committee bureaus appointed by the Central Committee of the RKP.

All guberniia control commissions located in areas where there are oblast central committee bureaus, are to send their resolutions, together with the pertinent materials, to the oblast bureau. If the latter does not agree with the resolution of the guberniia control commissions, it is to forward the materials together with its conclusions to the Central Control Commission.

Note 2 In places where there exist party bureaus elected at party conferences and confirmed by the Central Committee, control commissions can exist on the same basis as the oblast control commissions.

Note 3 The Far Eastern Central Control Commission is elected by the party conference of the Far Eastern Region ...

3   Wherever there is a control commission there shall be no conflicting subdivisions or analogous commissions or agencies (such as party courts, ethics commissions, etc.) – with the exception of the military party commissions attached to the politotdels.

4   All matters involving Red Army or Navy Communists that are subject to review by control commissions are to be submitted through the appropriate party commissions of the Red Army, and the latter are to give their preliminary conclusions on the matter. All cases received from the party commissions attached to politotdels are to be heard in the presence of the reporting official from the party commission.

2   ON THE REPORTING PROCEDURES FOR CONTROL COMMISSIONS

1   The control commissions, functioning alongside the party committee, report to the appropriate conferences – the guberniia control commissions to the guberniia party conference and the oblast commissions to the oblast conference. The Central Control Commission reports to the party congress.

2   The guberniia and oblast control commissions, as well as the Central Control Commission, give periodic reports to party organizations: oral reports at general party meetings and written reports in the party press.

3   THE COMPOSITION OF THE CONTROL COMMISSIONS

1   At the centre, the control commissions have an elected membership of five members and two candidate members; in the oblasts – three to five members and two to three candidate members and in the guberniia – three members and two candidate members.

2   A necessary condition for the control commissions is that they be

authoritative for the broad circles of party members. They are to be staffed by comrades with lengthy practical party experience, by the most steadfast comrades, those who enjoy universal trust and who are capable of implementing strict party control.

There is an obligatory term of party membership for members and candidate members of control commissions.

At the centre, the term is not less than ten years' membership in the party.

In the guberniia, one must have been a member since before the February (1917) Revolution.

In outlying areas, in exceptional cases, party comrades with three years' party service may be elected to control commissions, contingent upon confirmation by the Central Committee in each individual case.

This exception does not apply to former members of other parties.

It is desirable that there be at least one comrade on the control commission who has done service in the underground.

3   Members of control commissions cannot be at one and the same time members of party committees and cannot hold administrative positions of responsibility.

4   THE CONSTRUCTION (APPARATUS) OF THE CONTROL COMMISSIONS

1   In the interests of more successful work and the capability of investigating cases and conducting inquiries in a comprehensive fashion, a portion of the members of control commissions are to be freed from other work.

The Central Control Commission should have not less than three such members, and guberniia and oblast control commissions are to have one each.

2   Members of control commissions cannot be transferred to other work before the expiration of their term of office.

3   In their work, the control commissions utilize the apparatus of the corresponding party committee and have the authority to give assignments, within the sphere of their competence, to all party comrades and party organizations.

4   The control commissions must include a small investigatory apparatus of steadfast and knowledgeable party comrades – staffs of not more than five persons in the centre, and of from one to three in the oblasts and guberniias.

To handle current technical work, it is necessary to attach to the control commissions from one to three persons, depending on the concrete needs of the control commissions.

At the centre, the number of such workers may run as high as seven ...

2.27
Regulation on the Central
Revision Commission 2 April 1922

1   The Central Revision Commission is elected by the all-Russian party congress with a membership of three; it is elected for the same period and in the same fashion as the Central Committee, and members and candidate members of the Central Revision Commission must have not less than ten years' party membership.

2   The Central Revision Commission inspects:

a   the dispatch and correctness with which business is handled in the central party bodies and the proper functioning of the Central Committee Secretariat;

b   it periodically audits the treasury and enterprises of the Central Committee.

3   In carrying out their work, members of the Central Revision Commission use all materials obtained directly by the commission that have a direct bearing on the work of the Central Revision Commission, as well as all materials at the disposal of the central party bodies, including the reports by local inspection and control commissions, etc.

4   Members of the Central Revision Committee have the right to attend meetings of the Orgburo, and enjoy a consultative vote at such meetings.

5   Members of the Revision Commission have the right to be present at the places of work of Central Committee secretaries, department heads, and all staff workers, and to ask them for explanations concerning their work and their duties.

6   The Central Revision Commission has no apparatus of its own and conducts all practical work with the help of the apparatus of the Central Committee.

7   The Central Revision Commission, when conducting inspections, draws up official documents on the inspection in appropriate cases.

8   The Central Revision Commission reports as needed to the Central Committee on the work of the Central Committee bodies.

9   The Central Revision Commission presents its conclusions concerning the work of the central party bodies to all-Russian party conferences and to the all-Russian congress of the RKP.

The Congress instructs the Central Committee to work out, on the basis of this regulation, a corresponding one for the local revision commissions.

2.28
On the Question of the Russian Communist
Youth League   2 April 1922

I

1   The Russian Communist Youth League [Komsomol], which is a mass
organization for communist upbringing, serves the party as a powerful
weapon of communist ascendancy and influence over the broad strata of
worker and peasant youth. The Komsomol, while educating in its ranks the
most conscious and revolutionary segment of working youth, ensures the
healthy and regular growth of the party from the most active stratum of the
proletariat – the working youth who enter the party from the ranks of the
Komsomol fully trained for practical revolutionary work.

       The party, therefore, is profoundly interested in a most rapid and
painless adaptation of the Komsomol to work in the new conditions.

2   The object of the mass work of the Komsomol is the completely new
stratum of proletarian youth who have grown up in the era of the revolution, who have never experienced the oppression of the capitalist system
personally, and who are being subjected, in connection with the NEP to loss
of class identity, and to atomization, and who are experiencing an acute
deterioration in their economic situation (massive layoffs from production
work, reduction in earnings, violation of labour protection laws, etc.).

3   The maintenance of working youth in production and protection of
them against the forms of excessive exploitation that sap their physical and
spiritual forces are necessary prerequisites for a further strengthening of
the proletarian dictatorship and for the development of the industry of the
Soviet republic; these measures also ensure the Komsomol the capability
of fulfilling its basic tasks in both the organizational and educational
spheres.

       This maintenance of young workers in production is to be achieved
through energetic work on the part of the trade unions and state agencies,
with the direct participation and on the initiative of the Komsomol, by
means of:

       a ensuring that provision is made for a normal percentage of young
workers at production facilities;

       b ensuring conditions for the implementation of all norms of labour
protection by regulating pay rates in such a way that working youth are paid
for a shortened work day the same as if it had been an eight-hour day, and
by supervising the working conditions of youth in both state and private
industry;

       c reorganizing the work of youth, subordinating it to the aims of train-
ing and the acquisition of skills, building schools for working youth –
schools that combine practical production training with theoretical educa-

tion and socio-political upbringing. The material needs of these schools are to be served by the economic agencies and they are to command a central place in the attention of the People's Commissariat of Education.

4   The strengthening of the petty bourgeois elements has a particularly corrupting influence on working youth. Their resistance to these influences (particularly in everyday life) is extremely feeble, which, together with the worsening of the economic situation of working youth, lowers their interest in social and political questions.

On these grounds, counter-revolutionary parties are attempting in places to gain influence among working youth. Along with combatting these organizations, the Komsomol must oppose the corrupting influence of the petty bourgeois elements (motion pictures, cheap literature, etc.) with their own energetic cultural work, adapted to the needs of youth.

5   In the countryside, Komsomol organizations are to be one of the major support points of the party and Soviet government.

In connection with the NEP, which promotes a strengthening of the individual peasant holdings, the growth of petty property instincts, and strengthens peasant youth's dependence on the family, the work of the village Komsomol cells becomes exceedingly complicated.

The basic tasks of the Komsomol in the countryside are: to intensify work among the poorest segments of the village in order to protect them from the ideological influence of the kulaks, and to actively enlist peasant youth in the public life of the village and satisfy their cultural needs.

II

6   The cultural and political level of the basic mass of Komsomol members is little higher than the political level of the working youth who are not members.

The decline in the number of Komsomol members observable in recent times in many organizations is explainable by layoffs of youth from production work, the weakening of the Komsomol by various mobilization drives, etc., and above all, by the fact that the Komsomol is not sufficiently adapted to the needs of youth. Concurrently, one notes a weakening in the influence of the Komsomol on working youth.

These circumstances, as well as the extraordinary turnover of Komsomol membership, were the cause of weakness in the core of active Komsomol staff and have impeded the process of adaptation of the Komsomol to the new conditions, which should have found expression in the working out of new work habits, methods, and content.

One important reason for the difficult position in which the Komsomol finds itself is the lack of serious assistance from party organizations.

7   At the present time, the Komsomol is faced with the following, most basic practical tasks:

a to strengthen its proletarian representation and raise the age level of its membership through the addition of the working youth who succeed best at theoretical marxist training and practical training in economic matters;

b to develop among the mass of Komsomol members a sense of class identity on the basis of enlisting them in practical economic and cultural work that promotes mastery of the necessary organizational skills, and through participation in the day-to-day economic work and in the struggle of the trade unions. The extent to which the Komsomol is represented in the various state agencies is to be determined strictly by the requirements of practical work and by the tasks of education;

c to saturate all the Komsomol's educational work with the elements of marxism, to develop cultural and educational work on an extensive basis, and to adapt it to the psychological features peculiar to the various age groups;

d to prepare members of the Komsomol as well as non-members among worker and peasant youth for entrance into the ranks of the Red Army.

III

8   The tasks of the party with respect to the Komsomol are:

a to establish permanent and systematic ideological direction of the Komsomol on the part of the party organizations;

b to devote the particular attention of party cells to direct participation in the work of the Komsomol cells in all spheres;

c to select carefully the party representatives to Komsomol committees and to create for regular work in the Komsomol a cadre of party members who are interested in working with youth and who are capable of becoming rallying points for them;

d to ensure the Komsomol the necessary material and financial conditions both for development of its mass educational work and for education of the members of the Komsomol (clubs, schools, sports, etc.);

e to assist the Komsomol's educational work by means of serving it with various cultural institutions and with the publication of special literature for young people;

f to draw members of the Komsomol (in the first place, party members working in the Komsomol) into party work.

2.29
On the Press and Propaganda   2 April 1922

The growth of capitalist relations inevitably intensifies the bourgeois influence not only on the petty bourgeois strata of the population but also on the most backward part of the proletariat. Noting the striving of the bourgeoisie to influence the toiling masses through literature and cultural work, the Congress considers that this influence must be opposed by energetic political work. Therefore the party must in every way extend and deepen its agitation and propaganda.

I

One of the party's mightiest instruments for influencing the masses, for organizing them and educating them in communism, is the press.

But the soviet-party press is in a state of grave crisis. The most prominent characteristics of the crisis are: a) the sharp reduction in the number of newspapers and the smaller press runs of the remaining ones due to financial shortages, the shortage of paper and its high cost, and excessively high typographical expenses; b) weak ties with the masses, inadequate reflection of the current needs and demands of the toilers, poor coverage of local problems; c) the newspapers are insufficiently steadfast from the party political point of view; d) the distribution network is in total disorder, especially among the worker and peasant masses.

The overwhelming majority of the party committees, on whom lies the main responsibility for the state of the press, take a careless and inattentive attitude toward the demands and needs of the press. The resolution of the VIII Party Congress on the press, the Central Committee circulars on improving the local newspapers, on the registration of journalists, etc. have in most cases not been implemented by local organizations.

Considering the above, the Congress resolves:

I   In future the central and local party committees must devote immeasurably greater attention to the press than has been the case until now. Party-political leadership of the whole press must be intensified. Each party committee must assign a special cadre of press workers. The leading elements of each party committee are required to take charge of party publications. The Congress views the newspaper work of the communist-journalist as fundamental party work.

2   The character of the local press must be decisively altered. The basic content of the local newspapers must include questions of local construction, the lives, work, and struggle of the toilers, and these matters must be treated in the pages of the newspaper as a live and direct response to the demands and needs of the readers. The uezd press, except in specifically working-class areas, must be devoted exclusively to peasant matters; the guberniia press must devote considerable space to peasant questions; and special peasant newspapers must be organized in a number of oblast centres.

3   The Congress supports the Central Committee decision to designate

the tenth anniversary of *Pravda* (5 May 1922) as an all-Russian day of the press, and orders all local organizations to devote the most serious attention to the conduct of this day of the press.

4   The Congress permits Communists to participate in private publications only as an exceptional matter, with the permission of the appropriate party committees.

5   While considering that the normal way for a newspaper to work its way out of difficulties is by expanding its readership and increasing the number of paid subscriptions, the Congress, during the present transition period, recognizes the necessity of extending material support to the press and instructs the Central Committee immediately to adopt measures ensuring that the party newspapers will be provided with funds and newsprint.

6   In view of the fact that the party organs are disseminated in extremely insignificant quantities and that hundreds and thousands of party members do not read their party newspapers, the Congress hereby decrees that each party member is obliged to be a reader of, and subscriber (individually or collectively) to one of the party newspapers.

7   The Congress considers that the Komsomol press organs must find comprehensive support and that, in particular, its independent organs must continue to appear in a number of major guberniia centres; in the others, 'Youth Pages' in party and soviet papers will suffice. The Komsomol press must be under the overall leadership of the party guberniia committees.

8   Noting that many guberniia and oblast committees have not yet established an apparatus for press guidance, the Congress orders the guberniia and oblast committees immediately to set up press subsections on the basis of the decree passed at a meeting of guberniia and oblast committee secretaries (December 1921).

9   The Congress directs attention to the matter of issuing newspapers, and literature generally, for the national minorities, and especially in the Turkic languages.

II

1   The development of marxist education is quite impossible in the absence of appropriate literature. While noting the development of private presses hostile to the Soviet power, the Congress directs the attention of the Central Committee and of party committees – primarily in the oblast centres – to the necessity of publishing militant agitational-propagandistic and marxist literature. The Congress supports the Central Committee decision to convert the publishing house of the Main Political Education Administration into a direct party publishing house for popular, agitational, anti-religious, marxist literature. Party publishers must respond to the demands of the worker and peasant masses. In view of the inadequate

publication of marxist texts last year, all measures must be taken to ensure that they are written and published, with sufficient staff being assigned to this task and the work being co-ordinated at the local level. The Congress instructs the Central Committee to take steps to ensure publication in the very near future of the marxist classics, primarily the marxist publications of Plekhanov.

2   As regards the periodicals of guberniia party committees, they must include: in the first place, leading political articles; in the second place, materials for agitators and propagandists in the form of theses, etc.; in the third place, circular and informational material on the activities of the guberniia committee; in the fourth place, materials for discussion. Thus the specialized publications must be replaced by more general ones.

3   *Vestnik agitatsii i propagandy* [Agitation and Propaganda Herald, an organ of the Central Committee] must be issued as a bi-weekly and must be directed at the party members, giving them basic guiding material on political, economic, agitational, and propaganda matters. In all organs, party publications must take precedence over private ones.

4   The Congress recognizes the extraordinary need for literature directed at worker and peasant youth which could oppose the influence on youth exerted by rising gutter literature, and which could promote the communist education of the youth masses. The Congress supports the Central Committee decision to issue a major popular-scientific and literary-artistic magazine and instructs the Central Committee to broaden this initiative by setting up as soon as possible, with Komsomol participation, a popular-scientific and artistic series of books for youth.

III

1   The purge has revealed that the level of political preparation of party members is, on the average, extraordinarily low. Hence the task arises of systematically improving the political-marxist training of the mass of party members. This is accomplished mainly by the system of party and soviet-party schools – from the schools of elementary political education up to and including the higher party school.

The school propaganda functions of the cells must be reduced to a minimum. The cell's principal function must be to establish and in every way reinforce ties with the non-party masses. The cell must justify its designation as the primary level of the party organization, directly and constantly binding the party with the masses. Its internal work must centre on the day-to-day practical activities associated with current political questions which directly concern the material basis of the life of the masses. The tasks of systematic, in depth, theoretical marxist education must be carried out using the system of schools, circles, and clubs; therefore the following must be done in the immediate future:

a the network of soviet-party schools must be finally revised, struc-tured, and strengthened so that each guberniia town and, within the guber-niia – each two or three uezds, will have a school of the appropriate level;

b the existing network of party schools for eliminating political illiter-acy among party members must be extended. These schools must include several cells. The political literacy of party members is to be investigated. Party members who do not meet the elementary demands of political literacy are obliged to attend the schools of political literacy and while in these schools will be temporarily relieved of their party obligations; mem-bers possessing an elementary level of political training are to be organized into marxist circles;

c the organization of more advanced schools is to continue and be reinforced: the Red Professors' Institute, the courses at the Socialist Academy, the two-year courses in Sverdlov and Zinoviev Universities, the Communist University of National Minorities of the West, and the Univer-sity of Toilers of the East; the mission of each of these more advanced institutions is to be precisely defined, and their proper functioning is to be ensured. The Congress directs the attention of local party organizations, and of the Central Committee, to the necessity of a more thorough selection of students for these schools;

d The Congress orders the Central Committee and the guberniia com-mittees to assign a cadre of comrades well trained in marxism for speciali-zation in teaching and lecturing, adopting measures for covering fully their material needs. At the same time the Congress considers it necessary that each graduating class from a guberniia soviet-party school leave behind a group of its members for training as lecturers;

e the Congress recognizes the necessity of working out the methodological and pedagogical aspects of teaching in the spirit of marx-ism, both at the centre and at the local level;

f the Congress directs the attention of the party Central Committee to the necessity of improving the material position of the soviet-party schools. In view of the fact that the overwhelming majority of participants in the schools continued to work, despite the cold and famine in the schools, regarding their school work as a supreme party duty, the Congress consid-ers it essential, and hereby instructs the Central Committee, to find mea-sures for immediate improvement of the material position of the soviet-party schools.

2   Together with the school system, it is necessary to elevate and develop the activities of party clubs and marxist circles, converting them into instruments of party education which cultivate a strictly marxist outlook among party members. Special attention must be devoted to party clubs, which are to be converted into centres for the exchange of practical experience by party workers and, at the same time, centres of intra-party propaganda.

IV

In the view of the Congress, one of the principal tasks of the present period is to elevate political-educational work in the countryside to the necessary level. This work, on the whole, must be connected with the problem of elevating agricultural production. While noting that the NEP has led to the abolition of village reading rooms almost everywhere, the Congress considers the rebirth of the village reading rooms to be a necessity; they must be at the centre of all political-educational work in the village. Village reading rooms must become centres for disseminating correct and regular information to the broad peasant masses on the political life of the country (through a regular supply of newspapers, oral readings of newspapers, talks, etc.). The Congress considers it necessary that village reading rooms be locally financed by guberniia executive committees, and that they be subsidized by co-operatives, on the indispensable condition that the party and the political education organs retain the guiding role. The Congress instructs the Main Political Educational Administration to hold courses, conferences, and congresses of village reading-room workers in the very near future, both at the centre and at the local level. At the same time, the Congress directs the attention of party committees to the need for a more careful selection of these workers from among comrades who have organic ties with the village.

At the same time, party organizations must devote more attention to the cultural and political education work of the Agricultural and Timber Workers' Union by strengthening and extending the network of cultural and educational bases in the secretariats and the sovkhozes.

V

1   The Congress considers it necessary to strengthen agitprop sections by assigning to their leadership comrades who possess adequate marxist training and by converting them into militant centres of the struggle for marxist ideology and for the party's ideological influence upon the masses.

2   The Congress confirms the resolution of x Congress on the Main Political Education Administration and its organs and categorically condemns the strivings of some party committees to liquidate the work of the political education organs; in particular, the People's Commissariat of Education must allocate strictly guaranteed credits for these organs at all levels, from top to bottom. The Congress assigns to the guberniia committees the responsibility for the correct fulfilment of their functions by political education personnel; these committees are required to detail sufficiently tried and steadfast party workers to this work and are to assist the political education organs both by their instructions and by their authority.

3   As regards the mutual relations between Agitprop, the political education organs and the cultural sections of the trade unions, the Con-

gress confirms the resolution of the X Congress on this matter and finds that a personal union between the leading staffs of Agitprop and the political education organs would be advisable. The Congress directs the attention of party committees to the necessity of a more exacting selection of leaders for trade union cultural sections.

2.30
On Certain Members of the
Former Workers' Opposition   2 April 1922

1   The X Party Congress instructed the Central Committee 'to carry out the complete destruction of all manner of factionalism.' The Congress prescribed 'the immediate dissolution, without exception, of all groups that have been formed on the basis of some platform or other' and instructed all organizations 'to be very strict in ensuring that no manifestations of factionalism of any sort be permitted.' The Congress decreed that 'failure to comply with this resolution [of the Congress] must entail unconditional and immediate expulsion from the party.' The X Congress elected to the Central Committee two members of the former group of the so-called 'Workers' Opposition,' promoted to leading soviet positions comrades who had earlier belonged to this group, and the party as a whole took every measure to prevent any victimization for former factionalism. In special circulars the Central Committee confirmed to all organizations that during the party verification and purge, special instructions in the spirit of the most careful and attentive attitude toward former members of the 'Workers' Opposition' were to be given; many of these latter headed the verification commissions at both guberniia and oblast levels and at the centre; they even headed control commissions, and the party has thus manifested the greatest confidence in them.

2   Despite all this, the former members of the 'Workers' Opposition' have frequently violated the resolution of the X Congress; they have maintained and supported an illegal factional organization within the party itself. Because of this their factional statements both at the centre and at the local level have without any doubt introduced demoralization into the party's ranks. Several attempts have been made to select the leading organs of trade union associations such as, for example, the Central Committee of the Metal-Workers' Union, not on the basis of their business qualities but on a factional basis. Not only an open, but, as the commission has established, an underground struggle has been carried on for the seizure, by factionally inclined comrades, of the leading organs of the party, the trade unions, and the soviets at the local levels. Speeches made at meetings by members of the former 'Workers' Opposition' have often

been in terms of an opposition between themselves and all the rest of the party' – 'we and they.' It was precisely speeches of this sort against the party's resolutions which compelled the Central Committee on 9 August 1921, to raise the question of expelling from the party Central Committee member Comrade Shliapnikov, and already then more than half of the Central Committee members and candidates needed for adoption of such a measure were in favour of it.

The expulsion did not take place only because there was one vote less than the required two-thirds majority needed for application of this extreme measure.

The decision adopted unanimously on 9 August 1921 (with three abstentions) read as follows:

'In view of the frequent violations of party discipline by Central Committee member, Comrade Shliapnikov, the meeting hereby states that further speeches, statements, or criticisms by Comrade Shliapnikov outside the Central Committee, directed against Central Committee policy and in opposition to the decisions which truly express the opinion of the party congress, are absolutely inadmissible and raise point-blank the question of the possibility of Comrade Shliapnikov's further work in the Central Committee. In view of this the meeting categorically calls upon Comrade Shliapnikov to change radically his whole political behaviour in this connection, bringing it into agreement with the line of the Central Committee in whose ranks he remains. If Comrade Shliapnikov in future does not alter his behaviour, the Central Committee is hereby instructed to convoke a similar meeting (plenum of Central Committee and Central Control Commission members and candidates) for a second examination of the question.'

This conduct by members of the former 'Workers' Opposition' has induced the groups striving to set up a IV International to turn to the members of the former 'Workers' Opposition' as kindred spirits, offering support and calling for a united front; it has led these groups to reprint such writings as Comrade Kollontai's pamphlet, 'On the Workers' Opposition,' with the comrades from the former 'Workers' Opposition' not disowning this decisively, not stating publicly and officially that they have nothing to do with these groups which are harmful to the workers' movement, but limiting themselves to half-hearted statements.

Comrade Kollontai's public anti-party speech at the Comintern Congress was given a unanimously negative evaluation by the Congress and has been widely quoted by all the press hostile to us.

The nineteen-member commission specially elected by the XI Congress and representing the local organizations has ascertained that factional meetings have occurred at various times at which resolutions of a conspiratorial nature have been adopted, whose execution was entrusted to the leaders of this group, comrades Medvedev and Shliapnikov. Central Committee member Comrade Shliapnikov, and Comrade Medvedev, after receiving letters of the most anti-party character from their confederates (Savichev, Mitin), failed to raise for discussion in the Central Committee the matters dealt with in these letters, even though the letters were in no way personal but related entirely to the non-party attitudes and activity of the former members of the 'Workers' Opposition.'

3   Finally, with respect to the last meeting of the members of the former 'Workers' Opposition' group, resulting in the appeal to the Comintern, the commission has ascertained that comrades Medvedev and Shliapnikov convoked a special meeting of the adherents of the former 'Workers' Opposition' group, that G. Miasnikov was brought to this meeting even though already condemned and expelled from the party, and that this meeting, on the basis of completely unverified and unsupported facts and communications, compiled a bill of indictment against the party; further- more, as some who signed this document have testified, they did so merely out of group solidarity, without even possessing proper knowledge of the document's content.

4   The Congress is fully in agreement with the previous Central Com- mittee in considering that the comrades who signed the declaration in no way violated party discipline by the mere fact of submitting this declaration to the supreme organ of our class communist organization – the Comintern, and does not condemn the comrades for this. But the Congress views as anti-party in nature their perpetuation of a factional grouping for a year despite the resolute and unconditional resolution of the X Congress, their factional meetings, and the continuation of the factional struggle. The Congress views as entirely inadmissible the sending to the Comintern of information whose falsity was established by the special commission ap- pointed by the Comintern. The Congress most resolutely stigmatizes the conduct of certain members of this group whose explanations to the Com- intern commission contained false information about the party and dis- torted the actual pattern of relations between the RKP and the working class as a whole.

5   The commission also considers that not only have the above facts been established but also the fact that the former 'Workers' Opposition' group, whose conduct demoralized the organization from within, at the same time strove to consolidate its influence organizationally, and was willing under certain circumstances, to split our party, being prevented only by its feeling that the time was not yet ripe for this split. It was precisely Comrade Kollontai, whose pamphlet brought before the X Party Congress the idea that a split was inevitable and that it only remained to select the most suitable moment, who after the X Congress did not reject

this line of conduct and whose explanations before the commission of the XI Party Congress confirmed her view that a split is inevitable unless the party alters its line, i.e., unless the party adopts the views of comrades Kollontai, Medvedev, and Shliapnikov, which are both erroneous and harmful to the working class.

As regards factional meetings like the last one, Comrade Kollontai expressed her regret to the commission that there were so few of them. The Congress regards this group's attitude to the party as completely unacceptable, especially when the working class is experiencing a very difficult period of economic reconstruction, a certain strengthening of capitalist elements, unprecedented famine in the country, the threat of foreign intervention, an enhancement of petty bourgeois attitudes, when the primary condition of working-class victory is the unity of the party and the strictest discipline in its ranks.

On the basis of all of the above the XI Party Congress, having listened to the resolution of the enlarged plenum of the Executive Committee of the Communist International on the matter of the twenty-two, to the report of the nineteen-member commission appointed by the Congress to investigate the activities of certain members of the former 'Workers' Opposition,' as well as to the explanation of comrades Shliapnikov, Medvedev, and Kollontai, has resolved as follows:

1 It supports the resolution of the ECCI on comrades Shliapnikov, Medvedev, and Kollontai and instructs the Central Committee to expel these comrades from the party if, in the future, they display a similar anti-party attitude.

2 Comrade Mitin, who for sixteen years was an active member of the Menshevik party and entered the RKP in 1920, who organized a factional group which has steadily striven to demoralize the RKP organization in the Donbass, is hereby expelled from the party as a malicious disorganizer.

3 Comrade Kuznetsov, who betrayed the party's confidence by false testimony about his past, his years in the party and as a worker, who hid the fact that he was once a grocery dealer who only entered the ranks of the working class in order to evade military service, is expelled from the party as an element alien to the proletariat.

Izvestiia tsentral'nogo komiteta,   *KPSS v rezoliutsiiakh* II, 314–71
May 1922 (2.23, 2.26, 2.27, 2.28,
2.29); *Pravda*, 5 April 1922 (2.24,
2.25, 2.30)

XII Party Conference   4–7 August 1922

Meeting without Lenin and with only 129 delegates with a deciding vote and 92 with a consultative vote, the XII Party Conference nevertheless undertook a number of important tasks. Its principal achievement was the adoption of a new version of the party Rules, revising those adopted in 1919, particularly with respect to the admission of new members and the structure and procedures of the regional party bodies (2.31). This document had been prepared by a commission, headed by Molotov, which had been appointed following the XI Party Congress in May 1922. No minutes of the XII Conference have ever been published, so it is impossible to speak with any assurance about its proceedings.

The Conference passed resolutions dealing with co-operatives, foreign policy, the standard of living of party members (particularly the apparatchiki or full-time party employees), and on the forthcoming IV Congress of the Comintern. It also passed a resolution assessing the work of the trade unions in the light of the trade union resolution passed at the XI Party Congress and a resolution on 'Anti-Soviet Parties and Tendencies,' which once more concerned the Menshevik and Socialist Revolutionary parties, most of whose leaders found themselves by now abroad in exile. The Bolsheviks continued to fear a possible new impact of these parties because of the rise of the so-called NEP bourgeoisie and urged in the resolution intensified repression of these groups, or what was left of them, and the adoption of special agitation and propaganda measures to counterbalance their possible influence.

2.31
Rules of the RKP(b)   probably August 1922
[Replaces Rules adopted in 1919; see 2.10]

I   ON PARTY MEMBERS
1   [As in 2.10, art. 1, on definition of party member]
2   [Revises 2.10, art. 2]   New members are accepted from among candidates who have passed through a school of political literacy and have served the established period of candidacy.
Party members are accepted from among candidates in the following manner.
  a   Three categories are established; 1) workers and Red Army men of worker or peasant origin; 2) peasants (except Red Army men), whether engaged in farming or in cottage industry, who do not exploit another's labour; 3) others (white collar workers, etc.).
  b   To be admitted into the party, persons in categories 1 and 2 must have

recommendations from three party members of three years' standing; persons in category 3 must have recommendations from five party members of five years' standing.

Note Persons who give recommendations bear responsibility for those whom they recommend, and, in cases of unfounded recommendations, they are subject to party punishment, right up to expulsion.

 c Before admission the recommendations must be verified by the local party committee.

 d The question of admission into the party is first examined by the cell, is decided by the general meeting of the organization, and takes effect after approval by the party committee: for category 1 – by the uezd committee, for categories 2 and 3 – by the guberniia committee. In urban raion organizations the decision of the general raion meeting is final for persons of category 1.

 e Persons formerly in other parties are accepted on the recommendation of five party members of five years' standing and only after approval by the guberniia committee, regardless of the social position of the person accepted.

 f Persons twenty years of age or younger (except Red Army men) enter the party only through the Komsomol.

3 [Revises 2.10, art. 3] Any member of one [party] organization who moves into the area of work of another organization is registered with the latter as one of its members.

Note The transfer of a member within the boundaries of a guberniia may be carried out with the consent of the guberniia committee. A transfer from one guberniia to another is carried out in accordance with rules established by the Central Committee of the party.

4 [Revises 2.10, art. 4] The question of expelling anyone from the party is decided either by the general meeting of which the person is a member or by the guberniia control commission. The resolution on expulsion takes effect only after it has been approved by the guberniia committee, and the person is removed from party work pending this approval. The party press announces the expulsion of a party member and gives the reasons for the expulsion.

II ON CANDIDATE MEMBERS OF THE PARTY

5 [As in 2.10, art. 5, on candidate membership]

6 [New] The procedure for admission to candidate membership (division into categories, the character of the recommendations and their confirmation, the decision of the organization on admission and its approval by the party committee) is absolutely identical to that for admission to party membership.

7 [Revises 2.10, art. 7] For workers and for Red Army men of worker

or peasant origin the period of candidacy is set at not less than six months, for peasants in farming or cottage industries one year, and for others two years.

Note Persons formerly in other parties, regardless of their social position, must remain two years as candidate members.

8   [Revises 2.10, art. 8]   Candidates for party membership may participate in open general meetings of the party organization to which they belong.

9   [As in 2.10, art. 9, on candidates' dues]

III   ON THE ORGANIZATIONAL STRUCTURE OF THE PARTY

10   [As in 2.10, art. 10, on democratic centralism]

11   [As in 2.10, art. 11, on territorial principle]

12   [As in 2.10, art. 12, on local autonomy]

13   [As in 2.10, art. 13, on the directing organs at each level]

14   [As in 2.10, art. 14, on committee to deal with current work]

15   [Revises 2.10, art. 15]   The party's organizational structure is as follows:

  a   territory of the RSFSR – the All-Russian congress, the Central Committee;

  b   oblasts and Soviet republics within the RSFSR – oblast bureau of the central committee (or oblast conferences and congresses of national communist parties – oblast committees and the central committee of the national communist party);

  c   guberniias – guberniia conferences, guberniia committees;

  d   uezds – uezd conferences, uezd committees;

  e   volosts – volost meetings, volost committees;

  f   enterprises, villages, Red Army units, institutions – general cell meetings, cell bureaus.

16   [As in 2.10, art. 16, on hierarchy of authority]

17   [As in 2.10, art. 17, on special sections, e.g., national, except words 'among youth' omitted]

18   [As in 2.10, art. 18, on approval of membership of lower organizations by higher ones]

19   [As in 2.10, art. 19, on right of each organization to establish its own press]

IV   ON THE CENTRAL INSTITUTIONS OF THE PARTY

20   [As in 2.10, art. 20, on the party congress]

21   [As in 2.10, art. 21, on the convocation of an extraordinary party congress in the absence of action by the Central Committee]

22   [As in 2.10, art. 22, on the functions of a congress]

23   [Revises 2.10, art. 23]   The congress elects the Central Committee and determines its size.

   If the Central Committee loses members, they are replaced from among the candidate members of the Central Committee in manner determined by the congress.

24   [Revises 2.10, art. 24]   The Central Committee represents the party in its relations with other parties and institutions; organizes the various party institutions and directs their activities, appoints the editors of the central organs, who operate under its supervision; organizes and directs enterprises of social significance for the party; allocates party funds and personnel; and controls the central treasury.

   The Central Committee directs the work of the central soviet and social organizations through party fractions.

   The Central Committee holds a plenum at least once every two months. Candidate members of the Central Committee participate in Central Committee plenums with a consultative vote.

25   [Revises 2.10, art. 25]   The Central Committee organizes: for political work – a Political Bureau; for the general leadership of organizational work – an Organizational Bureau with five to seven members; and for current work of an organizational and executive character – a Secretariat of three members of the Central Committee who work continually in the Secretariat.

26   [Revises 2.10, art. 26]   Once a year during the interval between party congresses, the Central Committee calls an all-Russian party conference of the representatives of krai, oblast, and guberniia party committees, of the central committees of the national communist parties, of the oblast bureaus of the Central Committee, and of the politotdels of the Red Army and Navy.

27   [Revises 2.10, art. 27]   Once every two months the Central Committee circulates to the guberniia committees of the party a written report on its activities.

28   [Revises 2.10, art. 28]   The Central Revision Commission consists of three members who have at least ten years' party membership.

   The Central Revision Commission reviews: a) the speed and correctness with which business is conducted within the central organs of the party and the proper functioning of the Secretariat of the Central Committee of the RKP; b) the RKP Central Committees treasury and enterprises.

V   ON THE OBLAST ORGANIZATIONS

29   [Revises 2.10, art. 29]   With the permission of the RKP Central Committee the party organizations of an oblast may unite. The oblast

boundaries are determined by the oblast conference and are approved by the Central Committee.

30   [Revises 2.10, art. 30]   Party organizations serving the territory of a federative part of the RSFSR are equivalent to oblast (or guberniia) organizations of the party, i.e., they are wholly subordinate to the Central Committee of the RKP.

31   [New]   The oblast committee (or the central committee of the national communist party) is elected at the oblast conference (or congress of the national communist party).

In places where there are oblast economic organs (economic councils, etc.), or in regions located a long distance from the centre, oblast bureaus are created by special order of the Central Committee; these bureaus are appointed by the Central Committee of the RKP(b) with their membership in each case being determined by the Central Committee. Central Committee oblast bureaus are responsible only to the Central Committee of the RKP(b).

32   [Revises 2.10, art. 31]   The regular oblast conference (or congress of the national communist party) is convened by the oblast committee (central committee of the national communist party) every six months (in some oblasts this period may be extended to one year with the agreement of the Central Committee of the RKP); an extraordinary conference is convened by decision of the oblast committee (central committee of the national communist party) or of one-half of the total membership of the organizations in the oblast.

The standard of representation at the oblast conference (congress of the national communist party) is set by the oblast committee (central committee of the national communist party) by agreement with the guberniia committees within the oblast.

The oblast conference (congress of the national communist party) hears and approves the reports of the oblast committee (central committee of the national communist party), the revision commission, and the other oblast institutions, elects the oblast committee and the revision commission (the central committee and the central control commission of the national communist party).

33   [Revises 2.10, art. 32]   For the conduct of current work the oblast committee appoints a bureau of at least five of its members.

The oblast committee (oblast bureau of the central committee) organizes the various party institutions within the oblast, directs their activities, appoints the editors of the oblast party organ operating under its supervision, organizes and directs enterprises of general significance for the oblast, allocates party funds and personnel within the oblast, and controls the oblast treasury. The oblast committee (oblast bureau of the central committee) directs the activities of soviet executive organs through the party fractions and reports monthly to the RKP Central Committee on its activities.

The oblast committee (oblast bureau of the central committee) meets at least once a month.

VI ON THE GUBERNIIA ORGANIZATIONS

34 [Revises 2.10, art. 33] The regular party conference is convened by the guberniia committee once every six months, the extraordinary conference by decision of the guberniia committee or of one-third of the total membership of the organizations in the guberniia.

The guberniia conference hears and approves the reports of the guberniia committee, revision commission, and other guberniia institutions, elects the committee and revision commission.

35 [Revises 2.10, art. 34] The guberniia committee is elected by the conference and must include party workers of the guberniia centre and of the other major working-class centres of the guberniia.

The guberniia committee meets at least once a month. For the conduct of current work the guberniia committee appoints a bureau of five of its members, this number being subject to increase in case of necessity but only with the assent of the Central Committee (or, in the oblasts, of the oblast committee).

At least three bureau members are to be assigned strictly to party work.

The secretaries of a guberniia committee must have been party members before the Revolution of October 1917 and must be approved by the next higher party authority (whose sanction is also needed for waivers of the requirement on length of party membership).

36 [Revises 2.10, art. 35] The guberniia committee approves the membership of the uezd or raion organizations of the guberniia with the sanction of the oblast committees or of the Central Committee; organizes the various party institutions within the guberniia and directs their activities, appoints the editors of the guberniia party organ, working under its supervision; organizes all enterprises of significance for the guberniia; allocates party funds and personnel within the guberniia; and controls the guberniia treasury. The guberniia committee directs the activities of the soviet, the trade unions, and the co-operatives through the corresponding party fractions. The guberniia committee submits a detailed monthly report to the Central Committee on its activities and on the activities of the uezd committees. Oblast committees of autonomous oblasts are equivalent to guberniia committees.

37 [Revises 2.10, art. 36] During the intervals between conferences the guberniia committees make informational reports to the general meeting or conference of the city organization; furthermore, at least every three

months the guberniia committee convenes a guberniia conference of representatives of the uezd and city organizations (directly subordinated to the guberniia committee.)

38   [Revises 2.10, art. 37]   In guberniia cities, when the need arises, raion organizations are instituted with the rights of uezd organizations and subordinated directly to the guberniia committee.

VII   ON UEZD ORGANIZATIONS

39   [Revises 2.10, art. 38]   The uezd conference hears and approves the reports of the uezd committee, the uezd revision commission, and elects the committee and revision commission. The conference meets at least once every six months.

40   [Revises 2.10, art. 39]   The uezd committee is elected by the uezd conference and has a membership of seven to nine persons. The uezd committee appoints a bureau of three of its members, of whom at least two comrades must be released from all except party work.

The Secretary must have three years' party membership and must have the approval of the higher party authority (whose sanction is also needed for waivers of the requirement on length of party membership).

41   [Revises 2.10, art. 40]   The uezd committee approves the membership of the volost organizations and cells within the uezd with the sanction of the guberniia committee, organizes the various party institutions in the uezd, directs their activities, organizes all enterprises that have significance for the uezd, arranges meetings of volost cells at least once every three months, and controls the uezd party treasury.

Note Only the uezd committee may issue a party organ and party literature within the uezd (with permission of the guberniia committee).

42   [Revises 2.10, art. 41]   Through party fractions the uezd committee directs the work of the uezd executive committee, and also of trade union organizations, co-operative and other associations in the uezd.

VIII   ON VOLOST ORGANIZATIONS

43   [As in 2.10, art. 42, on the volost general meeting]

44   [Revises 2.10, art. 43]   The volost general meeting is convened at least once a month. The general meeting: a) decides questions on admission and expulsion of party members and submits its decisions for approval by higher party committees; b) elects the volost committee; c) discusses and approves the report of the volost committee; d) elects delegates to the guberniia, uezd, and other conferences; e) discusses and approves the report of the volost executive committee fraction.

45   [As in 2.10, art. 44, on election of the volost committee]

46   [Revises 2.10, art. 45]   The volost committee guides and directs the work of all organizations within the volost, registers all party members, organizes the distribution of literature, holds public rallies, lectures, etc.,

organizes new cells and submits them to the uezd committee for approval, controls the volost party treasury, reports on its activities once a month to the uezd committee, directs the work of the volost [soviet] executive committee through the party fraction.

[Art. 46, 1919 Rules, deleted, on review of volost treasury]

IX ON PARTY CELLS

47   [Revises 2.10, art. 47]   The basis of the party organization is the party cell. The cell is approved by the uezd or the raion committee and has at least three members.

48   [As in 2.10, art. 48, on the cell and the masses]

49   [Revises 2.10, art. 49]   For the conduct of current work the cell elects a bureau of three members, serving for three months.

The cell secretary must have been a party member for at least one year. Waivers of this requirement must have the sanction of the uezd (or raion) committee.

X   ON THE CONTROL COMMISSIONS

50   [New]   For purposes of promoting the consolidation of party unity and authority in the centre, the oblasts, and the guberniias, control commissions are organized through elections at the congress and at the oblast and guberniia conferences, and report to the organs electing them. At the centre the control commissions are elected with five members and two candidates, all with ten years' party membership; at the oblast level – with three to five members and two to three candidates, at the guberniia level – with three members and two candidates, all with party membership from before the February Revolution.

Control commission members have the right to be present with a consultative vote at all meetings of the corresponding party committees and at any other meetings or sessions of the corresponding party organizations.

Control commission resolutions may not be countermanded by the corresponding party committee but enter into force with the latter's agreement and are implemented by the latter.

In case of disagreement the matter is referred to a joint meeting. If agreement with the committee is not achieved, the matter is referred for decision to the appropriate party conference or higher control commission. *Note* Control commissions are not established in Central Committee oblast bureaus. If the decision of a guberniia control commission is protested, the matter is referred to the Central Control Commission together with the findings of the Central Committee oblast bureau.

XI   ON PARTY DISCIPLINE

51   [As in 2.10, art. 50, on party discipline]

52   [Revises 2.10, art. 51]   Failure to implement resolutions of higher organizations and other offences recognized as criminal by party opinion are punished as follows: in the case of the organization, by censure, appointment of a provisional committee from above, and general re-registration (dissolution) of the organization; in the case of the individual party members, by party censure, public censure, temporary removal from responsible party and soviet work, temporary removal from any party or soviet work, expulsion from the party, expulsion from the party with a report of the offence to the administrative and judicial authorities. Demotion to candidate membership is not permitted as a measure of party punishment.

[Art. 52, 1919 Rules, deleted, on holding special sessions to consider disciplinary questions]

53   [Revises 2.10, art. 53]   Disciplinary offences are examined by committees, general meetings, and by control commissions in the usual order through the established authorities.

XII   ON PARTY FINANCES

54   [As in 2.10, art. 54, on sources of funds]
55   [As in 2.10, art. 55, on amount of membership dues]
56   [Revises 2.10, art. 57]   In the case of persons, such as peasants, whose wages are indeterminate, membership dues are established by the local guberniia committee following the instructions of the Central Committee.

57   [New]   Unemployed persons and persons on social security (invalids, the aged) are entirely exempt from membership dues.

58   [Revises 2.10, art. 56]   Initiation dues of 3 per cent of salary are paid by party members and candidate members, and no one is excused from paying them.

59   [Revises 2.10, art. 58]   Party members and candidates are considered to have left the party if they have failed to pay dues for three months without an acceptable excuse; this is brought to the notice of the general meeting.

[Art. 59, 1919 Rules, deleted, on forwarding part of dues to higher organizations]

XIII   ON FRACTIONS IN NON-PARTY ORGANIZATIONS

[Entire section as in 2.10, arts. 60–66, except for minor changes in wording]

Izvestiia tsentral'nogo komiteta,   *KPSS v rezoliutsiiakh* II, 375–400
August 1922

XII Party Congress   17–25 April 1923

This was the last Congress held during Lenin's lifetime but he could not attend it because he suffered a stroke in December 1922 which partially paralyzed him and deprived him of speech. His final illness struck him at a time when he was growing more and more critical of the party apparatus and of some of its leadership. Specifically, Lenin was most concerned about the policy followed in Georgia by Stalin and Ordzhonikidze (at least partly connected with the formation of the USSR), although the recommendations he dictated at the end of December 1922 and at the beginning of January 1923, comprising his so-called Testament, also included a warning against Stalin, his views of other party members, as well as recommendations on reorganization of some of the central organs of the party. Evidence surrounding the handling of these documents is not entirely clear. So far as can be judged, Lenin addressed them to and wanted them discussed by this Congress. However, it appears that only his notes on the question of nationalities reached the Politburo which, on Stalin's insistence, decided to keep them secret. Rumours began circulating about the existence of these documents and as a result they could not be entirely ignored at the Congress. The situation was further complicated by the already existing split between the troika of Stalin, Zinoviev, and Kamenev, on the one hand, and Trotsky and his supporters on the other hand. At this moment, however, both sides, for a variety of reasons, preferred to keep their differences from breaking out into the open. Consequently, on 16 April 1923, a day before the opening of the Congress, a new kind of preparatory session was held by a decision of the Central Committee dated 15 April 1923 (this party resolution is omitted from R.H. McNeal, *Guide to the Decisions of the Communist Party of the Soviet Union, 1917–1967*, in which it should have appeared as entry number 230415; the document was first published in *Dvenadtsatyi s''ezd RKP(b), Stenograficheskii otchet*, Moscow, 1968, 768). The meeting was called a *senoren konvent* – a session of the elders – a term drawn from the practice of the Imperial Duma. Each oblast or guberniia delegation was to elect one representative for each ten Congress delegates to attend this meeting, which meant an attendance of about forty out of the 408 delegates to the Congress (not counting the 417 with a consultative vote). It was summoned, as the resolution put it, 'in the interest ... of securing the best conditions of information to the delegates ...' The meeting obviously touched, perhaps only in a general way, on the subject of Lenin's notes, but no decision was announced. It was only on the 18 April that the presidium of the Congress issued a protocol on the subject. It decided, under Kamenev's chairmanship, to make public to the konvent 'once again' (apparently an allusion to the first senoren konvent meeting) Lenin's notes and all connected material, and after that to acquaint the various delegations with the material. However, it was also decided that the material was not going to be announced in the Congress section on the national question and, therefore, not on the floor of the Congress. This ruling was strictly adhered to. Although all the delegates must have been familiar at least with the content of Lenin's notes on nationality, when Mdivani (during the discussion of Stalin's report on the national question) wanted to quote from Lenin's letter to Mdivani, in which he supported the Georgian against his fellow countryman Stalin, he was ruled out of order.

The senoren konvent, at its first meeting on the eve of the Congress, probably also approved an arrangement for the agenda: Zinoviev would deliver the political report of the Central Committee, which had been Lenin's prerogative in the past, Stalin and Trotsky having turned down the offer to do so. Stalin did deliver, however, the less prestigious organizational report of the Central Committee, which was his function as General Secretary.

The changed atmosphere from the XI Congress was readily noticeable at the very opening of the Congress. When Rudzutak nominated members to the Congress presidium and various other committees, no voices from the floor were heard adding new names or commenting, as was the case in the past. The procedural rules still included the provision that forty delegates had the right to submit their own co-reports – only by now it was an even less meaningful provision than before.

Neither Stalin's nor Zinoviev's reports aroused great controversy and no negative votes were reported on the resolutions based on them. However, echoes of the old opposition were still heard. Lutovinov charged that if there were opposition groups underground it was because they were driven there, because there no longer existed a possibility to discuss different viewpoints in a normal way. Osinsky launched a bitter attack on Zinoviev for the latter's obvious desire to step into Lenin's shoes: 'When there is a sign on a cage saying "lion,"' he said, 'and the lion is not there, I do not believe the sign.' Osinsky's remarks brought about a strong retort from Stalin who came to Zinoviev's defence.

Krasin, the commisar of foreign trade, also engaged in a controversy with Zinoviev, in which he tried, in vain, to convince the leadership that they should 'render unto Caesar what is Caesar's,' i.e., they should not interfere in the work of the experts in the Soviet apparatus.

Mdivani and Makharadze, the two Georgian opponents of Stalin, exposed the high handed methods and russification policies of the latter in Georgia. None of this was to any avail – the leadership prevailed.

Some signs of the split between the troika and Trotsky came to the surface at the Congress. Kosior, a supporter of Trotsky, attacked what he called a leading group in the Central Committee for packing the leading party organs with their supporters and excluding other members from work because they spoke against the official line. He objected, somewhat naively, to the appointments of party members from below, claiming that, as a result, a number of experienced party workers from Trotsky to Shliapnikov were without sufficient work. In his reply to Kosior, Stalin accused Trotsky of refusing to accept additional work. Significantly, at Stalin's request, these remarks were deleted from the stenographic report of the Congress.

On the economic side, the state of the country was still chaotic, especially in industry, but the NEP began to have some beneficial effects and the leadership could afford to start – but only to start – thinking seriously about the organization of industrial planning. The theses on industry were prepared for and delivered to the Congress by Trotsky and were accepted, with minor alterations, in the final resolution (2.33). A further modification of the NEP policy in the countryside was also implemented, replacing the tax in kind with a monetary levy (2.34).

The Congress adopted resolutions concerning the Revision Commission, Central Control Commission, the Comintern, the establishment of raions, the nationality problem, press and propaganda, work in the countryside, work among women, and the Komsomol (2.36). Last but not least, the Congress passed a resolution 'On the Organizational Question' (2.35) which established new admission rules to the party and provided for a reorganization of Rabkrin and for enlargement of the Central Committee and the Central Control Commission. All these recommendations were included in Lenin's notes. He proposed to increase the membership in the Central Committee and in the Central Control Commission in order to reduce the power of the top leadership in the leading organs. Lenin's proposals also included turning the Joint Plenum of the Central Committee and Central Control Commission into a party conference and some fusion between the Central Control Commission and Rabkrin (*Collected Works* XXXVI, 593–7; XXXIII, 481–6).

Ironically, these measures played into Stalin's hands. He was not in full control of the Politburo and the number of Zinoviev's supporters in the twenty-seven-member Central Committee was too large for his comfort. Since Stalin was in full control of the Secretariat, however, he was able to see to it that a majority of the new members of the Central Committee, enlarged to forty members and sixteen candidates, were his supporters. It is not clear what role the senoren konvent played in this case, but it did discuss the composition of the new Central Committee at its second session. The actual choice of Central Committee members took place again during a secret session of the whole Congress. A new Central Control Commission was also appointed with fifty members and ten candidates.

After the Congress the new Central Committee chose a Politburo, adding Rudzutak as a candidate member. One other innovation was introduced at the Congress. For the first time a whole session, in the Bolshoi Theatre, was devoted to ceremonial greetings from various workers' organizations, a practice which became a ritual in subsequent years.

2.32
On the Central Committee Report   19 April 1923

The XII Congress entirely supports the Central Committee's political and organizational lines which, in the past year again, have given the party substantial successes.

In particular, the Congress entirely supports the Central Committee's foreign policy and resolutely condemns any vacillation in this matter. The Congress categorically affirms the unwavering monopoly of foreign trade, and the inadmissibility of any evasion or wavering in its implementation, and instructs the new Central Committee to take systematic steps to strengthen and develop the foreign trade monopoly.

The attitude of the broadest working masses to the RKP is one of the best criteria of the correctness of the party's policies during the past year. The party has won the undivided support of the whole proletariat and inspired confidence in the work of the RKP even among the more backward strata of workers who during the five years of revolution, one way or another, shunned the work of the Communists and viewed the Soviet power with certain scepticism. Labour productivity and the pay of the workers have been raised, the workers are more interested in questions of political and economic construction, the authority of the trade unions has been significantly enhanced, and the co-operative movement has made considerable strides.

The first signs are at hand of the country's incipient economic rebirth. The period is beginning when the NEP business methods, whose significance has been assimilated by the whole party, must be made more precise and concrete.

For a long time to come agriculture will remain the basis of the Soviet economy. The working class, led by our party, bears this firmly in mind but at the same time is making the most energetic efforts to advance state industry in the cities, especially heavy industry, which alone can become the solid foundation of a truly socialist development.

The problem of the most suitable way to export Russian wheat surpluses has become of first-class importance, since its solution will stimulate the peasant to increase his sown area, will make possible the establishment of a more correct relationship between grain prices and the prices of industrial products, will also enhance the possibility of providing agriculture with the necessary amounts of industrial products, and thanks to the overall increase in the means at the country's disposal, will help heavy industry to get back on its feet more rapidly. The basic practical problems facing the party in the immediate future are: establishing an even closer tie between the city and the peasantry which make up the overwhelming majority of the population of Russia, supplying the villages comprehensively with progressive workers under the guidance of our party, organizing encouragement by the party etc., on a broad scale, and a careful tax policy taking into account the peasants' actual ability to pay.

Closely connected with this is the most important *political* task of the party, one which determines the whole outcome of the revolution: to *guard and develop* with extreme attention and care the *union of the working class and the peasantry*. This is the point of view from which the party must approach the solution of all the major current problems, bearing in mind that the relative importance of state industry in the country's whole economy can only increase gradually, and only through steady and systematic work by the party to improve the organization of industry, heighten its profitability, etc.

The XII Congress confirms for unwavering execution the resolutions of previous congresses on the need for a precise division of labour between party and Soviet organizations, on greater specialization by economic and administrative personnel in each line of work, on strict observance of the principle of personal responsibility for assigned work. The XII Congress confirms the decision of the XI Congress that 'party organizations themselves settle economic questions only in those cases where, and to the extent that, such questions actually require a decision of principle by the party.' But the Congress warns against an excessively broad interpretation of these decisions, as this could create political dangers for the party. At the present time the RKP is guiding, and must guide, all the political and cultural work of the organs of state power, is directing and must direct the activities of all the economic organs of the republic. The party's job is not only to distribute its personnel correctly among the various branches of state work but also to define and verify in all essentials the actual course of this work. In no way can the party now limit its role merely to general propaganda and agitation. The dictatorship of the working class cannot be assured in any other way than as the dictatorship of its progressive vanguard, i.e., the Communist Party. While systematically involving in economic and state work all valuable non-party workers and peasants, the party at the same time cannot forget for a minute that the RKP bears principal responsibility for the functioning of economic and state organs, for it alone has been historically summoned to be the actual bearer of the working-class dictatorship. *Still closer to the economy, still greater attention, guidance, effort to the economic organs – this is the party's slogan for the immediate future.*

As the party intensifies its economic work, the planning principle must gradually take on increasing significance. The Congress reminds all that the plan for the electrification of Russia, which must remain the cornerstone of all the republic's economic efforts, will for many years be the principal planned economic effort.

The task of a correct policy on the nationality question is tied in with the absolute necessity of a binding link with the peasantry. The greatest danger for the party would be an insufficiently attentive attitude to the interests of the toiling masses of the large numbers of formerly oppressed nationalities on the territory of the USSR. Above all, the party must struggle resolutely against the remnants of Great Russian chauvinism. Only a resolute struggle against Great Russian chauvinism can ensure a firm union and can ensure the party's influence among the toiling masses of other countries.

Now that the Civil War is entirely over, the task of radical reconstruction and systematic improvement of the whole state apparatus can for the first time be placed on the party's agenda as a task of prime importance which will only be resolved in a number of years and only if the reorganization measures are undertaken extremely cautiously and are carefully thought through. The task of creating an inexpensive and truly new, truly socialist apparatus is the prime task of the years to come. Only its successful solution will ensure the unbreakable union of workers and peasants.

On the other hand, the party itself is gradually being restructured and purged, it is regrouping its ranks, it is subjecting decisions to the test of experience and reformulating a number of its basic tasks – in response to the whole NEP transitional period.

In particular, the party must bear in mind that its economic wing (a part of its economic personnel), which is of enormous significance for the fate of the revolution, is now through the very conditions of its work subject to a certain danger of being influenced by the bourgeois elements of the NEP. The party is putting forward its best people to work in the economy. But in this it must take into account not only strict party spirit, length of party service, etc., but also practical economic talent and business sense. These two criteria are not always easily combined in one person. It is necessary to waive sometimes one, sometimes the other. The selection of the cadre of economic personnel therefore becomes a major matter, and one of great difficulty. The reduction, here and there, of the number of worker-communists in economic organs is a dangerous phenomenon for the party, and the Central Committee must adopt measures against this threat. The Congress fully confirms the resolution of the August 1922 All-Russian Party Conference ['On the Improvement of the Material Situation of RKP Members'] aimed at reducing material inequalities in the party (the ban on participation in profits, compulsory deductions from high salaries for the party's benefit and for mutual-assistance funds, etc.), which under NEP conditions was fraught with special danger.

The Congress hereby notes that the Central Committee of the party has never for a moment closed its eyes to the existing threat of the degeneration of certain party cells. This is precisely what has enabled it to take the necessary measures in time.

The reorganized Rabkrin and Central Control Commission may and should become the party's main lever for resolving these tasks.

While supporting the plan for the radical reorganization of Rabkrin and the Central Control Commission, the Congress is convinced that an appropriate improvement in the central state and party control apparatuses, given the necessary organizational connection between them and the systematic combination of their efforts, will make it possible to attain both goals: 1) to undertake a decisive improvement of the state apparatus, and 2) to secure the party against the distortion of its line and against an actual breakaway of some groups of party workers from the party as a whole.

The Congress notes with satisfaction the improvement of the Central Committee's organizational apparatus and of all the organizational work of the party centre generally, and instructs the new Central Committee to give high priority to the work of the Accounts and Assignment Section, which is now to play an especially important role in the correct assignment of personnel to ensure that the party exerts real leadership in all areas of the administration without exception. The Congress also notes the improved party work in such areas as the party press, work with the Komsomol, work with female workers and peasants, educational work (soviet-party schools, communist universities, workers' educational programmes, and institutions of higher education) to prepare a proletarian intelligentsia.

The Congress instructs the Central Committee to devote particular attention to two tasks: a) a systematic improvement of the party's social makeup – meaning that the absolute numerical preponderance of industrial workers in the party is to be ensured, and b) a very great intensification of work to enhance the cultural level of the ordinary party member through more intensive party-educational work, etc.

The XII Congress cannot close its eyes to the fact that the NEP environment prepares the ground for deviations whose danger the party must foresee and to which it must give a decisive ideological rebuff from the very outset. Those deviations which set the Soviet state against the working class, and the party against the Soviet state, are particularly dangerous and destructive for our party's historic mission.

Now the main agitational instrument of all enemies of our party is to set the Soviet state, resting on an alliance between the workers and peasants, against the interests of the working class and the dictatorship of the party. But this same pattern of thought takes other forms as well – the form of well-intentioned 'criticism' of our party's policy from the 'left' or 'right' (taking the form of attempts to increase the 'independence' of Soviet and economic organs from the party) – which sometimes does not encounter a sufficiently resolute rebuff in the ranks of our party, especially among its youthful elements and among those with insufficient party training. However, this circle of ideas, when developed, is nothing other than a revision of the party's tested tactics of the last five years and inevitably leads to liquidationist conclusions.

Therefore, the XII Congress especially stresses the need, in the future as well, to adhere strictly to the tactics which have served to strengthen the peasants' confidence in the proletariat and, on the other hand, have secured the party's de facto leadership of the whole soviet, especially the economic, apparatus of the Soviet republic.

The XII Congress registers its firm conviction that the Central Committee will resolutely sweep away any efforts to introduce any sort of vacillation into our ranks with respect to these matters which are of the utmost importance for the dictatorship of the proletariat.

The XII Congress, in particular, repeats the assignment given to the Central Committee at the XI Congress with respect to the former 'Workers' Opposition' group, and extends it to anyone who will disturb party unity during the present decisive period of the revolution. The Congress is convinced that the iron will for *unity* to be observed in the broadest strata of party members will ensure that the party in the years immediately ahead will be even more cohesive and welded together than has been the case up until now.

The Congress orders the Central Committee not to lose sight of the danger of possible new attempts at intervention by the most irreconcilable elements of the imperialist camp. The more complex the international political situation becomes for the bourgeoisie (the Ruhr events, etc.), the greater will be the growth of the international bourgeois reaction (fascism), and the more chance that at some moment a new attempt will be made to apply military pressure against the USSR. The Congress feels that the party as a whole must, as before, devote comprehensive attention to the material and cultural needs of the Red Army and Navy.

2.33
On Industry

25 April 1923

...

3 TASKS AND METHODS OF PLANNING

... It is perfectly obvious that the basic planning of industry cannot be effected within industry itself, i.e., merely by the efforts of its leading administrative organ – the Supreme Council of the National Economy, but must be the function of a special planning organ which stands above the organization of industry and binds the latter to finance, transport, etc. By its very position Gosplan is such an organ. However, Gosplan must be accorded a more definite position, a firmer organization, clearer and better-recognized rights and, in particular, obligations. The unwavering principle must be established that no state economic problem is dealt with in the higher organs of the republic without the participation of Gosplan. Whether or not the initiative comes from Gosplan or from one of the departments, Gosplan must analyze the new problem, project, or proposal in the light of all its other economic work and thereby define its proportionate weight and significance. Both at the centre and in the field a clean sweep must be made of all attempts by departments and institutions to secure some decision or other by circuitous methods, by stating that they are urgent or must be taken at once, by improvising – with all such attempts being viewed as manifestations of economic short-sightedness and as the most pernicious remnants of *administrative partisanship* [avoidance of central authority, strict organization, discipline].

The success of each department's functioning must be evaluated to a considerable extent as a function of its timeliness in submitting drafts and proposals to Gosplan for comprehensive elaboration and co-ordination. The more so as the success of Gosplan's own functioning must be evaluated as a function of its own timeliness in spotting economic problems, in correctly foreseeing what tomorrow will bring, and in stimulating individual departments to the timely budgetary and practical co-ordination of those areas and lines of work which require such co-ordination.

Gosplan must be an instrument for combating the creation of the various temporary and accidental commissions: investigating, directing, verifying, preparatory, etc., which are a major evil of our government's work. Proper operation must be provided by the normal and continuing organs. Only in this way can these organs improve and develop the necessary flexibility through all-round adaptation to the assigned task on the basis of continuing experience.

Without deciding ahead of time the question of whether or not in the future the leading planning organ, the general staff of the state economy – Gosplan, will have to be endowed with some administrative rights or other, and with which, for the immediate future it would seem sufficient to determine that when planning leadership requires the use of compulsion, sanction for this must be given by the appropriate central organs (the individual economic commissariats, Council of Labour and Defence, Sovnarkom, the Presidium of the VTSIK).

Especially under the conditions of economic and cultural backwardness of the USSR, a general economic plan can be worked out successfully only to the extent that the individual economic oblasts are granted the necessary independence to solve the economic problems deriving from their natural and production conditions. At the all-union level planning must consist primarily in taking properly into consideration and guiding the work of the individual oblasts and in unifying organically the oblast plans and the economic tasks of all-Union significance into a single USSR plan.

The interests and rights of the national republics must be fully taken into account in resolving the basic economic problems. The overall planning tasks falling to the national republics must be resolved through their appropriate organs and in permanent and close collaboration with them. This is the only way in which the most appropriate distribution of industry can be effected, in accordance with conditions of nature, sources of raw materials and energy, etc. ...

2.34
On Tax Policy in the Countryside   25 April 1923

...

3   The transition from food requisitions to the tax in kind has meant recognition of the peasant's right to dispose freely of the product of his labour, but this right has been limited by the need of the Soviet state to have at its own disposal certain grain reserves as a basic stock with which to supply the army and to restore industry and transport.

4   In view of the incipient overall recovery of economic life in the Soviet republics, as expressed both in the revival and in the greater magnitude of commercial exchange, the party now can and must take the next step towards expanding the opportunities of the peasants to dispose freely of the product of their labour. As the amount marketed increases, the Soviet authority can and must release the peasant from the obligation of making payment in kind to the state and grant him the possibility of making a part of these payments in monetary form.

5   Replacing part of the payments in kind by monetary payments will alleviate the position of the peasantry and benefit the peasant economy not only by reducing the incidental costs of paying taxes in kind but also by making it possible for the peasant freely to adjust to the market, to select the most advantageous crops, to engage in commerce, etc. At the same time, this measure will also improve the overall economic position of the country in that it will lead to a further expansion of trade, will serve as a way of liquidating the financial collapse, and will ensure stability in the circulation of money. This last is absolutely essential for the development of trade between the city and the countryside, this being impossible as long as the steady depreciation of the currency undermines the circulation of money and impedes the marketing of both agricultural and industrial products. This measure, therefore, while directly alleviating the position of the

peasantry, strengthens the whole economy of the country which, in turn, will help the peasantry more rapidly to escape from ruin and poverty, to replace their stocks, and to heighten the technical level of their operations.

6   In addition to the transition from taxation in kind to monetary taxation, the Communist Party must, if it is to alleviate the position of the peasantry, consolidate all direct state taxes on the peasants (the tax in kind, the household tax, and the cartage tax), as well as all direct local taxes, into a single direct agricultural tax. A unified agricultural tax will have a decisive effect in ending the multiplicity of taxes which rightly causes the peasants to complain and makes it difficult for them to calculate firmly their income and expenses for purposes of conducting their operations. The Communist Party must introduce a system of taxation which will enable the peasant to know precisely, and beforehand, what his entire direct tax will be and which will require him to deal with only one collector of this tax ...

2.35
On the Organizational Question   25 April 1923

I

I   THE CENTRAL COMMITTEE PLENUM

The Congress elects forty Central Committee members and fifteen to twenty candidate members.

The purpose of the expansion is to bring new members into the Central Committee – primarily local party workers, and, in particular, those from the working class who have the best ties with the proletarian masses.

In addition to the forty persons with deciding votes, a) candidate members of the Central Committee and b) members of the Central Control Commission presidium, are entitled to participate in Central Committee plenums with a consultative vote.

The same persons can be simultaneously candidate members of the Central Committee and members of the Central Control Commission; when becoming a member of the Central Committee, the candidate must relinquish his position in the Central Control Commission.

The Central Committee plenum meets regularly at least once every two months. Each plenum decides on the date of the next plenum, which date may be changed only as an exceptional measure by a joint decision of the Politburo and Orgburo. The plenum meets for two to three days in order to be able to discuss seriously the items on the agenda. All of the most fundamental issues are to be decided by the plenum. Especially during the two or three weeks preceding the ordinary meeting of the plenum the Politburo must systematically include on the agenda of the plenum all important questions whose decision can be postponed. The preparatory work for plenums must be done more thoroughly than has been the case up until now. All materials for the forthcoming plenum, at least on the most important items, must be distributed in time to all Central Committee members. At each plenum the Politburo will submit a report on its activities in the intervening period.

Extraordinary meetings of the plenum are convoked by decision of the Politburo or at the demand of one-fourth of the members of the plenum.

2   THE POLITBURO

The Politburo is elected by the Central Committee plenum, with a membership not to exceed seven members and four candidate members.

In addition to Central Committee members, three permanent representatives of the Central Control Commission, from the latter's presidium, have the right to be present at Politburo meetings. The new Central Committee is hereby instructed to determine how Central Committee members who are not in the Politburo, and also the Central Control Commission presidium, are to be supplied with Politburo documents.

The new Central Committee is instructed to take all necessary steps to improve the Politburo's work in respect of its planned guidance of state – and, in particular, of economic – organs.

3   THE ORGBURO

The Orgburo consists of seven members and four candidate members.

Three representatives of the Central Control Commission are to be present at Orgburo meetings. Guberniia committee secretaries making reports will have a consultative vote at Orgburo meetings. Members of oblast central committee bureaus and of krai committee bureaus will also have the right to be present at Orgburo meetings with a consultative vote.

Members of the Central Committee may appeal Orgburo decisions to the Politburo, and Secretariat decisions to the Orgburo; in both cases the execution of such decisions is suspended.

4   THE CENTRAL CONTROL COMMISSION

It is understood that there must be a division of labour between party and state organs (in the spirit of the resolution of the XI Party Congress) [2.25], but without any infringement on the party's guiding role. To ensure that the party exercises not merely verbal, but real leadership of state and economic organs, the closest organizational tie must be established between leading state and party control organs at such central points as, for example, the reorganized Rabkrin.

The Congress will elect fifty Central Control Commission members, primarily workers and peasants with substantial length of party membership who are suitable for party-control and soviet-control work. The principal task of the Central Control Commission will be to ensure observance of the party line in all respects by all soviet organs. The Central Control Commission's functions are to be extended in line with this while at the same time it retains the tasks assigned to it by the party Rules. The Central Control Commission plenum will elect a presidium of nine comrades whose qualifications are high in all respects, i.e., party workers more or less of Central Committee quality. Rabkrin is appointed by the party Central Committee, where possible from the members of the Central Control Commission presidium. At the same time, the board of the commissariat must include several members of the Central Control Commission presidium. Not less than half of the remaining Central Control Commission members are assigned to Rabkrin and, with regard to the execution of their Soviet assignments, work under the guidance of the board of Rabkrin in accordance with the directives of the instructions, and the resolution on concerted action elaborated by the Central Control Commission presidium together with the commissariat board, and approved by the party Central Committee.

As a rule, plenums of the Central Control Commission will take place every two months immediately prior to the Central Committee plenum.

The party Central Committee will delegate its representatives with a consultative vote, to plenums of the Central Control Commission.

Proposals on necessary changes and measures to improve the state apparatus, economic-administrative work, etc., and also those relating to the replacement of leading party workers at the local level and at the centre are submitted by the Central Control Commission presidium to the party Central Committee – to the plenum, the Politburo, or the Orgburo, depending upon the nature of the problem.

All basic issues relating to the functioning of the Rabkrin and to improving the state apparatus, as well as major practical measures and the assignment of Central Control Commission members to work in Rabkrin, are to be discussed at the permanent joint meetings of the Central Control Commission presidium and the board of Rabkrin; these meetings are to be convoked periodically, not less than twice a month.

The statutory position of the conference remains as before, i.e., its decisions must be approved by the Central Committee.

All Central Control Commission members and candidate members participate in the all-Russian conference with a consultative vote.

II

THE ORGANIZATIONAL REGULATION OF THE COMPOSITION OF THE RKP

The threat represented by the NEP to the internal composition of the RKP should not be under-rated. The possibility that certain party cells will degenerate is not excluded. Remaining the only legal party, and at the same time being in power, the party cannot fail to take into account the fact that for several years to come its ranks will inevitably be infiltrated by alien elements. That being the case, the following measure, among others, is necessary: *most probably it will be necessary, every year at the party congress, to carry out major organizational manoeuvers aimed at regulating the party's composition* (admission to membership, etc.) *in order systematically to improve the composition of the RKP.*

The party accepts, and must accept, not only workers, but also peasants, Red Army men, employees, students, etc., as members of RKP. But, as a proletarian party, it must systematically heighten the percentage of industrial workers in the party and, at the same time, regulate and limit the admission to the party of all other elements. In the final analysis, one of the most important guarantees against the above dangers is, above all, the proletarian make-up of the party itself.

In recent years the percentage of working-class party members has been systematically increasing. There are large numbers of workers in leading state, party, and trade union posts. But the party has not yet achieved a sufficient preponderance of industrial workers among the whole 500,000 members and candidate members of the RKP.

This is even more true for the candidates, as was disclosed by the party census and subsequently.

The Congress hereby notes that in recent years there has been a particularly powerful influx of persons desiring to join the RKP, and, it is once again becoming necessary to adopt the most attentive and painstaking attitude toward the matter of admission into the party, the Congress recognizes the following measures as necessary:

a the number of persons required to give references for industrial workers engaged in production is for the next year (until the XIII Congress) to be reduced from three to two – with two years' party membership; the same procedure is also to be applicable to Red Army men (of worker or peasant origin) with not less than one year's membership in the Komsomol;

b working-class members of the Komsomol may be admitted into the RKP upon the recommendation of one party member of three years' standing together with an affirmative decision of the local committee of the Komsomol;

c while for non-working-class persons the existing statutory conditions for admission into the party remain unchanged, the absolute obligation of the strict fulfilment of all statutory requirements relating to this matter is hereby confirmed, with the guberniia committees bearing particular responsibility;

d during 1923 and 1924 (up to the XIII Party Congress) *only* industrial workers engaged in production are to be promoted from candidate member to member, all others being left as candidates for one more year in order to enable these candidates to obtain the best party preparation;

e certain special practical measures must be taken to facilitate the admission of industrial workers into the party.

To this end the Congress orders party committees to organize special missions (repeated not once but several times), of comrades with substantial party experience and appropriate length of time as party members, to industrial areas; and also to organize systematic visits by them to factories and plants in order to meet workers desiring to enter the party. After attentive examination and collection of the necessary attestations on workers desiring to enter the party (candidates), and with the co-operation of the party cells, the party comrades who have participated in these missions to factories and plants must in appropriate circumstances act as sponsors before the party committee. This measure must in no way weaken the work of the party cells themselves on bringing new working-class members into the party.

Deviations from the established procedure for admitting members into the RKP are in each case permitted only as an exceptional measure and, in each case, only by special decision of the Central Committee.

The Congress considers it necessary to adopt systematic measures to improve the party's composition, imposing a series of limitations on the admission into the party of persons from non-proletarian strata as well as from other parties. But once accepted into the party, after passing all the preliminary tests and limitations, the party members must, of course, enjoy all the rights of party members generally. It would be entirely inadmissible to continue to regard such comrades with distrust after their admission, because of their social origin or their prior adherence to other parties. A resolute struggle must be conducted against the slightest attempt to create an atmosphere of dividing party members into those with full rights and those with less than full rights.

In view of the motley social make-up of certain party organizations, and the necessity of strengthening them, the Congress considers it advisable when necessary to conduct a verification and purge of the party members of some organizations. Such a verification may be conducted only by decision of the Central Committee.

III

PARTY ORGANIZATIONAL WORK AND THE SELECTION OF PARTY WORKERS

The most important method for strengthening the party organization, other than a purge, is the already broadly employed system of improving and selecting the leading cadre of party workers, from the guberniia and oblast committee secretaries to the cell secretaries.

This has been done in the following way: by requiring the secretaries of party organizations (starting with the cell) to have been party members for a certain period of time, thus concentrating in party work those party comrades who have undergone the best political training and testing; by replacing the previous cell secretaries who carried out technical functions in the raion, by party organizers capable of conducting the cell's party work and of involving all cell members in this work, and – which is particularly important – by beginning to carry out the selection of these cell organizers (primarily cells in industrial enterprises) under the active guidance of party committees; by setting up a network of instructors from the Central Committee to the uezd committee and the raion committee which was, on the one hand, a way of tying together and raising party work and, on the other, a way of practically training new cadres of party workers; by placing party work in working-class centres under special observation and giving it intensified support by party forces, funds, and literature (both in industrial areas and in certain larger enterprises), and by a series of other measures.

The Congress supports these measures and recognizes the need to continue and intensify the work already undertaken in this connection by the party organizations.

At the same time the Congress recognizes that the party's immediate task is to strengthen party leadership in selecting leaders for soviet, in particular, economic, and other organs, which must be done by means of a correct and comprehensive system of evaluating and selecting leaders and responsible workers in soviet, economic, co-operative, and trade union organizations.

To this end the Congress instructs the Central Committee to take all steps to expand and fortify the party's evaluating and assigning organs at the centre and at the local level in order to encompass the whole mass of communists and communist sympathizers in all areas of the economy and administration without exception.

IV
THE GUBERNIIA CONFERENCES
It is hereby decreed that ordinary guberniia party conferences are not to be held twice a year, but once a year.

V
PARTY EDUCATIONAL WORK, ESPECIALLY AMONG YOUTH
The existing circumstances make the consolidation of party organizational work among the mass of party members, at the present time, a task of primary importance.

The Congress hereby notes that *too little attention is still being devoted to work with youth*. The Congress instructs the Central Committee to take the most decisive measures to ensure that party organizations at the uezd, guberniia, and all-Russian levels devote to work with youth as much attention and staff as this most important branch of work deserves, the party's future depending upon it.

The older party members must direct particular attention to this very important work. In addition to everything else, effective assistance by the older party members to the training of the younger generation of communists for work will bring about the radical elimination of any and all friction among the different age groups within the party. The party's strength will reside precisely in its success in *establishing an uninterrupted bond between the adolescent youth and the older generation of revolutionaries*, unifying in the party's ranks all that is viable in the revolutionaries of both generations.

A Central Committee school for uezd party committee secretaries, enrolling 200–300 persons, is to be organized on an urgent basis.

The Central Committee is instructed to take urgent steps to ensure that the staffs of periodical publications, especially in the provincial industrial regions, work in a businesslike way and in the party spirit.

The new Central Committee is instructed to take steps to ensure that party comrades in responsible positions, who need further education, be enabled to secure the necessary leave for this purpose.

VI
THE ORGANS CONCERNED WITH PARTY HISTORY
To ensure the regular and most rapid implementation of the tasks assigned to the Institute of Party History, the Congress resolves:

1   The existing Central Committee resolution that the Institute's organs are sections of corresponding party committees is hereby confirmed.

2   The Central Committee must provide, both at the centre and at the local level, the necessary staff for work exclusively in party history.

3   The monetary resources needed to support the Institute of Party History and its organs, as well as to cover their publication activity, are to be found and firmly included in budgetary estimates.

2.36
On the Work of the Komsomol   25 April 1923

During the past year the Komsomol has passed through a severe crisis, as a result of which its membership declined significantly in the first half of the year. However, as a result of broadly implemented economic and political-educational work, the Komsomol recovered during the second half of the year, attracted into its ranks tens of thousands of new workers, adolescents, and youths, strengthened the proletarian nucleus of its organization, and increased its membership.

The period which the communist youth movement has just entered in its development is defined, above all, by the exceptionally rapid rate of growth of the Komsomol – by the fact that almost half of its membership has been replaced by new youth, devoid of any revolutionary experience, and whose consciousness has been formed in the conditions of Soviet life.

Now is the time when the party is confronted more acutely than ever before with the problem of training a new communist generation of skilled and class-conscious workers, and also of peasants who are concerned with building the Soviet republic. At the same time, systematic work must be done to create in this new generation a serious urge to master science and technology. The revolutionary energy and enthusiasm of the youth must find their broad application in achieving success in the area of specialized knowledge. Only under these conditions will the workers' and peasants' republic obtain new cadres of truly excellent technicians, managers, professional men, staff for co-operatives, etc.

All this confronts the party with a number of fundamental tasks with respect to the Komsomol.

1   The party has the primary task of handing over to the new generation of youth all its experience in revolutionary struggle and of painstakingly acquainting it with the party's past. It is exceptionally important, for the revolutionary training of youth, to acquaint it with the class struggle and the contradictions in capitalist society, considering that the present generation of working-class youth started its conscious life under Soviet conditions and has little acquaintance with capitalist conditions; at the same time, it is important to guide the education of youth in the spirit of international solidarity, of intensifying the flow of information on the international workers' movement, etc. The party must devote the most serious attention to the creation of an adequate network of political schools and political circles, which all members of the youth league would attend. This is the goal to which the Komsomol press must be subordinated, and party organizations must devote attention to supporting this press both materially and by literary efforts.

2   The renewal of Komsomol membership raises the question of training its commanding officers. The collectives of propagandists whose purpose is to develop leaders for workers and village cells must be supported in every way by the party organizations.

The party must strive to ensure that this cadre of Komsomol propagandists is formed as rapidly as possible. Therefore, the party organizations must participate actively in consolidating the network of propaganda groupings and other techniques for training active workers (courses, seminars, etc.) attaching an experienced party propagandist to each propaganda group or other unit of active Komsomol workers.

3   Thus far the educational work of Komsomol village cells has not been properly organized. But now, more than ever before, the village cells – because they are attracting a new youth cadre – can be used as a significant buttress of party work in the village. It is necessary to intensify in every way the systematic agitational-propagandistic influence on the peasant youth in the spirit of the policy of the Soviet power, of promoting agriculture, of broadening the political horizon and raising the cultural level of the village youth, of providing it with literature, etc. At the same time the Congress feels it is essential in every way to involve the village cells of the Komsomol in village social life and in Soviet construction which, however, should in no way push into the background the basic task of the Komsomol in the countryside – educational work among the peasant youth.

4   Under the present conditions of relatively peaceful development all work with youth must be so arranged that the organizations of the new growing generation receive not only cultural training but also revolutionary hardening. The Congress also emphasizes that the educational work of the Komsomol must be supplemented by mass campaigns designed to elicit the active participation of the youth and must have a strikingly pronounced revolutionary character.

5   The broad scope of the youth movement leads to a numerical weakening of its party core. To ensure party influence within the youth movement and the inflow of working-class youth into the party, the Congress considers it essential to facilitate entry into the party by working-class Komsomol members and a greater involvement of active Komsomol workers in party life, party meetings, etc.

More than ever before, the party's leadership of the Komsomol must be based on practical assistance to the Komsomol educational work and on a strengthening of its political leadership, while ensuring the broad initiative and activity of youth organizations and involvement of the Komsomol in political and trade union work. While approving the decisions of previous party congresses on work with youth, the Congress resolutely opposes reducing the role of the Komsomol to one of a purely 'cultural' organization.

6   While noting the achievements of the Komsomol in its support of the navy and the cavalry, the Congress considers it necessary to intensify this work in every way, strongly stressing the necessity of the closest tie between the Komsomol and the Red Army.

7   The intensified urge of working-class youth to participate in sports must be used by the party both for improving the physical health of the upcoming working-class generation and for reinforcing the bond between

the Komsomol and the youth masses generally. The working-class youth in factories and plants must be brought together in physical education circles.

8   Given the existing prospects for the development of industry, the comprehensive development and reinforcement of factory apprentice schools takes on paramount importance not only for the Komsomol but also for the whole party and Soviet power. By training skilled and class-conscious workers, they fulfil a very important role in filling the ranks of the progressive industrial proletariat.

Therefore, the Congress considers it necessary to give comprehensive support to the network of factory apprentice schools which are indissolubly tied in with production, and to expand this network whenever possible, to enhance education work and especially political work in them, and also to improve the material conditions of these schools.

9   The growth of the children's movement under the guidance of the Komsomol, in the form of the 'Young Pioneers,' confronts the party organizations with the task of giving comprehensive assistance to the development of this work.

Party organizations must help the Komsomol to unify revolutionary pedagogical forces around the communist children's movement.

10   Noting that the female proletarian and peasant youth are insufficiently attracted into the Komsomol, the Congress assigns the Komsomol the task of increasing its efforts among the female proletarian-peasant youth.

11   Recognizing that the state and trade union organs must intensify their assistance to working-class youth and thus relieve the Komsomol of excess state and trade union work, the Congress instructs the Central Committee to work out the patterns of ties and inter-relations between the Komsomol and the state and trade union organizations.

12   A closer tie between the party and the Komsomol will make it possible to raise the question of employing the party apparatus to assist in part of the work of the Komsomol. However, this should in no way violate the harmony of the Komsomol organizational structure which is based on the principle of independent action and is adapted to the advancement of party workers and the development of their organizational skills.

Pravda, 20 April 1963 (2.32); 29   *KPSS v rezoliutsiiakh* II, 404–85
April (2.33); 26 April (2.34); 28
April (2.35): *Spravochnik par-
tiinogo rabotnika* II, 80 (2.36)

Joint Plenum of the Central Committee and the
Central Control Commission   25–27 October 1923

After the XII Congress Stalin continued to tighten his stranglehold over the party, which culminated in his follower Dzerzhinsky's proposal that party members should act as informers of the GPU in order to help maintain party discipline. The proposal triggered Trotsky's open opposition to the leadership which took the form of a letter to the Central Committee on 8 October. In the letter Trotsky attacked the Secretariat, blaming it for discontent not only in the party but in the country as well. He also challenged the right of the leaders to continue in their positions. Trotsky's stand may have encouraged some of the former opposition members such as Sapronov and Osinsky who, together with forty-four others, sent the so-called 'Declaration of the 46' to the Politburo in which they strongly criticized the dictatorship of the troika.

Stalin swiftly responded by convening this plenum, which was deliberately packed to add weight to its condemnation of the opposition. Not only were the fifty-six members and candidate members of the Central Committee joined by the sixty members and candidate members of the Central Control Commission, but also by an unspecified number of representatives from ten party organizations, which probably put the total near 150 participants. Their resolution 'On the Intra-party Situation' (2.37) may have been adopted unanimously. Trotsky was absent from the plenum owing to illness, but surprisingly, he approved the resolution, with the proviso that he could continue to argue his case.

2.37
On the Intra-party Situation   27 October 1923

The plenums entirely support the movement toward intra-party democracy undertaken in timely fashion by the Politburo, and also the intensified struggle, proposed by the Politburo, against excesses and against the demoralizing influence of the NEP on certain elements of the party.

The plenums instruct the Politburo to do all that is necessary to accelerate the work of the commissions appointed by the Politburo and the September plenum: 1) the commission on the 'scissors' [rise in prices of manufactured goods; fall in agricultural prices], 2) on wages, and 3) on the situation within the party.

After elaborating the necessary measures on these issues the Politburo must immediately start to implement them, reporting on this to the next Central Committee plenum.

The Joint Plenum of the Central Committee and the Central Control Commission, meeting jointly with the representatives of ten party organizations, consider Comrade Trotsky's speech, at this crucial moment for the international revolution and the party, to be a serious political error, especially because Comrade Trotsky's attack on the Politburo took on the objective character of a factional speech threatening to strike a blow at the party's unity and to create a crisis within the party. The plenums note with regret that in raising these issues Comrade Trotsky followed the course of appealing to individual party members instead of the only permitted course – of first submitting these questions for discussion by the boards of which Comrade Trotsky is himself a member.

The course selected by Comrade Trotsky was a signal to a factional grouping (the Declaration of the 46).

The Central Committee and Central Control Commission plenums, together with the representatives of the ten party organizations, resolutely condemn the Declaration of the 46 as a step in the direction of a factional-splitting policy, taking this form perhaps against the will of those signing the declaration. This declaration could place the whole life of the party in the months to come under the threat of an intra-party struggle, thus weakening the party at the most crucial time for the fate of the international revolution.

VKP(b) v rezoliutsiiakh I (4th edition), 639–40   *KPSS v rezoliutsiiakh* II, 495–6

XIII Party Conference   16–18 January 1924

The debate on Trotsky's letter and on Declaration of the 46, started at the October Joint Plenum, was seemingly ended on 5 December 1923 when the Politburo adopted a resolution in the name of the Central Committee and the Central Control Commission, professing to accept at least some of the criticism of the two documents. However, on 8 December Trotsky published another letter called 'The New Course,' in which he welcomed the resolution but at the same time continued his attack on Stalin, the party bureaucracy, and the resulting economic inefficiency. 'The New Course,' published in *Pravda* on 11 December 1923, was followed by a new widespread discussion culminating in the XIII Conference.

With Trotsky still ill and absent and with Lenin on his deathbed, Stalin, supported by Zinoviev and Kamenev, was free to lead the counter-attack with a resolution 'On the Results of the Discussion and on Petty Bourgeois Deviation in the Party' (2.38), which condemned Trotsky and his followers in no uncertain terms. The resolution was passed by an overwhelming majority of apparently handpicked delegates and included two warnings. The first was Stalin's inclusion in the resolution of paragraph 7 of the 'On Party Unity' resolution of the X Congress (2.13) giving the Central Committee power to expel party members for factional activity; the second was an inclusion of a paragraph (10) threatening expulsion from the party to all those guilty of 'spreading unverified rumours and prohibited documents' – obviously a reference to Lenin's Testament with its unflattering remarks about Stalin.

The Conference, attended by 128 delegates with a deciding vote and 222 with a consultative vote, also passed resolutions on party construction, on the international situation, and on current tasks of economic policy. The last, with its stress on the support of and co-operation with the peasants was a further manifestation of the lack of influence of Trotsky who favoured a more rapid industrial development.

2.38
On the Results of the Discussion and on
Petty Bourgeois Deviation in the Party   18 January 1924

I   THE ORIGINS OF THE DISCUSSION

The September (1923) Central Committee Plenum and, even earlier, the Politburo of our party's Central Committee, long before any speeches by the opposition, had already raised the question of the need to stimulate party work and strengthen workers' democracy within the party.

On the one hand, the advance of industry, which ended the declassing of the proletariat, the cultural growth of the working class, the growth of activity within it, all created more favourable conditions for a genuine implementation of the principles of intra-party democracy. On the other hand, the economic conflicts of the summer, although in themselves representing no threat and much smaller in size than has been the case in the past, showed that in places the party organizations had insufficiently firm ties with the non-party working-class masses.

The Central Committee of the party realized that the transition to the new course had to be accomplished deliberately, carefully, and after serious preparation. With this awareness the party Central Committee in September 1923 set about the preparatory work in this area.

During this time the old opposition groups and groupings, whose policies had already been more than once condemned by the party, decided that the moment was opportune for an attack on the Central Committee of the party. Calculating that the question of intra-party democracy would arouse the keenest attention of all party members, the opposition groups decided to exploit this slogan for factional purposes. After the September resolution of the Central Committee plenum Trotsky's letter appeared, and right after it the letter of the 46. These documents gave a completely incorrect and ultra-factional evaluation of the country's economic situation and of the party's internal situation, foretold a severe economic crisis in the republic and an internal crisis in the party, and accused the party Central Committee of incorrect leadership ...

Since the appearance of Trotsky's factional manifesto the struggle has intensified still further. In Moscow, and especially in military cells and in the cells of higher educational institutions, the opposition has undertaken a campaign against the Central Committee which is unprecedented in our party's history, sowing mistrust in the party's Central Committee. The representatives of the opposition are being dispatched throughout Russia. The struggle is assuming an unprecedentedly bitter form. The members of the former 'Democratic Centralism' group, who for many years have struggled against the party line, form the nucleus of the opposition. Several former Central Committee members who, on Lenin's proposal, were not re-elected at the X Congress (Preobrazhensky, Smirnov, Serebriakov), have attached themselves to this nucleus. This whole opposition bloc is headed by Trotsky and, therefore, has initially acquired a certain authority ...

3   POSITIVE RESULTS OF THE DISCUSSION

... The whole party's anxiety to ensure party unity has been emphasized with particular acuteness. The least hint of the possibility of a threat of schism has aroused and continues to arouse the sharpest and most violent protest on the part of the whole mass of party members. The party will politically annihilate anyone who makes an attempt on the unity of the party ranks. Party unity is more assured now than ever before.

4   PRACTICAL CONCLUSIONS

Considering the whole state of affairs in the party, the Conference considers the following to be necessary:

1   The size of the proletarian nucleus within the party, and its proportionate weight in the party's whole policy, must be augmented at whatever cost. During the forthcoming year an intensive effort must be made to recruit production workers so that not less than 100,000 new members will be brought into the RKP ranks from among these genuine proletarians. To this end it is necessary to facilitate in every way the entry of workers into the party. At the same time, during this very period, entry into the party for all non-proletarian elements must be absolutely closed. Within the party systematic propaganda must be conducted in order to make the whole party equal to its basic working-class nucleus.

2   To effect a stronger tie between the party and non-party persons the

effort must be made to ensure that in all soviets and in all Soviet organs non-party workers have adequate representation, not in words but in fact. The Central Committee of the party must exercise the strictest surveillance of the implementation of this decision and must resolutely call to order any local organizations which violate it.

3   Party organizations must be especially attentive in their explanations to those cells which in previous discussions have to some extent wavered in the matter of the party line. Explanation, explanation, and once again explanation – this is the main task that the party's basic cadre, above all, must shoulder.

4   Special attention must be given to explanatory work among youth. In view of the lack of financial means, the party must prefer to have a smaller contingent of students but improve their material situation and enhance the qualitative side of work in the institutions of higher education. Special measures must be taken to ensure correct party guidance of work with youth. The party cannot go so far as to flatter the youth, but neither can it permit a system of reprimands and bureaucratic tutelage. The only way to reach the goal is through patient explanation of the foundations of leninism.

5   One of the most important tasks is to attribute due importance to the study of RKP history and, above all, of the principal facts of the struggle of bolshevism with menshevism, the role of the various factions and tendencies during that struggle and, in particular, of those eclectic factions which strove to 'reconcile' bolshevism with menshevism. The Central Committee of the party must adopt a number of measures aimed at publishing suitable numbers of texts on the history of the RKP and also making it obligatory to teach party history in all party schools, institutions of higher education, circles, etc.

6   It is necessary to follow the lead of the largest proletarian organizations and set up, in all our organizations, circles for the study of leninism; as their basic texts they will use, primarily, the collected works of Comrade Lenin and will make sure that such circles have adequate guidance.

7   The party's Central Organ (*Pravda*) must be given the appropriate staff to enable it to explain systematically the foundations of bolshevism and to conduct a campaign against all deviations from it.

8   The current discussion should be removed from the pages of *Pravda* and transferred to a special *Discussion Sheet* appearing jointly with *Pravda*.

9   Freedom of discussion within the party in no way means freedom to undermine party discipline. The Central Committee of the party and all local party centres must immediately take the strictest measures to maintain iron bolshevik discipline wherever attempts are being made to weaken it.

10   Decisive measures, up to expulsion from the party, must be adopted against the spreading of unverified rumours and prohibited documents, and

against analogous techniques preferred by unprincipled groups infected with petty bourgeois attitudes.

11   Information on the activities of the Central Committee, and on intra-party life generally, must become more available. To this end, stenographic reports of the meetings of Central Committee plenums must be circulated to all members and candidate members of the Central Committee and the Central Control Commission, as well as to oblast and guberniia committees. *Pravda, Izvestiia tsentral'noga komiteta*, and other newspapers at the centre and at local levels must give broad coverage to party life. A special information section must be set up in the Central Committee of the party.

12   Special attention should be given to a correct and sound organization of party work in the army. The party must punish with particular severity any attempts to engage in factional 'work' in the ranks of the Red Army.

13   The Conference considers it entirely appropriate once again to support wholeheartedly and unreservedly the resolution of the X Congress which prohibited factional groupings. The Conference considers it necessary to propose that the XIII Congress confirm this resolution in the name of the supreme organ of the party.

14   The Conference orders the Central Committee to publish the previously unpublished seventh paragraph of the resolution 'On Party Unity' adopted, at Comrade Lenin's proposal, by the X Congress, which entitles a joint meeting of the Central Committee and the Central Control Commission by a two-thirds majority to demote from member to candidate member, or even to expel from the party, any Central Committee member who has violated party discipline or has 'tolerated factionalism.'

15   The Conference cannot overlook the decision of the last Moscow guberniia conference, brought to the attention of the whole party, to create a factional grouping in Moscow undermining party unity. The Conference assumes that the party Central Committee and Central Control Commission will at once take the most resolute measures, up to expulsion from the party, against those who, in the main political centre of the USSR, are attempting to split the party's ranks.

Considering the all-Russian discussion of these issues to be terminated, the Conference calls on all party organizations to pass to business-like work. The fundamental premise of the further successes of the proletarian revolution is the unwavering unity of the party – the leading party of the proletarian dictatorship. Party unity must be guarded as the apple of one's eye. The Conference is convinced that the Central Committee, around whom, as the outcome of the discussion has shown, the whole party has once again rallied, will firmly guard this unity.

Plenum of the Central Committee   29, 31 January 1924

As was stipulated at the XII Congress (2.35), all decisions of a party conference had to be approved by the Central Committee. This Central Committee
plenum publicly demonstrated that superior position by approving resolutions, with minor additions, adopted earlier in the month at the XIII Party
Conference: on party construction, on the current tasks of economic policy,
and on the 'petty bourgeois deviation' (2.38). It also took the occasion of
Lenin's death to announce the 'Lenin Enrolment' of ordinary industrial
workers into the party (2.39), a policy shift favoured by Lenin which tended
to submerge the role of the intelligentsia in the party but also in the long run
strengthened Stalin's position in relation to his various rivals.

2.39
On the Admission of Production Workers
to Party Membership   31 January 1924

I

Along with the recovery of industry in this past period, and the recovery
and growth of the proletariat, there has been a growth in the appeal of our
party to the workers. The last Conference took note of this increased
interest of production workers in entering the ranks of our party and
adopted a resolution calling on the RKP to draw not less than 100,000
production workers into its ranks. The death of V.I. Lenin has aroused
tremendous sympathy on the part of the workers both for Comrade Lenin
himself and for the Communist Party whose leader he was from the moment of its birth. The enhancement of the party's appeal for the workers
has recently become exceptionally great. All this confronts the party with
the task of conducting a broad and energetic campaign to bring production
workers into our party's ranks. At the same time this campaign must
subsequently serve to enhance the party's continuing and systematic work
to bring production workers into the party and to increase the proportionate weight of this part of the party. The slogans of this campaign must be:
'Production workers, steadfast partisans of the proletarian revolution –
join the RKP! Proletarians! Send the best, progressive, honourable, and
bold fighters into the ranks of the party!' The immediate goals of this
campaign are to be met in three months.

II

All party organizations from top to bottom must set as their foremost party
goal the planned conduct of this campaign to draw production workers into
the party. All the party's organizational and ideological educational work

must concentrate its principal effort in the months to come on this basic party task.

III

Only production workers are to be taken into the party. The conditions established by the XII Party Congress governing the number and period of party membership of sponsors remain in force. Whenever production workers are unable to submit the statutory recommendations, party committees must within one month organize meetings between comrades who are party members with the right to issue recommendations for entry into the party and workers who want to enter the RKP. Party committees are entitled to examine the applications of comrades for entry into the party without recommendations (if the comrade cannot supply them) provided that the party organization, helped by general meetings of workers, shall have adequately verified these candidacies.

IV

It is desirable that the candidacy of workers applying for entry into the party be first discussed at a general meeting of the workers of the enterprise, thus to facilitate the party's task of conducting the necessary verification of these candidacies. The effort should be made to secure the most active possible participation of non-party workers in the evaluation of the worker candidate for entry into the party. In this way it is necessary to strive to select the best, the staunchest, and the most active workers for admission into the party on the one hand, and the overall strengthening of our party's ties with the broad non-party working-class masses on the other. The candidacy of those desiring to enter the party are submitted to the cell for its approval after the opinion of the general workers' meeting has been made known.

V

Applications for admission into the party may be submitted both by individual workers and by groups of workers. But persons are admitted into the party only after preliminary examination of each individual candidacy.

The resolution of the XII Party Congress calls for especially painstaking examination of the candidacies of those who have formerly been members of other parties.

VI

The task of bringing production workers into the party's ranks means that particular attention must be directed to intensifying the recruitment of the Komsomol working-class youth, especially in view of the fact that this will reinforce the party nucleus of the Komsomol and, at the same time, strengthen its purely proletarian part.

VII

The Central Committee recognizes the necessity of reviewing the existing resolution on schools of political education for candidate members of the party to ensure that these schools of political education concentrate principal attention on party history and the exceptional role in it played by the guiding ideas of Comrade Lenin.

The Central Committee places all party organizations under the obligation of concentrating their attention and the principal forces of the party on ensuring that the newly admitted production workers pass most rapidly and correctly through the candidates' schools of political education.

Izvestiia tsentral'nogo komiteta,   *KPSS v rezoliutsiiakh* III, 14–16
2 February 1924

2.40
The Main Current Tasks of the Party
in the Sphere of the Press   6 February 1924

As a result of the internal and external situation of the republic and the growing upsurge in the cultural and political level of the advanced stratum of workers and peasants, the role of the press is growing rapidly. It is of particularly vital importance:

1   As one of the most important forms of ties between the party and the working and peasant masses, and of influence of the towns on the countryside;

2   As a tool for strengthening the party and achieving a closing of party ranks.

3   As a means for disseminating knowledge among the worker and peasant masses and for raising their cultural and political level.

In accordance therewith, it is necessary that press matters be placed in the centre of the party's attention.

I

IN THE SPHERE OF THE PEASANT PRESS

A *a*   The task for the coming year is to raise the mass of workers and peasants which is, as yet, untouched by the press, to the level already achieved by workers in industrial areas, as concerns the supplying of the population with newspapers. The circulation of the central *Krest'ianskaia gazeta* [Peasant Gazette] is to be brought up to 200,000 copies by spring, with particularly intensive work being done among Red Army men and among teachers.

b In the field of serving the peasant, it is necessary to render all possible support to the uezd and gubernia peasant newspapers. The Press Section of the Central Committee is to work out a concrete plan for the network of uezd peasant newspapers, with provision for the network to conform to the particular conditions of the various regions, while striving to enlarge the areas that these newspapers serve (the okrug newspapers in the Ukraine), and to reorient them toward serving the peasantry, while at the same time closing down uezd newspapers that do not serve the peasants or the workers. It is essential that the instruction of the uezd newspapers be strengthened and that their staffs be improved; model uezd newspapers (as many as ten) are to be set up in a number of agricultural guberniia.

c Over the entire range of peasant newspapers, primary importance is to be accorded to questions of the republic's economic and political situation as viewed from the standpoint of strengthening the union of the working class and the peasantry, together with elucidating questions of co-operatives and disseminating agronomic measures susceptible of mass application and capable of yielding at least a minimum strengthening and improvement of the peasant farm. It is also necessary that particular attention be devoted in the peasant newspaper to elucidating questions of everyday life, particularly for the peasant woman.

d The People's Commissariat of Education and the Central Committee of the State Committee on Workers' Education are to take all possible measures to establish ties between both the central peasant newspaper and the local peasant newspapers, on the one hand, and village teachers, on the other, in order to turn them into one of the support points for the dissemination and reading of the peasant newspaper and for the organization of a network of village correspondents.

e The network of Red Army newspapers is to be strengthened by providing them with the appropriate funding and with qualified staff. The management of the Red Army press is to be strengthened and this press is to be used not simply for the purpose of military and political education for the Red Army masses, but also to exercise influence on the village through the Red Army. In connection with the present-day situation, the entire press, both central and local, is to devote greater attention to making known the daily life and conditions in the Red Army and Navy. Moreover, every effort is to be made to facilitate the supplying of Red Army personnel (the nationalities) with newspapers in their native languages.

f It is recommended that the Komsomol central committee, together with the Press Section of the Central Committee, proceed to a review of their press and to the creation of weekly organs of the Komsomol, above all in the national republics in the local languages.

IN THE SPHERE OF THE NATIONAL PRESS

B *a*   It is deemed necessary to allocate to the budget of national republics and oblasts, certain material resources earmarked for the press in the non-Russian languages, and to cover deficits out of the subsidies provided for in the all-union budget and disbursed through the appropriate oblast sections of the press.

b   It is advised that the Russian-language press published in the national republics be reviewed with a view toward reducing to the greatest possible extent sectional publications of the type intended for the apparat, and to use the resources freed in this way to develop the press in the local languages.

c   The Press Section is ordered to study, as a first priority, all forms of newspapers in local languages (wall newspapers, printed newspapers, etc.) and to set up – in accordance with the cultural level and local conditions of the given national oblast – a newspaper for the peasants (oral, wall, printed, and adapted for reading aloud), and in so doing, to bear in mind the experience of the Ukraine in organizing readings of the press by 'readers.'

d   The Accounts and Assignment Section is ordered, together with the Press Section, to strengthen the press of the various nationalities with politically sound editorial and writing staff, while at the same time strengthening at the Press Section the work of supervising and guiding the press in the autonomous and independent republics.

e   At the same time, leading newspapers for party members in the local languages must be strengthened in the larger republics.

IN THE SPHERE OF THE WORKERS' PRESS

C *a*   The work of strengthening ties between the party and the working class is to be continued through the workers' newspapers, with a maximum of attention being devoted to questions of the republic's political situation, to questions of economic policy, wage rates, politics, earnings, etc., on both an all-republic and local scale.

b   Party committees are to devote particular attention to the content of workers' newspapers in order to achieve a businesslike discussion in them of the basic economic and political questions of interest to the working masses, as well as of questions of everyday life. Regular coverage is to be given to the work and line of the directing bodies, and of the party directing bodies in particular.

c   Wall and oral newspapers are to be developed at places of work and army posts, and they are to be adapted to the political and economic tasks of the moment.

IN THE SPHERE OF THE TRADE UNION PRESS

Party organizations are to devote particular attention to the trade union press and to provide it with the necessary cadres of journalistic party staff workers. The trade union newspapers that presently exist, which are not intended to serve the broad circles of workers, must be reorganized into mass weekly workers' newspapers and magazines. They must concentrate primary attention on serving the day-to-day economic and cultural needs of the working class, linking them with the general tasks of the trade union movement, and must – as a first order of business – focus attention on the work of the factory trade union committees, of the meetings of delegates and of the all-union organizations, enhancing their authority and linking to them the broad masses of the proletariat.

II
IN THE SPHERE OF THE LEADING PRESS
In the leading press organs, which are of particularly great importance as a means for unifying the party, it is essential that first prominence be given to questions of party policy, both in the sphere of international relations as well as in that of domestic economic and general policy. The leading party newspapers must give the party member a party orientation, avoiding superficial agitation and a narrowly departmental elucidation of questions, while giving more facts and giving them in a more planned and systematic fashion. A start is to be made on systematically exposing basic deviations and on waging a systematic ideological struggle against them. The 'Party Life' section of the newspapers is to be improved. Attention is to be given to the need to simplify the language (particularly in the workers' newspapers and in those for peasants).

The leading press is to be set the task of exposing the basic questions that are of interest to the broad party masses. It is to continue and deepen the broad discussion of the questions of party life in the area of the 'scissors crisis,' earnings, etc., enlisting in the discussion on as broad a basis as possible, Communists who work in the primary party cells.

It is necessary that the press provide a full and comprehensive discussion of all the new party tasks resulting from the immense growth in the worker core of the party, that it provide a comprehensive service to the new party members in the sphere of political education, and that it enlist them in the work of the workers' correspondents. In the present circumstances, the role of party newspapers as 'collective organizers' must be developed to the utmost.

III
IN THE SPHERE OF BOOK PUBLISHING
A   It is necessary to step up the work of creating popular books for

workers and peasants. The necessary regrouping of human and financial resources must be carried out in order to strengthen as much as possible the editions of popular, inexpensive books for peasants – political works, reference books, entertaining fiction on revolutionary themes, and works on agronomic methods susceptible of mass application. Particular attention is to be devoted to the creation and dissemination of a Soviet textbook for the peasant elementary school, a task that has great cultural and political significance.

B   In the sphere of book publishing in the non-Russian languages, the Press Section, together with the People's Commissariat of Education and representatives of the central and local publishing houses of the various nationalities, are to work out measures to put the local publishing houses on a sound footing, such that they respond to the true needs of the popular masses and are capable of creating a mass readership. The work is to centre on the publication of the necessary quantity of popularized marxist literature and political literature for the village, and of textbooks for the peasant school. In so doing, however, no duplication of effort is to be permitted. In the national republics, and in particular in the Ukraine and Central Asia, the number of Russian books being published and republished is to be cut to the maximum extent possible. The centre of gravity of book publishing is to be moved to the various local areas. It is considered imperative that a special party publishing house of the *Krasnaia Nov* [Red Virgin Soil] type be set up under the central committee of the Ukrainian Communist Party.

C   With a view toward assisting the efforts at self-education of both non-party and Communist workers who have no opportunity to study regularly, a series of 'libraries' is to be created on questions of the history of the party and of the international workers' movement, on the natural sciences, technology, etc. Publication of a cycle of books of the 'home university' type is to be undertaken; in particular, a series is to be created for the average party member, consisting of ten to fifteen books covering the basic questions of the development of society toward communism, party construction, and the Soviet system.

IV

A basic condition for achieving success is that of reducing the cost of newspapers and books and improving the distribution apparatus. In order to accomplish the necessary regrouping of means, there is to be a further decisive cutback in official literature (of not less than 50 per cent by 1 January), including the literature serving the guberniia party apparatus. All the basic elements in the price of books are to be reviewed with a view toward a decisive price reduction. State price reductions and subsidies are to be concentrated on peasant and non-Russian books and newspapers, and the necessary sums are to be allocated to the all-union budget within two weeks' time. The size of the sum is to be determined by a commission composed of Comrade Sokolnikov, who is to serve without replacement, and comrades Iakovlev and Rudzutak, with Comrade Molotov as their replacement. In the sphere of distribution, it is recommended that all distribution agencies (contracting agencies, the Central Union of Consumer Co-operatives, the People's Commissariat of Posts and Telegraph) concentrate their forces and monetary resources on moving books and newspapers from the guberniia centre to the uezd and village.

V

The Press Section, with the help of the People's Commissariat of Education and with the co-operation of Rabkrin, is to strengthen its guidance and overseeing of the work of the state and party publishing houses (the Main Russian Literature Administration) of the central press, the nationality press, and the distribution agencies; it is to conduct the work of studying the activities of the publishing houses jointly with the latter organizations. The Central Committee's Accounts and Assignment Section and Press Section, in accordance with the resolution of the xii Party Congress [On the Questions of Propaganda, Press, and Agitation], are advised to improve systematically the quality of the people who staff the press, both by transferring to newspaper work comrades with extensive party and political experience – in the first place those in the larger worker centres, in border areas and in the Ukraine, as well as by training new staff in schools.

The editorial and publishing staffs of the major party and Soviet publishing houses are to be reviewed and strengthened. An exact accounting of press staffing arrangements is to be completed not later than 1 January. The Press Section is to strengthen its live instruction in the local areas by arranging more frequent trips by instructors and also by meetings of staffers from newspapers and publishing houses of the same type. In Moscow, Kharkov, Leningrad, and Tiflis, regular meetings of the responsible editors of the central newspapers are to be held under the direction of the Central Committee Press Section.

At the same time, it is deemed necessary quickly to create and strengthen agencies for the direction of the press in all oblast centres and central guberniia cities where major press and publishing activities are carried on ...

Izvestiia tsentral'nogo komiteta,
March 1924

XIII Party Congress   23–31 May 1924

The attacks on Trotsky by Stalin, Zinoviev, and Kamenev continued at the XIII Party Congress, the first after Lenin's death. Zinoviev did not waste any time, in his political report of the Central Committee (this was the last time he had the opportunity to deliver it) to ridicule and isolate Trotsky by accusing him, unjustly, of responsibility for the formation of factions and groupings. He taunted Trotsky for his charges of lack of intra-party democracy and secretarial bureaucratism by arguing that the party needed '... a thousand times bigger monolith than so far ...' and concluded by issuing a challenge to Trotsky to get up before the Congress, as was worthy of a Bolshevik, and admit: 'I made a mistake, and the party was right.'

Trotsky accepted the challenge and made what may well be the most inept speech of his career. On the one hand he argued that he may have exaggerated the meaning of intra-party democracy by turning the slogan into an absolute, but if these exaggerations did take place, did not the Central Committee resolution (resolution of the Politburo of 5 December 1923) 'give us the full right to say that they stemmed from other negative and painful phenomena?' and 'Were these exaggerations in the sphere of intra-party democracy not a reaction to exaggerations in the intra-party bureaucracy which threatens to alienate the masses from the party?'

On the other hand, he argued that no one could be right against the party for 'In the final analysis the party is always right because it is the only historical instrument given to the proletariat for the solution of its fundamental problems.' He concluded with what, at least temporarily, amounted to a capitulation: 'When the party passes a decision which one or another among us finds unjust then he says: just or unjust, but this is my party, and I shall bear the consequences of its decisions to the end.'

The debate, which also included Kamenev's vitriolic attack on Trotsky and Stalin's noncommital organizational report but far more outspoken concluding remarks, was finally ended by Lenin's widow, Krupskaia, who, rather inconsistently, remarked that, 'Comrade Trotsky said that the party is always right. If this were so it would not be necessary to have such bitter discussions' and then fully endorsed the Central Committee policy of Stalin and Zinoviev. Her motion to end the debate was carried.

Krupskaia's endorsement of Stalin and Zinoviev was all the more surprising since her attempt to make the Congress familiar with the most crucial note of Lenin's Testament, in which Lenin criticized the individual leaders and especially Stalin, whom he proposed to remove as General Secretary, was thwarted by the two. The Testament was, however, read to the senoren konvent, which was again set up at this Congress, with instructions that while the delegations were to be informed about the contents, they were not to discuss the notes on the floor or divulge them to the public. Trotsky, who was present at the meeting of the senoren konvent, did not take advantage of this unique opportunity and remained silent. Stalin, as a result of the notes, offered to resign at the Central Committee meeting following the Congress, but the whole meeting, which included Trotsky, insisted that he continue in his work. (Stalin volunteered this information at the Joint Plenum of the Central Committee and the Central Control Commission on 23 October 1927; see Stalin, *Works* x, Moscow 1954–5, 13 volumes, 181; hereafter cited as *Works*).

The acceptance of the Central Committee report [2.41], which was moved by the presidium 'in the name of many delegations,' was announced as unanimous. According to the official record, this vote was followed by stormy, prolonged applause after which the delegates rose and sang the 'International,' yet another sign of the ponderous stalinist style in public party politics which placed any dissident in a difficult position.

Another manifestation of this style was apparently engineered by Zinoviev, on his own behalf. During one of the Congress sessions there appeared 'tens of thousands of teachers' in the Red Square 'to greet the XIII Congress.' A delegation of these was admitted to the Congress hall and their spokesman delivered a brief speech in which he showered praise on Zinoviev.

After the initial excitement the Congress settled down to a seemingly businesslike treatment of other matters among which were the control commissions (2.42), press (2.43), agitprop (2.45), as well as treatment of the Revision Commission, Comintern, party construction, guberniia party conferences and secretaries, domestic trade, co-operatives, work in the countryside, work with youth, cultural work, and work among women workers and peasants.

The Congress, attended by 748 delegates with a deciding vote and 416 with a consultative vote, was very clearly packed by Stalin and Zinoviev supporters, many of whom were present illegally. The Politburo, before the Congress, gave to those new candidate members admitted to the party under the so-called Lenin Enrolment the right to elect delegates to the Congress. This was, as Kamenev admitted himself, at the opening of the Congress, 'a formal violation of our Rules.' As he further explained, the Central Committee felt the gesture reflected the general view of the party and believed that the Congress would approve it – which it did unanimously.

While the Congress in its entirety was well prepared and conducted, there occurred one incident when the delegates got out of hand, to the obvious embarrassment of the presidium. The incident was a result of a rather innocuous suggestion by Molotov in his report on party construction to the effect that the guberniia conference should meet twice a year instead of once a year as was resolved at the XII Congress [2.35]. The proposal, apparently for purely technical reasons, aroused considerable hostility and was defeated by 266 votes to 259. Molotov proposed a compromise resolution which would relieve certain party organizations of the second yearly conference provided the Central Committee gave its approval. The motion passed by 322 votes to 246. The large number of abstentions in both instances was not explained.

Still in the spirit of Lenin's recommendations to the XII Congress and still playing into Stalin's hands, the Congress once more significantly enlarged the Central Committee to fifty-three members and thirty-four candidates. After the Congress, the Central Committee elected Bukharin to a full member of the Politburo to fill Lenin's place, and added Dzerzhinsky, Sokolnikov, and Frunze as candidates, all of whom, with the exception of Sokolnikov, were supporters of Stalin at the time.

2.41
On the Central Committee Report 27 May 1924

The XIII Congress entirely supports the Central Committee's correct political line and organizational work, which have brought the party major successes in all areas of work in a difficult and complex time. The Congress notes with satisfaction that for the last reporting period, which was the first year of Central Committee work during which the Central Committee and the whole party were deprived of Comrade Lenin's immediate leadership, the Central Committee's work was correct.

The Congress fully and completely affirms the resolutions of the XIII Party Conference 'On Party Construction' and 'On the Results of the Discussion and on Petty Bourgeois Deviation [2.38] resolving that these resolutions be included among the resolutions of the XIII Party Congress. The Congress gives its full support to the party Central Committee for the firmness and bolshevik implacability which it displayed during the discussion – defending the foundations of leninism against petty bourgeois deviations.

The Congress supports the Central Committee's foreign policy which has led to the de jure recognition of the Union of Soviet Socialist Republics by a number of major bourgeois states.

The Congress instructs the Central Committee to continue to display maximum caution in the granting of concessions, with all resoluteness to uphold the foreign trade monopoly, to develop the export of grain, and to give thought to securing a favourable balance in our foreign trade.

In view of the new international situation, and, in particular, in view of how insistently all sections of the international bourgeoisie are attempting to force the USSR to pay off tsarist debts and to pay for nationalizing the property of the major foreign capitalists, the Congress considers it especially important to acquaint the working population of the USSR, and of the villages in particular, more carefully and systematically with all the most important resolutions of the party and the Soviet power on questions of international politics.

The Congress notes with satisfaction that the formation of the Union of Soviet Socialist Republics has been successfully completed, thus creating a firm foundation for the brotherly and peaceful coexistence of all the nationalities inhabiting the USSR.

The Congress instructs the Central Committee to take pains to ensure that all nationalities of the USSR, without exception, possess the rights prescribed by the resolutions on the national question adopted at the XII Congress of the RKP.

The Congress notes that the party's NEP has coped with the tasks which the party set.

An overall economic advance has been clearly outlined on the basis of this new economic policy; without any doubt, agriculture is moving forward; state industry is growing and becoming more highly concentrated; wages are gradually rising, and definite successes are being registered in the increase of labour productivity.

The party has conducted and is conducting a successful struggle against divergence in the prices of agricultural and industrial products. On this basis the confidence of the working class in the party is growing and becoming increasingly firm and whole-hearted.

The party sees no grounds for revising the NEP and considers its next task to be the systematic strengthening of socialist elements in the economy on the basis of the NEP.

The party's unchanged task remains the strengthening and consolidation of the peasants' confidence in the proletarian state by adopting a number of real measures to forge an economic bond between the city and the countryside, to promote the peasant economy (agricultural credit, etc.) and to elevate the cultural level of the village.

The Congress notes that the Central Committee put through a timely and broadly thought out currency reform which is of gigantic significance for the whole economic advance of the socialist proletariat. The firm implementation of this major reform will serve to place the whole economic life of the USSR on a healthy basis. Noting with satisfaction the successes achieved in this area, the Congress instructs all local organizations to ensure the most precise and exact implementation of all decisions of central organs relating to the currency reform, bearing in mind that difficulties in this area may be anticipated and that they will be avoided only through application of maximum discipline.

The Congress notes with approval the timely initiative of the Central

Committee in such fundamental questions as that of internal trade and co-operation. These questions become central for a whole period of time. Further successes in the economic construction of the USSR depend upon the correctness of party policy in these questions. The Congress notes that the Central Committee clearly perceives the inevitability, in the present NEP period, of the growth of a new bourgeoisie and is taking all the necessary economic and political measures which this fact implies.

The Congress notes with special satisfaction the Central Committee's political initiative and work in connection with the Lenin Enrolment. After the loss of class consciousness had ceased among the proletariat, after Soviet power had achieved its first significant successes on the economic front, it became possible to bring into the party ranks hundreds and thousands of new members – production workers. The party was and remains a workers' party. The party's tie with numerous non-party workers is strengthening and growing. The time is drawing near when the whole basic mass of the proletariat of our Union will come into the party. The Congress instructs the Central Committee to conduct all its work in such a way that in the very near future the overwhelming majority of party members will consist of workers directly occupied in production.

The Congress directs the particular attention of the whole party to the need for strengthening efforts among women workers and peasants and for advancing them into all party and Soviet electoral organs. The Congress supports the Central Committee's allocation of particular attention to the Komsomol and to all work among the worker and peasant youth.

The rise in the political activity of the working masses confronts our party with the serious task of involving the broad masses in active work in the soviets, the unions, and in the co-operatives.

The Congress instructs all party organizations to devote intensified attention to establishing closer ties with the best part of village and city teachers, the agronomists, and the other strata of the toiling village intelligentsia. To this end the party must first of all devote serious attention to improving the material position of these strata. If it follows a correct line in this matter the party can rapidly make these strata the bearers of the fundamental ideas of the party and Soviet power among the broad peasant masses. All party organizations must, in particular, devote sufficient attention to preparing the first all-union congress of teachers, and must ensure that the great majority of teachers from the rural areas are enabled to participate in this congress so that it will really carry out the gigantic task imposed upon it by the whole current situation.

As regards the promotion of state industry, the major task of the ensuing period is the advancement of metallurgy. Now that the fuel problem is settled, transportation improved, and currency reform begun – it is the turn of metal. Securing production of the means of production within the Union means creating a genuinely solid basis for a socialist economy and to a considerable extent freeing ourselves of the necessity to place large orders abroad. The Congress instructs the Central Committee to devote serious attention to this problem.

The Congress instructs the Central Committee to devote more attention than hitherto to the electrification of the USSR, to do everything possible for the implementation of the whole electrification plan which is of such gigantic significance for the consolidation of our economy and, thus, for the strengthening of socialism.

The Congress welcomes the measures undertaken by the Central Committee to put through the very timely reform in the military area and to increase the number of party workers in it. In connection with the role of territorial formations in the country's defence, the Congress directs the party's attention to the need for the most energetic work on strengthening the communist influence in them. The Congress instructs the Central Committee to adopt a series of measures to heighten the number of Communists among Red Army soldiers and Red sailors.

The Congress notes the regular fruitful work of the Central Committee plenum and of the joint sessions of the Central Committee and Central Control Commission plenums. Experience has shown that increasing the composition of the Central Committee by bringing into it those local party workers who have the best ties with the masses has been very beneficial. The Congress recognizes the necessity of further increasing the composition of the Central Committee and the Central Control Commission.

The Congress finds that the Central Committee should devote particularly serious attention to the reduction and simplification of the state apparatus.

The Congress feels that an immediate task of the party is to improve the functioning of the co-operatives and of trade and credit institutions, and to increase the number of party members in them.

The Congress considers it necessary that even more serious and extensive support be given by the party to the communist institutions of higher education than has previously been the case. The Congress instructs the Central Committee to devote full attention to the improvement of work in the institutions of higher education. By a serious approach to the work, by propaganda for leninism, and by elucidating disputed questions the party will succeed in gaining the support of the best among the young students.

The Congress finds that the verification of the individual composition of certain groups of party cells, undertaken with the approval of the Central Committee, was timely and will be very useful for the party.

The Congress instructs the Central Committee to continue, just as firmly and resolutely as before, to protect party unity and the enduring bolshevik line from any sort of deviation. Now that the party has lost Comrade Lenin, the task of ensuring full party unity has become even more important and necessary than before. The smallest factional activity must be punished in the severest fashion. A firm and monolithic RKP, based on the unwavering principles of leninism, is the major prerequisite for further successes of the revolution.

2.42
On the Work of the Control Commissions 27 May 1924

While confirming the resolution of the previous congress on the tasks of the Central Control Commission and Rabkrin and also on their methods of work, the XIII Party Congress considers it necessary, in the light of the experience acquired, to give the following supplementary instructions:

1 The interest displayed by all guberniia and oblast party conferences in the reports of the control commissions and Rabkrin manifests how urgent is the need for a reorganization of the local control commissions and Rabkrin on the basis of the resolutions of the XII Party Congress on the Central Control Commission and Rabkrin and demonstrate that adequate conditions for this reorganization exist. In the light of this the Congress resolves that the merger of the control commission and Rabkrin shall be extended to all local organs and that the Central Control Commission will have one of the principal tasks of guiding the operations of the local organs and of establishing the closest link between them and the centre.

2 Concentration of the efforts of Central Control Commission members in the centres, as provided by the previous Central Control Commission structure, is of great positive significance for reasons already given by Vladimir Ilyich: precisely this circumstance makes it possible to mold the Central Control Commission members into a cohesive group which collectively develops measures to improve the state apparatus and to counteract attempts to violate party unity. But, on the other hand, such a concentration of Central Control Commission members in the centre makes it much more difficult for them to be constantly aware of everything occurring in the party and among the broad working masses. In order to retain the positive aspects of the previous Central Control Commission organization and at the same time to fill the above organizational gap and further to implement Comrade Lenin's planned reorganization of the Central Control Commission and Rabkrin, the Congress resolves that:

   a Seventy Central Control Commission members are to work constantly in the Central Control Commission and Rabkrin at the centre, and approximately twenty of these must be production workers, primarily from the bench, and peasants actually engaged in farming.

Central Control Commission members destined for work in the Central Control Commission and Rabkrin must be entirely released from any prior assignments.

b Fifty Central Control Commission members are to be elected from among party members who are production workers and, after being elected, are to continue in production work.

c Thirty Central Control Commission members, after election, are to remain at the local level to work with the local organs of the control commissions and Rabkrin in the largest and most important oblast and guberniia organizations.

d The Central Control Commission members who will be working directly in the Central Control Commission and Rabkrin (except for the twenty production workers and peasants) should have been party members for at least ten years. The Central Control Commission members working in the local organizations must have been members since at least before February [1917], and the peasants and factory workers – since at least before October [1917].

Individual exceptions can be made to the party membership requirements which must be met by candidates for Central Control Commission membership, especially in national oblasts and republics.

e The rights and obligations of Central Control Commission members, both those remaining in production and those working in the central and local organs of the control commissions, are defined in the special instruction being worked out by the Central Control Commission.

f The XIII Congress resolves to change the resolution of the XII Congress as follows: the Central Control Commission plenum elects a Central Control Commission presidium of fifteen persons and six candidates from among comrades of the highest qualifications in all respects, i.e., party workers of the Central Committee type.

g The XIII Congress resolves to change the resolution of the XII Congress as follows: the period of party membership required for members of the guberniia control commissions may be reduced from before February to before October [1917].

3   Comrade Lenin defined in the following way the party's task in the struggle for the state apparatus: 'We must strive to construct a state in which the workers would retain their guidance of the peasants as well as the peasants' confidence and with the greatest economy would eliminate from their social relations any traces of any sort of excesses whatsoever. We must reduce our state apparatus to the minimum. We must eliminate from it all traces of the excesses of which so many have remained from tsarist Russia, from her bureaucratic-capitalistic apparatus.'

The party can carry out this gigantic task only by turning 'for new forces to the deepest roots of our dictatorship,' i.e., by 'mobilizing the best of our workers' to study and improve the state apparatus and to eliminate all short-comings.

In addition to involving workers directly in administrative and economic organs, the efforts of the workers must also be mobilized around Rabkrin and the Central Control Commission which, according to the thoughts of Comrade Lenin and the resolution of the XII Congress, are organs for furthering the improvement of the state apparatus.

In view of this the Congress confirms the decision of the party Central Committee and the Central Control Commission to establish a close tie between Rabkrin organs and the factory committees and to call upon the trade union organs and the organs of party and soviet supervision to assist each other in improving production and administration.

The success of all efforts to improve the state apparatus is guaranteed only if the heads of the given organ or enterprise are involved in this work.

Therefore Rabkrin and trade union organs must avoid any work on improving the state apparatus, if done in isolation from the leaders of the corresponding organs, and must put through any improvements of the apparatus by working with these leaders who are the ones responsible for the affairs of the given organ or enterprise.

With the same aim of involving the broad worker and peasant masses in the improvement of the state apparatus, the work of the Central Control Commission and Rabkrin, as well as of the administrative and economic organs, must be publicized to the maximum, and there must be maximum agitation and propaganda of the ideas upon which V.I. Lenin based the reorganization of the Rabkrin and the Central Control Commission and a popularization of the tasks with which these organs have been entrusted by party resolutions.

The Congress directs the Central Control Commission in its day-to-day work to direct attention to the fact that often the party workers and the leaders of economic and trade union organs have no common language and no common line. The control commissions must have the task of helping both the Central Committee and the local party organs to unify and straighten out the policies of trade union and managerial staffs in constructing a workers' dictatorship and strengthening the union of the working class and the peasantry.

4   As regards the work of the party boards, the control commissions should not be transformed into exclusively judicial organs for the trial of violations of party Rules and of communist ethics. The control commissions must conduct a broad and systematic study of unhealthy phenomena in the party, both in the area of ideology and in that of organizational practice and the lives of party members. On the basis of this study the control commissions must work jointly with party committees to develop measures for eliminating the conditions which give rise to these unhealthy

phenomena and in their practice, before resorting to punishment, must make use essentially of party educational measures, in particular with respect to party members of worker or peasant origin, bearing in mind the cultural level of the party members, their conditions of life, national characteristics, etc. The control commissions must organize their work in such a way that random petty violations by party members, which do not harm the life of the organization and do not indicate that the party member committing the violation is fundamentally unsound, do not come before the control commission but are handled by the person's comrades.

In the adjudication of a case the control commissions must in no way follow a stereotyped approach in determining how best to act upon a given party member; a completely individualized approach must be adopted with respect to each party member who is called to account for some transgression, and all the circumstances and conditions of the particular transgression must be taken into account.

To ensure application of this line in the struggle against unhealthy phenomena, violations of the party Rules and of communist ethics, maximum attention must be devoted to the work of the party boards of the control commissions, and they must be selected from among the staunchest, most thoughtful, and most sensitive comrades. The party board must function under the direct and close supervision of the presidium of the control commission, and the head of the party board must be a member of the control commission presidium.

The Congress confirms the decision of the Central Control Commission to the effect that all control commission members in turn must participate in the adjudication of cases in party boards, and that ordinary party members from production cells must participate as party assessors.

5   To ensure a comprehensive and profound study of the state apparatus, leading to long-lasting and cardinal improvements, the Congress orders the control commissions and Rabkrin to limit to the utmost the number of objects of investigation and study, selecting from them those links of the state apparatus which are decisive for ensuring a close tie between the working class and the peasantry. The control commissions and Rabkrin must base their work on a definite plan which is approved by the party committees and the appropriate higher soviet organs (the Sovnarkom, the guberniia executive committee) and which is co-ordinated in advance with the national economic plan organs (Gosplan, the guberniia planning commission, the economic council, etc.) and with the leaders of the corresponding institutions.

6   Multiplicity and lack of co-ordination in the supervision of soviet and economic organs must be eliminated, since the presently existing situation disorganizes the administration and the economy, deprives the leader of

the institution or department of responsibility for the situation in his section of the state apparatus, and represents an irrational and uneconomical waste of effort which does not lead to any substantial results in the normalization of the administration and the economy.

In order to unify and co-ordinate the supervisory and revisional activities of the corresponding organs to a greater or lesser extent with the same or other tasks of those bodies which are concerned with the study or supervision of the state apparatus (Rabkrin, Gosplan, the Central Statistical Administration, the trade unions, the Financial Administration of the People's Commissariat of Finance, the Economic Administration of the GPU, etc.), the Congress hereby recognizes the necessity of obliging the Central Control Commission and Rabkrin to develop measures for unifying the activities of the above organs and concentrating in the control commissions and organs of Rabkrin the practical co-ordination of their supervisory and revisional functions and their study of the state apparatus.

7   In their study of the state apparatus and their investigations the control commissions and Rabkrin organs should not proceed from any preconceived ideas as to the unsuitability of the directors of the organs under study or investigation for the conduct of the affairs entrusted to them. Even at the present time the party's work on selecting the directors of institutions and economic organizations has yielded great and positive results, placing staunch and tested party members at the head of state and economic organs.

Communist managers are one detachment of the RKP who have been advanced to responsible work which is necessary for the whole working class. It must be borne in mind that their position is exceptionally complex under NEP conditions, surrounded by bourgeois elements, and that the party, following all their work attentively, must be extraordinarily solicitous with these workers who, in addition to their complete devotion to the party, have given proof of ability to acquire the experience needed for industrial administration. The party must assist these comrades in every way in their work and at the same time take care to ensure that such managers do not become isolated from the party organization and from the working masses.

But it must at the same time be borne in mind that the responsible role which the party assigns to these managers imposes precisely upon them the duty of carrying on their work of constant protection of state interests together, and in close connection, with the broad working masses and that the struggle against excesses of all kinds in the state apparatus, against a non-businesslike approach, bureaucratism, excesses in personal life, and abuse of official position can in no case be weakened by the party.

8   The Congress imposes upon the Central Control Commission and

Rabkrin the special task of watching over the correct implementation of all party resolutions on specialists, struggling resolutely against the various deviations observed in certain party members, in this area.

9   In order to fully ensure unity of leadership by party organizations and by the party as a whole, the Congress considers it essential to maintain a close tie between the control commissions and the party committees; this is to be expressed particularly in the obligatory participation of the representatives assigned by party committees in the sessions of the control commissions and in the latter's work generally.

10   The principal condition of success of Rabkrin and the control commissions is the selection of workers of genuinely good quality both with regard to the Communists and with regard to the specialists in various branches of the state administration and the economy. The Congress orders all party organizations to assign their best and most skilled members to work in organs of Rabkrin and the control commissions. All organizations must promote the selection of the best and most tested specialists for these organs, offering them the best, and not the worst, existential conditions when they are transferred to work on improving the state apparatus.

This selection of party workers of good quality for work in the control commissions and Rabkrin is possible only if the number of party workers in Rabkrin is reduced to the minimum, and if they are granted improved facilities, as was firmly pointed out by Comrade Lenin in his articles. In the light of this the Congress assigns the Central Committee and the higher soviet organs the task of supplying all Rabkrin organs, including the local ones, with means sufficient to raise employees and party workers in Rabkrin and the control commissions to a position which is not worse than that of the organs which they are investigating and reviewing.

Particular attention must be devoted to selecting the staff of inspectors of Rabkrin organs. Besides including members of the Central Control Commission and the guberniia control commissions, this staff of inspectors must be made up of responsible party members who must view their work of leading the investigations of the state apparatus, because of its responsible nature and decisiveness for the results of the work of the Rabkrin and the control commissions as a whole, as highly important creative work in governmental and party construction.

11   The Congress confirms the decision of the Central Committee and the Central Control Commission to carry out a verification of party members in soviet and higher educational cells and considers that the Central Committee and the Central Control Commission must henceforth conduct this purge in a planned manner, gradually encompassing one organization after another. This purge of the party members in soviet and higher educational cells must in no way be viewed as implying blanket distrust of all party members in soviet and economic work, nor of the teachers and students; it

was undertaken to help party members in the conduct of their work by removing those party members who are compromising the party and who ultimately impede the implementation of genuine party leadership and the proper ordering of the state apparatus.

2.43
On the Press 31 May 1924

1   The past year has been characterized by a growth in the volume of the periodical press (from two to three million), by a consolidation of its material position, by qualitative improvement, and by a strengthening of its ties with the broad toiling masses through worker, peasant, military, and other correspondents – who are elements of a true workers' democracy. Together with the major conquests in the dissemination of the workers' and party press, one must note the growth of the village press, headed by *Krest'ianskaia Gazeta*, which is winning over the individual subscriber, and also certain successes in increasing the printing of the nationality press. All of these achievements must serve only as the point of departure for further systematic work of increasing the printing of our papers and improving their quality. The task of the forthcoming year must be: *no party member who does not subscribe to and read the party newspaper; not one man or woman worker, or Red Army man, who does not read a newspaper; two million newspapers into the villages – not less than one newspaper for each ten peasant homes.*

2   Under present conditions the press takes on particular significance as an instrument for educating and organizing the toiling masses. The tie between the press and the masses must be strengthened, the press must be brought closer to the masses, and the principal effort must be concentrated on explaining the fundamental questions of life of the millions of workers and peasants. This must determine the tasks and the contents of the party, worker, and peasant newspapers and the books for the corresponding strata.

3   In accord with the cultural and political growth of the working class, the mass workers' press must intensify and deepen its elucidation of political and economic questions (the international position of the USSR, the world workers' movement, questions of finance, co-operation and trade, of wages, industry, and agriculture, of the activities of the control commissions and Rabkrin in improving the state apparatus), linking this with questions of factory life and production (the experience of *Gudok* [Whistle]). The workers' press must also satisfy readers' demands in matters of general education and must devote systematic attention to scientific, technical, and literary questions (columns, surveys, bibliography). Workers'

papers must systematically discuss village life from the viewpoint of consolidating the union of the working class and the peasantry.

Further work must be done on the language of the newspapers and on the skilful combination of maximum popular appeal and clarity of exposition with serious and comprehensive content.

4   A very important task of the workers' press is to service the needs of the Lenin Enrolment, its training in the bolshevik spirit, and its involvement in practical work (party and social).

In this connection it is necessary to create an all-union mass party newspaper and at the same time to intensify the discussion of matters of party policy, party construction, party life, and the propaganda of leninism in all organs of the mass workers' press.

5   The Congress considers it necessary to impress upon our party, Soviet, and trade union press their duty of especially careful analysis of the work of the co-operatives, especially their lower-level organs and of a businesslike presentation of propaganda for the co-operatives, noting true practical achievements, local initiative, and experience, unmasking speculation and abuse of private trading capital, unifying the masses in the struggle against private capital and at the same time subjecting to severe criticism all abuses, bureaucratism, sloppiness, and incorrect conduct (choice of goods, false expenses) of co-operative construction. Party organs must be more attentive to the co-operative press and must assign party workers to it.

6   The Congress notes with satisfaction the considerable successes achieved by *Pravda* in expanding its press run and improving its contents, and, in particular, as regards its handling of questions of party life. The Congress instructs the Central Committee to assign the necessary staff to the party's central organ, *Pravda*, to enable it systematically to explain the foundations of bolshevism and to wage a campaign against any deviations from it. It is also necessary to strengthen and improve the leading party organs in the national republics and the major centres, incorporating in them generally sections on 'party life.'

7   The trade union press must become a mass press and must concentrate its principal attention on servicing the daily economic and cultural needs of the working class, tying them in with the overall tasks of the trade union movement; it must devote attention, in the first place, to the work of the factory committees, delegates' meetings, and union organizations, heightening their authority and uniting them with the broad proletarian masses. The trade union press must be in closer contact with its readers and subscribers (mass recruitment of trade union correspondents at the lower levels, transition to individual subscriptions). The mass trade union journals must take the course of servicing the broad circles of lower-level trade union workers and leading members of the unions. The party organs must promote the improvement and consolidation of the trade union press.

8   The press must be obliged to listen with maximum sensitivity to the demands and proposals emanating from the masses. The institution of worker correspondents must be consolidated in every way, and they must be carefully safeguarded from any sort of red tape or bureaucratism. The basic form of worker-correspondent organization must be their unification at the newspaper. Party assistance and guidance of the worker-correspondent movement must take the form of intensifying their communist education, of helping the newspapers to select worker-correspondents, of organizing political-educational work among the worker-correspondents (circles, clubs, short-term courses, congresses, etc.), and of helping them improve their professional skills as worker-correspondents. Intensified attention by the party and the trade unions to the worker-correspondents should in no way be transformed into tutelage (censorship of the lower-level cells, the factory committees, etc.). Party work in the worker-correspondent movement must be oriented toward the further mass involvement of fresh working-class cadres in this movement (especially those from the Lenin Enrolment) and toward a comprehensive strengthening and enhancement of the ties of the worker-correspondents with the masses, both in the production process and in everyday life.

9   In our press system wall newspapers take on ever-increasing significance as instruments of influence on the masses and as a technique for bringing to light their activity. The factory and plant newspapers already play a major role in the improvement of production, in its correct organization and in building a new way of life, in the struggle against illiteracy and religious prejudices. Wall newspaper work in the factories must be done with all possible assistance from, and under the leadership of, the party cells and the Komsomol. The party committees must enhance their leadership of wall newspaper work.

In the countryside the wall newspaper must become one of the most important forms of the work of village party and Komsomol cells. It must struggle for an improvement of the peasant economy, for the co-operatives, for an improvement in the cultural level of the village, for the interests of the weaker peasants, against the exploitative tendencies of the kulak and against administrative abuses. The village wall newspaper must be closely tied in with the reading room, the agricultural station and the school.

10   The network of peasant weekly newspapers must be extended, the existing peasant newspapers must be strengthened, their press runs increased, their content improved, and their ties with the peasants strengthened by a massive involvement of village correspondents through the 'reading aloud,' 'friends of the press,' 'recitation,' and other circles. The work of village correspondents must be comprehensively assisted by the party and soviet organs. An attentive attitude to letters from the peasants, the processing of all peasants' complaints in the soviets, legal

assistance to the peasants, the skilful combination of agricultural information with the explanation of general political and economic issues, in particular, the problem of co-operation, and finally, a presentation which is accessible to the peasant without any false over-simplification or unnecessary vulgarization – are all essential qualities of a mass peasant press.

The press of the Red Army and Red Navy is of great significance for serving the peasantry; it must be strengthened in every way, and its content and language must be adapted to the young men who are pouring into the army. Wide use must also be made of conscripts from the countryside to establish a link between the peasantry and the Red Army and peasant newspapers.

11   The transition of the national republics press to the local languages must be completed, an effort must be made to increase the press run of the nationality press and to strengthen its union with the masses through worker and peasant correspondents, and through the development of a newspaper format which is adapted to the level of the backward peasantry of the national republics. The national press in particular needs to be reinforced by party leadership and must be strengthened by politically steadfast party worker-journalists. With regard to publication, all national publishing houses must come over on the whole to the use of the non-Russian languages, to the output of high-quality and low-priced texts for primary schools, mass popular books for the worker and peasant, and a popular leninist series accessible to the broad masses of the local population.

12   The developing work of the Komsomol is far from being adequately serviced by literature. A network of young people's oblast newspapers (for workers, peasants, and national minorities) must be established and secured. An all-Russian Komsomol newspaper must be created. Particular attention must be directed to the peasant and nationality papers and to extending the network of young worker and peasant correspondents.

Komsomol publication work must be strengthened, especially by adding to the Komsomol editorial boards marxist editors who are party members.

The primary task of the Komsomol must be the creation of a literature for the peasant youth masses. Party leadership must be strengthened, and strict ideological steadfastness ensured, in the issuance of youth literature by soviet, party, and other publishers. All work in this area must be co-ordinated with the educational activities of the Komsomol. Particular attention should be directed to popular youth literature on the history of the RKP and especially on the bolshevik struggle against opportunism and intra-party deviations.

A start must be made in creating a children's literature under the painstaking supervision and leadership of the party in order to increase the class, international, and labour educational aspects of this literature. In particular, publication of Young Pioneer literature must be developed, with party, trade union, and soviet organizations helping the Komsomol in this effort.

13   The existing periodicals for women workers and peasants must be strengthened, and in the general press organs more attention must be directed to explaining the problems of the daily life and work of the broad masses of women workers and peasants. The participation of women workers and peasants in our press must be enhanced (women worker, peasant, and trade union correspondents), with primary emphasis on women leninists, women delegates, etc.

Particular attention must be directed to involving women workers and peasants in wall newspaper work. Party members working in the public press must also be brought in to service publications for women workers and peasants.

In the eastern republics the general press must devote the greatest possible attention to the emancipation of women and to the adoption of measures leading to the creation of a periodical and non-periodical press in the national languages directed at the toiling eastern women.

14   All published material must become cheaper. In the matter of distribution, staff and funds must be concentrated on making the maximum numbers of books and newspapers available to the broad masses by developing a locally based network of book dealers using all existing distribution apparatuses (contractors, the post offices, and especially the cooperative system). The distribution of printed matter must become less expensive, and party leadership in this matter must be strengthened. The offices of the People's Commissariat of Post and Telegraph must improve their distribution of printed materials, particularly in the villages, and all possible support must be given to the voluntary mass associations for the distribution of literature (Komsomol, factory, and plant associations, village 'books and newpaper' circles, etc.).

15   Special state financial assistance must be concentrated on *support for the nationalities, peasant, and Red Army press*, specialized mass literature for peasants, and publication of the works of V.I. Lenin by allocating appropriate funds from the state budget and, in the national republics, from the local budgets as well.

16   Urgent measures must be adopted to issue, in all the languages of the Union, national editions in many printings of the works of V.I. Lenin, devoting particular attention to the editorial aspects of these editions, their accessibility, low cost, and distribution. A series of condensations of the works of V.I. Lenin is to be organized for use by party members of the Lenin Enrolment and by non-party persons. The Congress instructs the Central Committee to publish without undue delay a complete edition of

the works of V.I. Lenin in Russian and of his selected works in all the major non-Russian languages of the Union.

17   While noting the strengthening of our publishing houses and the considerable expansion of publishing, the Congress feels that efforts must be intensified: 1) to ensure greater differentiation and specialization of publishing houses with respect to basic types and forms of publication 2) to develop and strengthen the publishing houses in the principal nationality and oblast centres; 3) to merge party, soviet, trade union, and co-operative publishers both in the centres and at the local level in order to intensify the influence of party committees on the work of publishers, and to ensure the best co-ordination of their publishing schedules as well as the best organization of publishing and distribution.

18   Work must be intensified on the creation and publication of mass, high-quality popular books and pamphlets which are entirely accessible to the workers and peasants, so that serving the broad masses will be the fundamental and primary task of our publishers; the publication of popular and low-cost peasant literature must be improved and strengthened, with particular attention to the lowest, semi-literate, peasant reader and to the output of publications of practical use and interest for the village.

As regards academic materials, the fundamental task must be the final transition to the publication of new, high-quality, political and methodical text, as well as teaching and methodical materials. Particular attention is to be directed to the formulation and distribution of a Soviet text for the peasantry, which would be of the greatest cultural and political significance, and also to the preparation and publication of a series of texts on political and social matters for mass use in urban and rural schools. While the principle of state monopoly on the publication of educational materials is to be preserved, other major soviet-party publishing houses are to be invited to publish such materials in co-operation with the state publishing houses of the union republics.

In order to further the self-education both of non-party workers and of worker-communists, the establishment of suitable libraries and the publication of books of the 'home university' type is to be intensified.

The party's leadership of critical and bibliographical work in our newspapers, magazines, and publishing houses is to be intensified, with permanent and systematically functioning sections being organized in the newspapers and special attention being devoted to mass editions and problems of party education.

19   In artistic literature the party's basic task must be oriented toward the creativity of workers and peasants who are becoming worker and peasant writers through the process of the cultural advance of the broad national masses of the Soviet Union. Worker and peasant correspondents must be viewed as reserves from which new worker and peasant writers will come forward.

There must be an overall increase in the material support for, and promotion of, proletarian and peasant writers who have come to our literature in part from production and the plow and in part from the stratum of intelligentsia which in the October days and during the era of War Communism entered the ranks of the RKP and the Komsomol.

Particular attention must be paid to writers and poets from the Komsomol, who are active in the very midst of the working-class youth.

The primary prerequisite for the growth of worker and peasant writers is their release from narrow clanishness in order to work more seriously on themselves, both artistically and politically, with the party – and particularly the party's literary critics – giving them all possible encouragement.

At the same time it is necessary to continue the existing systematic support of the most gifted of the so-called fellow-travelers who are being trained in the school of comradely work together with Communists. The party must organize firm criticism which, while singling out and supporting talented Soviet writers, at the same time points out their errors, which derive from an inadequate understanding of the Soviet order, and induces them to overcome bourgeois prejudices.

While considering that no one literary trend, school, or group can or should speak for the party, the Congress stresses the necessity of settling the problem of literary criticism and of the fullest possible explanation by the party of the standards of artistic literature on the pages of the soviet-party press.

The Congress directs particular attention to the necessity of creating a mass artistic literature for the workers, peasants, and Red Army men.

20   The increasing significance of the press and the increasingly complex demands of readers compel party organs to make the most attentive and painstaking selection of persons for the mass press from among comrades who possess sufficient authority, are steady in party matters, and possess good workmanlike sense. The transfer of party member-journalists to press work must be continued.

In electing party committees, especially in industrial centres, comrades must be selected who are capable of guiding the work of the most important local press organ. The systematic training of new staff from among the worker and peasant correspondents must also be intensified, especially through the State Institute of Journalism which must be strengthened by party journalists. Particular attention must be directed to the training of workers for the nationality presses.

The party organs must also make a painstaking selection of the leading, especially editorial, staff of the major local publishers with the aim of strengthening and consolidating them.

21   The increased significance of the press as a means of binding the party to the masses requires the setting up and strengthening of organs of

press guidance, the intensification of party supervision and leadership through the press sections and subsections of party committees and through the party committees as a whole. The party committees must take a closer interest in the solution of all basic problems of press guidance, including such problems in their work plans. The consolidation of the supervision and guidance of newspapers and publishers, in particular, demands a consolidation of the press sections of the oblast committees, the national central committees, and of the Central Committee bureau.

22   It is necessary to change to a system of oblast and krai party magazines oriented toward the middle peasant party member, with a number of the guberniia party magazines being converted into small party bulletins. The party-educational guiding character of party magazines is to be strengthened, and they are to explain, in addition to problems of leninism and of intra-party life and practice, also questions of economic and cultural construction, primarily using local materials and experience.

23   Through the press sections and subsections at the centre and at the local level, a firm policy must be followed of liquidating all varieties of departmental literature with the aim of releasing corresponding resources for the support of the peasant and nationality press. State expenditures on departmental literature are to be rigidly reduced.

2.44
On Agitprop Work   31 May 1924

I   IN THE SPHERE OF AGITATION

1   The favourable conditions for strengthening the party's influence among the worker and peasant masses, created by the general economic advance of the USSR and the massive inflow into the party's ranks of men and women production workers, require a radical break in the party's agitprop work in the direction of expanding and deepening its mass forms both within the party and among the non-party workers and peasants. This is also required, on the one hand, by the party's tasks of serving the Lenin Enrolment and involving it in the active work of the party, the trade unions, and the state, and, on the other, by the party's firm course toward intra-party democracy.

2   It is necessary, in the first place, to develop mass political agitation. While reducing the number of campaigns and limiting them to the most important ones, it is necessary steadily and regularly to explain, during the process of current work, the most important international and domestic political events, the most important measures taken by Soviet power, and the major issues of local life: the activities of soviet organs and trade union organizations, economic problems of enterprises, the activities of the co-operative movement, of the municipal services, etc., without in any way playing down or curtailing analyses of the overall tasks confronting the

party and the Comintern. It is necessary to struggle against the repetition of platitudes, seeking maximum concreteness, and tying the issues to the current demands and needs of the particular audience.

3   The inflow into the party of 150–200,000 production workers, their completion of schools of political education, and the heightened interest in the party all make it essential to raise, on the largest scale, the question of individual and group agitation and propaganda; the principal obstacle to their development in the past has been the insufficiency of party members in factories. Each man or woman worker who is a party member must be converted into an active party agitator. In private group and personal conversations with workers, during breaks, at the factory bench, in the apartment, etc. – these comrades must conduct agitation on behalf of the party on the major political events and on all issues which are of greatest concern to the workers (currency reform, wages, co-operation, the trade union movement, questions of municipal services, housing, production propaganda, daily life, etc.).

4   Work must be intensified on the selection, training, and promotion of agitators and propagandists from worker cells and on the guidance of their activities; the work of collectives and red corners in shops, barracks, dormitories, and cafeterias must be broadened and deepened. All agitators must be regularly supplied with the needed materials through newspapers and magazines, and must be given timely instructions. Special attention must be devoted to working out an agitation method which takes into account previous agitational experience. As far as this is possible, speakers should specialize in particular questions (economic, trade union, etc.).

5   To intensify far-reaching mass agitational work which encompasses the most backward strata, in the largest and most important lower-level cells, comrades from the cell bureau must be appointed to agitprop work ...

2   IN THE SPHERE OF PROPAGANDA

8   In accordance with the overall change in the work of Agitprop and in the sphere of propaganda, emphasis must now be placed on the mass forms of this work, and among these the most prominent must be the workers' club, the red corner, the reading room, and cultural patronage of the countryside.

9   It is even more necessary now than before to bring about a genuine conversion of workers' clubs into centres for the communist education of the broad masses of men and women workers. The maintenance of the Lenin Enrolment – its involvement in the organizational work of the club, its conversion into an instrument for organizing the working mass and rallying it around the tasks of the party, the state, the co-operative movement, and the trade unions, and for drawing more workers into the party's ranks – must become the goal of all club activities in the period to come. To this goal must be subordinated all basic types and forms of the club's

educational work – socio-political, economic, production, and that pertaining to everyday life.

The club must be organized on the basis of voluntary membership, ensuring the maximum activity of its members.

Mass forms of club work must be in the forefront, and to these must be subordinated the activities of all club circles and the work of the club's audience as a whole.

As for the content of club work, primary emphasis must be placed upon the propaganda and explanation of the basic tasks confronting the party, the state, and the trade unions in economic, state, and trade union construction, in party tactics, and the policy of the Soviet power on the bases of leninism. In the overall work of the club the most prominent place must be given to the propaganda of leninism. The club's library must become an instrument of such propaganda, and for this a suitable selection of literature must made.

Considerable attention must also be devoted to natural scientific (anti-religious) propaganda.

The tasks of the clubs demand a genuine unification of all club work under the immediate guidance and supervision of the party. This guidance must be political and organizational as well as methodical; it must tie in the activities of the workers' clubs with the work of all other clubs (party, Komsomol, Red Army, etc.) and must be implemented through special club commissions in the agitprop sections of the party committees; the communist members of each club are to organize party collectives headed by the fractions of the club administration and maintaining constant contact with the club commissions of the party committees ...

12   In developing mass forms of its work in the city and the village the party in the near future, more than ever before, can and must rely on its steadily growing worker composition. Therefore its preparation for the role of the bearer of party influence among the worker and peasant masses must be the first and most important business of intra-party propaganda.

Any further raising of the level of political development and political knowledge of party members, in particular, of the Lenin Enrolment, will require the expansion and consolidation of the network of standard five to six-month schools of political literacy and their supplying with materials (under the local budget); the courses offered in these schools would concentrate on the history of the revolutionary struggle and the Communist Party, questions of party tactics and party construction, and the basic questions of the policy of the Soviet state – particularly in economic matters ...

Pravda, 28 May 1924 for 2.41; 1   *KPSS v rezoliutsiiakh* III, 38–129
June (2.43); 3 June (2.42); 4 June (2.44)

2.45
On One-Man Control in the Red Army 6 March 1925

At the present time one of the most important elements in building up the Red Army is the transition to the practical implementation of one-man leadership.

Entirely favourable conditions for implementation of the principle of one-man leadership have been created as a result of all the previous work done by the party and the military organs on the overall strengthening of the command staff (by selecting its best elements, through broad involvement of command staff in political-educational work, and through the steady increase in the number and role of staff of the party committees).

In this connection the task of the commissars, who played a major role in the struggle and in building up the Red Army, must be radically changed.

According to the most recent decisions of the USSR Revolutionary Military Council, one-man leadership in military units will be implemented in two forms.

In the first place, all operational, training, administrative, and economic functions will be fully concentrated in the hands of the chief commanding officer and the combat commander.

Hence the commissar is relieved of the obligation of day-to-day supervision of the commanding officer's training, administrative, and economic functions and retains his supervision of political and party work in the unit as well as bearing responsibility for its morale. The military commissar does not participate directly in the commanding officer's one-man performance of all training and administrative-economic functions but uses all his influence and authority to assist the commanding officer in strengthening and enhancing the training and technical economic condition of the unit.

In the second place, commanding officers, who are party members and satisfy the requirements of party-political leadership (i.e., who can at the same time act as commissars), will combine in their hands the functions of training, administrative-economic, and party-political leadership.

One-man leadership on this basis will first of all be implemented in units of the Red Army.

In the Navy and the national units one-man leadership in the above form will be implemented more gradually, and as a general rule, the institution of the comissar will continue to be employed in them as before.

The transition to one-man leadership will undoubtedly heighten the socio-political weight of the command staff and will draw them closer to the local soviet and party organs – this will result from the requirements of all their day-to-day work in the service.

Implementation of one-man leadership will at the same time demand a maximum intensification of political work and a comprehensive strengthening of party influence in the units.

In this connection, the role of the political organs, as party and army institutions, is especially increased.

Considering the overwhelming significance of the reorganization of the armed forces of the country on the basis of one-man leadership and the resulting increase in the party's role in the army, the Central Committee orders party committees to give maximum assistance to political organs in their institution of practical measures for the implementation of one-man leadership and for strengthening party influence in the Red Army.

Spravochnik partiinogo rabot-
nika v, 476

XIV Party Conference   27–29 April 1925

The campaign against Trotsky continued until January 1925 when at a meeting of the Central Committee Plenum (17–20 January 1925) Trotsky was relieved of his post as chief of the army. It is characteristic of Stalin's caution that he resisted the demands of Zinoviev and Kamenev for the expulsion of Trotsky from the party and, for the time being, was satisfied with depriving him of a position which could have served Trotsky as a power base. Later at the XIV Party Congress, Stalin explained his reasons, rather incongruously in view of his subsequent steps, by pointing out the danger of 'chopping off one today, another tomorrow' and 'what would then be left in the party?'

With Trotsky isolated, Stalin was no longer in need of the support of Zinoviev and Kamenev and shortly after the January 1925 Plenum began to take concrete steps against Zinoviev and his powerful Leningrad organization. These measures were not the first sign, however, that the troika alliance was not as real as it may have appeared. It did not escape Zinoviev's notice after the XII Party Congress that the enlargement of the Central Committee and the ever-growing power of the General Secretary were a threat to his own position. As he revealed at the XIV Party Congress, Zinoviev organized a meeting in the Caucasus (during the summer of 1923) of several high ranking party members, including Bukharin, to devise ways for preventing Stalin's rise to unlimited power. Stalin, who was informed about the meeting by Zinoviev, through Ordzhonikidze, later arrived and took part in the discussions. A compromise was arrived at under which Bukharin, Zinoviev, Trotsky, and Korotkov became members of the Orgburo. As Zinoviev himself admitted, the compromise turned out to be of no practical significance.

The following year, in June 1924, Stalin took both Zinoviev and Kamenev to task, ostensibly for ideological reasons. Zinoviev was criticized for identifying the dictatorship of the proletariat with the dictatorship of the party and

Kamenev was attacked for arguing that Russia, under the NEP, was not yet a socialist country. Zinoviev and Kamenev, until then firm supporters of Stalin's pro-peasant policy, began to turn left to the position previously advocated by Trotsky in his dispute with the troika.

Trotsky, instead of taking advantage of the strained relations in the troika, committed yet another tactical mistake by the publication, in the autumn of 1924, of a book of articles under the title *1917*, with an introduction called 'The Lessons of October,' in which he attempted to work out a theory on the betrayal of the revolution by the 'right.' He documented his case partly by pointing to Zinoviev's and Kamenev's opposition to the bolshevik seizure of power in November 1917. The result was a postponement of Zinoviev's and Kamenev's policy switch and a strengthening of Stalin's position. Stalin did not remain aloof in this fracas, but for the time being glossed over Zinoviev's and Kamenev's indiscretions in November 1917 and concentrated the full force of his attack on finishing off Trotsky by falsely minimizing his role in the bolshevik seizure of power, and by accusing him of ideological distortions of leninism.

It was against this background that the XIV Party Conference met in April 1925. The sign that neither Stalin nor Zinoviev or Kamenev (Trotsky was absent) were ready to bring their disagreements into the open was indicated by their being among the 392 delegates with a consultative vote, outnumbering the 178 with a deciding vote. All three were elected to the Conference presidium. Kamenev chaired all the Conference sessions and Zinoviev delivered a report on the Comintern which was approved as a resolution without debate. Otherwise, none of the three were elected to any of the commissions to draft the final versions of the proposed resolutions nor did they participate in the discussions. While the Conference once again gave its approval to the pro-peasant policy in resolutions on co-operation with the peasants and a single agricultural tax (which was reduced and the alleged danger stemming from the rich peasants minimized) there was little indication of any opposition.

Molotov gave a major report on party construction which was approved unanimously as a resolution (2.46), expressing once again concern about the composition and growth of party membership. Resolutions on metal industry and revolutionary legality were also adopted.

2.46
On Party Construction   29 April 1925

...

III   IMPROVEMENT OF PARTY COMPOSITION AND REGULATION OF PARTY
GROWTH

During the past year, since the XIII Congress, the party has, on the whole, continued to grow normally, mainly by taking in more workers. Noting, however, that the fundamental decision of the XIII Party Congress on regulating the party's composition, namely, the decision to the effect that our party should be composed of at least 50 per cent of workers directly engaged in production, has not yet been carried out, the Conference states that this decision of the XIII Congress should in future continue to be the basic guiding directive regulating party growth.

At the same time, as has already been stated, village party organizations must take in the best, stable, revolutionary, and politically trained farm labourers and rural toilers, poor peasants, and those of the middle peasants who are closest to the party. Party organizations should also have their attention drawn to the need for strict adherence to the resolution of the XIII Congress on the admission of white collar workers and intellectuals into the party which calls for the observance, in such cases, of both the established formal requirements and the other requirements mentioned in the resolution of the Congress and which relate to the capacity of the new party member really to assist the party and the organs of the proletarian dictatorship. With regard to the further growth of the party it is necessary to be guided by the task of maintaining the party as a genuine communist proletarian vanguard, and therefore under existing conditions more attention must be devoted to improving the party's qualitative composition, compelling all newly entering party members to meet the same requirement.

In view of the above:

I   The Conference recognizes that two recommendations by party members who have been in the party for one year are sufficient for acceptance, as candidate members of the party, of workers directly engaged in production. It is necessary to continue the existing practice of discussing at open cell meetings the new candidacies of those wishing to enter the party. This decision is to be transmitted to the regular party congress for its approval.

2   To make it easier for farm labourers, peasant tillers, and worker or peasant Red Army men to enter the party, such persons will henceforth require recommendations from only two party members of only two years' membership. Approval of new party candidates of this category is to be transferred from the guberniia committees to the uezd (and okrug) committees. In those rural areas where there is an influx of peasants and farm labourers into the party but where there are no party members with the right to give recommendations, party workers must be sent to acquaint themselves with the peasants wishing to enter the party and, if appropriate, to issue them the necessary party recommendations.

3   The struggle must be intensified against the red tape involved in examining applications (in particular, of peasants) for entry into the party

and against the impermissible delay in transferring candidates to full party membership.

4   The campaigns of mass recruitment into the party, both in the city and in the country, must be ended absolutely.

5   Local party organizations are forbidden to admit persons into the party on the basis of previously established admission allotments or on the basis of a percentage relationship among the various categories of those to be admitted.

6   In view of the overall party growth and the need for greater organizational clarity in party construction, the continued existence in either the city or the country of any kind of special organizations of helpers or sympathizers (with their own separate meetings, etc.) is considered unsuitable ...

Draft in *Pravda*, 25 April 1925   *KPSS v rezoliutsiiakh* III, 173–216

2.47
Party Policy in the Sphere of Literature   18 June 1925

1   The recent advance in the material well-being of the masses due to the upsurge in people's minds caused by the revolution, the intensification of mass activity, the gigantic expansion of outlook, etc., cause an enormous growth in cultural demands and needs. In this way we have entered a period of cultural revolution which is the preface to further advance to a communist society.

2   Part of this mass cultural growth is made up of the growth of a new literature – proletarian and peasant in its initial embryonic stages but at the same time unprecedentedly broad and comprehensive in its forms (worker and peasant correspondents, wall newspapers, etc.) and leading to conscious literary and artistic productions.

3   On the other hand, the complexity of the economic process, the simultaneous growth of contradictory and even directly hostile economic forms, the inception and strengthening of a new bourgeoisie caused by this development; the inevitable, although initially not always conscious, craving for this by a part of the old and new intelligentsia; the chemical secretion from out of the depths of society of ever-new ideological agents of this bourgeoisie – all of this must inevitably be felt also on the literary surface of social life.

4   Thus, however curtailed the class struggle may be in our country generally, the literary front is the one place where it does not cease. There

is not and cannot be a neutral art in a class society, although the class nature of art generally, and of literature in particular, is expressed in far more variegated forms than, for example, in politics.

5   However, it would be quite incorrect to lose sight of the basic fact of our social life, namely, the fact that the working class has won power, that there exists a proletarian dictatorship in the country.

Although before seizing power the proletarian party fanned the class struggle and followed the line of splitting the whole of society, in the period of proletarian dictatorship the proletarian party is faced with the problem of how to get along with the peasantry and how slowly to refashion it; the problem of how to admit a certain degree of co-operation with the bourgeoisie and how slowly to squeeze it out; the problem of how to place the technical, and any other, intelligentsia at the service of the revolution and how to win it over ideologically from the bourgeoisie.

Thus, although the class struggle is not curtailed, it alters its form, since before seizing power the proletariat is striving to break down the given society while in the period of its dictatorship 'peaceful organizational work' comes to the fore.

6   While preserving, strengthening, and continually broadening its leadership, the proletariat must also take a suitable position on a whole series of new sectors of the ideological front. The penetration of dialectical materialism into completely new areas (biology, psychology, natural sciences generally) has already begun. And sooner or later the conquest of positions in literature must also become a fact.

7   It must be borne in mind, however, that this task is infinitely more complicated than the others which are being resolved by the proletariat since even within the limits of capitalist society the working class could prepare itself for the victorious revolution, train cadres of fighters and leaders, and work out the magnificent weapon of political struggle. But it could not give an ideological analysis of natural scientific or technical questions, nor could it, as a culturally depressed class, create its own literature, its own special artistic form, its own style. Although the proletariat already has in its possession faultless criteria of the socio-political content of any literary production, it does not yet have such definite answers to all questions about artistic form.

8   The above considerations must determine the literary policy of the leading party of the proletariat. The principal questions involved are the following: the relationship between the proletarian and peasant writers, the so-called fellow-travellers [writers who were sympathetic to the party but did not wish to join] and others; the party's policy with respect to the proletarian writers themselves; questions of criticism; questions of the style and form of artistic productions and methods of working out new artistic forms; finally, questions of organization.

9   The relationship among the various writers grouped in terms of their social class or social group content is determined by our overall policy. However, here it must be borne in mind that in literature, leadership belongs to the working class as a whole, with all of its material and ideological resources. Proletarian writers do not yet have hegemony, and the party must help these writers to earn their historic right to this hegemony. Peasant writers must meet with a friendly welcome and must have our unconditional support. The task is one of switching their growing cadres over to the tracks of proletarian ideology and in no sense one of eliminating from their creations the peasant literary and artistic forms which are the very basis of any influence upon the peasantry.

10   As regards the 'fellow-travellers,' the following must be borne in mind: 1) their differentiation; 2) the significance of many of them as skilled 'specialists'; 3) the presence of wavering in this stratum of writers. Here the overall directive must be to adopt a tactful and solicitous approach to them, i.e., the sort of approach which would ensure all the conditions for their transfer, as rapidly as possible, to the side of communist ideology. Eliminating the anti-proletarian and anti-revolutionary elements (which are today very insignificant), struggling against the incipient new bourgeois ideology on the part of the fellow-travellers of the smenovekh tendency [an allusion to a white émigré publication, *Smena vekhi* (Change of Landmarks), which maintained that the Soviet Union was ceasing to be revolutionary], the party must be tolerant of intermediate ideological forms, patiently helping these inevitably varied forms to live out their lives in increasingly close and comradely co-operation with the cultural forces of communism.

11   With respect to proletarian writers, the party must adopt the following position: in every way helping them to grow and supporting them and their organizations, the party must by all means prevent the appearance in this group of the ruinous phenomenon of communist boasting. Precisely because it sees in them the future ideological leaders of Soviet literature, the party must struggle in every way against a frivolous or neglectful attitude toward the old cultural heritage or toward specialists in belles lettres. Equally deserving of condemnation is the position of belittling the very significance of the struggle for the ideological hegemony of the proletarian writers. Against capitulationism, on the one hand, and against communist boasting on the other – this should be our party's slogan. The party must also struggle against attempts at a purely hothouse 'proletarian' literature; a broad treatment of phenomena in all their complexity, refusal to keep to the framework of the factory alone, a literature not of the shop but of a great struggling class which is leading millions of peasants – this should be the framework of the content of a proletarian literature.

12   The above considerations by and large determine the tasks of criti-

cism, which is one of the principal educational instruments available to the party. Without for one instant yielding the positions of communism, without backing away from the proletarian ideology by one iota, disclosing the objective class meaning of various literary productions, communist criticism must struggle mercilessly against counter-revolutionary manifestations in literature, must unmask the smenovekh liberalism, etc., and at the same time must display the greatest tact, caution, and tolerance of all the literary strata which can and will go along with the proletariat. Communist criticism must cease its customary use of the tone of literary command. This criticism will be of profound educational significance only when it relies on its ideological superiority. Marxist criticism must resolutely rid itself of all pretentious, semi-literate, and self-satisfied communist boastfulness. Marxist criticism must set itself the slogan – 'learn,' and it must eliminate from its midst all literary garbage and works distinguished only for their 'originality.'

13   While infallibly bringing to light the social class content of literary tendencies, the party can in no way bind itself to a preference for any particular direction as regards *literary form*. Although giving guidance to literature as a whole, the party can as little support any *one* literary faction (these factions being classified according to their different views about form and style) as it could by resolutions decide matters relating to the form of the family, even though in general it undoubtedly guides and must guide the building up of a new way of life. Everything makes us assume that a style will be created to match the epoch, but it will be created by other methods, and no resolution of this problem is yet in sight. Any attempts to bind the party in this way to a given phase of the country's cultural developments must be rejected.

14   Therefore the party must speak out for free competition among the various groupings and tendencies in this area. Any other decision of this question would be an official bureaucratic pseudo-decision. It would be equally impermissible through a decree or party decision to *legalize a monopoly* in literature and publishing by some group or literary organization. While giving material and moral support to a proletarian and proletarian-peasant literature, helping the fellow-travellers, etc., the party cannot grant a monopoly to any particular group, even to the one with the most proletarian ideological content: this would signify, first of all, the death of proletarian literature.

15   The party must in every way eradicate attempts at home-made and incompetent administrative interference in literature; the party must concern itself with the careful selection of staff in the institutions charged with press matters to ensure a genuinely correct, useful, and tactful guidance of our literature.

16   The party must indicate to all workers in literature the need for a

correct delimitation of the function of critic from that of writer. The latter must move the centre of gravity of their work to literary production in the real meaning of the word, using for this the gigantic material offered by contemporary reality. Greater attention must also be devoted to the development of the national literatures of the numerous republics and oblasts of our Union.

The party must emphasize the necessity of creating a literature aimed at the truly mass reader, worker, and peasant; a bolder and more decisive break must be made with aristocratic prejudices in literature; and appropriate form, which is understandable by the *millions*, must be developed using all the technical achievements of the old craft.

Only when Soviet literature and its future proletarian vanguard have solved this great task will they be able to carry out their cultural-historic mission.

Spravochnik partiinogo rabotnika
V, 349–52

2.48
On Party Commissions in Red Army and Navy
Politotdels   26 October 1925

I   THE ORGANIZATION OF PARTY COMMISSIONS

1   Red Army party commissions are organized in the political administration of okrugs, fronts, armies, and navies, in the politotdels of divisions and brigades, and in other equivalent formations.
Note A special decision provides for the organization, in the Political Administration of the Red Army, of a dispute commission acting as the military investigation apparatus of the party Central Control Commission.
2   Party commissions are elected at okrug, front, army, navy, divisional, and equivalent party conferences. Okrug, navy, front, and army commissions are elected with nine members and three candidates; divisional and equivalent commissions are elected with five members and three candidates. Party commissions are elected for the period between regular party conferences.
3   Party members who have been in the party for not less than three years may be elected members of divisional and equivalent party commissions. Responsible secretaries of divisional party commissions must have six years' of party membership. Five years' of membership are required for members of okrug, front, army, and navy party commissions. Responsible secretaries of okrug party commissions must have been party members since October [1917].

Note In exceptional cases with the approval of the higher party commission, and each time by special decision of the party conference, and also by intervention of the chief of the corresponding political organ, the stipulated period of party membership may be waived; waivers for members of okrug, front, and army party commissions must be approved in the Central Control Commission.

4   The members of divisonal and equivalent party commissions are approved by okrug party commissions; the members of okrug and equivalent party commissions are approved by the Central Control Commission through the control commissions of the Political Administration.

5   Before expiry of their terms of office, members of divisional and equivalent commissions may not be shifted from one formation to another without the agreement of the higher – okrug / front – party commissions. In the same way, transfers of members of okrug and equivalent party commissions require the assent of the Central Control Commission and the control commission of the Political Administration.

II   RIGHTS AND OBLIGATIONS OF PARTY COMMISSIONS

6   Party commissions have the right to discuss and take decisions in respect of all matters associated with violations of the party Rules and party ethics; they also have the right to approve candidacies for party membership and transfers from candidate to full membership.

7   Divisional and equivalent party commissions conduct preliminary investigations and issue conclusions in respect of violations of the party Rules and party ethics. In matters of admission to candidate membership and transfer to full membership, decisions of the divisional party commission are final for persons of the first category.

8   As regards admission to the party of persons of the other categories, the decisions of divisional party commissions enter into force only upon approval by okrug and equivalent party commissions.

9   All decisions of party commissions are implemented by the corresponding chiefs of political organs.

In case of disagreement the questions are referred to the higher political organ and party commission for final decision.

10   Decisions of divisional and equivalent party commissions may be appealed to okrug party commissions, and decisions of okrug and equivalent party commissions – to the Central Control Commission through the control commission of the Political Administration.

11   Members of party commissions have the right to participate in all meetings and conferences of the corresponding political organs.

12   Party commissions report on their activities to the divisional party conference and the okrug party commission. Okrug party commissions report to the okrug party conference and to the Central Control Commission through the Political Administration.

III WORKING STAFF OF THE PARTY COMMISSION

13   The party commission elects from its members a responsible secretary for the practical day-to-day conduct of work.

Note Responsible secretaries of party commissions are included as members of special staff categories of the corresponding political organs.

14   The duties of the responsible secretary of the party commission include:

a   implementation of the decisions of corresponding and higher party commissions;

b   the preparation of materials and convocation of commission meetings;

c   the examination of preliminary investigational materials and, when necessary, the remission of cases for further inquiry;

d   the distribution, among party commission members and candidate members, of materials for the conduct of investigations;

e   the summoning of all persons needed to testify in the case under consideration;

f   guidance and supervision of the conduct of business correspondence in the party commission;

g   the compiling of reports and accounts of the party commission's work.

15   In its work the party commission makes use of the apparatus of the corresponding political organ.

Note The procedures for handling the business correspondence and accounts of party commissions are set forth in a special decision.

16   By agreement with the corresponding chief of the political organ, the responsible secretary of the okrug party commission calls periodic conferences and calls in the secretaries of divisional and equivalent party commissions to report.

IV CONNECTIONS AND RELATIONS AMONG PARTY COMMISSIONS, PARTY COMMITTEES, AND CONTROL COMMISSIONS

17   Local party committees give guidance on the admission of candidates, and on the transfer of candidates to membership, by periodically hearing the reports of divisional and okrug party commissions and adopting decisions on them. Guberniia (and okrug) control commissions implement their leadership in the same way, in combating violations of the party Rules and party ethics.

Note If, after hearing a report, the okrug and its equivalent party commission disagree with a decision of the corresponding party committee and the control commission, the matter is referred for a decision to the Central Committee and the Central Control Commission through the control commission of the Political Administration.

18   Party commissions and control commissions maintain contact with

one another through mutual representation. Through its representative the control commission conveys its views on matters connected with the work of the party commission. The party commission conveys its view to the control commission in the same way.

19   If the representatives of control commissions in the party commissions, and of the party commissions in the control commissions, are not elected members of the latter, they have an advisory vote.

Spravochnik, partiinogo rabotnika
v, 476–9

XIV Party Congress   18–31 December 1925

After the XIV Conference both sides in the intra-party struggle tried to take the initiative: Zinoviev by attacking the pro-peasant policy of Stalin and Bukharin, and Stalin by attempts to penetrate or weaken Zinoviev's Leningrad party organization. On 3 October 1925 an enlarged meeting of the Central Committee plenum took place at which the opposition consisting of Zinoviev, Kamenev, Sokolnikov, and Krupskaia charged that their freedom of criticism of the right wing deviation was being hindered by the leadership and demanded a discussion of the question at the plenum. Agricultural policy was discussed at the plenum and, surprisingly, a compromise was adopted in the form of a resolution which emphasized both the necessity to struggle against the danger stemming from the 'kulaks' and at the same time insisting on the need for support from the rest of the peasantry – a so-called two-front policy later advocated by Stalin at the Congress. It is not clear why Stalin agreed to a compromise at this juncture. It may have been his proverbial caution or he simply may have wanted to lull Zinoviev into a sense of false security. On the eve of the Congress, as a result of Stalin's persistent attempts to infiltrate the Leningrad delegation with his own supporters and the equally persistent refusal of the Leningraders to allow this to happen, a vicious campaign broke out in the newspapers controlled by the Moscow and Leningrad organizations respectively. As is evident from the Congress debates, Stalin offered Zinoviev a compromise two days before the Congress opened, which in fact would have amounted to a complete capitulation and which Zinoviev flatly rejected, although by now he was prepared to let Stalin control the whole party apparatus provided he himself retained the leadership of Leningrad. It was too late for such a concession because it merely recognized the status quo. The Leningrad organization attempted, on the basis of the XIII Congress decision, to have the XIV Congress meet in Leningrad, apparently hoping that the Leningrad atmosphere might temper Stalin's attack. It is doubtful that it would have made much difference but Stalin probably shared their view and, as a result, as was announced at the XIV Congress, the Central Committee 'found it impossible' to abide by the decision of the XIII Congress and decided to hold the meeting in Moscow instead. When this decision was put to a vote it was passed unanimously with three abstentions.

It must have been clear to Zinoviev at the very opening of the Congress that he would not carry the day. Out of the 665 delegates with a deciding vote and 641 with a consultative vote, the Leningrad delegation had only 62 and 17 respectively. As Lashevich, a follower of Zinoviev, remarked in a speech to the Congress, 'everything was prepared exceptionally skilfully' (by Stalin). With the exception of the Leningrad delegation and a handful of their supporters elsewhere, the delegates were handpicked by Stalin. The outcome – the defeat of the Zinoviev opposition – was a foregone conclusion. Nevertheless, or perhaps because of it, the debates were the noisiest and most unruly of any Congress up to that time. Trotsky, who had only a consultative vote, had not yet entered into a coalition with Zinoviev and did not participate in the debates. The Leningraders applauded their own speakers, the stalinists jeered them, and the chairmen of each session frequently had to ring the bell for order. The opposition spokesmen were always reminded by the chairmen when their allotted time was up, although in most instances it was extended by a few minutes, while the stalinists spoke without interruptions from the chair.

For the first time in his career, Stalin gave the principal address, the political report of the Central Committee (*Works* VII, 267–361, 362–403) while the organizational report was delivered by Molotov. Stalin reminded the Congress how the party dealt with 'anti-party trotskyism' and, pointing out that a new discussion occurred, expressed confidence (to the accompaniment of applause) that 'the party will deal speedily even with that discussion.'

In the initial stages of the debate at least, the opposition was not to be cowed. They submitted a petition, signed by forty-three delegates, in which they demanded, and received, the right for Zinoviev to deliver a Central Committee co-report with Stalin. In its own way, Zinoviev's co-report (which curiously enough received the same prominent display on the front page of *Pravda* – 23 December 1925 – as that of Stalin) was a masterpiece. Zinoviev touched upon all the disputed points of ideology such as state capitalism, socialism in one country, or whether or not the NEP was socialism, and more specifically, the policy toward the peasants; but not once did he mention Stalin by name. Instead, he directed his remarks to Bukharin, who some time before the Congress called upon the peasants 'to enrich themselves' and not to fear confiscation. Perhaps Zinoviev still entertained a faint hope that by sparing the General Secretary he might be able to strike some bargain with him.

What followed was a prolonged and stormy debate in which Kamenev delivered a courageous and bitter attack on Stalin, accusing him of establish-

ing himself as a one-man ruler. When he concluded with the remarks that 'We
are against the theory of one-man rule, we are against the creation of a
leader,' a pandemonium broke out on the floor. The delegates got up, shouting 'Stalin, Stalin, Hurrah, Hurrah,' accompanying the shouting with
'stormy, long-lasting applause' – all signs of a carefully staged demonstration. Krupskaia, too, intervened in the debate, and to point out that a majority
was not always right, somewhat recklessly referred to the 1906 Stockholm
Party Congress in which the Mensheviks had a majority and the Bolsheviks a
minority. Her remarks caused considerable furor and she felt compelled,
perhaps under pressure, to withdraw her remarks later in the proceedings.
However, the last words on the issue belonged to Stalin when he told the
delegates that the party wanted unity and would accomplish it 'with comrades Kamenev and Zinoviev, if they so wish, or without them if they do not
wish so.' Obviously smarting under Kamenev's attack he sought to reassure
the Congress that 'To lead the party on any other basis than a collective one is
impossible. It is silly to dream of that after Ilyich [Lenin], silly to talk about
it'.

In spite of Zinoviev's co-report, the opposition did not introduce its own
resolution on the Central Committee report – in the interest of unanimity,
explained Kamenev – but it did oppose the official version (2.49), in a vote of
559 to 65, which suggests that either 41 delegates were absent or else abstained, meaning that they were not fully committed to Stalin. Stalin's report
included some strong statements on industrialization which may have been a
continuation of the compromise made at the October Central Committee
Plenum or may indicate that he contemplated adopting the programme of the
left opposition even before he routed them.

After these dramatic sessions the opposition declined in strength and was
not able to muster as large a number of votes in the face of the aggressive
campaign to intimidate them. One such step was the introduction of an
'Appeal to All Members of the Leningrad Organization' (2.50) by Kalinin.
Supported by alleged messages from various workers' organizations in
Leningrad, disowning Zinoviev, the campaign to unseat him was launched.
On the floor of the Congress the opposition attempted to protest the drive but
could find only thirty-six delegates who were prepared to attach their signatures to the protest. A resolution castigating the activity of the Leningrad
newspaper produced only thirty-eight opposition votes against it, again illus-
trating the tendency of any vanquished force to suffer defections.

Other resolutions of the Congress concerned the adoption of new party
Rules (2.52) and trade unions, (2.51) and contained further measures towards
improvement of central control over the local organizations. The new Rules
also changed the name of the party to the 'All-Union Communist Party
(bolshevik).' A resolution on the Central Control Commission also passed
(on the basis of a report by Kuibyshev) which made it once more clear that the
Commission served as a policing tool of the leadership to keep control and

discipline in the party. Other resolutions dealt with the Revision Commission, Komsomol, and the Comintern (the report on which, ironically, was still delivered by Zinoviev).

The Congress elected a new and further enlarged Central Committee of sixty-three members and forty-three candidates, still including Zinoviev, Kamenev, and Trotsky, in spite of their political defeats. The new Politburo reflected the tide of battle more accurately. Kamenev was demoted to candidate member, and Kalinin, Molotov, and Voroshilov, all of whom could be counted upon to support Stalin, although for different reasons, were promoted to full membership. Of candidate members, Frunze had died since the XIII Congress, the Trotskyite Sokolnikov was dropped, and Petrovsky and Uglanov were added.

2.49
On the Central Committee Report   23 December 1925

The XIV Party Congress entirely supports the political and organizational line of the Central Committee which has secured a general economic advance for the party, the working class, and the whole country, and has consolidated the position of socialism both outside and inside the country.

Thanks to this policy, in the *international* sphere the Soviet Union has newly been recognized by a number of capitalist states, has concluded with them a number of new trade agreements and concessions, has increased its foreign trade, and has strengthened its international position.

Thanks to the same policy in the *domestic* sphere, the Soviet Union is in a position to ensure a firm state budget, rapidly to move ahead with the development of industry and with further development of agriculture, accompanied by a general advance in wages and in labour productivity, raising their production almost to the pre-war level and ensuring an increasing role of socialist elements in the whole economy.

Thanks to this same policy, Soviet power has consolidated the alliance between the working class and the peasantry and has ensured its leadership by the proletariat; has raised the actual role and significance of co-operation; on the basis of socialist construction has rallied large strata of the technical and other intelligentsia under proletarian leadership; has strengthened co-operation among the peoples of the Soviet Union and, as a result of successful regionalization, has started establishing a material-economic base in the oblasts, autonomous republics, and union republics.

While taking note of all these successes, the Congress at the same time calls attention to the errors in grain deliveries and foreign trade which have created a threat to the stability of our currency, this necessary condition of our economic development, and have led to a negative trade balance. While supporting the decisions taken by the party Central Committee in the beginning of November of this year, which are correcting these errors, the Congress instructs the Central Committee to intensify its guidance of the work of the economic commissariats and to be vigilant in ensuring that such errors do not occur in future.

In the forthcoming year the party starts its work in new conditions, both external and domestic.

As regards *international relations*, there is a consolidation and expansion of the 'breathing space', which has turned into a whole period of so-called peaceful coexistence of the USSR with the capitalist states, despite the fact that the contradictions between these two camps are not weakening but increasing. This ensures both the possibility of internal construction and – primarily because of the economic ties with foreign countries – definite benefits for accelerating this construction in the USSR. On the other hand, our economy's expanding ties with world capitalism heighten our dependence upon the latter, which leads to a whole series of new dangers and which our party cannot fail to take into account in its work on socialist construction and on ensuring our country the necessary economic independence.

Within the capitalist countries mention must be made of the partial stabilization of capitalism and the relative consolidation of the political power of the bourgeoisie in Europe; the unprecedented growth in the role of the United States of North America which verges on world financial hegemony; the gradual decline in the role of the British Empire as a world power; the contradictions between the vanquished and the victors in the imperialist war, the contradictions in the camp of the victors themselves, the contradictions between the United States of America and Europe; the undermining of the whole system of imperialism by the awakening colonial and semi-colonial peoples (China, India, Syria, Morocco) whose movement, which in places takes the form of national liberation wars, has attained gigantic and hitherto unprecedented dimensions; finally, the growth – in new forms – of the workers' movement in Europe and its close ties with the proletariat of the USSR (the struggle for unity in the trade union movement, workers' delegations to the USSR, etc.).

The relative stabilization and the so-called pacification of Europe under the hegemony of Anglo-American capital has led to a whole system of economic and political blocs, the most recent of which was the Locarno Conference and the so-called 'guarantee pacts', which were directed against the USSR. These blocs and agreements, which take cover behind the supposedly pacifistic League of Nations and the hypocritical hullabaloo of the II International about disarmament, in substance mean nothing other than an arrangement of forces for a new war. Against these blocks of capitalist states under Anglo-American hegemony, accompanied by the frenzied growth of armaments and therefore fraught with the danger of new wars, including the danger of intervention, there is a growing rapprochement between the proletariat of the advanced countries and that of the USSR under the slogan, above all, of the struggle for peace, the struggle against new imperialist wars and against armed attacks on the USSR.

Considering these circumstances, the Congress instructs the Central Committee to be guided in its policy by the following fundamental considerations:

a the alliance between the proletariat of the USSR, as the base of world revolution, and the Western European proletariat and the oppressed peoples, must be strengthened in every way, keeping a course toward the development and victory of the international proletarian revolution;

b it is necessary to conduct a policy of peace, and this must be at the centre of the government's whole foreign policy and determine all its basic moves;

c economic construction must be conducted from the viewpoint of converting the USSR from a country which imports machinery and equipment into one which produces them, so that the USSR, in circumstances of capitalist encirclement, could in no way become an economic appendage of the world capitalist economy but would represent an independent economic unity being constructed along socialist lines and, because of its economic growth, capable of serving as a powerful instrument for revolutionizing the workers of all countries and the oppressed peoples of the colonies and semi-colonies;

d when possible, economic reserves are to be prepared for use in preserving the country from any and all contingencies, whether in the domestic or in the foreign market;

e all measures are to be taken to strengthen the country's defence capacity and to intensify the power of the Red Army and the Red Navy and Air Force.

As regards *economic construction*, the Congress considers that our country, the land of the proletarian dictatorship, possesses "all that is needed to build a full socialist society" (Lenin). The Congress considers that the basic task of our party is to struggle for the victory of socialist construction in the USSR. The current year has fully confirmed the correctness of these considerations. Before the seizure of power by the proletariat in other countries but with its indisputable assistance, without any so-called 'assistance' from foreign capital and in continuous struggle against private capital in our own country, the working class in alliance with the basic mass of the peasantry has already achieved its first serious successes in socialist construction.

The past year was marked by a rapid growth of the economy as a whole, to the point where it is close to the pre-war level, and by the growth of certain of its branches: industry, agriculture, transport, foreign trade, internal trade, the credit system and the banks, state finances, etc. Within the economy, with all the variety of its component parts (the barter economy of the peasants, petty commodity production, private-owner capitalism, state capitalism, and socialism), there is a sharp increase in the proportionate share of *socialist* industry, of state and co-operative trade, of nationalized credit, and of the other commanding heights of the proletarian state.

Thus the proletariat is taking the *economic offensive* on the basis of the NEP and is moving the economy of the USSR toward socialism. The state socialist industry increasingly becomes the vanguard of the economy, leading the way for the economy as a whole.

The Congress notes that these successes could not have been attained without the active participation of the broad masses in the common undertaking of building a socialist industry (the campaign to heighten labour productivity, production conferences, etc.).

At the same time, however, there also develop the particular *contradictions* of this growth and the specific *dangers and difficulties* which this growth entails. These include: an absolute growth in private capital together with a relative decline in its role, in particular that of private commercial capital which converts its operations to servicing the countryside; the increased number of kulak farms together with increasing differentiation of the village; the growth of a new bourgeoisie in the cities which is striving to make economic contact with the commercial capitalists and the kulaks in their efforts to subjugate the basic mass of middle-peasant farms.

In the light of the above, the Congress instructs the Central Committee to be guided in its economic policy by the following directives:

a at the head of the list is the task of ensuring in every way the victory of socialist economic forms over private capital, of consolidating the foreign trade monopoly, of developing the socialist state industry and, under its leadership and with the assistance of the co-operative movement, attracting an ever greater mass of peasant farms into the channel of socialist construction;

b the economic independence of the USSR must be assured, as this safeguards the USSR from becoming converted into an appendage of the world capitalist economy; for this it is necessary to hold the course for the industrialization of the country, the development of the production of means of production, and the formation of reserves for purposes of economic manoeuver;

c on the basis of the decisions of the XIV Party Conference, every effort is to be made to promote the growth of production and trade in the country;

d all resources are to be used, the strictest economy is to be observed in the expenditure of state funds, the rate of turnover of state industry, of trade, and of the co-operatives is to be accelerated in order to heighten the tempo of socialist accumulation;

e our socialist industry is to be developed on the basis of an elevated technical level but at the same time in strict accordance both with the capacity of the market and with the financial possibilities of the state;

f all efforts are to be made to promote the development of soviet local industry (at the raion, okrug, guberniia, oblast, and republic levels), in every way stimulating local initiative to organize this industry which is aimed at satisfying the most varied needs of the population as a whole and of the peasantry in particular;

g the development of agriculture is to be maintained and advanced along the lines of increasing the agricultural crops, developing industrial crops, improving agricultural technology (introduction of tractors), the industrialization of agriculture, an orderly approach to land use, and comprehensive support for the various forms of collectivization of agriculture.

The Congress considers that one of the essential conditions for resolving these tasks is the struggle against the lack of belief in the building of socialism in our country and against attempts to view our enterprises as state-capitalist when they are actually enterprises 'of a consistently socialist type' (Lenin). Such ideological currents which make it impossible for the masses to have a conscious attitude toward the building of socialism generally and toward socialist industry in particular, are only capable of impeding the growth of socialist economic elements and of making private capital's struggle with them easier. Therefore, the Congress considers it necessary to conduct a broad educational effort to overcome these perversions of leninism.

As regards the *relations among classes*, the Congress notes the following principal phenomena which are basically determined by the economic development of the USSR: the growth of the industrial proletariat, the strengthening of the kulaks in the countryside, the growth of a new bourgeoisie in the cities, the increased activity of all classes and groups in our country. At present one of the fundamental forms of class struggle is that between capitalist and socialist elements in the economy, the struggle between the bourgeoisie and the proletariat for domination of the basic mass of peasants. This struggle also takes on a political expression, principally in the attempts of the kulak elements of the village to dominate the middle-peasant strata and thus to subject the soviets to their own influence.

While the poor peasants and, above all, the farm labourers are the proletariat's *support* in the countryside, the middle peasant is and must be its *firm ally*. It should not be forgotten for a single moment that the abolition of landlord property rights and the transfer of the landlord lands into the hands of the peasantry, the policy of establishing committees of the poor and of dispossession of the kulaks in the village, and finally, the removal of the land from commercial exchange (its nationalization) have all served to strengthen the middle peasant strata to an extraordinary degree, so that, despite the process of differentiation, these strata now constitute the fundamental mass of peasantry. Now that the dictatorship of the proletariat has been consolidated, socialism cannot be constructed by merely neutralizing these strata, without having in this mass a firm ally. For the fundamental course of the building of socialism in the village is, with increasing economic leadership by the socialist state industry, the state credit institutions, and other commanding heights in the hands of the proletariat, to draw into the co-operative organization the basic mass of the peasantry and to ensure that this organization develops along socialist lines – using, overcoming, and supressing its capitalist elements. Therefore, any underestimation of the middle peasant, any failure to understand his exceptionally important role, any attempt to turn the party away from the slogan of a firm alliance with the middle peasant to the outmoded one of his neutralization, any *'fear* of the middle peasant,' lead objectively to an undermining of the proletarian dictatorship, for this serves to undermine the worker-peasant bloc.

The struggle against the kulaks must follow the path of organizing the poor peasants against the kulaks and of consolidating the alliance of the proletariat and the poor peasantry with the middle peasants, for the purpose of splitting the middle peasants away from the kulaks and thus isolating the latter.

Failure to understand the full importance of the struggle along both these lines is associated with the two deviations from the correct party line pointed out by the XIV Party Conference and the October Plenum of the Central Committee.

The Congress decisively condemns the deviation which consists in underestimating the differentiation in the village, in failing to see the dangers involved in the growth of the kulaks and of the various forms of capitalist exploitation, in not wanting to understand the full necessity of rebuffing the kulaks and limiting their exploitation strivings, in failing to see how obligatory it is for the proletarian party to organize and weld together the poor peasants and the farm labourers against the kulak and in a struggle with him.

But at the same time the Congress equally decisively condemns attempts to gloss over the basic issue in communist policy toward the village, the question of the struggle against the middle peasant, as the central figure in agriculture, and of co-operation, as the fundamental organizational form of the movement of the village to socialism.

The Congress especially emphasizes the necessity of struggling against this last deviation. While the party is relatively better prepared for a direct struggle against the kulak and for overcoming the first deviation, the overcoming of the second deviation represents a far more difficult task, for this demands more complex techniques of struggle which combine methods of political isolation of the kulaks with methods of pulling the basic mass of the peasantry into the channel of socialist construction. This second deviation is the more dangerous in that under present conditions it threaten a return to the policy of dispossession of the kulaks, frustration of the party's present line in the village, a line which has already yielded major political successes, a break in the union between the proletariat and the peasantry and thus the frustration of our whole construction effort.

The Congress wholly and completely supports the decisions of the XIV Party Conference on the peasant question (including those relating to the expansion of rental rights and the right to hire labour, assistance for cottage industry, the transition from the system of administrative pressure to one of economic competition and economic struggle, the revival of the soviets, etc.) aimed at further improving the party's policy of reinforcing the bond between the proletariat and the peasantry. The Congress notes that it was only this change in the party's policy, resulting from the altered relations among classes, which radically improved the situation in the village, heightened the authority of the proletariat and its party among the peasantry, and thus created a firm foundation for extensive organizational work aimed at involving the peasants in the building of socialism.

At the same time the Congress wholly and completely supports the decisions of the October Plenum of the Central Committee on work among the village poor. Only to the extent that the advance in the productive forces of the village is accompanied – in the present conditions of increased activity by all class groupings – by the organization of the farm labourers and peasants with relatively small holdings, will the appropriate correlation of class forces and the leadership of the industrial proletariat be assured. In supporting the Central Committee decisions on material assistance to the poor and on organizing groups of the poor, the Congress emphasizes that here there can be no question of a return to the committees of the poor nor of a return to the system of pressure used in the period of War Communism, to dispossession of the kulaks, etc. It is a matter of organizing the village poor who, with the help of the party and the state power in the struggle on the economic and political front (kolkhozes, artels, associations, co-operatives, peasant committees, soviets), must overcome the remnants of the psychology of dependence, take the course of an organized class repulsion of the kulak, and become a reliable support of the proletarian policy in its struggle to rally the middle peasants around the proletariat.

The Congress hereby notes that the agricultural co-operatives are still far from fulfilling their important role both with respect to economic work and from the point of view of involving the masses in their work, and also from the viewpoint of correct socialist leadership. The Congress directs the attention of all party members to their duty of watching over the development of agricultural co-operation in the most attentive manner and of adopting all measures designed to ensure its correct growth.

The increased *activity of the masses*, together with the increased activity of all class groups and strata, has itself become – on the basis of the economic advance – a factor of first-rate political importance. The proletariat and its party, as the fundamental guiding force of society, must use this growth for a still greater involvement of the masses on all fronts of socialist construction and for the struggle against the bureaucratism of the state apparatus. The growth of mass activity *in the cities* is reflected in the revival of the city soviets, trade unions, workers' co-operatives, etc. *In the village* the growing activity of the masses of middle and poor peasants is reflected in the revival of the soviets and the co-operatives. The Congress once again stresses that under existing conditions the dictatorship of the proletariat cannot be strengthened by the methods of War Communism and by administrative pressure; that the co-operatives cannot be built up unless they are voluntary, unless the elected organs are responsible to their electors, and unless the shareholders have confidence in these organs; that the revival of the soviets, the growth in their ties with the broad circles of the toiling population, are a necessary prerequisite of all subsequent work by the party and Soviet power.

From the viewpoint of preserving and consolidating proletarian leadership the revival of the village soviets and co-operatives, unleashing the initiative and activity of the peasantry, presupposes the revival and cohesiveness, the increasing activity, and the organizational consolidation of the proletariat. Only on this condition can the proletarian dictatorship be strengthened and a correct political line, from the socialist viewpoint, assured. From this, above all, stems the slogan of reviving the trade unions – this mass workers' organization which strives to include every single member of the proletariat. Trade union democracy must be the method which facilitates the participation of the masses in their common work, expands the possibilities of selecting new persons promoted from below, renews the leading staff of the trade union organizations, and promotes class cohesiveness and the increase in class consciousness of the proletarian masses.

In order to carry out all this work of reviving the mass organizations of the proletariat and the peasantry in the proper way, it is necessary that the leading force in all these organizations, i.e., the vkp, also follow in all of its components the course of a consistent intra-party democracy. The Congress approves the October appeal of the Central Committee plenum on intra-party democracy and orders party organizations to bear in mind the following tasks in this respect:

a   enhancement of the activity of the broad party masses in the discussion and resolution of the major problems of party policy;

b   consistent application of the principle that leading party organs are to be elected, with new forces to be advanced to leading work, the party aktiv to be expanded, and new party cadres to be formed to assist the old;

c   increase in qualifications of the party aktiv, in particular, its knowledge of theory;

d   dissemination among the broadest party circles of the foundations of the leninist doctrine.

The strengthening of the *party* and of its leading role in all areas of our construction effort, which in the present complex situation is more necessary than ever before, also presupposes the proper regulation of the party's composition. In this respect the Congress considers it necessary to conduct a policy directed at improving the qualitative composition of the party organizations, at an ever-increasing involvement of the workers in the party, and at a continual rise of the relative weight of the proletarian party nucleus. At the same time as it confirms the necessity of strict application of the established measures for limiting access to the party to non-proletarian elements, the Congress rejects any policy leading to an excessive swelling of the party's ranks and to filling them with semi-proletarian elements which have not passed through the school of the trade unions and the proletarian organizations generally. The Congress condemns such attempts as having nothing in common with leninism, as the negation of the correct relationship between the party (the vanguard of the class) and the class, and as rendering communist leadership impossible.

The party's leading role may be fully secured only through the absolute unity of will and cohesion of the party ranks, the maintenance and consolidation of bolshevik proletarian discipline in the party.

The Congress supports the Central Committee's policy aimed at preventing an open discussion with certain leaders of the Leningrad organization and certain of their sympathizers in the Central Committee, at attempting to overcome differences internally, and at ensuring the party's collective leadership.

The Congress instructs the Central Committee to struggle resolutely against all attempts to undermine party unity, from wherever they may come and by whomever they may be headed. The Congress is firmly convinced that the Leningrad organization will be in the foremost ranks of those struggling for the unity and cohesion of our leninist party, a unity which must be preserved and strengthened at all cost.

The Congress welcomes the strengthened ties between the proletariat of the Soviet Union and that of all other countries. In this the Congress sees a growth in the influence of the Soviet Union as the base for the international workers' movement. The Congress orders the Central Committee to continue in future to strengthen in every way the ties of international solidarity under whose sign the dictatorship of the proletariat was born, battled for its rule, and has grown strong.

2.50
Appeal to all Members of the Leningrad
Organization   28 December 1925

Comrades! The party Congress appeals to you in view of the completely incorrect behaviour of the Leningrad delegation which at the Congress put forward its own co-reporter against the Central Committee and issued a special 'Declaration of the Leningrad Organization,' over the signature of Kamenev and others, which threatens to undermine our party's unity.

Your *conference* voted for *confidence* in the Central Committee and gave instructions to vote for this confidence at the Congress. Your *delegation* at the Congress voted *against confidence* in the Central Committee.

Your *conference* considered the party's *unity* to be essential. Your delegation voted *against* the whole Congress, placing itself in opposition to the party Congress.

All the Leningrad worker-communists agreed beforehand that it was necessary to march in step with their party. But the *Leningradskaia Pravda* has already launched a campaign against the decisions of the Congress, i.e., has launched a campaign aimed at *disrupting party unity*.

At the same time the Leningrad guberniia party committee prohibited the Vyborg raion from meeting to express its solidarity with the whole party and its Congress, and justified this by references to party discipline. This decision of the guberniia committee is completely incorrect. It is in contradiction with the foundations of intra-party democracy. This decision, and the others which violate the elementary rights of party members and are in contradiction with intra-party democracy, must immediately be revoked by the guberniia committee.

The Congress calls upon all members of the Leningrad organization to end all such attempts at subverting the unity of our leninist party.

The opposition completely unmasked itself at the Congress. While the opposition leaders did not mention any disagreements with the Central Committee at the raion conferences or even at the guberniia party conference, but gathered votes under the banner of fidelity to the party leadership, at the Congress they appeared as a separate group, one in opposition to the Central Committee of our party.

Their assertion that the party is unaware of the kulak danger is untrue.

Their attempt to lessen the significance of the leninist slogan of the union of the proletariat and the village poor with the middle peasants, under the cover of a hue and cry about the kulak danger, is dangerous.

The assertion that the Congress did not accept the opposition amendment is untrue. The opposition did not submit an amendment but an ultimatum against which the Congress could hardly fail to object.

The Congress gave its own precise decision in the resolution adopted upon the proposal of the Moscow, Ural, Ukrainian (together with the Donbass), Tula, Ivanovo-Voznesensk, and Nizhny Novgorod delegations. This decision (like the others) of the Congress is binding upon all party members. Discussion of Congress decisions cannot and should not be permitted. Any worker-communist can see that the resolution on the Central Committee's report is permeated with leninism from its first line to its last. Any worker-communist can see that it is permeated with great concern for party unity. For the sake of this unity the Congress was willing to soften certain formulations of the resolution. And your delegates voted against this resolution.

The XIV Congress hereby declares that any statement that the party wants to belittle the significance of the Leningrad organization is a slander against the party.

The XIV Congress does not doubt that the Leningrad organization, which has always been in the vanguard of the party's ranks, will succeed in correcting the errors committed by the Leningrad delegation.

Long live the Leningrad organization of the vKP(b)!

Long live the unity of the leninist party!

2.51

On the Work of the Trade Unions 31 December 1925

...

PARTY AND THE UNIONS

38 The Communist Party, as the organized vanguard of the working class and the leader of the whole proletarian movement, unifies and directs all forms and aspects of this movement, all the workers' organizations, toward the implementation of the ultimate goal of the working class – the struggle for communism.

The trade unions can fulfil their tasks only under the guidance of the vKP as the vanguard and leader of the working class as a whole. The task of the party as a whole and of the individual party organs is to ensure correct and systematic guidance of the trade unions, effecting this through the corresponding communist trade union fractions.

However, despite the numerous resolutions of party congresses and conferences and the directives of the Central Committee, the Central Committee Plenum of 3 October 1925 disclosed inadequacies in the guidance of trade union fractions by the party organs.

Along with petty interference by party organs in the day-to-day work of trade union organizations, the following were revealed: a frivolous approach to selecting the leading party workers of trade union organizations, their frequent replacement which at times violated trade union democracy, the referral of most questions relating to working conditions, wages, collective agreements, etc., to party organs for their decision which is a violation of normal methods of trade union work and lowers the authority of the trade unions in the eyes of the broad working masses.

These deviations and errors in the guidance of trade union fractions by many local party organizations, which to a considerable extent were caused by the difficulties of the struggle to restore industry and increase labour productivity, are *especially inadmissible* now in view of the indubitable and ever-increasing successes in all branches of the economy.

39   The Congress hereby reminds all party organizations that the trade unions are broad organizations of the non-party worker masses, that work can be conducted successfully in them only by employing methods of persuasion, of comradely discipline, by developing the broad initiative of their members in all branches of union work. The trade unions must embody the fullest implementation of a healthy worker democracy. Methods of commanding and petty supervision are least of all permissible in the trade unions.

In addition to the tasks involved in reviving the soviets and developing intra-party democracy, the party is confronted with the task of rehabilitating, strengthening, and consolidating the trade unions, strengthening and deepening trade union democracy, and raising the authority of the unions in every way.

40   The trade unions were created and built up by our party. They have grown and achieved major successes under party leadership. Their achievements and failings are also the achievements and failings of our party and of the Soviet power whose support they are. In the trade unions the party has a mighty apparatus for bringing communist influence and its own policies to the whole mass of non-party workers, and through the latter to many millions of peasants.

The trade unions can successfully fulfil this role only if they support the party as a whole and if they have the unconditional confidence of the non-party workers, who view them as organs for defending and expressing their economic interests.

The Congress is obliged to indicate to all party organizations the need for a more attentive, sensitive, and solicitous attitude toward the trade unions and for a change in methods of implementing party leadership. Therefore, all party leadership of the trade union movement must be exercised through the fractions and groups of Communists in the trade unions.

41   While recognizing as correct the structuring of the trade union organizations along raion lines, in accordance with the similar structuring of the soviets, and the creation of republican and oblast trade union councils on normal electoral principles as well as the granting to them of expanded rights ensuring their independence and initiative in all areas of union activity, the Congress instructs its fraction in the All-Union Central Council of Trade Unions to maintain undeviatingly the unity of the general line, the unity of action, and the unified organizational structure of the trade unions over the whole territory of the USSR, combatting any possible manifestations of federalism in the trade union movement.

The principles of democratic centralism and trade union discipline which underlie the structure of the USSR trade unions must be strictly supported and consolidated by all – both by members of the party working in the trade unions and by the party organizations ...

2.52
Rules of the VKP(b)   31 December 1925
[Replaces Rules adopted in 1922; see 2.31]

I   ON PARTY MEMBERS

1   [As in 2.31, art. 1, on definition of party member]

2   [Revises 2.31, art. 2]   New members are accepted from among candidates who have passed through a school of political education and have served the established period of candidacy.

Party members are accepted from among candidates in the following ways:

a   Three categories are established: 1) workers and Red Army men of worker or peasant origin, 2) peasants (except Red Army men), whether engaged in farming or in cottage industry, who do not exploit another's labour, and 3) others (white collar workers, etc.).

The first category is divided into two groups:

The first group of category 1 includes industrial workers regularly engaged in physical labour for wages.

The second group of category 1 includes non-industrial workers, Red Army men of worker or peasant origin, and farm labourers.

b   To be admitted into the party, persons in the first group of category 1 must have two recommendations from two party members of one year's standing; persons in the second group of category 1 – recommendations from two party members of two years' standing; persons in category 2 – recommendations from three party members of two years' standing; persons in category 3 – recommendations from five party members of five years' standing.

Note When Komsomol members of category 1 and 2 are taken into the party, the recommendation of the Komsomol committee is equivalent to the recommendation of one party member.

c Persons formerly in other parties are accepted in exceptional cases on the recommendation of five party members of five years' standing and only through a production cell with obligatory approval by the Central Committee, regardless of the social position of the person accepted.

Note The Central Committee may grant to certain krai party committees or to central committees of national communist parties the right of ultimate approval of persons formerly in other parties.

d Before acceptance the recommendations must be verified by the local party committee.

e The question of admission into the party is first examined by the cell, is decided by the general meeting of the organization, and takes effect after approval by the party committee: for category 1 – by the uezd and raion committees (in cities and industrial centres), for 2 and 3 – by the okrug or guberniia committee. In city raion organizations the question of admission into the party is decided by the general meeting of party members. When the city raion contains more than 1000 members and candidates, admission is by the raion committee plenum, without the sanction of the general meeting.

f Youth up to twenty years of age (except Red Army men) enter the party only through the Komsomol.

3   [As in 2.31, art. 2, note to point 'b']

4   [New]   Seniority of party membership of candidates who are accepted as party members is counted from the day on which the general meeting of the appropriate cell decides to confirm a given comrade as a party member.

5   [Revises 2.31, art. 3]   Any member of one [party] organization who moves into the area of work of another organization is registered in the latter as one of its members.

Note The transfer of a party member from one organization to another is conducted according to rules established by the Central Committee of the party.

6   [Revises 2.31, art. 4]   The question of expelling anyone from the party is decided at the general meeting of the organization of which the person is a member and is approved by the guberniia (okrug) control commission or directly [decided] by the guberniia (okrug) control commis-

sion. The resolution of expulsion takes effect only after it has been approved by the guberniia (okrug) committee, the given person being removed from party work from the day of expulsion by the general meeting or by the guberniia control commission (okrug control commission). The party press announces the expulsion of a party member and gives the reasons for the expulsion.

II ON CANDIDATE MEMBERS OF THE PARTY

7   [As in 2.31, art. 5, on the period of candidacy]

8   [As in 2.31, art. 6, on procedure for admitting candidates]

9   [Revises 2.31, art. 7] The period of candidacy is at least six months for category 1; at least one year for category 2; and at least two years for category 3.

Note Persons formerly in other parties, regardless of their social position, must remain two years as candidate members.

10   [Revises 2.31, art. 8] Candidates for party membership participate in open meetings of the organization to which they belong. While participating in party meetings, party candidates do not have a deciding vote but participate only with a consultative vote.

11   [As in 2.31, art. 9, on dues for candidates]

III ON THE ORGANIZATIONAL STRUCTURE OF THE PARTY

12   [As in 2.31, art. 10, on democratic centralism]

13   [As in 2.31, art. 11, on the territorial principle]

14   [As in 2.31, art. 12, on autonomy in local matters]

15   [As in 2.31, art. 13, on the authority of the general meeting, conference, or congress]

16   [As in 2.31, art. 14, on the election of committees to function in the interval between general meetings, etc.]

17   [Revises 2.31, art. 15] The party's organizational structure is as follows:

  a Territory of the USSR – the All-Union Congress, the Central Committee;

  b Oblasts, republics, guberniias – oblast / krai conferences, congresses of the national communist parties, guberniia conferences – oblast / krai committees, central committees of national communist parties, guberniia committees.

  c Okrugs / uezds – okrug / uezd conferences – okrug / uezd committees.

  d Volosts / raions – volost / raion conferences – volost / raion committees.

  e Enterprises, villages, Red Army units, institutions – general cell meetings – cell bureaus.

18   [Revises 2.31, art 16]   The order of subordination and accountability, precedence and priority of party decisions (from the highest instance to the lowest): the all-union congress, the Central Committee, the oblast / krai conference, the oblast / krai committee, conference of national communist parties, the central committee of national communist parties, guberniia conference, etc.

19   [As in 2.31, art. 17, on special sections in committees; words (national, work among women, etc.) omitted]

[Art. 18, 1922 Rules, on approval of membership of lower organizations by higher deleted]

20   [As in 2.31, art. 19, on the right of each organization to establish its own press]

IV   ON THE CENTRAL INSTITUTIONS OF THE PARTY

21   [Revises 2.31, art. 20]   The party congress is the highest organ of the party. Regular congresses are convened annually. Extraordinary congresses are convened by the Central Committee on its own initiative or at the request of at least one-third of the party members represented at the preceding party congress. The convocation of a party congress and its agenda are announced at least a month and a half before the congress. Extraordinary congresses are convened on two months' notice.

A congress has a quorum if at least half the party members who were represented at the previous congress are represented at it.

Standards of representation at a party congress are set by the Central Committee.

22   [As in 2.31, art. 21, on the convocation of an extraordinary congress in the absence of action by the Central Committee]

23   [Revises 2.31, art. 22]   The congress:

    a   hears and approves the reports of the Central Committee, the Central Control Commission, the Central Revision Commission, and other central institutions;

    b   revises and alters the party Programme and Rules;

    c   defines the party's tactical line on current problems;

    d   elects the Central Committee, the Central Control Commission, and Central Revision Commission, etc.

24   [As in 2.31, art. 23, on the election of the Central Committee]

25   [Revises 2.31, art. 24]   In the intervals between congresses the Central Committee directs all party work, represents the party in its relations with other parties, organizations, and institutions, organizes the various party institutions and directs their activities; appoints the editors of the central organs, which work under its supervision; and approves the appointment of editors of party organs of major local organizations; organizes

and directs enterprises of social significance; distributes party funds and personnel; and controls the central treasury.

The Central Committee directs the work of the central Soviet and social organs through party fractions.

The Central Committee holds at least one plenum every two months. Candidate members of the Central Committee participate in the plenums with a consultative vote.

26   [Revises 2.31, art. 25]   The Central Committee organizes: for political work – a Political Bureau; for general leadership of organizational work – an Organizational Bureau; and for current work of an organizational and executive character – a Secretariat.

27   [Revises 2.31, art. 26]   Once during the intervals between party congresses, the Central Committee calls an all-union party conference of the representatives of local party organizations.

28   [Revises 2.31, art. 27]   The Central Committee regularly informs party organizations about its work.

29   [New]   The size of the elected Central Control Commission is determined by the party congress.

30   [Revises 2.31, art. 28]   The size of the elected Central Revision Commission is determined by the party congress; those elected must have at least ten years' party membership.

The Central Revision Commission reviews: a) the speed and correctness with which business is conducted in the central organs of the party and the good order of the apparatus of the Secretariat of the Central Committee of the VKP(b); b) the treasury and enterprises of the Central Committee of the VKP(b).

V   ON OBLAST / KRAI ORGANIZATIONS

31   [As in 2.31, art. 29, on formation of oblast organizations, with the word, 'krai' added as an alternative term and with the name of the party changed from RKP to VKP]

32   [Revises 2.31, art. 30]   Party organizations that serve the territories of the national republics (or oblasts) of the USSR or RSFSR are equivalent to oblast (or guberniia) organizations of the party, i.e., they are wholly subordinate to the Central Committee of the VKP(b).

33   [Revises 2.31, art. 31]   The oblast / krai committee (or central committee of the national communist party) is elected at the oblast / krai conference (or congress of the national communist party).

Note Presidiums or bureaus of krai and equivalent committees are approved by the Central Committee of the VKP(b).

34   [As in 2.31, art. 31, second paragraph, on oblast bureaus, with minor changes in wording and change in party name]

35   [Revises 2.31, art. 32]   The regular oblast / krai conferences (or congresses of national communist parties) are convened by the oblast / krai committee (central committee of the national communist party) once a year; extraordinary conferences by decision of the oblast / krai committee (central committee of the national communist party) or of one-third of the total membership of the organizations in the oblast / krai.

Standards of representation at the oblast / krai conference (congress of the national communist party) are set by the oblast / krai committee (central committee of the national communist party).

The oblast / krai conference (congress of the national communist party) hears and approves the reports of the oblast / krai committee (central committee of the national communist party), control commission, revision commission, and other oblast / krai institutions, discusses problems of party, soviet, economic, and trade union work in the oblast / krai or republic, and elects the oblast / krai committee, the oblast / krai control commission and revision commission (central committee, central control commission, and central revision commission of the national communist party).

36   [Revises 2.31, art. 33]   For the conduct of current work the oblast / krai committee appoints a bureau of at least five of its members.

The oblast / krai committee (central committee of the national communist party) organizes the various party institutions within the oblast / krai, directs their activities, appoints the editors of the oblast / krai party organ working under its supervision, organizes and directs its own enterprises of general significance for the oblast, allocates party funds and personnel within the oblast / krai, and controls the oblast / krai party treasury. The oblast / krai committee (central committee of the national communist party) directs the activities of the organs of the soviets, trade unions, co-operatives, and other organizations through their party fractions; it also directly guides the work of the Komsomol organizations and submits to the Central Committee detailed reports on its activities at the time and in the form determined by the Central Committee of the VKP(b).

The oblast / krai committee (or central committee of the national communist party) holds a plenum at least once every two months.

VI   ON GUBERNIIA ORGANIZATIONS

37   [Revises 2.31, art. 34]   The regular guberniia party conference is convened by the guberniia committee at least once a year, the special conferences by decision of the guberniia committee or of one-third of the total membership of the organizations in the guberniia.

The guberniia conference hears and approves the reports of the guberniia committee, the guberniia control commission, revision commission, and the other guberniia institutions, discusses problems of party, soviet, economic, and trade union work in the guberniia, elects guberniia committee, the guberniia control commission and revision commission, and the delegates to the all-union congress.

38 [Revises 2.31, art. 35] The guberniia committee is elected by the conference and must include party workers of the guberniia centre and of the other major working-class centres of the guberniia.

The guberniia committee meets at least once a month. For the conduct of current work the guberniia committee appoints a bureau of at least five of its members.

At least three of the bureau's members must be assigned only to party work.

The secretary of the guberniia committee must have seven years' party membership and must have the approval of the higher party authority (whose sanction is also needed for waivers of the requirement on length of party membership).

39 [Revises 2.31, art. 36] The guberniia committee approves the membership of the uezd and raion organizations of the guberniia with the sanction of the oblast / krai committees or of the Central Committee, organizes the various party institutions within the guberniia, directs their activities, appoints the editors of the guberniia party organ working under its supervision, organizes all its own enterprises of significance for the guberniia, allocates party funds and personnel within the guberniia, and controls the guberniia treasury.

The guberniia committee directs the activities of soviets, trade unions, co-operatives, and other organizations through their fractions; it also has immediate direction of the work of the Komsomol. The guberniia committee submits to the Central Committee reports on its activities at the times and in the form determined by the Central Committee. Oblast committees of autonomous republics and oblasts are equivalent to guberniia committees.

40 [Revises 2.31, art. 37] During the intervals between conferences the guberniia committee makes periodical informational reports to the general meetings or conferences of city or uezd / raion organizations; furthermore, the guberniia committee holds expanded plenary sessions or guberniia-wide meetings of the representatives of uezd and raion committees (directly subordinate to the guberniia committee).

41 [As in 2.31, art. 38, on raion organizations in cities]

VII ON OKRUG ORGANIZATIONS

42 [New] The okrug party conference is convened by the okrug committee at least once a year, extraordinary conferences – by decision of the okrug committee or of one-third of the total membership of the organizations within the okrug.

The okrug conference hears and approves reports of the okrug committee, control commission, revision commission, and the other okrug institutions; it elects the okrug committee, control commission, revision commission, and the delegates to the all-union party congress.

43   [New]   The okrug committee elected by the conference must include party workers of the okrug centre and of the other major working-class centres of the okrug.

44   [New]   The okrug committee meets at least once a month. For the conduct of current work the okrug committee appoints a bureau of at least five of its members.

At least three of the bureau's members must be assigned to party work only.

The secretary of the okrug committee must have five years' party membership and must have the approval of the higher party authority (whose sanction is also needed for waivers of the requirement on length of party membership).

45   [New]   The okrug committee approves the membership of the raion organizations and party cells (the membership of raion organizations must then be approved by the oblast / krai committee or the central committee of the national communist party), organizes the various party institutions within the okrug and directs their activities, appoints the editors of the okrug party organ working under its direction and supervision, organizes all its own enterprises of significance for the okrug, allocates party funds and personnel within the okrug, and controls the okrug treasury. The okrug committee directs the activities of the soviets, trade unions, co-operatives, and other associations through their fractions and also has the immediate direction of the work of the Komsomol. The okrug committee submits to the oblast / krai committee (or to the central committee of the national communist party) reports on its activities at the times and in the form determined by the Central Committee.

46   [New]   During the intervals between conferences the okrug committee makes periodic informational reports to the general meetings or conferences of city or raion organizations; furthermore, the okrug committee holds enlarged plenums or okrug-wide meetings of the representatives of raion committees and large cells (directly subordinate to the okrug committee).

47   [New]   If the higher party committee gives its assent, raion organizations equivalent to the raion committees of guberniia cities may be established in large okrug cities.

VIII   ON UEZD ORGANIZATIONS

48   [Revises 2.31, art. 39]   The uezd conference hears and approves the reports of the uezd committee, the revision commission, and the

plenipotentiary of the guberniia control commission, discusses problems of party, soviet, economic, and trade union work in the uezd, elects the committee, the revision commission, and the delegates to the guberniia conference. The conference is convened once every six months.

49 [Revises 2.31, art. 40] The uezd committee is elected at the uezd conference. The uezd committee appoints a bureau of not more than five to seven of its members, of whom at least three comrades must be released from all except party work.

The secretary of the uezd committee must have three years' party membership and must have the approval of the higher party authority (whose sanction is also needed for waivers of the requirement on length of party membership).

50 [Revises 2.31, art. 41] The uezd committee approves the volost and raion organizations and cells in the uezd with the sanction of the guberniia committee, organizes various party institutions in the uezd, directs their activities, organizes all its enterprises of general significance for the uezd, arranges meetings of volost cells and controls the uezd party treasury.

Note The uezd party committee may issue party literature and a party organ only with the permission of the guberniia committee.

51 [Revises 2.31, art. 42] Through party fractions the uezd committee directs the work of the uezd executive committee and also of trade union organizations, co-operative, and the other associations in the uezd; it also gives immediate direction to the work of the Komsomol organization.

IX ON VOLOST / RAION ORGANIZATIONS

52 [Revises 2.31, art. 43] The highest organ of the volost is the general meeting of the party members of the volost.

Note. In large volosts (raions), where it is difficult to convene a general meeting, a volost (raion) conference may be substituted for the general meeting. Such conferences are convened at least once every three months.

53 [Revises 2.31, art. 44] The volost / raion general meeting is convened at least once a month; the general meeting (*a*) decides questions on admission and expulsion of party members and submits its decisions for approval by higher party committees; (*b*) discusses and approves the report of the volost / raion committee; (*c*) elects the volost / raion committee; (*d*) elects delegates to uezd and other conferences; (*e*) discusses and approves the report of the volost / raion executive committee fraction.

54 [Revises 2.31, art. 45] The volost / raion committee is elected by the volost / raion party meeting or conference and serves for six months.

The secretaries of the volost committee must have one year's party membership.

Note No volost committee is organized in volosts with less than three village cells; in such volosts the uezd committees may entrust the cells of the volost centres with implementation of certain of the duties of the volost organizations.

55   [New]   The volost / raion committee meets at least once every two weeks.

56   [As in 2.31, art. 46, on the work of the volost / raion committee, except for the word raion added after volost, and the word okrug added after uezd]

X   ON PARTY CELLS

57   [Revises 2.31, art. 47]   The basis of the party organization is the party cell. The cell is approved by the okrug, uezd, or raion committee and has at least three members.

58   [New]   In major enterprises with large numbers of workers trade cells may be organized within the factory cell covering the whole enterprise, provided the okrug / uezd committee or raion committee (in cities) give their assent in each individual case.

59   [As in 2.31, art. 48, on the cell and the masses, except for addition of 'and their education' in point 2]

60   [Revises 2.31, art. 49]   For the conduct of current work the cell elects a bureau serving for six months.

The cell secretary must have at least one year's party membership; exceptions are permitted only with the sanction of the okrug / uezd committee or the raion committee (in cities).

XI   ON THE CONTROL COMMISSIONS

61   [Revises 2.31, art. 50]   In order to assist the party in the task of consolidating the unity and authority of the VKP(b), of attracting the best part of the working class into the party ranks, of struggling against violations of the VKP(b) Programme and Rules by party members, of comprehensively implementing the party line in the activities of soviet organs, and of developing measures to improve and strengthen the soviet and economic apparatus – control commissions are organized through elections at the congress and at oblast, krai, guberniia, and okrug conferences and report to the organs which have elected them.

Note Okrug control commissions are organized only with the permission of the VKP(b) Central Committee and the Central Control Commission.

62   [Revises 2.31, art. 50]   Control commission resolutions may not be countermanded by the corresponding party committee but enter into force only with the latter's agreement and are implemented by the latter.

In case of disagreement the matter is referred to a joint meeting. If agreement with the committee is not achieved, the matter is referred for decision to the appropriate party conference or to the higher control commission or to the party congress.

A *On the Central Control Commission*

63 [New] The Central Control Commission is elected mainly from among workers and peasants possessing the necessary party, soviet, economic, or direct production practice. Central Control Commission members who are to work directly in the Central Control Commission or the Rabkrin must have at least ten years' party membership; Central Control Commission members working in local organs – at least seven years', and production workers and peasants – at least five years'.

64 [New] Central Control Commission members may not be simultaneously members of the Central Committee and may not occupy administrative and economic posts.

Note Waivers of this rule require, in each case, the special permission of the vkp(b) Central Committee and the Central Control Commission Presidium.

65 [New] The Central Control Commission holds one plenum every three months. For the direction of all current work of Central Control Commission organs during the periods between plenums a presidium of twenty-one members and nine candidates is formed together with its executive organ, the secretariat; a Central Control Commission party board is also formed to examine violations of party ethics and of the vkp(b) Rules and Programme.

66 [New] Central Control Commission members participate with consultative vote at all-union party congresses and conferences, at congresses and conferences of national communist parties, and at the krai, oblast, guberniia, okrug, uezd, and other levels, as well as at plenums, meetings, sessions, and assemblies. Only members and candidate members of the Central Control Commission Presidium are present at vkp(b) Central Committee plenums. Central Control Commission members participate with deciding vote at joint plenums of the Central Committee and the Central Control Commission.

The Central Control Commission Presidium delegates three members, with their three deputies, to meetings of the Central Committee Politburo and five members, with their five deputies, to meetings of the Central Committee Orgburo and Secretariat, with a consultative vote in all cases.

67 [New] The Central Control Commission has the right to assign tasks, within the limits of its competence, to all party members and party organizations.

B *On the control commissions of national communist parties and of oblast / krai, guberniia, and okrug parties*

68 [New] The number of members and candidates in the central control commissions of national communist parties and of oblast / krai, guber-

niia, and okrug control commissions is determined by the Central Control Commission of the vKP(b) in proportion with the size of the organization, the economy of the region, and other considerations.

Control commission members and candidate members are elected mainly from among those workers and peasants who are most steadfast in party matters, who have – for the central control commissions of the national communist parties and for oblast / krai control commissions – at least seven years' party membership, and for the other control commissions – at least five years' party membership, who possess the appropriate party, soviet, and trade union practice, and are capable of assuring effective party and soviet control.

Note Waivers are permitted with the agreement of the vKP(b) Central Committee and the Presidium of the Central Control Commission.

69   [New]   Control commission members may not at the same time be members of party committees and may not occupy responsible administrative positions.

Note Waivers are permitted with the agreement of the Presidium of the vKP(b) Central Control Commission.

70   [New]   The control commission plenum elects a presidium and a party board and nominates the membership of the board of Rabkrin.

71   [New]   Control commission members and candidates take part with consultative vote in meetings of the corresponding party committee plenum and in party conferences and meetings in their organizations.

The control commission presidium delegates some of its members to participate, with consultative vote, in meetings of the corresponding party committee bureaus.

72   [New]   Divergences between decisions of the control commission and of the party committee are referred to a joint meeting. If agreement is not reached, the matter is referred, in the case of the central control commissions of the national communist parties, oblast / krai control commissions, and guberniia control commissions which are not under the central control commission of a national communist party or under an oblast / krai control commission to the Central Control Commission of the vKP(b); in the case of the guberniia control commissions and oblast control commissions which are under a central control commission of a national communist party or a krai control commission the matter is referred to the corresponding central control commission of the national communist party or to the oblast / krai control commission.

73   [New]   The control commission has the right to assign tasks, within the limits of its competence, to all party members and party organizations.

c   *On control commission plenipotentiaries*

74   [New]   The institution of control commission plenipotentiary is hereby created in the okrug and uezd party organizations in order to effect a

direct and vital connection between the control commission organs and the lower-level party organizations together with the worker and peasant masses.

75 [New] The okrug and uezd party conferences will propose as control commission plenipotentiaries primarily those workers and peasants who are most steadfast in party matters and have at least five years' party membership; they must be approved by the corresponding control commission.

Note It is desirable that control commission members be proposed as plenipotentiaries.

76 [New] In large raions of major political and economic significance the control commission plenipotentiaries are released from all except party work – in all other raions they do this in addition to their other work.

77 [New] Control commission plenipotentiaries have the right to take part, with consultative vote, in meetings of the corresponding party committee, in party conferences, and in control commission meetings and sessions.

XII ON PARTY ORGANIZATIONS IN THE RED ARMY

78 [New] The Political Administration of the Army, as the military section of the Central Committee, has the overall direction of party work in the Red Army and Navy. The Political Administration exercises its leadership through its appointed politotdels (fronts, districts, fleets, armies, divisions) and military commissars and through the party commissions elected at the corresponding army conference.

Cells and party collectives in the Red Army and Navy work on the basis of special instructions approved by the Central Committee.

79 [New] Commanders of politotdels of districts, fleets, and armies must have seven years' party membership; commanders of politotdels of divisions and brigades four years'.

80 [New] Party commissions are concerned with questions of admission and expulsion of party members and candidates; they also watch for violations of the party Programme and Rules. Commission members must have five years' party membership.

81 [New] Party members and candidates in the Red Army and Navy are appointed and transferred by the appropriate political organ.

Transfers of leading party workers in the army (commanding officers and political personnel) are co-ordinated with party organs according to Central Committee instructions.

82 [New] Political organs in the armed forces must maintain close ties with local party committees by means of constant participation by leaders of political organs and by military commissars in local party committees, and also by the systematic hearing by party committees of reports by commanders of political organs and military commissars on political work

in military units. Local party committees and control commissions direct the work of party commissions with respect to admission to candidacy, transfer from candidacy to party membership, and the struggle against violations of party Rules by means of a systematic hearing of reports on the organization of this work in divisional and district party commissions and through issuing appropriate directives to the latter.

XIII   ON PARTY DISCIPLINE

83   [As in 2.31, art. 51, on party discipline in general]

84   [Revises 2.31, art. 52]   Failure to implement instructions of higher organizations and other offences recognized as criminal by party opinion are punished as follows: in the case of the organization, by censure, appointment of a provisional committee from above and general re-registration (dissolution of the organization); in the case of individual party members, one or another aspect of censure (publicize the offence, reprimand, etc.), public censure, temporary removal from responsible party and soviet work, expulsion from the party, expulsion from the party with a report of the offence to the administrative and judicial authorities. Demotion to candidate membership is not permitted as a measure of party punishment.

85   [Revises 2.31, art. 53]   Disciplinary offences are examined by general meetings and by control commissions in the usual order through the established authorities.

XIV   ON PARTY FINANCES

86   [As in 2.31, art. 54, on sources of funds]

87   [Revises 2.31, art. 55]   Membership dues are set at not less than one-half of one per cent of salary. There are four categories of membership dues, depending on the amount earned. The first category pays one-half of one per cent; the second one per cent; the third two per cent; and the fourth three per cent.

88   [Revises 2.31, art. 56]   In the case of persons, such as peasants, whose wages are indeterminate, membership dues are set by local guberniia committees.

89   [As in 2.31, art. 57, on persons who are excused from dues, with minor changes in wording]

90   [Revises 2.31, art. 58]   Initiation dues of 3 per cent are paid by candidate members and no one is excused from paying them.

91   [As in 2.31, art. 59, on penalty for non-payment of dues]

92   [New]   The procedure for collecting membership dues and party contributions is set out in a special instruction.

XV   ON FRACTIONS IN NON-PARTY ORGANIZATIONS

93   [As in 2.31, art. 60, on the organization of party fractions in non-party

organizations, with addition of last sentence, which is transposed from art. 61 and with minor changes in wording]

94 [As in 2.31, art. 61, on representation of fractions in party committees when they are being discussed, with deletion of last sentence, which is transposed to art. 60 and with minor changes in wording]

95 [Revises 2.31, art. 62] Fractions, regardless of their importance, are entirely subordinate to the corresponding party organizations. In all matters with respect to which there exist legal decisions of the corresponding party organization fractions must adhere to these decisions strictly and undeviatingly. The committee has the right to introduce any member into the fraction or recall him from it but must inform the fraction of the reasons for such a step, with the recall or introduction of a new member taking place in accordance with the Rules and the resolution on the non-party organ in which the fraction is working. The fraction is autonomous in matters of its internal life and current work.

If there is a substantial disagreement between the party committee and the fraction on any matter within the latter's competence, the committee must examine the matter a second time with the representatives of the fraction and adopt a final decision which is immediately to be carried out by the fraction.

96 [As in 2.31, art. 63, on nomination of persons for the most important positions in the organization in which the fraction is working]

97 [As in 2.31, art. 64, on matters of political significance]

98 [Revises 2.31, art. 65] Any matter subject to decision by the non-party organization in which the fraction is working, and which is important in principle, as well as all matters which necessitate co-ordinated statements of Communists, must be discussed beforehand in the general meeting or in the bureau of the fraction.

99 [As in 2.31, art. 66, on unanimity of voting in the fraction, words 'according to the Rules' are added at the end of the paragraph]

100 [New] Fractions in non-party organs do not maintain direct contacts with fractions in lower-level organs. When a fraction has to carry out its decisions according to the party line, this is done through the appropriate party committee (signed by the secretary of the committee and by a member of the bureau of the fraction).

Pravda, 25 December 1925 (2.49); 26 December (2.50); *Spravochnik partiinogo rabotnika* VI, 268–71 (2.51); 481–94 (2.52)

KPSS v rezoliutsiiakh III, 243–311

2.53
On the Procedure for Transferring Responsible
Workers of the OGPU   25 May 1926

As a supplement to the instruction of 16 November 1925 ... the Central Committee orders the following guidelines to be adopted for transfers of responsible OGPU workers who are not included in the Central Committee nomenclature:

I   The transfer or recall of plenipotentiary representatives, the chiefs of guberniia / oblast or okrug OGPU sections, and their deputies is effected by the OGPU by agreement with the corresponding party committee.

Note The transfer of OGPU workers who are designated for assignment by the Central Committee must be approved by the VKP(b) Central Committee following the established procedure.

2   The OGPU may independently (departmentally) transfer, with notification of the appropriate party committee, OGPU personnel who are party members, occupying the following positions:

a   Chiefs and deputy-chiefs of the Secret-Operational and Administrative-Organizational administrations of plenipotentiary OGPU offices.

b   Branch and section chiefs of plenipotentiary OGPU offices and their assistants, representatives and deputy-representatives of OGPU organs, and agents who have completed the TOGPU school.

c   Inspectors of plenipotentiary OGPU offices as well as of guberniia, oblast, and okrug OGPU sections.

d   Chiefs of units and branches of guberniia / oblast and okrug OGPU sections.

e   Uezd representatives of guberniia / oblast OGPU sections and raion representatives of okrug OGPU sections.

3   Other party members working in organs of the OGPU may be recalled by party committees only by agreement with the corresponding OGPU organ, and if possible, with replacement of each recalled worker by another of equal value.

> *Spravochnik partiinogo*
> *rabotnika* VI, 567

Joint Plenum of the Central Committee and
the Central Control Commission   14–23 July 1926

The message of the XIV Congress was evidently well understood in Leningrad. It was thus comparatively easy for Stalin's emissary Molotov, sent to Leningrad, to cleanse the organization of all anti-Stalin elements. Within a few weeks after the Congress the Leningrad organization was under Stalin's control and S. M. Kirov became its leader instead of Zinoviev, who was left without a power base.

It was only now, when powerless, and after he contributed considerably to the destruction of Trotsky and the preceding opposition groups, that Zinoviev began, in Trotsky's words, to knock on his door (L. Trotsky, *Stalin*, London, 1947, 400). In fact, Zinoviev hinted at such a possibility at the XIV Congress. Sometime during July 1926 an uneasy alliance was formed between Trotsky, Zinoviev, Kamenev and some of the members of the former Democratic Centralists and Workers' Opposition. Both Trotsky, on the one hand, and Zinoviev, on the other, issued amnesty to each other (as Stalin put it) by declaring that their mutual attacks in the past had been mistaken (*Works* VIII, 248–9). The alliance was doomed to fail from the start. Not only did they have little chance of support from below, but various groups in the alliance also held each other in utter contempt. Furthermore, Trotsky, allegedly under Stalin's pressure, strengthened Stalin's hand and weakened his own (if that was still possible) by publicly rejecting as slanderous and malicious, the information on Lenin's Testament, published in 1925 by Max Eastman in his book *Since Lenin Died* (New York, 1925; *Bol'shevik*, no. 16, 1 September 1925, 68; Stalin, *Works* X, 180). The United Opposition (also referred to as new opposition) under Trotsky's guidance prepared its own programme and warned against the dangers of a possible 'Thermidor' in Russia. Stalin did not wait long with his answer. The July Plenum provided the first opportunity for a party gathering at which he was able to confront the United Opposition. It was apparently a lively encounter, the stress of which may have contributed to the death of Felix Dzerzhinsky, the founder of the Cheka and a prominent supporter of Stalin. He collapsed during the session of the plenum. Although Stalin was assured of a considerable majority (no voting records are available), he sought to enhance the plenum's prestige and add weight to its decisions by inviting the membership of the Central Revision Commission to participate at its meetings.

The principal anti-opposition move of the plenum was the adoption of the resolution 'On the Affair of Lashevich and Others' (2.54) which led to the expulsion of Zinoviev's supporter Lashevich from the Central Committee (and also from his position on the Revolutionary Military Council) and to the expulsion of Zinoviev from the Politburo. A stern warning was issued to the other opposition members.

Other resolutions of the plenum dealt with the re-election of the Soviets, the housing problem, and the date of the forthcoming XV Party Conference.

To replace the expelled Zinoviev, the plenum appointed Rudzutak as a full member of the Politburo, and Ordzhonikidze, Andreev, Kirov, Mikoyan, and Kaganovich, as candidate members of the Politburo.

2.54
On the Affair of Comrade Lashevich and
Others and on Party Unity   23 July 1926

1   The preservation of our party's unity has always been the concern of
the whole party and of its central organs – the Central Committee and the
Central Control Commission. Headed by Comrade Lenin, the party has
successfully warded off any manifestations of factionalism, any attempts at
combatting the party made by factions and groupings 'with platforms of
their own and with a will to close ranks to a certain extent and create their
own group discipline' (from the resolution of the X Congress [2.13]). The X
Congress, which met precisely at the watershed in the life of the country
and the party, during the transition to the NEP, adopted a resolution on
party unity which was written and submitted by Lenin. In this resolution
'the Congress draws the attention of all party members to the fact that the
unity and cohesion of their ranks, and the achievement of full trust among
the party members and of truly friendly work that truly embodies the unity
of will of the proletarian vanguard, are particularly necessary at the present
moment when a number of circumstances are intensifying the waverings of
the petty bourgeois population in the country.' And the Congress further
indicates that 'It is essential that all class-conscious workers clearly realize
the harmfulness and inadmissibility of any factionalism whatsoever, which
inevitably leads, in practice, to less friendly work and to repeated and
intensified attempts by enemies of the ruling party, who have attached
themselves to it under false pretenses to deepen divisions and use them for
purposes of counter-revolution.'

    The resolution on unity proposed by Lenin and adopted by the X
Congress has been the guiding directive of the party and all its organs for
preserving the cohesiveness of its ranks, and, relying on the will of the X
Congress, the party has coped with all manifestations of factionalism up
until the XIV Congress. At the moment of the XIV Congress the party has
once again been confronted with the factionalism of the so-called 'new
opposition.'

    The XIV Party Congress decisively rejected the political and organi-
zational views of the opposition, which pervert the leninist line, but despite
that, the Congress and the new VKP(b) Central Committee thought it
possible and necessary to introduce supporters of the opposition into all the
party's leading organs, including the Central Committee and its Politburo.
The party hoped that the opposition would realize its errors and correct
them in the process of businesslike work. The opposition was thus afforded
a full opportunity to defend its views in the normal party way whenever
differences of view arose on one question or another. Although the opposition still continued to adhere to its errors, as pointed out by the XIV

Congress, and has introduced elements of clear factional irreconcilability into the work of the Politburo and the Central Committee, this advocacy of opposition views within the Central Committee in the normal party way did not provoke any serious concern about preserving party unity on the part of the Central Committee or on that of the Central Control Commission.

2   But, unfortunately, the opposition has not confined its struggle to the legitimate advocacy of its views within the limits of the party Rules and has recently passed to direct violations of the resolutions of the X and XIV congresses on maintaining unity in party ranks, resorting in its anti-party struggle to attempts at setting up an illegal factional organization opposed to the party and directed against its unity.

The party has recently been confronted with a whole series of such factional moves by the 'new opposition,' taking the form of: the holding of illegal conspiratorial meetings; the reproduction and distribution in Moscow and other cities of specially selected secret party documents aimed at discrediting the party line (similar secret Politburo documents have been distributed among party members and obtained by organizations in Briansk, Saratov, Vladivostok, Piatigorsk, Omsk, Gomel, Odessa, etc.); the dispatching of its agents to other party organizations with the aim of setting up underground factional groups there (the trip of Comrade G. Belenky to Odessa in order to organize an illegal faction with its special code, attendance, etc.).

It must be noted that all the threads of the opposition's factional moves lead to the apparatus of the ECCI headed by Politburo member Comrade Zinoviev.

Particular mention must be made of the illegal factional meeting called by the ECCI worker, Comrade G. Belenky, in the woods near Moscow which was a schismatic step unprecedented in the life of our party. This meeting, held with all the rules of conspiracy (patrols, a strictly factional selection of those invited, etc.), was not only led by an ECCI worker who presided over it but, what is also unheard of in our party, a candidate member of the VKP(b) Central Committee, Comrade Lashevich, makes a report at this secret meeting in which he calls upon those assembled to organize for a struggle against the party, against the Central Committee which it had elected.

All of these disruptive steps by the opposition already show that the opposition has resolved to move from the legal advocacy of its views to creating an illegal all-union organization which is in opposition to the party and thus is preparing a split in its ranks ...

Taking into account all of the above, the Central Committee and Central Control Commission plenum resolves:

a considering it intolerable that a member of the Central Committee Politburo should assume the de facto leadership of the opposition's fac-

tional struggle, Comrade Zinoviev is hereby expelled from the Central
Committee Politburo, and at the same time all opposition members, regardless of their position in the party, are warned that continuation of their work
on setting up a faction in opposition to the party will force the Central
Committee and the Central Control Commission to defend party unity by
drawing certain organizational conclusions also with respect to them ...

Without firm party discipline, without subordination of the minority
to the majority, the party would be unable to carry out the historic tasks
imposed upon it by the October Revolution, would be unable to preserve
and strengthen the power of the proletarian dictatorship and thus to ensure
the triumph of socialism. The Central Committee and the Central Control
Commission are firmly convinced that our party will find within itself
sufficient strength to repulse any attempts at violating party unity, will
repulse any attempts at splitting the party and at demoralizing it.

Down with factions and factional struggle, which prevent the party
from leading the great building of socialism!

Long live the unity and cohesion of the leninist party!

Pravda, 25 July 1926   *KPSS v rezoliutsiiakh* III, 332–54

Joint Plenum of the Central Committee and
the Central Control Commission   23, 26 October 1926

This meeting was called primarily to approve the agenda for the forthcoming
XV Party Conference, and specifically to prepare the strategy with which to
confront the opposition at the Conference. Once again Stalin was prepared to
go to any length to provide the greatest possible impression of his own
legitimacy by including in the plenum not only the Central Committee, the
Central Control Commission, and the Central Revision Commission but also
a delegation from the Executive Committee of the Communist International.
The participation of foreigners at the plenum was an exceptional occurrence,
to be sure, but it was made necessary, from Stalin's point of view, by the fact
that Zinoviev was still the head of the Comintern and also by the support of
Zinoviev against Stalin by some foreign communists. Through these selected
foreign delegates Stalin wished to demonstrate that the denunciation of
Zinoviev and his allies had international communist approval as well. Stalin's
position was made easier once more by yet another blunder of the opposition,
who, before the meeting took place, began campaigning at party meetings in
factories against the leadership, in order to hang on to some power within the

party, as Kamenev explained at the XV Party Conference. Stalin swiftly counter-attacked; the oppositionists (Trotsky, Zinoviev, and Kamenev among them) panicked and, it would seem, on their own volition, published in *Pravda* (17 October 1926) a statement confessing to a violation of party discipline, and at the same time denouncing their few supporters in the Comintern as well as the few remaining former members of the Workers' Opposition with whom they had allied only a few short months before. Provided with this ammunition, the plenum passed a resolution 'On the Situation in the Party' (2.55) based on a report by Kirov, Zinoviev's successor in Leningrad. The resolution relieved Zinoviev of his position as the head of the Comintern, expelled Trotsky from the Politburo, and Kamenev as a candidate member of the Politburo. The plenum also adopted theses on the opposition which formed the basis of a resolution passed at the XV Conference (2.56).

Also in preparation for the Conference, the plenum approved resolutions, presented by the Politburo, on trade unions and on the economy.

The two sessions of the plenum were split by an interval of two days, not a common occurrence, which may be explained by the role of the plenum in setting the agenda for the forthcoming Conference that opened during the day of the last session of the plenum.

The plenum promoted Orakhelashvili from candidate member to full member of the Central Committee to replace the late Dzerzhinsky.

2.55
On the Situation in the Party as a Result of Factional Activity and the Violation of Party Discipline by a Number of Central Committee Members 23 October 1926

The following draft resolution submitted by Comrade Kirov in the name of the Leningrad members of the Central Committee is hereby approved:

1   In view of the violation of party discipline by Central Committee members comrades Trotsky, Zinoviev, Kamenev, Piatakov, Evdokimov, Sokolnikov, Smilga, and candidate member of the Central Committee, Comrade Nikolaeva – the Central Committee and Central Control Commission plenum warns all these comrades and calls to their attention the inadmissibility of such conduct by members of the party's leading institution.

2   In view of the fact that Comrade Zinoviev does not represent the VKP(b) line in the Communist International, and because of his leading factional work in the Communist International, he has lost the confidence of many communist parties (the German, English, French, American, etc.), which have stated this in their resolutions, the Central Committee and the

Central Control Commission find it impossible that Comrade Zinoviev should continue to work in the Communist International.

3   Because comrades Trotsky and Kamenev have been leaders of factional activity since the July Plenum of the Central Committee and the Central Control Commission, the Central Committee and Central Control Commission plenum resolves to release Comrade Trotsky from the duties of member of the Central Committee Politburo, and Comrade Kamenev from those of candidate member of the Central Committee Politburo.

In connection with the death of Comrade Dzerzhinsky the plenum resolved to admit into the Central Committee, the first candidate member of the Control Committee, Comrade Orakhelashvili.

Pravda, 24 October 1926   KPSS v rezoliutsiiakh III, 360–1

XV Party Conference   26 October–3 November 1926

The result of the United Opposition is 'the adding together of emasculated forces,' remarked Stalin, to the accompaniment of laughter and prolonged applause, in his report to the Conference (*Works* VIII, 245–310, 311–72). His observation was correct. The opposition lost whatever little support it may have had among the rank and file by their inexplicable surrender of a few days before. The surrender combined with Stalin's control over the selection of delegates put those oppositionists who were allowed to participate at the Conference in an untenable position.

There were 194 delegates with a deciding vote, a relatively small but dependable number of stalinists, while the delegates with a consultative vote numbered 640 and included Trotsky, Kamenev, Zinoviev, and other unreliables. The latter delegates could not, of course, influence the unanimity of the votes, but did participate in the discussions.

The stalinist leadership completely dominated the Conference and each of its reports led to the adoption of a resolution: Bukharin's on the Comintern, which included an attack on the left wing supporters of the Soviet opposition in the German Communist Party; Rykov's on economic matters; Tomsky's on the trade unions; and Stalin's on the opposition.

The last was the central point of the discussions at the Conference. Stalin set out his position by once again defending the slogan 'socialism in one country,' copiously quoting and distorting, when his case required it, Marx, Engels, Lenin, as well as the writings of the opposition and splitting hairs over whether victory or final victory of socialism was possible in Russia under contemporary conditions. Ideology was not Stalin's strongest point but political tactics were, and he exploited the former antagonism among the now allied opposition with consummate skill. Invoking Trotsky's 'my party – right or wrong' he challenged the opposition 'to renounce openly and sincerely' their 'errors of principle' (one thing the opposition did not admit in their previous surrender) and concluded by a threat that if they did not do so then 'the party which gave you a beating yesterday will proceed to finish you off tomorrow.'

Trotsky, Zinoviev, and Kamenev tried to answer Stalin's attack as best they could over the constant, loud, and crude interruptions by hecklers. Inevitably, fully conscious of their vulnerability, they remained on the defensive throughout the proceedings.

Not surprisingly, the theses of the October Plenum were passed unanimously in the form of a resolution 'On the Opposition Bloc in the VKP(b)' (2.56) in response to Stalin's report. Unexpected support came to Stalin from Krupskaia, who at this time no longer collaborated with the oppositionists, and while present at the Conference as a delegate with a consultative vote, did not intervene in the discussions. She later explained that she came to the conclusion that the opposition overdid its attacks on the leadership, that 'quantity turned into quality' and 'comradely criticism gave way to factional criticism' (in a letter to *Pravda*, 20 May 1927). A few months later, invoking Lenin's authority, she came forward once more in support of Stalin against the United Opposition (in a speech to the Bauman raion party conference reprinted in *Pravda*, 5 November 1927).

2.56
On the Opposition Bloc in the VKP(b)   3 November 1926

The characteristic trait of the period through which we are passing is the complication of the struggle between the capitalist nations and our country on the one hand, and between the socialist elements and the capitalist elements within our country on the other.

If the attempts of world capital toward the economic encirclement of our country, toward its political isolation, toward a disguised blockade, and finally toward direct revenge because the workers of the USSR help the struggling workers of the West and the oppressed peoples of the East, create external difficulties [for the USSR], then the transition of our country from a period of recovery to a period of reconstruction in industry and agriculture on the basis of a higher technology – complicating the struggle between capitalist and socialist elements of our economy – creates domestic difficulties.

The party sees these difficulties and is able to overcome them. The party, with the help of the proletarian millions, is already overcoming these difficulties, confidently leading the country along the road to socialism. But not all the detachments of our party believe in the possibility of continued progressive movement. Some parts of our party, few in number it is true, are intimidated by the difficulties, experience fatigue and hesitation, fall into despair and generate defeatist morale, are infected with scepticism with regard to the creative strength of the proletariat, and give way to the ideology of capitulation.

In this sense, the present period of crisis is quite reminiscent of that of October 1917. Then as now, the complex situation and difficulties in the transition from a bourgeois revolution to a proletarian revolution engendered in one section of the party hesitation, defeatism, and scepticism regarding the possibility that the proletariat could seize and hold power (Kamenev, Zinoviev). So now, in the present crisis, the difficulties of changing to a new phase in the building of socialism engender hesitations in some circles of our party, disbelief in the possibility of victory for the socialist elements of our party over capitalist elements, lack of trust in the chance for the triumphant building of socialism in the USSR.

The opposition bloc is an expression of these low and defeatist moods in the ranks of one part of our party.

The party sees the difficulties and is able to overcome them. But, in order to overcome these difficulties, first and foremost it is necessary to overcome the low spirits and the defeatist ideology in the ranks of one part of the party.

The opposition bloc in its document dated 16 October 1926, while repudiating factionalism and disassociating itself from the clearly menshevist groupings within the VKP and outside it, at the same time declares that it stands firm on its old positions of principle, does not reject these mistakes of principle and will defend these mistaken views in the framework of the party Rules.

It follows from this that the opposition bloc intends henceforth to generate defeatist morale and capitulation in the party, intends henceforth to propagandize its mistaken views in the party.

Therefore the immediate task of the party consists in revealing the principal failure of the basic views of the opposition bloc, in explaining their incompatibility with the foundations of leninism, and in conducting a vigorous ideological struggle against the mistakes of the opposition bloc in matters of principle with the aim of overcoming them completely.

I   THE TRANSITION OF THE 'NEW OPPOSITION' TO TROTSKYISM ON THE
    BASIC QUESTION OF THE CHARACTER AND THE PERSPECTIVES OF OUR
    REVOLUTION

The party proceeds from the fact that our revolution is a socialist revolution, that the October Revolution is not only a signal, a stimulus, and a point of departure for a socialist revolution in the West, but is at the same time, first, a basis for the subsequent development of world revolution and, second, the opening of the transitional period from capitalism to socialism in the USSR (the dictatorship of the proletariat), during the course of which the proletariat – given a correct policy regarding the peasantry – can and will successfully build a complete socialist society, if, of course, the power of the international revolutionary movement on the one hand and the power of the proletariat of the USSR on the other, will be great enough in order to guard the USSR from the military intervention of imperialism.

Trotskyism adheres to completely different views on the character and perspectives of our revolution. Despite the fact that trotskyism went along with the party in October 1917, it proceeded and continues to proceed from the point that our revolution *in itself* is not, *in essence*, socialist; that the October Revolution is *only* a signal, a stimulus, and a point of departure for a socialist revolution in the West; that if delay ensues in the world revolution and the victorious socialist revolution in the West does not come very soon, then proletarian power in Russia must collapse or degenerate (which is one and the same) under the pressure of unavoidable clashes between the proletariat and the peasantry.

While the party, in organizing the October Revolution, proceeded from the fact that 'the victory of socialism is possible originally in a few or even in one capitalist country taken separately'; that 'the victorious proletariat of this country, having expropriated the capitalists and having organized its socialist production,' can and must stand up '*against* the rest of the capitalist world by attracting to itself the oppressed classes of other countries by encouraging them to rise up against the capitalists, if necessary by coming out even with armed might against the exploiting classes and their states' (Lenin). Trotskyism, on the contrary, collaborating with the Bolsheviks in the October period, proceeded from the view that 'it is hopeless to think ... that, for example, revolutionary Russia could stand its ground in the face of conservative Europe' (Trotsky).

While the party proceeds from the fact that in the Soviet Union there is 'everything necessary and sufficient' for the construction of a full socialist society' (Lenin, 'On Co-operation'), Trotskyism, conversely, proceeds from the view that 'a genuine advance in the socialist economy in Russia will become possible only after the victory of the proletariat in the most important countries in Europe' (Trotsky).

While the party proceeds from the principle of 'ten to twenty years of proper relations with the peasantry and the securing of victory on a world scale' (Lenin), Trotskyism, on the contrary, proceeds from the view that the proletariat can have no proper relations with the peasantry until the victory of the world revolution; that the proletariat, having taken power, will have hostile clashes not only with all groups in the bourgeoisie which supported it at first in its revolutionary struggle, but with the broad masses of the peasantry with whose assistance it came to power'; that 'the contradictions in the position of a worker government in a backward country with the overwhelming majority of the peasant population will find their solution only on an international scale, in the arena of the world revolution of the proletariat' (Trotsky).

The Conference asserts that the views of Comrade Trotsky and those of one mind with him on the fundamental question of the character and perspectives of our revolution have nothing in common with the views of our party, with leninism.

The Conference considers that such views, in deprecating the historic role and position of our revolution as bases for the subsequent development of the world revolutionary movement, in weakening the will of the Soviet proletariat for the future building of socialism and thus hindering the release of the forces of the international revolution, contradict the principles of true internationalism and the basic line of the Communist International ... The Conference therefore considers the views of Comrade Trotsky and those who think like him to be a *social democratic deviation* in our party on the fundamental question of the character and perspectives of our revolution.

The basic fact in the development of intra-party relations in the VKP after the XIV Congress (which discussed the principal views of the 'new opposition') is the circumstance that the 'new opposition' (comrades Zinoviev, Kamenev), which earlier fought against trotskyism, against social democratic deviation in our party, went over to the side of the ideological position of trotskyism; that it wholly and fully gave up its former all-party positions for trotskyism and now comes out *for* trotskyism with the same fervour with which it came out *against* trotskyism before.

The transfer of the 'new opposition' to the side of trotskyism was determined by two major circumstances:

a   the fatigue, the hesitations, the defeatist morale that is alien to the proletariat and the defeatism amongst the supporters of the 'new opposition' in the face of new difficulties in the crisis we are passing through. The current vacillations and the defeatism of comrades Kamenev and Zinoviev arose not by chance, but as a repetition, a relapse of those vacillations and defeatist morale which these comrades displayed nine years ago, in October 1917, in the face of difficulties during the crisis period of that time;

b   the utter defeat of the 'new opposition' at the XIV Congress and the endeavour, which arose in this connection, to achieve at all costs a unification with the trotskyists in order that, with the union of the two groups – the trotskyists and the 'new opposition' – the weakness and the isolation of these groups from the proletarian masses could be compensated for; the more so since the ideological positions of trotskyism were completely matched by the current defeatist mood of the 'new opposition.'

It is necessary to explain the fact that the opposition bloc turned into a gathering place for each and every person who was denounced by the party and the Comintern, for every bankrupt trend within the vKP(b) and outside of it, from the 'Democratic Centralists' and the 'Workers' Opposition' in the vKP(b) to the 'ultra-leftist' opportunists in Germany and the liquidators like Souvarine in France.

From this follows the unscrupulousness and lack of policy principles which lay at the base of the existence of the bloc of trotskyites and the 'new opposition' and without which they could not bring together the various anti-party trends.

In this way, the trotskyites on the one hand and the 'new opposition' on the other completely naturally met on the *common* platform of the social democratic deviation and the unprincipled union of diverse anti-party elements in a struggle against the party, thus forming an opposition bloc that represents – in a new form – something akin to the relapse of the August bloc (1912–14).

II THE PRACTICAL PLATFORM OF THE OPPOSITION BLOC

The practical platform of the opposition bloc is a direct continuation of the basic mistake of that bloc on the question of the character and perspectives of our revolution.

The most important features of the practical platform of the opposition bloc centre on these basic points:

a The questions of the international movement. The party proceeds from the fact that the advanced capitalist countries are experiencing by and large a state of partial, temporary stabilization, that the current period is an inter-revolutionary period, committing the communist parties to a preparation of the proletariat for the forthcoming revolution, that the capitalist offensive, vainly trying to consolidate stabilization, cannot but cause a reciprocal struggle and a union of the forces of the working class against capital, that the communist parties must intervene in the intensifying class struggle and turn the attacks of capital into counter-attacks of the proletariat in order to achieve the dictatorship of the proletariat, that to achieve these goals the communist parties must seize the working class millions who still side with the reformist trade unions and with the II International, that the tactics of the united front are thus necessary and required for the communist parties.

The opposition bloc proceeds from completely different premises. Not believing in the inner strength of our revolution and falling into despair in the face of delay in the world revolution, the opposition bloc is sliding off the ground of marxist analysis of class forces of revolution onto the ground of 'ultra-leftist' self-deception and 'revolutionary' adventurism, denies the presence of partial capitalist stabilization and thus takes to the road of putschism.

Hence there is the demand of the opposition for a review of the tactics of the united front and of the breakdown of the Anglo-Russian committee, the misunderstanding of the role of the trade unions and the slogan on the replacement of the trade unions with new, invented 'revolutionary' organizations of the proletariat.

Hence there is the support on the part of the opposition bloc of the ultra-leftist squawkers and opportunists in the Communist International (for example, in the German party).

The Conference believes that the policy of the opposition bloc in the international sphere does not answer the interests of the international revolutionary movement.

  b The proletariat and the peasantry in the USSR. The party proceeds from the fact that the 'supreme principle of dictatorship is the maintenance of the union of the proletariat and the peasantry so that it could retain a leading role and state power' (Lenin), that the proletariat can and must be a predominant force with regard to the basic mass of the peasantry in the economic sphere, in the sphere of building socialism, just as the proletariat was in October 1917 a predominant force with regard to the peasantry in the political sphere, in the matter of overthrowing the power of the bourgeoisie and establishing a dictatorship of the proletariat; that the industrialization of the country can be started only if it will be supported by the gradual improvement of the material status of the majority of the peasants (the poor, the middle peasants) who offer a basic market for our industry; that in view of this there must be introduced an economic policy (a price policy, a fiscal policy, etc.) which strengthens the union of industry and peasant economy and preserves the union of the working class and the basic mass of the peasantry.

The opposition bloc proceeds from completely different assumptions. Departing from the basic lines of leninism on the peasant question, not believing in the hegemony of the proletariat with regard to the peasantry in the matter of building socialism and viewing the peasantry mainly as a hostile environment, the opposition bloc suggests economic and financial measures that are capable only of dissolving the union of town and country, of pulling down the union of the working class and the peasantry and thereby undermining any chance for real industrialization. Thus, for example: a) the suggestion of the opposition of raising the selling prices for manufactured goods. Such an increase cannot but cause a rise in retail prices, an impoverishment of the poor peasants and of many strata of the middle peasantry, a decrease in the domestic market capacity, discord between the proletariat and the peasantry, a fall in the exchange rate of chervonets [currency partly based on gold and foreign reserves], and finally a lowering of real wages; b) the suggestion of the opposition on the maximum fiscal pressure on the peasantry, a pressure which cannot but open breaches in the union of the workers and peasants.

The Conference considers that the policy of the opposition bloc on the peasantry does not answer the interests of the industrialization of the country and the dictatorship of the proletariat.

c *The struggle against the party apparatus under the banner of a struggle with bureaucratism in the party.* The party proceeds from the fact that the party apparatus and the party masses comprise a single whole; that the party apparatus (the Central Committee, the Central Control Commission, the oblast organizations of the party, the guberniia committees, the okrug committees, the uezd committees, the cell bureaus, etc.) embodies in itself the leading element of the party on the whole; that the party apparatus contains in itself the best people of the proletariat who must and need be criticized for errors, who must be and need to be 'refreshed,' but who cannot be defamed, without risking demoralization of the party and leaving it unarmed.

The opposition bloc, conversely, proceeds by contrasting the party masses with the party apparatus; tries to disparage the leading role of the party apparatus, reducing it to functions of registrar and propagandist; sets the party masses against the party apparatus and thus discredits the party apparatus, weakening its position in the matter of state leadership.

The Conference believes that the policy of the opposition bloc, not having anything in common with leninism, is capable of leading only to the disarming of the party in its struggle against the bureaucratism of the state apparatus, for the real alteration of this apparatus and thereby for the strengthening of the dictatorship of the proletariat.

d *The struggle against the 'regime' in the party under the banner of a struggle for intra-party democracy.* The party proceeds from the fact that 'who weakens, however so little, the iron discipline of the party of the proletariat (especially during its dictatorship) in fact helps the bourgeoisie against the proletariat' (Lenin); that intra-party democracy is essential not for weakening and breaking down the proletarian discipline in the party, but for strengthening and consolidating it; that without iron discipline in the party, without a firm regime in the party which is strengthened by the sympathy and support of the proletarian millions, the dictatorship of the proletariat is impossible.

The opposition bloc, on the contrary, proceeds by juxtaposing intra-party democracy to party discipline, confuses the freedom of factions and alignments with intra-party democracy and tries to use this sort of democracy for breaking down party discipline and for undermining the unity of the party. Naturally the summons of the opposition bloc to a struggle against the 'regime' in the party, which leads in reality to a defence of freedom for the factions and alignments in the party, is thereby a summons which, in expanded form, was seized upon by anti-proletarian elements of our country as an anchorage of salvation from the regime of the dictatorship of the proletariat.

The Conference considers that the struggle of the opposition bloc against the 'regime' in the party, having nothing in common with the organizational principles of leninism, is capable of leading only to the destruction of party unity, to the weakening of the dictatorship of the proletariat and to the unleashing of anti-proletarian forces in the country that try to weaken and break down the dictatorship.

As one of the means to dislocate party discipline and to aggravate the struggle within the party, the opposition bloc chose the method of all-union discussion. It tried to press this discussion in October of this year. Considering the free discussion of questions on disagreements in the theoretical journals of our party as necessary and recognizing that each member of the party has the right of free criticism of the deficiencies in our party work, the Conference at the same time recalls the words of Lenin to the effect that our party is not a debating club, but a militant organization of the proletariat. The Conference considers that an all-union discussion can be recognized as necessary only in the event: a) if this need is recognized at least by several local party organizations from the guberniias or oblasts; b) if within the Central Committee there is not a firm enough majority present on the most vital questions of party policy; c) if, despite a firm majority in the Central Committee that holds to a definite point of view, the Central Committee still considers it necessary to verify the correctness of its policy by means of a discussion in the party. In all these instances an all-union discussion can begin and can be carried out only after a corresponding decision by the Central Committee.

The Conference states that at the moment when the opposition bloc demanded the convening of an all-union discussion, not a single one of these conditions was met.

The Conference therefore considered that the Central Committee of the party acted completely properly, having deemed the discussion unsuitable and having condemned the opposition bloc for its attempts to impose an all-union discussion on the party concerning questions already decided by the party.

In summing up the analysis of the practical platform of the opposition bloc, the Conference determines that this platform signals the departure of the opposition bloc from the class line of the proletarian revolution on the most vital questions of foreign and domestic policy.

III   'REVOLUTIONARY' WORDS AND OPPORTUNISTIC DEEDS OF
       THE OPPOSITION BLOC

The characteristic feature of the opposition bloc is the fact that, while actually being an expression of the social democratic deviation in our party, indeed defending an opportunistic policy, it tries none the less to invest its actions with revolutionary phraseology, it tries to criticize the party 'from the left,' tries to dress itself up in a 'leftist' toga. This circumstance can be explained in that the communist proletarians to whom the opposition bloc mainly appeals are the most revolutionary of all proletarians in the world; that they, educated in the spirit of revolutionary traditions, simply will not hear open criticism from the right; in view of which the opposition bloc, in order to palm off its opportunistic wares, is forced to paste onto them a label of revolutionary character, knowing well that only with such a ruse can the attention of the revolutionary proletarians be attracted.

But since the opposition bloc is in any case a champion of the social democratic deviation, since it in fact defends an opportunistic policy, then the words and deeds of the opposition bloc invariably come into conflict with each other. Hence there is an inner discrepancy in the work of the opposition bloc. Hence there is discord between word and deed, between revolutionary phrase and opportunistic deed.

The opposition clamorously criticizes the party and the Comintern 'from the left' and suggests at the same time a review of the tactics of the united front, breakdown of the Anglo-Russian committee, breaking with the trade unions, their replacement by new 'revolutionary' organizations, believing by all these means to promote the revolution; but in fact what comes from this is help to Thomas and Udegest [European right-wing socialists], breakaway of the communist parties from the trade unions, the weakening of the positions of world communism – that is slowing down the revolutionary movement. 'Revolutionaries' – in words, but accomplices of the Thomases and the Udegests – in deeds.

With much fanfare the opposition 'berates' the party 'from the left' and demands at the same time a rise in selling prices for manufactured goods, thinking in this way to hasten industrialization; but in fact what comes from this is a disorganization of the domestic market, a break in the union between industry and peasant economy, a fall in the chervonets exchange rate, a fall in real wages and thus – a detriment to industrialization of any kind. Industrialists in words – but accomplices of the opponents of industrialization – in deed.

The opposition accuses the party of unwillingness to struggle with the bureaucratism of the state apparatus and at the same time suggests a rise in selling prices, thinking, obviously, that this rise has no relation to the question of bureaucratism in the state apparatus; and in fact it turns out that this must mean the full bureaucratization of the state economic apparatus, for high selling prices are the surest means of decay of industry and of bureaucratization of the economic apparatus. Against bureaucratism – in words, but defenders and champions of bureaucratism of the state apparatus – in deed.

The opposition fusses and shouts against private capital and suggests at the same time to take state capital out of circulation for the benefit of industry, thinking with this to undermine private capital; but in fact what comes from this is every conceivable strengthening of private capital, for taking state capital out of circulation that represents the basic sphere of work of private capital cannot but place trade at the complete disposal of private capital. A struggle with private capital – in words but aid to private capital – in deed.

The opposition shouts about the degeneration of the party apparatus; but in fact it turns out that when the Central Committee brings up the question of expelling one of the truly degenerate communists, Mr Ossovsky [a minor party official], the opposition displays highest loyalty to this gentleman by voting against his expulsion. Against degeneration – in words but accomplices and defenders of degeneration – in deed.

The opposition shouted about intra-party democracy and demanded at the same time an all-union discussion, thinking with this to realize intra-party democracy; but in fact it turned out that in imposing discussion on the huge majority of the party by an insignificant minority, the opposition committed the foulest act of violation of any democracy whatsoever. For intra-party democracy – in words but violation of the basic principles of any democracy – in deed.

In the period of aggravated class war that we are living through in the workers' movement, only one of two possible policies can have bearing: either a policy of menshevism or a policy of leninism. The attempts of the opposition bloc to take the middle course between two opposing lines, under the cover of 'left revolutionary' phraseology and with emphasis on criticism against the VKP had to lead and in truth did lead to the slipping down of the opposition bloc into the camp of the opponents of leninism.

The enemies of the VKP and the Comintern know the worth of the 'revolutionary' phraseology of the opposition bloc. Therefore, disregarding this phraseology as nothing worthy, they unanimously praise the opposition bloc for its non-revolutionary deeds while adopting as their own the opposition slogan of the struggle with the basic lines of the VKP and the Comintern. It cannot be considered mere chance that the Socialist Revolutionaries and the Constitutional Democrats, the Russian Mensheviks and the German 'left' Social Democrats, that all of them found it possible to express openly their sympathy for the struggle of the opposition bloc against the party while banking on the fact that the struggle of the opposition bloc would lead to a split and that a split would unleash the anti-proletarian forces of our country to the joy of the enemies of revolution.

The Conference considers that the party must pay special heed to unmasking the 'revolutionary' disguise and to revealing the opportunistic essence of the opposition bloc.

The Conference believes that the party must protect the unity in its ranks as the apple of its eye, considering that the unity of our party is the basic antidote for each and every counter-revolutionary feeble impulse of the enemies of revolution.

IV   CONCLUSIONS

Summing up the past stage of the intra-party struggle, the XV Conference of the VKP states that the party manifested its great ideological growth in this struggle, repudiated without hesitation the views of the opposition on matters of principle and achieved a swift and decisive victory over the opposition bloc by forcing it to repudiate openly factionalism, and by compelling it to disassociate itself from clearly opportunistic groupings within and without the VKP.

The Conference states that, as a result of the attempts of the opposition bloc to thrust a discussion on the party and to break its unity, the party masses rallied even more around the Central Committee, thereby isolated the opposition and in this way ensured real unity of the ranks of our party.

The Conference considers that only with the active support of the wide party masses could the Central Committee achieve such successes; that the activity and the consciousness shown by the party masses in the struggle with the disorganizing work of the opposition bloc are the best indications that the party is living and developing on the principles of real intra-party democracy.

Fully and completely approving of the policy of the Central Committee in its struggle to attain unity, the Conference feels that the tasks of the party in the future must consist in the following:

1   To take care that the achieved minimum, necessary for party unity, had really been implemented.

2   To conduct a decisive ideological struggle with the social democratic deviation in our party, explaining to the masses the erroneousness of the views of the opposition bloc on matters of principle and bringing to light the opportunistic content of these views no matter with what 'revolutionary' phrases it covers itself.

3   To ensure that the opposition bloc recognizes the erroneousness of its views.

4   In every way possible to preserve party unity, suppressing each and every attempt to resume factionalism and to violate discipline.

Pravda, 13 November 1926   *KPSS v rezoliutsiiakh* III, 363–412

2.57
The Regulation of [Party] Growth in
Connection with the Census Results   13 October 1927

The review of the regulation of party growth and the preliminary results of the party census show that the party has continued to grow since the XIV Congress (from 1,078,185 members and candidate members on 1 January 1926, to 1,199,616 on 1 July 1927) and that the basic mass of those admitted during the past three years have remained in its ranks (more than 800,000 persons, and of these more than half a million workers, were taken into the party between 1924 and 1926).

The party, on the whole, has coped with the task of educating the vast stratum of proletarians taken into its ranks, especially in connection with the first Lenin Enrolment and the mass enrolment of 1925. Not only has the overwhelming majority (more than 90 per cent) of those newly admitted remained in the party's ranks but, at the same time, out of this stratum has grown and been trained a very considerable party aktiv which is working in party, trade union, soviet, and other organs.

This rapid party growth was inevitably accompanied by a weeding out of a certain part of those newly admitted. Thus, in 1925 – 3.7 per cent, in 1926 – 4.3 per cent, and in the first half of 1927 (the period of the party census) – 5 per cent were expelled for various reasons or left the party voluntarily. Thus the party census led to an additional departure of about 3 per cent of the party's membership (i.e., 36,000 persons of whom about 20,000 were production workers). Data from the Central Control Commission's selective investigation of thirty-four cells indicate that the overwhelming majority of the workers who left the party during the census were candidates and persons who had been party members only since 1924 or later, i.e., who entered the party during the mass recruitment. And the greater part of those who left the party (more than 80 per cent) never participated in social work – either before entering the party or subsequently. This shows that poor work by the cells prevented the party from retaining the allegiance of these more backward elements of the working class. An investigation of sixty-five large enterprises has also confirmed that the number weeded out was still larger due to the weak involvement of newly admitted workers in both educational and party organizational work.

The intensified attention, during the last two years, of the Central Committee and local organs to the regulation of party growth through the composition of new admissions has led to a systematic increase in the number of production workers (from 42 per cent in 1925 to 56 per cent in 1927), with a corresponding reduction in the number of white collar workers (from 25.6 per cent to 16.3 per cent). But the rate of this increase is, without any doubt, inadequate, since as a result of the inevitable weeding out of a part of those admitted, the advancement of production workers to leading economic, trade union, and soviet positions, transfers to study in high educational institutions, etc. (preliminary calculations indicate that every year more than 20,000 persons transfer to work outside factories or higher educational institutions, which is about 6 per cent of the production workers in the party or about 2.5 per cent of the total party membership), the party not only fails to take in enough production workers to cover the losses but there is even a slight reduction in the ratio of production workers to total party membership (from 40.8 per cent on 1 January 1926, to 37.5 per cent on 1 July 1927) with an absolute increase in the number of party members of worker origin (from 582,000 on 1 January 1926, to 621,000 on 1 July 1927).

The overall increase in the activity of the worker masses and the growth of the non-party worker aktiv in enterprises makes possible a significant intensification of the admission of production workers into the party (data from a survey of sixty-five enterprises indicate that only about 30 per cent of the non-party worker aktiv has been brought into the party). It must be noted in particular that the Komsomol and the meetings of women delegates have done too little to prepare their activists for admission into the party.

On the basis of the resolutions of the XIII and XIV Party Congresses on intensifying the admission of production workers into the party, and considering the observed increase in working-class activity, the Central Committee directs the attention of all party organizations to the necessity of intensifying the recruitment of production workers into the party so that within two years production workers will make up not less than half the party's total membership.

On the basis of the above, the Central Committee orders as follows:

1   While developing the recruitment of workers into the party, principally and primarily in the large enterprises, party committees must carry this effort into the shops and devote primary attention to bringing into the party activist workers who are involved in trade union, soviet, and other social organizations. Workers are to be drawn into the party in this way through systematic selection of the best elements of the working class. It is necessary, in particular, to strengthen the individual ties between the most politically developed party members and the non-party activists, to attract more of them to open cell and party school meetings, and to involve them in practical work on party assignments.

2   In view of the weakness of the Komsomol and party organizations in training Komsomol and worker youth for entry into the party, and in view of the presence in many enterprises of a significant number of persons who are backward in this respect; finally, in view of the fact that the greater part

of the worker youth activists must, as they develop politically, be drawn into the party's ranks, the party organizations are hereby ordered to intensify their assistance to Komsomol organizations in the party training of youth.

3   In view of the low percentage of Communists among women workers, especially in the textile industry, party organizations are hereby ordered to take steps to intensify the work of meetings of women workers dealing with political education of women worker delegates, especially those working in production, for the purpose of their joining the party. Greater attention must be directed to improving the work of political cells, to involving women worker activists in political education schools, and to strengthening the organizational links between party organizations and delegates' meetings, by assigning a cadre of party workers to assist the delegates' meetings and also by having women delegates participate in open party cell meetings, etc.

4   Noting the still inadequate recruitment, by village party organizations, of farm labourers and agricultural workers, and also of the poor peasants' aktiv, the Central Committee orders party organizations to concentrate their attention on the training, and on drawing into the party, of the farm labourer and poor peasants' aktiv which is developing in the union of agricultural workers, in poor peasant groups, in practical soviet and co-operative work, etc., by having them participate in open cell meetings, schools of political education and advancement, etc.

Village organizations must direct attention to intensifying the political education of women farm labourers, through meetings of delegates and through the union of agricultural workers.

5   The limitations on the admission of white collar workers established by the XIII Congress must be strictly applied, and before each new member is admitted a thorough check must be made of his activity in social work among workers and his readiness and capability to be of genuine and substantial assistance to the party and the proletarian dictatorship. Before admitting white collar workers to party membership or candidate membership, party committees must become personally acquainted with them and must interrogate the persons giving them recommendations.

Izvestiia tsentral'nogo komiteta,
22 October 1927

Joint Plenum of the Central Committee and the Central Control Commission   21–23 October 1927

While Stalin appeared to be in full control of the domestic situation during the previous year or so, matters were not going so well for him on the international front. The British General Strike in 1926, the Arcos raid and the resulting break of diplomatic relations with the Soviet Union by Britain, did not enhance Stalin's stature. But his worst blunder was the mismanagement of the Chinese revolution. Needless to say, this provided material for the opposition, who, in their last desperate attempts to save themselves, tried to exploit it to their own advantage. In May 1927 a group of party members signed the so-called Declaration of 84 (later signed by as many as 300 members) which proclaimed support for Trotsky and Zinoviev and criticized Stalin for his international and domestic excesses. Stalin could not afford to tolerate such a challenge. The XV Party Congress, already overdue, had to be called in the not too distant future, and Stalin did not cherish the prospects of the oppositionists exposing his blunders before such a gathering. This was especially so because the break of diplomatic relations by Britain also brought about a war scare which provided an opportunity for Trotsky to present himself as an alternative leader to Stalin. Trotsky argued in his so-called Clemenceau statement that Stalin and his followers were incapable of leading the country in war and that, should war come, he would do his utmost to take over its direction.

As a result, Stalin not only unleashed the OGPU who subjected the oppositionists to a variety of harassments but at the same time tried, at a joint plenum of the Central Committee and the Central Control Commission in July-August 1927, to have Trotsky and Zinoviev expelled from the Central Committee, accusing Trotsky, on the basis of the Clemenceau statement, of defeatism and disloyalty. However, the unexpected happened. The plenum, composed of a vast majority of Stalin's supporters, at first approved the expulsion of Trotsky and Zinoviev but later (mainly because of Ordzhonikidze's efforts) worked out a compromise under which the two opposition leaders once more declared their loyalty to the Central Committee. The oppositionists, encouraged by this unexpected turn of events, began to make preparations for the forthcoming congress and worked out a platform (later published by Trotsky in exile under the title *The Real Situation in Russia*, London, 1928) on the basis of which they sought to bring about a change of leadership. However, on Stalin's insistence, the Central Committee, invoking the resolution of the X Party Congress on party unity, refused to grant the opposition permission to circulate their material freely as a basis for the pre-congress discussion. When the oppositionists set up their own printing shop it was closed down by the OGPU and several of them, including Preobrazhensky, were expelled from the party and some arrested.

Trotsky, seeing his last opportunity slipping through his fingers, took the occasion of the October Joint Plenum to attack Stalin (for the first time in public) on the basis of Lenin's Testament, only to be rebuffed by the General Secretary who quoted back at him Trotsky's own article of 1925 in which he

denied the existence of any such document (see above p. 285). On this
occasion, the joint plenum gave in to Stalin's pressure and passed a resolution
(2.58) expelling Trotsky and Zinoviev from the Central Committee.

2.58
On the Expulsion of Comrades Zinoviev and Trotsky
from the Central Committee of the VKP(b)   23 October 1927

The joint plenum of the Central Committee and the Central Control Commission in August 1927 showed a high degree of tolerance and flexibility
with regard to comrades Trotsky and Zinoviev by giving them an opportunity to keep their promise of 8 August on the destruction of elements of
factionalism and by confining themselves to a warning which was a final
warning.

However, comrades Trotsky and Zinoviev for the second time de-
ceived the party and in the rudest manner broke the commitments to which
they pledged themselves, and not only did not obliterate 'the elements of
factionalism,' but, on the contrary, brought the factional struggle against
the party and its unity to a stage that verged on the formation of a new
anti-leninist party together with bourgeois intellectuals.

In view of this, the Joint Plenum of the Central Committee and the
Central Control Commission resolves: to *expel* comrades Trotsky and
Zinoviev from membership in the Central Committee.

The Joint Plenum of the Central Committee and the Central Control
Commission resolves, further, to submit for the consideration of the XV
Party Congress all data on the schismatic activity of the leaders of the
trotskyite opposition (the organization of the illegal anti-party printing
house for the destruction of the party, the bloc with renegades Maslow,
Ruth Fischer, Souvarine for the destruction of the Comintern, and so forth)
as well as the groups of comrades V. Smirnov – Sapronov.

Pravda, 25 October 1927   *KPSS v rezoliutsiiakh* III, 542

2.59
On the Anti-party Statements of
the Leaders of the Opposition   14 November 1927

On 7 November 1927, the tenth anniversary of the bolshevik revolution, the
oppositionists staged demonstrations in Moscow and Leningrad. One week

later, on 14 November, 'the question of anti-Soviet activities of the leaders of the Trotskyite-Zinovievite bloc was discussed by the Central Committee and the Central Control Commission of the VKP(b) which resolved to expell Trotsky and Zinoviev from the party.' In addition, Kamenev was now expelled with four others from the Central Committee.

The Central Committee offer to publish opposition material mentioned in the decision below must be properly understood. The Central Committee insisted that the material appear in official party publication. The opposition, with good reason, suspected that it would be censored and made the attempt, as we saw above, to publish it separately.

The decision (2.59) was issued under the name of the Central Committee and the Central Control Commission but did not emanate from a joint plenum of these bodies.

1   In order to ensure for the entire party a correct and normal preparation for the XV Congress, the Central Committee of the VKP(b) published, in accordance with the party Rules, the theses of the Central Committee more than a month before the congress. It published in the 'Discussion Leaflet' the counter-theses of the opposition soon after receiving them and also the speeches and articles of the opposition. It accorded the opposition a complete opportunity to come out in defence of its views in print as well as in party organizations and in party cells. But neither Comrade Zinoviev nor Comrade Trotsky considered it necessary to appear at party meetings, continuing, however, to arrange illegal meetings without the participation of delegates from the party.

2   Despite this, the opposition not only did not renounce the policy of dissension and the breach of party unity, but, on the contrary, it strengthened its destructive work even more. Repudiated by all cells in which discussion took place, not collecting even one per cent of the votes of party members, the opposition: a) continues to put out illegal anti-party leaflets where party activity is depicted in a slanderous fashion. It continues to print its publications in illegal printing houses, equipped by means of stealing print, paper, and so forth; b) organizes a series of anti-party illegal meetings, attracting non-proletarian elements which are alien to the party and the working class; c) prepares at anti-party underground meetings an anti-party demonstration. It discusses plans for a future struggle with the party and draws into this discussion bourgeois elements alien to the party, unleashing in this way anti-Soviet forces which are hostile to the proletariat; d) willfully seizes the premises of the auditorium of the Moscow Higher Technical College for its anti-party meeting, subjecting the representatives of the party to a beating; e) turns to setting up open meetings with speeches directed against the VKP(b), against the Soviet

government; f) on the day of the tenth anniversary of the October Revolution, instead of coming to the common tribune at the Lenin Mausoleum and greeting the working-class millions of Moscow and Leningrad together with other comrades, the leaders of the opposition depart for the byroads and lanes, where they try to organize speeches against the party. They spread about and paste up illegal anti-party leaflets, appealing against the party to elements alien to the party and to the Soviet government. They seize premises, replacing Soviet superintendents and setting up their armed guard, and thereby transgress the limits of Soviet legality and in this way openly become the mouthpiece of powers hostile to the regime of the proletarian dictatorship.

3   The Central Control Commission and the Central Committee of the vkp(b) recognizing these actions as completely intolerable for party members and moreover for members of the Central Committee and the Central Control Commission, resolve:

a   to expel from the Central Committee and the Central Control Commission the members and candidates of the Central Committee comrades Kamenev, Smilga, Evdokimov, Rakovsky, Avdeev, and the members of the Central Control Commission Muralov, Bakaev, Shklovsky, Peterson, Soloviev, and Lizdin;

b   to consider it necessary to withdraw these comrades from leading party and Soviet work;

c   with regard to comrades Trotsky and Zinoviev, who are the main leaders of this entire anti-party activity which is clearly developing into an anti-Soviet activity and undermining the dictatorship of the proletariat, noting that the categorical demand directed at comrades Zinoviev and Trotsky at the session of 11 November 1927 to immediately stop the organization of illegal anti-party meetings and to renounce the extension of intra-party discussions beyond the limits of the party was answered by them with an ostentatious exit from the session of the presidium of the Central Control Commission, and several hours later by a written answer dated 11 November 1927 in which essentially they reject these commitments to the party which are most fundamental for each party member – to expel comrades Trotsky and Zinoviev from the ranks of the vkp(b);

d   to warn comrades Kamenev, Smilga, Evdokimov, Rakovsky, Avdeev, Radek, Muralov, Bakaev, Shklovsky, Peterson, Soloviev, and Lizdin that the question of the compatibility of their factional activity with their remaining in the ranks of the vkp(b) is being placed by the presidium of the Central Control Commission for discussion by the XV Party Congress.

Izvestiia tsentral'nogo komiteta,   *KPSS v rezoliutsiiakh* III, 545–7
15 November 1927

XV Party Congress   2–19 December 1927

Although the party Rules called for annual congresses, two years had elapsed between the XIV and XV congresses. This was due, in all likelihood, to Stalin's desire to rout the opposition before the Congress met. In spite of his well-organized and substantial majority over the opposition, he felt vulnerable to the charges levelled at him.

Trotsky, Zinoviev, and some others had been expelled from the party before the Congress, which meted out this punishment to those of their cohorts who were spared up to that time (2.63). Six of the oppositionists, Kamenev among them, were (on the decision of the Central Committee) included among the 771 delegates with a consultative vote (there were 898 delegates with a deciding vote at the Congress). While allowed to speak to the Central Committee report, they were subjected to incessant jeers and insults from the floor. In two instances the heckling was so severe that the chairman, Petrovsky, declared that the presidium of the Congress shared the delegates' indignation and put it to a vote whether or not the speakers should continue. In both cases, to the refrain of insults, the delegates voted for cutting the speakers off. Completely routed, many of the oppositionists signed several appeals requesting to be readmitted to the party only to have their requests rejected. As a last resort, twenty-three of them, including Zinoviev and Kamenev, but not Trotsky, signed a degrading petition denouncing their previous actions and confessing to 'anti-leninism.' They were not even admitted into the hall of the Congress to submit their petition but a short resolution was passed referring the petition to the Central Committee and the Central Control Commission for judgment in individual cases six months after the receipt of each petition. Some were later readmitted into the party – until their final expulsion during the terror of the thirties. The resolution concerning these penitents was passed with one negative vote. This appears to be the last gesture of its kind in the history of the party, at least at a Congress, although the lonely dissenter explained to the Congress presidium just before closing of the last session that his disagreement was not one of principle and therefore he was changing his vote. The resolution was then recorded as having passed unanimously.

The Central Committee's political and organizational reports delivered by Stalin (*Works* x, 275–363, 364–82) and S.V. Kosior (not to be confused with V.V. Kosior, the supporter of Trotsky, who some time before was 'exiled' by Stalin to a diplomatic post at the Soviet Embassy in Paris) respectively, were the subject of a resolution that was approved unanimously (2.60), as was the resolution approving Molotov's report on work in the countryside (2.62).

In a major symbolic act the XV Congress ordered the Central Committee to supervise the preparation of the Five-Year Plan for the National Economy

(2.61). The resolution to this end had already been passed at the October Joint Plenum. The presentation of this project to the Congress by two reporters, Rykov and Krzhizhanovsky, and its unanimous adoption, was mainly a formality.

At this stage, it was not made clear how far-reaching and grandiose the actual process of collectivization and industrialization would be. However, the leadership was preparing its ground carefully. Stalin exploited the war scare for all it was worth (which does not mean that he did not believe it) and argued that the period of 'peaceful coexistence' was coming to an end, giving place to a period of imperialist attacks against the USSR. Implicitly, at least, he forewarned his listeners that the country had to industrialize as rapidly as it could, to be able to withstand such attacks.

There was, in all likelihood, another reason behind Stalin's decision to adopt the policy of the left. We saw that both Lenin and Stalin were concerned about the effects of the NEP on the population and the steps which they took to counterbalance them. It is entirely possible that by 1927 Stalin became convinced that if the economic freedoms enjoyed by the peasants and others were not drastically curtailed, the future of socialism, as he saw it, was very much in question. It cannot be denied that the policy served his own personal purposes but it would be a mistake to view his tactical and ideological switches solely in the light of the power struggle.

To make collectivization easier, the kulak had to be eliminated through economic measures, Stalin stressed, but not to the exclusion of administrative measures, which as he admitted, meant the employment of the OGPU. The dreaded organization was beginning to come into its own. Molotov also referred to 'the great public benefit' which it already brought and would bring in the future, in the fight against the petty bourgeoisie, a term which included all the foes of stalinism.

The Congress also amended the party Rules. The interval between congresses was extended from one to two years, legitimizing the two-year period which elapsed between the XIV and XV congresses. The plenums of the Central Control Commission were made mandatory every three months, and current work of that organ was to be conducted by a presidium of twenty-one members and nine candidates. Four of the presidium members and four of the candidates were to be delegates to the Politburo, instead of the three, as had been the case until then. In addition, two other brief resolutions were passed: one which stipulated that any member who refused to answer truthfully questions submitted to him by the Central Control Commission would be liable to immediate expulsion from the party. The second, in the spirit of the XV Party Conference resolution on opposition (2.56), for all practical purposes, forbade any 'all-union' discussion of any subject unless specifically allowed by an appropriate decision of the Central Committee. Other resolutions of the Congress dealt with the Central Revision Commission, the Central Control Commission, and the Comintern.

The Congress elected a new Central Committee, purging the defeated opposition and rewarding those who helped in the triumph. The number was increased to seventy-one members and fifty candidates. After the Congress, the Central Committee elevated Kuibyshev to full membership of the Politburo, where he joined Bukharin, Voroshilov, Kalinin, Molotov, Rykov, Rudzutak (who became a full member in 1926), Stalin, and Tomsky. The candidate members were all stalinists with the exception of Uglanov who was a protegé of Bukharin; they included Petrovsky (who with Uglanov had been a candidate since 1925), Andreev, Kirov, Mikoyan, Kaganovich, Chubar (who had been promoted to this position in 1926), and S. V. Kosior, the one new candidate member.

2.60
On the Central Committee Report 7 December 1927

The XV Congress of the All-Union Communist Party (Bolsheviks) entirely supports the political and organizational line of the Central Committee.

The Congress hereby notes that under the very difficult conditions of the reporting period the correct policy of the Central Committee strengthened the international power of the USSR, enhanced our country's role as a factor for international peace, and ensured the growth in authority of the USSR as the home of the world-wide revolutionary movement.

Within the country the Central Committee's policy led to major successes in socialist construction, the steady growth of productive forces in the city and the countryside with the increasing preponderance of socialist elements throughout the whole economy, elevation of the material and cultural level of the worker and peasant masses, a strengthening of the Union of Soviet Socialist Republics through correct implementation of the leninist nationality policy, consolidation of the union of the working class and the peasantry, a growth in the leading influence of the proletariat and its party, and on the whole, a systematic strengthening of the position of the proletarian dictatorship.

At present the proletarian state, the working class, and the party are commencing their work in international and domestic circumstances which in many respects have changed.

As regards the *international* situation, the reporting period has disclosed a number of new elements and characteristics both within the imperialist camp and in the relations between the capitalist countries and the Soviet Union. The partial stabilization of capitalism already noted by the XIV Congress has by now sufficiently revealed its essence and displayed its latent contradictions. Despite a certain forward movement by the capitalist states, despite the growth of world production to the pre-war levels, despite the restoration of world commodity trade and the strengthening of currencies, despite a certain 'normalization' of international relations, despite the partial technical progress and rationalization of capitalism, despite all this – and to a certain extent as a result of it – the irreconcilable contradictions within the world capitalist system have become *intensified*. The unevenness in the development of the capitalist countries has become more intense and, consequently, so has the struggle for spheres of economic and political influence and for the division of the world. The international *struggle for markets*, for raw materials, for spheres of capital investment, has become more intense because of the discrepancy between the productive capacities of the imperialist economy and the purchasing power of the popular masses disinherited by capitalism, because of the chronic underutilization of the capitalist productive apparatus, because of the loss of the gigantic USSR market to the world capitalist economic system.

The contradictions have become intensified between the European-American metropolitan areas, on the one hand, and the dependent countries and colonies on the other, with the struggle of the dependent countries against imperialist oppression assuming the form of armed uprisings, colonial wars, and colonial revolutions (China and Indonesia).

There is an intensification of the class struggle in the imperialist countries where, in response to the capitalist onslaught against the working class and its standard of living, in response to the liquidation of the eight-hour day and the rationalization of exploitation, in response to the reactionary-militaristic policies of the ruling bourgeois groupings, the working class is starting to take the counter-offensive.

Contradictions have become intensified between the countries of the bourgeois encirclement and the USSR whose triumphant development has undermined the foundations of world capitalist rule. The growth of socialist elements in the USSR, the collapse of bourgeois hopes for a degeneration of the proletarian dictatorship, and the increased international-revolutionary influence of the USSR are the principal factors in this intensification.

Thus the whole development of capitalism has disclosed a tendency to reduce the historical period of the 'breathing space,' to bring nearer a new era of major imperialist wars, and to speed up the revolutionary outcome of world conflicts. For the USSR this means, above all, increasingly tense relations with the bourgeois states whose policies, despite a number of internal contradictions among states and individual bourgeois groups which still impede the formation of a unified capitalist front, become increasingly hostile to the USSR and give rise to the immediate threat of an imperialist attack from the outside.

The preceding two-year period of international development has once again graphically demonstrated the futility of the efforts of bourgeois and pacifist politicians to 'bring together' and 'conciliate' states on a capitalist basis. The endless unifying conferences and commissions of the League of Nations, the so-called 'Bankers' Manifesto' (declaration against a post-Versailles tariff bacchanalia), the international economic conference, the pacificist 'Pan-Europe' project, the tripartite Geneva 'disarmament' conference, have all shown themselves to be new deceptions of the working class. The attempts at 'unification' only concealed the frenzied behind-the-scenes competition of the imperialists, the struggle for division of the colonial spoils, the unending armaments race, the formation of secret and open military blocs which directly prepare new imperialist wars. As a matter of fact fascist, chauvinist, and militarist tendencies have been growing. Under the guidance of the conservative cabinet in London, reactionary elements of the international bourgeoisie have started to prepare the ground for an armed assault on the USSR, after entangling it in a whole cluster of provocations (assaults on USSR diplomatic representatives, murder of Soviet diplomats).

The XV Congress of the VKP(b) notes that, together with the growth and intensification of fascist and militaristic-aggressive tendencies in the policies of the capitalist states, preconditions are being created for a revolutionary solution of contemporary international and internal contradictions. The British general miners' strike of 1926, the Indonesian uprising, the great Chinese Revolution, the revolutionary behaviour of the workers in 'stabilized' Austria (July 1927), together with the consolidation of the proletarian dictatorship in the USSR – abruptly lay bare the contradictory nature and the rottenness of the world capitalist regime. In Europe, at present, the brief ebb of the revolutionary surge (after the defeat of the 1923 German Revolution) has again become a flow, with a heightening of the militant activities of the proletariat, differentiation and radicalization of the workers' movement, the closing of ranks in the Comintern and its sections, growth of the mass revolutionary movement (the demonstrations in connection with the murder of Sacco and Vanzetti, the electoral successes of a number of communist parties, the October delegations of foreign workers to the USSR, etc.).

Considering these circumstances, characterizing the present international situation, the XV Congress orders the Central Committee to continue its work:

a on the basis of the continued implementation of an undeviating policy of peace, which is nothing other than a policy of struggling against the threat of imperialist wars and which at the same time is the fundamental condition of the further growth of socialism in the USSR;

b on the basis of the comprehensive consolidation of the fraternal ties of the USSR workers with the workers of the Western European countries and with the toiling masses of the oppressed countries;

c   on the basis of the continued systematic development of economic ties with capitalist countries, at the same time ensuring the growth of the economic independence of the Soviet Union;

d   on the basis of the continued strengthening of the defence capacity of the country, of the power and military capacity of the workers' and peasants' Red Army, Air Force, and Navy;

e   on the basis of the accumulation of the necessary economic reserves (grain, commodity, monetary, special defence reserves).

The XV Congress also views as completely correct the Central Committee's line and its efforts in *domestic policy and economic construction*.

The Central Committee's leninist policy has ensured the development of state industry to the pre-war level with an increase in the number of workers employed and a growth in labour productivity and wages. The development of state heavy industry has been accompanied by a continuous growth in the share of production of the instruments of production. Industry's surpassing of its pre-war levels, the renovation of the fixed capital of socialist industry, the initiation of radical technical and productive transformation, the considerable successes of electrification, the creation and development of whole new branches of industrial production (machinery, machine tools, automobiles, turbines, the aviation, and chemical industries), the building of new factories, large constructions and installations, and the radical re-equipping of old factories – such are the substantial achievements of the party and the working class on the road to the industrialization of our country as proclaimed by the XIV Party Congress.

Along with the growth of socialist state industry, there has also been an enhancement of the significance of the remaining system of the economic commanding heights of the proletarian state: transport, the state budget, the banking and credit network, the trade apparatus. The state co-operative sector has taken a decisive position in the market and is systematically squeezing out private commercial capital. And despite the semi-boycott manoeuvers of the capitalist encirclement, our foreign trade relations have also expanded on the basis of the foreign trade monopoly, and a favourable trade balance has been achieved.

Through a gradual strengthening of the leading role of the socialist city the party's economic policy in the period covered has promoted the further development of agriculture, an increase in the sown area and in the marketed share of the crop, and the introduction of elements of a more advanced agricultural technique: multi-field crop rotation systems, technical crops, and the mechanization of agriculture. The economic bond between the city and the countryside has been considerably strengthened. Together with the growth of agriculture, the supply of the countryside with urban industrial goods also grew and the significance of agricultural co-operation increased.

However, the XV Congress of the vkp(b) considers it necessary to point out that the above achievements are inadequate and that the level of agriculture still remains extremely low. Therefore the Congress directs the Central Committee to take practical measures to intensify the advance of agriculture, one of these fundamental measures being, in the view of the Congress, the speediest introduction of land management measures. The primary task must be – on the basis of continued peasant co-operation – the gradual transition from fragmented peasant farms to large-scale production (collective cultivation of land through the intensification and mechanization of agriculture), in every way supporting and encouraging the beginnings of collectivized agricultural labour. Such an intensification of the advance of agriculture is necessary both to heighten the well-being of the basic mass of the peasantry and to expand the market for heavy industry (as an outlet and as a source of raw materials), and also for the technical reconstruction of the village and the establishment of socialist co-operation there – in this way overcoming the capitalist elements in the countryside.

The elapsed period of economic development is an undoubted step forward to socialism. This overall success, however, does not signify the disappearance of the difficulties, dangers, and contradictions associated with the characteristics of our growth, with our country's technical and economic backwardness, and with the pressure exerted by social class forces harmful to the proletariat; only through systematic struggle against these forces can the above difficulties be overcome and further progress be made toward socialism. To the number of major difficulties must be added the following: the problem of exports and imports, which has become extremely complex due to the aggravation of the international situation; the problem of fixed capital; the problem of production costs and of the reduction of industrial prices; the problem of unemployment and of agrarian overpopulation; the problem of the scarcity of goods, on the one hand, and of an improved supply of agricultural products to the cities, on the other; finally, the problem of accumulating reserves (commodity and currency). The Congress directs the attention of the whole party to the fact that these problems may be successfully solved only if the party makes a special effort to apply all its forces, maintains its will unified, and carries out party directives in a concerted manner.

The XV Congress considers that a policy of economic displacement should and can be applied even more resolutely to the private capitalist economic elements whose absolute mass is increasing although to a much lesser extent than the socialist sector of the economy. The prerequisites for a further economic offensive against the capitalist elements have been created by the previous successes of economic development on the basis of growing commodity exchange and the liquidation of the remnants of War Communism (by decision of the XIV Party Conference), which have concentrated in the hands of the proletarian state suitable material and economic resources both for successfully overcoming capitalist elements in the countryside (a joint offensive with the middle peasant against the kulak, more help for the poor peasants, the strengthening of co-operation between the poor and middle peasants, production co-operatives) and for continuing to displace private capital in the city.

The XV Congress instructs the Central Committee to continue, without slowing down, its policy of socialist *industrialization* which has already yielded its first positive results. In every way consolidating the industrial power of the USSR, the party must continue, using available financial and economic means, to develop production of the means of production, in particular, metallurgy and machine building, to develop within the country the production of industrial raw materials (cotton, wool, leather, etc.), to reduce production costs, and steadily to reduce the prices of industrial products.

The general objective of industrializing our country must be accompanied by a resolute course aimed at the *rationalization* of production and administration. Along with the improvement and simplification of the state and co-operative apparatus, the rationalization of production is the main task in the forthcoming period. In the interests of heightening the material and cultural standard of living of the proletariat and also in the interest of rationalization of the productive process the party has proclaimed gradual transition to the seven-hour working day, to be accompanied by a continued improvement in the living standard of the working class; this is the principal difference between our methods of rationalization and those of capitalism where rationalization, on the contrary, is accompanied by a reduction in the living standard of the masses and by a lengthening of the working day. While appealing to all party, economic, trade union, and soviet organizations to apply all their energy to the solution of this most important task of socialistic rationalization, the XV Congress of the VKP(b) holds that only on its basis will it be possible to industrialize the country (including the industrialization of agriculture), to absorb unemployment, to root out bureaucratic perversions of the proletarian state, increasingly to satisfy the needs of the worker-peasant masses, to ensure their continued cultural growth, and to overcome the principal difficulties of socialist construction.

Despite the leading and still growing role of the socialist economic nucleus, the advance of the productive forces of the USSR economy is inevitably accompanied by a partial growth of class contradictions. The private capitalist strata of the city and village join forces with certain bureaucratic elements in the soviet and economic apparatus and strive to intensify their opposition to the working-class offensive, to exert influence on certain strata of employees and intellectuals, on backward strata of handicraftsmen and artisans, peasants and workers, which are hostile to the dictatorship of the proletariat. This influence is also manifested in the cultural-political and the ideological realms (the smenovekh doctrine, [that the USSR is returning to capitalism] the kulak slogan of a 'peasant union,' chauvinism, anti-semitism, the doctrine of bourgeois-democratic 'liberties' and the petty bourgeois opposition 'two-party' slogan associated with it, etc.). The working class headed by the VKP(b) has counteracted this harmful influence, and the growing activity of capitalist elements, by strengthening the proletarian dictatorship, by a still greater advance in the activity, initiative, and culture of the proletarian masses (stimulation of the soviets, development of trade union democracy and the co-operatives, strengthening the ideological influence of the proletariat on the village, mass cultural-educational work, etc.) as well as by strengthening the ideological influence of the proletariat upon the broad strata of the Soviet intelligentsia. While noting a series of unquestioned victories on this battlefront, the Congress considers it necessary in future to mobilize the proletariat in every way and to intensify the struggle on the ideological and cultural front.

While noting that our *party* has grown quantitatively and qualitatively since the XIV Congress, wholly supporting the Central Committee's policy on regulating the social composition of the party, and noting the success of the 'October Enrolment' of workers in the party on the tenth anniversary of Soviet power, the XV Congress of the VKP(b) hereby states that the directing role of the VKP(b) as the fundamental lever of the dictatorship may be preserved, secured, and strengthened only through the leninist cohesiveness and proletarian discipline of the party ranks, through a steady heightening of the ideological-theoretical and cultural level of its members, through the consistent implementation of intra-party democracy, and through a systematic improvement of the party's social composition by steady recruitment into the party of men and women production workers.

Especially in view of the complexity of the tasks before the party and in order to increase the activity of the whole mass of party members, the Congress considers it necessary to develop intra-party democracy, to subject defects in the soviets, and in the party itself, to businesslike criticism, to intensify the struggle against careerism, etc. At the same time the Congress directs the party's attention to the necessity of intensifying work in the Komsomol, among working youth generally, and among women.

The XV Congress notes that, despite the warning of the XIII Party Congress against the 'petty bourgeois deviation' of Trotsky's group and despite the warning of the XV All-Union Party Conference against the 'social democratic deviation' of the opposition united under Trotsky's leadership, the latter continues from month to month to deepen its revisionist errors, to struggle against the vKP(b) and the teachings of Lenin, having formed its own special party, carrying the struggle outside the vKP(b), and appealing to non-proletarian elements in the country against the regime of the proletarian dictatorship. The ideology of the opposition, who have openly formed a bloc with renegades of international communism (Maslow, Souvarine, and Co.), has now taken the shape of a particular trotskyite form of *menshevism*. Denial of the socialist character of Soviet state enterprises, denial of the possibility of the victorious construction of socialism in our country, denial of the policy of a union between the working class and the basic masses of the peasantry, and denial of bolshevik organizational principles (the policy of splitting the vKP(b) from the Comintern) have logically led the trotskyite-menshevik opposition to slander the USSR as a degenerate thermidorian state, to deny the proletarian dictatorship in the USSR, and to wage a counter-revolutionary struggle against it.

The outcome has been the opposition's ideological break with leninism, its degeneration into a menshevik group, its taking the course of capitulating before the forces of the international and domestic bourgeoisie, and its objective transformation into an instrument of a third force against the regime of the proletarian dictatorship. That is why the opposition has been so overwhelmingly rejected both by the mass of the party members and by the working class as a whole.

The XV Congress views all decisions of the Central Committee and the Central Control Commission directed against the disruptive work of the troskyites as absolutely correct and as the necessary minimum and directs the Central Committee to continue in future to ensure the leninist unity of the party at whatever cost.

Considering that the tactical differences between the party and the opposition have grown into programmatic ones, that the trotskyite opposition has become an objective factor in the anti-Soviet struggle, the XV Congress declares that adherence to the trotskyite opposition and the propogation of its views are incompatible with membership in the ranks of the bolshevik party.

In the name of the vKP(b) and of the working class of the Soviet Union, the XV Congress declares its firm proletarian conviction of the victory of socialism in our country, despite all difficulties. The world-wide historic experience of the decade of existence of the proletarian dictatorship have brilliantly confirmed the correctness of the leninist path followed by the vKP(b). The XV Congress orders the Central Committee to proceed undeviatingly along this path, to rally ever greater masses of the toilers of our country under the banner of socialist construction, to strengthen the fraternal ties of solidarity with the proletariat of all countries, and with each year to make the USSR an ever mightier outpost of the world socialist revolution.

2.61
On the Directives on the Establishment of a
Five-Year Plan for the National Economy   19 December 1927

I RESULTS AND PREREQUISITES OF SOCIALIST CONSTRUCTION

1   The results of the decade elapsed since the October Revolution disclose the gigantic international significance of this revolution as a component part of the great international revolutionary process which is transforming capitalist society into a socialist one. The dictatorship of the proletariat, the proletarian nationalization of the means of production, of transport, of credit, and of foreign trade, the nationalization of land – all are preconditions of the development of the USSR economy on essentially different, socialist principles. The *social class content of the economic commanding heights*, determining the development of the economy as a whole, has become essentially different. The *relationship between the city and the village* has become essentially different, for industry has 'turned its face toward the countryside' and has become a mighty factor in its socialist transformation, and the growth of the domestic market has started to take the form of increased village prosperity – not, as under capitalism, of its destruction. The *organizational form* of the economy has become essentially different inasmuch as the possibility has arisen of *planned guidance of the economy*, increasingly suppressing the anarchy of the capitalist commodity market, on the basis of the nationalization of heavy industry and of the other commanding heights. The *distribution of national income* has also become essentially different as a result of the virtually complete liquidation of the former ruling classes and the concomitant destruction of a considerable part of the non-productive consumption generally. These distinguishing characteristics of the USSR economy have made possible a much more rapid reconstruction process than in the capitalist countries and a much more rapid rate of economic growth generally.

2   The results of economic development since the so-called 'New Economic Policy', which laid the foundation for the correct combination of state socialist industry and the small or very small businesses of simple commodity-producing peasants, have completely confirmed Lenin's thesis that in our country we have everything that is necessary and sufficient for the building of socialism, that the objective internal conditions of the economic and social development of the USSR by no means make the collapse or degeneration of the proletarian dictatorship inevitable, that the

existence of a large number of peasant farms and the tie between them and the state economy by no means transforms our country into a land of peasant narrowmindedness ...

4   ... With regard to the relationship between *production* and *consumption*, it must be borne in mind that they cannot both be maximized *simultaneously* (as the opposition is now demanding), since this is an insoluble problem. Similarly, at the present time, the policy of one-sided (capital) *accumulation* (as Trotsky demanded when in 1923 he adopted the watchword of rigid concentration and intensified pressure on the workers) or the policy of one-sided *consumption* cannot be adopted. Considering both the relative degree of contradiction among these aspects and their interaction and the constraints they exert upon one another, and also the fact that from the point of view of long-term development these interests generally coincide, what is required is to find the optimum combination of both of these factors.

The same must be said about the city and the village, socialist industry and peasant economy. It is wrong to demand the maximum transfer of funds from the peasant economy into industry, as this demand would mean not only a political break with the peasantry but also undermining of the raw-materials basis of industry itself, undermining of its domestic market, undermining of export, and upset of the equilibrium of the whole economy. On the other hand, it would be incorrect to refrain from taking funds from the village in order to build industry; that, at the present time, would slow down the rate of development and would upset the balance to the detriment of the country's industrialization.

With regard to the *pace* of development, it is equally necessary to bear in mind the extreme complexity of the task. Here the aim must not be to maximize the pace of accumulation for the *immediately following* year or years, but to combine economic elements in such a way as to ensure the most rapid *long-term* pace of development. From this point of view the opposition's slogan of raising prices is to be condemned resolutely and once and for all: this slogan would not only lead to the bureaucratic degeneration and monopolistic decay of industry, not only would it strike a blow at the consumer and, in the first place, at the working class and the city and village poor, not only would it deal considerable trump cards to the kulak – but after a time it would sharply lower the rate of development, narrowing the domestic market, subverting industry's agricultural base, and bringing technical progress in industry to a standstill.

It is equally necessary to reach an optimum combination of both factors as regards the relationship *between the development of heavy and light industry*. While we consider it correct to transfer the centre of gravity to production of the means of production, here note must be taken of the danger of tying down too large a proportion of state capital in heavy industry, which is amortized in the market only in a number of years; on the other hand, it is also necessary to bear in mind that the more rapid turnover in light industry (production of goods of foremost necessity) enables its capital to be used also for heavy industrial construction, provided that *light* industry itself develops.

Only if both of these facts are taken into account and combined in a planned fashion will it be possible to conduct the economy along the course of a more or less planned, more or less crisis-free, development.

5   From the point of view of the *class struggle* and the *deployment of class forces* the period we are entering is characterized by the growing class power of the proletariat and the consolidation of its alliance with the mass of poor and middle peasants, with a relative decline – although still possibly an absolute increase – in the private capitalist elements in the city and countryside.

The decisions of the XIV Conference and the XIV Party Congress have served as the basis for a correct policy toward the village in the present period in that they strengthened the alliance between the working class and the basic mass of the peasantry. Having overcome the anti middle peasant deviation in its party, and on the basis of the consolidation of the worker-peasant bloc, the proletariat can now proceed, *together* with the whole mass of the poor and middle peasants, to more systematic and insistent restrictions on the kulak and the private property owner. This must be the basic class orientation of the Five-Year Plan for the National Economy.

II   THE PROBLEM OF THE FIVE-YEAR PLAN AND THE PARTY'S ECONOMIC
     POLICY

1   The basic difficulties and problems of the economic policy of the proletariat are in regulating the *relations between the city and the village*. The Five-Year economic plan must be structured in such a way as to resolve the problems arising out of the fundamental disproportions of our economy: the disproportion *between industry and agriculture* which is far from overcome despite the more rapid growth of industry over that of agriculture; the disproportion between the prices of industrial and agricultural products (market 'scissors'); the disproportion between the demand for *industrial raw materials* (cotton, leather, wool, etc.) and its supply; and finally, the disproportion between the quantity of working hands in the countryside and the real possibility of their economic employment (the so-called 'rural overpopulation') ...

3   *The only correct way to overcome these disproportions* is by lowering the *production costs of industrial products* through an energetic rationali-

zation of industry and its expansion, consequently, on the basis of a policy of *lowering industrial prices*; by developing *labour-intensive crops in the countryside and industrializing* agriculture (primarily by developing industries involved in the primary processing of agricultural products); by the comprehensive *encouragement of small-scale savings* (internal loans, savings banks, by encouraging the acquisition of shares in co-operatives and building new co-operative factories) and by tying them in with the credit system ...

5   With respect to *industry* the following major problems must be noted: in the first place, the correlation between *production of the means of production* and *the production of consumer goods*, i.e., between heavy and light industry; in the second place, the correlation between *the number of industrial units under construction* and *their scheduled dates of completion* (because of the danger of freezing excessive funds over too broad a front of capital construction with too long a period of amortization); in the third place, the correlation between production costs and wages; and, finally, the correlation between production for the internal market and for export, on the one hand, and for the country's defence, on the other.

The policy of industrializing the country requires, in the first place, a strengthening of the *production of the means of production* so that the growth of heavy and light industry, transport, and agriculture, i.e., their production requirements, will be basically met from the domestic industrial production of the USSR. Those branches of heavy industry must develop most rapidly which in the shortest time strengthen the economic might and defence capacity of the USSR, guarantee the possibility of developing in case of an economic blockade, lessen our dependence on the capitalist world, and promote reorganization of agriculture on the basis of higher technology and collectivization of the economy. Therefore, particular attention must be devoted to the fastest possible implementation of the electrification plan, the development of heavy and light metallurgy especially as regards high-quality metals, the development of chemical production especially of artificial fertilizers, the further development of coal and peat mining and of oil production, the building of general and agricultural machinery, ship building, electrical industry, and the gold and platinum industry.

The *consumer goods* industry must improve the quantity and quality of its production to a level which will ensure a substantial elevation of the per capita consumption of the toilers. Particular attention must be directed to the development of textile, leather, and food industries which, since they ensure the growth of agricultural raw materials production, particularly stimulate the increasing industrialization of agriculture and absorption of the agricultural overpopulation ...

7   The plan for *agriculture* must take into account, not only the categor-

ical necessity of an overall advance of agriculture (in the first place, increasing yield and expanding the sown area) but also a correct combination of the basic economic elements in the regional as well as in the branch sectors (grain crops, technical crops, and animal husbandry), while these agricultural branches must develop with sufficient rapidity to: 1) ensure an expansion of mass consumption, 2) ensure a sufficient increase in exports to meet the import and currency accumulation needs of the Five-Year Plan, 3) increase the coverage of industrial demands by our own raw materials. The Five-Year Plan's price policy for agricultural products must ensure that the relations among the various developing branches of agriculture will be stable and will correspond to the plans for the country's industrial and personal consumption and for export. The *distribution of resources* among the various branches of agriculture is determined by the above factors and also by the need to eliminate the disproportion between the available labour power and its actual employment: hence the need to force the development of *labour-intensive crops* and to *industrialize agriculture* rapidly, mainly by increasing the primary processing of agricultural products.

Hence also the inadmissibility of an overall approach to problems of agricultural technology and the necessity to distinguish from one another the grain-producing regions (requiring tractors, machinery, select seed, etc.), regions of intensive technical crops (requiring land improvements, drainage, irrigation, fertilizers, etc.), and finally, animal-raising regions (requiring improved breeds and the organization of marketing). In particular, the plan must expand the area sown to wheat and barley and heighten yield and the marketed share of these crops in such a way as to cover both the growing demand within the country and the necessary volume of exports. At the same time the plan must incorporate measures relating to forestry, especially regarding their rational management (forest management and amelioration, reforestation) to ensure a proper and fuller use of the country's forest resources.

The plan must provide for *capital investments* in agriculture, both by the peasants themselves and from the state budget, aimed at the mechanization of agriculture and at accomplishing the most important irrigation projects and land improvement generally, with particular attention being directed at projects designed to prevent possible crop failures. The plan must incorporate measures for supplying the villages with complex agricultural machinery, especially tractors, which in our conditions is one of the means of strengthening the collectivization of agricultural production.

The Five-Year Plan must foresee accelerated work on *land management* as the elementary prerequisite for a general transition of all agriculture to a higher level and for introducing collective methods of farming, as well as for securing the interests of the poor and middle peasants in the struggle against the kulak. It is also necessary to make up a plan for resettlement and on its basis to intensify resettlement efforts which, promoting the advance of the productive forces of agriculture and improving the situation of the peasant groups which possess little or nothing, will serve to reduce 'agrarian overpopulation.'

The plan must be based upon the party's fundamental class orientation, namely, the policy of relying on the poor peasants, a firm alliance with the middle peasants, and an offensive against the kulak. Therefore the plan must aim at supporting the *co-operatives* (here decisively rejecting the opposition's proposal that the co-operatives be deprived of their capital, which would be a blow against Lenin's whole co-operative plan); it must be based upon a correct policy *within the co-operatives* (credit to the smallholders, struggle against kulak tendencies, and a corresponding policy within the farm machinery associations, etc.); it must, furthermore, proceed from the premise that, together with the comprehensive development of *marketing* co-operatives, now extensive support must be given to all viable forms of *producer* co-operatives (communes, kolkhozes, artels, production associations, co-operative factories, etc.), and also to sovkhozes which require advancement to a higher level.

8   A major task of socialist construction in the organization of trade is *to overcome the anarchy of the market*, and the waste of materials inherent in the capitalistic mode of distribution, through the further development and rationalization of the socialized sector of commodity trade.

The socialized trade sector, which is expanding by displacing private capital and is introducing the planning principle into commodity trade by rationalizing the trade network and by minimizing non-productive expenditures in trade, will secure all the gigantic economic advantages of the new social system of distribution and, in the future, with the successes of socialist construction, will be transformed into an apparatus for the socialist distribution of products ...

Confirming the correctness of the Central Committee's economic policy during the preceding period, the Congress is of the view that the implementation of the Five-Year Plan, which must considerably enhance the well-being of the masses and consolidate the position of socialism, depends first and foremost upon the harmony, cohesion, and creative energy of the *party itself*. From this point of view the Congress categorically condemns the activities of Trotsky's opposition faction which is disrupting the great constructive effort and disturbing its course and is trying to disorganize the whole soviet apparatus as well.

The Congress categorically condemns the opposition's economic line. Contrary to Lenin's statement that complete victory of socialism in our country is possible provided the party follows a correct policy and there are no attacks from the outside, the opposition assumes that the victory of socialism is impossible. Therefore, instead of a confident and well thought-out policy, it proposes to the party either the greatest unprincipled vacillations or a policy which has nothing in common with leninism. In the sphere of economic rationalization the trotskyite opposition, accusing the opponents of its policy of an 'agitator's approach,' has gone from the slogan of 'rigid concentration' and pressure on the workers (with the closing of such giants of proletarian industry as the Putilov factory, the Briansk factory, etc.) all the way to essentially denying rationalization itself.

Lenin's major proposition, which is at the *basis* of the whole economic orientation, namely, the proposition that proletarian industry must give the peasant *cheaper* goods than he got from the capitalist system, has clearly been scorned by the opposition. In complete opposition to Lenin, it has advanced the proposition that more must be taken from the peasants than was taken by the old regime, that the policy must be to *elevate* the already *extremely high* prices, etc., etc. Only the pressure of extremely severe criticism compelled the opposition to break away from this policy which was a policy of breaking with the peasantry and fleecing the worker-consumer, a policy of helping the kulak in the village, a policy of monopolistic parasitism and bureaucratic degeneration of the industrial apparatus. In full and in principle contradicting *Lenin's whole co-operative plan* which insisted on the *financing* of the co-operatives, the opposition has put forward the proposition that co-operative capital must be withdrawn from trade, in this way thinking to lighten the position of industry. But this bureaucratic-administrative policy would hand over the real and vital tie with the peasants to *private capital*, would be a blow against the economic initiative of the peasants, would block off their road to socialism, placing private capital in command, during the conversion process, between state industry and the peasantry. Fully contradicting Lenin, who issued a direct *warning* against the 'super-industrializing' point of view, pointed out the necessity of moving ahead with the whole basic mass of the peasants, and swept aside lightweight *phrases* about 'peasant narrow-mindedness', the trotskyite opposition fully *adheres* to the 'peasant narrowmindedness' thesis ridiculed by Lenin and proposes moving ahead without this peasant mass, thus inevitably condemning the party's policy to failure. Deriving from this the thesis of 'degeneration, Thermidor,' and others taken from the Ustrialov-Menshevik arsenal [Ustrialov propagated in exile the idea that the Bolsheviks were ceasing to be revolutionary], the opposition is trying to demobilize the working class ideologically, abandoning the bolshevik track of the very energetic construction of socialism in favour of the menshevik track of a 'critical' attitude toward the very class essence of this construction. Taking a negative, or at best a 'neutral', attitude toward the rationalization of industry, the opposition in its demagogic-agitational demands is attempting to find support in the prejudices and khvostism [tail-endism; following in the wake of events] of the ·

most backward proletarian strata with a semi-peasant consumer psychology. From this attitude of the opposition toward rationalization, and its lack of confidence in the latter's success, flows its negative attitude toward the seven-hour working day, whose successful implementation is a function of the harmonious and energetic accomplishment of rationalization.

The objective result of this policy would be the bureaucratic *stagnation* of our industry and the proletariat's conversion from allies and leaders of the peasantry into *consumers* who do not set themselves the task of *remaking* the peasant economy. Such a policy would inevitably lead to the collapse of the proletarian dictatorship. On the other hand, the opposition hides behind the banner of *internationalism* while in fact it advocates the sort of economic tie with *international capital* which would lead to a loss of economic independence by the Union and to the thwarting of socialist construction.

The Congress instructs the Central Committee to have a Five-Year Plan developed for consideration by the next Congress of Soviets and to ensure that all local soviet, trade union, party, and other organizations are involved in the thorough and comprehensive discussion of the draft plan.

2.62
On Work in the Countryside 19 December 1927
...

III THE STATE OF PRACTICAL WORK AND ITS INADEQUACIES.
PERVERSION OF THE PARTY LINE

17 Although the general policy is entirely correct and the growing influence of the proletarian state, its organs, and the co-operatives upon agriculture is becoming increasingly powerful, it is necessary to point out a number of major inadequacies, errors, distortions, and sometimes even scandalous violations of the party's political line.

With respect to the activities of *state organs*, errors must first of all be noted in the regulation of prices for agricultural products (mistakes of 1925/26) which led to the disruption of our export-import plan and thus of the production programmes of industry, a reduction in the area sown to technical crops, etc. It must be noted that the *land organs*, the organs of co-operation and agricultural credit, devote far from adequate attention to implementing a correct proletarian policy in the village (machinery supply, credit, rental policies, land management, etc.) and frequently do not adequately repulse the claims of the kulaks. It is equally necessary to note that the organs of the *People's Commissariat of Finance*, despite major successes in implementing a progressive tax structure, do not always cope with the task of accounting for all taxable income of kulak groups and of establishing a suitable tax rate. It is further necessary to point out that the state delivery organs frequently under-rate the significance of the co-operatives as mass organizations whose goal is to socialize agricultural production, and tend to play down the role of the co-operatives and convert the co-operative movement itself into nothing but a branch of the corresponding state delivery organizations.

18 In the co-operative movement itself are to be noted a number of unhealthy phenomena which signal a distortion of the party's policy. The *composition* of the co-operatives, on the whole unconditionally poor peasant and middle peasant, none the less frequently reveals relatively slight involvement of the poor peasants in the co-operatives and a disproportionately extensive involvement of the prosperous village apex. The make-up of the *electoral organs* of the co-operatives manifests the same inadequacies despite the decision that kulaks are not to be admitted to these organs. The result is that in the matter of *machinery supply* there have been frequent instances where precisely the upper village strata have had relatively better access to machinery. The same must be said about the distribution of *credit*. It must also be pointed out that party directives are not obeyed by co-operative organs which often do not use up funds directly allocated for the poor peasants in the co-operatives. Despite the recent turn for the better with respect to these facts, and despite the vкp(b) Central Committee straightforward directives on the matter, such distortions of the party line continue to occur. Attention should also be directed to the existence of false co-operatives which serve to mask kulak 'associations' enjoying all the rights and privileges of co-operatives. Another considerable inadequacy in the organizational work of the co-operatives is the existence of a mass of so-called 'wild' co-operatives not yet incorporated into the centralized co-operative system.

A general defect in the work of the land organs, economic organs, co-operatives, and credit institutions, is the frequent absence of co-ordination among them leading even to the mutual incompatibility of the measures which they practice.

19 With regard to the *work of the soviets*, the party's policy of rehabilitating the village soviets has been an undoubted success. The soviets (their sections and commissions) are increasingly becoming centres for organizing economic and political life, schools of administration, instruments for promoting new poor peasant and middle peasant cadres, etc. The organization of the non-party aktiv around the soviets has enhanced their authority in the eyes of the broad masses. At the same time it is necessary to mention the increasing degree of self-discipline of the poor peasants and agricultural labourers displayed in the elections to the soviets, the co-operative organs, etc.; at the same time it must be recognized that this work is still far from adequate.

20   With regard to *party work*, it must next be noted that it is still inadequate among the farm workers (as is also reflected in the composition of the village cells), and that party political work in the village generally is still insufficiently tied in with economic and cultural construction. However, the campaigns for re-elections to the soviets, conducted under party direction and on the basis of broad democracy for the toilers, show that the authority of the party organizations has grown among the peasant masses. A very important role in the village is played by the *Komsomol* organization which at the present time must set itself the task of regulating its composition so as to increase its nucleus of farm labourers and poor peasants, of training extensive new cadres of Komsomol activists from among its members, of implementing the party line more precisely, of giving the party active assistance in organizing the poor peasants and agricultural workers, and of educating its members politically. In the village the Komsomol organization must be the party's principal lever for the advancement and collectivization of agriculture, the development of broad cultural initiative, and the training of new cadres of workers for socialism. In the matter of transforming farm worker and poor peasant women into activists, of elevating the cultural level of the peasantry and improving their co-operatives, an important role is played by the delegates' meetings of women peasants which must intensify their work on the comprehensive involvement, in all village socialist construction, of the peasant strata which are closest to the party.

IV   CURRENT TASKS OF THE PARTY

In that way we can state: 1) that the socialist sector of the economy has grown very significantly, and together with it, the relative influence of the working class; 2) that private capital has been forced out of a number of very important positions; 3) that in the countryside both the fundamental contradictions and the levers of socialist development have become outlined with perfect clarity, i.e., on the one hand, some growth of the kulaks, and on the other hand, strengthening of the middle peasant group and growth in the organization of the village poor, rapid development of the co-operatives which, according to Lenin, under conditions of the proletarian dictatorship is equivalent to the 'growth of socialism,' and strengthening of the role of the state organs in planning and regulating the peasant economy.

The corresponding party policy since the XIV Party Conference and the XIV Party Congress has led to a number of major changes in another respect: 1) the sown area has increased, and there has been a sharp reduction in the amount of uncultivated land, this being due to the overall economic advance of the basic mass of the peasantry; 2) the middle peasant has moved further away from the kulak politically, the union between the working class and the mass of middle peasants has become stronger, and there has been a decisive breakthrough in the matter of isolating the kulaks.

Thus the goals set by the party at the XIV Conference and the XIV Congress must basically be considered as having been attained. The party won these successes by struggling both against an underestimation of the kulak threat and, especially, against the opposition's anti middle peasant deviation. The party would not have been able to achieve these successes if it had not concentrated its fire against the opposition's opportunistic anti middle peasant deviation, as this deviation, undermining the bond between the proletariat and the middle peasant masses and making it more difficult to split the middle peasant away from the kulak, in fact serves to heighten kulak influence in the village. The party's leninist policy of union with the middle peasant must be continued. The successes of party policy in the village, and the new situation thus created, permit the party of the pro- letariat, by employing the whole power of the economic organs, and relying, as before, upon the poor and middle peasant masses, to develop further the offensive against the kulaks and to adopt a number of new measures limiting the development of capitalism in the countryside and leading the peasant economy along the road to socialism.

This is the background of the following current tasks of the party:

1 *Elements of regulation of agriculture by the state plan*

   a   the successes of the state organs and the co-operatives in taking over the sale of industrial goods (including the products of cottage industry) in the village and the deliveries of agricultural products to the city are to be consolidated and developed as the prime condition for overcoming the anarchy of the market, extending the planning principle to agriculture, and safeguarding the guiding role of socialist industry throughout the whole economy.

   b   the policy of bringing down the prices of industrial goods while maintaining the stability of agricultural prices is to be maintained undeviat- ingly as the major condition for improving the material position of the toiling masses and strengthening the bond between the city and the village.

   c   the developing practice of establishing contractual relations ... be- tween the peasants in co-operatives and the state organs is to be supported in every way since it creates a direct link between the peasant economy and the corresponding branches of socialized industry (sugar and textile indus- tries, etc.) and facilitates regulation by the state plan of the agriculture of these raions and branches.

   d   in accordance with the task of comprehensive encouragement of the unification of small peasant farms into large collective farms, the agricul- tural credit system must direct its main attention to the support and de- velopment of producer co-operatives among the broad masses of poor and middle peasants, devoting increased attention both to securing peasant deposits in the co-operatives and especially to organizing processing co-operatives, etc.

e   with the strengthening of the co-operatives (agricultural, consumer, and cottage industry) and with the exclusion of the kulak and the small private trader from the area of commodity circulation, it will be necessary to establish such relations between the co-operatives and the state organs which will ensure a further expansion of the sphere of work of the co-operatives by unconditional safeguarding of the interests and the leadership of the Soviet state.

2   *Taxation*
a   The decision of the party and the Soviet power releasing peasant smallholders (35 per cent of the peasant farms in the Union) from the agricultural tax is to be implemented with all due precision.

b   In order to tax the growing income of the most prosperous village strata, the Central Committee is charged with developing the question of transfer to a fully progressive income tax.

3   *The co-operatives*
a   The network of consumer, agricultural, and cottage industry co-operatives is to be broadened and strengthened with the aim of drawing all the poor peasants and most of the middle peasants into the co-operatives in the near future; the funds made available by the co-operatives for organizing poor peasant co-operatives are to be increased.

b   The involvement of peasant women in the co-operatives is to be intensified, especially of those who are working in agricultural branches employing considerable amounts of women's labour (poultry farming, various branches of cottage industry, etc.)

c   In order further to exclude private capital from cottage industry, the state organs are to give more extensive support to cottage industry co-operatives, their mechanization is to be intensified, etc.

d   The so-called 'wild' co-operatives which have arisen through the organizational weakness of the co-operative movement, are to be included immediately in the co-operative system.

e   Approval is hereby given to the practice of forming specialized forms of agricultural co-operatives (reorganized Agricultural Union, bread centre, butter centre, flax centre, sugar beet co-operative, etc.) and, since these are the most reliable instruments for inducing the individual peasant farmers to pass gradually from marketing and supply co-operatives to socialized forms of production, their further development is recognized as essential.

f   The struggle to free the smallholders who lack equipment from their dependence on kulak elements, who use their equipment (agricultural machines, etc.) to enslave the poor peasants, must be intensified and to this end a broad network of equipment supply points must be developed in the agricultural co-operatives, in addition to the state equipment supply points, for renting machinery to smallholders on advantageous terms and for furthering the development of socialized land cultivation techniques, harvesting techniques, etc.

g The supplying of agricultural equipment to the kolkhozes and the peasant smallholders is to be facilitated in every way, with special credit advantages, repayment conditions, etc., being worked out. In order to limit the supply of agricultural machinery to kulak elements appropriate norms are to be developed (reduction of the kulak share in the sum total of equipment produced, payment in cash, etc.)

h The funds assigned by state and local budgets to poor peasant needs must be increased and employed for the development of producer co-operatives (kolkhozes); at the same time the poor peasants' share of other credits is to be increased.

i Existing successes in advancing the most reliable poor peasant and middle peasant elements to leading positions in co-operatives must be consolidated, and from them must be created new and broad cadres of socialist co-operative members; the struggle must be intensified against the attempts of kulak elements to take over the lower-level co-operative organizations.

j Approval is hereby given to the creation of a union of agricultural co-operative unions as a centre for unifying all aspects of agricultural co-operation and as an organ called upon to broaden the co-operative base in the village, together with the consumer and the cottage industry co-operatives, and to instil socialist co-operative methods in the millions of peasants.

4 Kolkhozes and sovkhozes

a The Central Committee decision on the results of kolkhoz and sovkhoz construction since 30 December 1926, is hereby approved, and all party organizations and party workers in soviet and co-operative organs are ordered to intensify their assistance to kolkhoz construction and to strengthen the sovkhozes, converting them into truly exemplary large-scale farms of the socialist type and at the same time intensifying their assistance to the peasant farms (organizing equipment supply points, agricultural information points, tractor columns, etc., in the sovkhozes).

b While rendering all possible support to the expansion of the network of poor peasant and middle peasant associations for the purchase and joint use of agricultural machinery, a resolute struggle must be conducted against pseudo associations (and against pseudo co-operatives generally) which usually act as shields for kulak elements in their acquisition of all sorts of illegal advantages in matters of credit, supply, etc.

5 *Land use and management*

  a The foundations of the nationalization of land are to be consolidated in every way, and any (direct or indirect) attempts to undermine the nationalization of the land, such as buying and selling or the giving of land as occurs, for example, in certain regions of the Caucasus and of Central Asia, are to be prosecuted as serious crimes.

  b In those regions where the leasing of land leads to the growth of kulak elements the amount of land leased is gradually to be reduced. The period of the lease is to be limited to not longer than one crop rotation, but in any case no longer than six years. With regard to persons who, despite the assistance extended to them by the state and the co-operatives, do not cultivate their assigned land themselves or with the help of their families but lease it out from year to year, their right to lease land is to be limited by decision of the volost (raion) executive committees to from three to six years in a row, at the expiry of which they are to be deprived of the right to hold land, and their lands are to be transferred into the possession of the land association.

  Persons guilty of violating the law prohibiting all and any forms of sublease are to be resolutely punished as criminals.

  State land funds are primarily to be leased to farms of the labouring type, with the period of lease being limited to six years. Waivers of this rule with respect to state land funds are permitted in individual raions only with the assent of the central land organs.

  c Those forms of land use which most favour the development of agricultural co-operatives and mechanization (small settlements set apart from the village, etc.) are to be comprehensively encouraged and extended; the practice of assigning land to separate holdings, and especially to individual farmsteads, is to be limited, and completely ended wherever it leads to the growth of kulak elements.

  d The state is to be in charge of the organization of land use by the poor peasant and smallholder strata. This must be closely tied in with other organizational and economic measures (agricultural assistance, credit, land improvement, supply of equipment, etc.). Care must be taken to ensure that in the organization of land use the interests of the poorest strata are safeguarded even with respect to the quality and location of the land allocated.

  The planned deadline for completing work on the organization of land use in the USSR is to be shortened.

  e The urgency of establishing the fundamental principles of land management and land use on an all-union scale is hereby recognized.

6 *Hired labour and the Union of Agricultural and Timber Workers*

  a Care must be taken to ensure undeviating implementation of the Labour Code with respect to men and women agricultural workers on farms of the kulak type, with Code violators being held strictly account-able.

b The 'Provisional Rules' must be implemented undeviatingly in peas-ant farms employing hired labour, and violators of the 'Provisional Rules' are to be held strictly accountable.

c The laws on social insurance of agricultural and forest workers, both men and women, must be implemented strictly.

d To recognize as necessary, the intensification of efforts of the Ag-ricultural and Timber Workers' Union to organize the still unorganized farm labourers, and similarly the facilitation of admission, into the Agricultural and Timber Workers' Union, of those semi-proletarian elements in the village who are still outside the union and for whom hired labour is the basic means of subsistence.

7 *Insurance for smallholders. Peasant assistance associations*
    a The Central Committee is hereby ordered to undertake to prepare the conditions necessary for the adoption, at the next Congress of Soviets, of laws on the old-age insurance of peasant smallholders.

b The peasant mutual assistance associations are to be strengthened in every way so that they would become a truly mass organization of the poor peasant and middle peasant village strata for extending mutual assistance and for organizing economic measures alleviating the position of the smallholders. While work is to be continued on individual assistance to poor peasants, the efforts of the Peasants' Mutual Aid Society are more and more to be concentrated on extending collective-production assis-tance to peasant smallholder strata.

8 *Soviets. Cultural work*
    a While continuing the policy of reactivation of the soviets as centres for political education of the broad masses of toiling peasants under the leadership of the proletariat, particular attention is to be directed to form-ing and enlarging a non-party aktiv of poor and middle peasants, intensify-ing the involvement of the farm labourers and smallholders in this aktiv. Here attention must be directed to enlisting in the aktiv women peasants and farm labourers (women delegates, members of soviets) and to promot-ing them to leading positions in the soviets.

b In connection with the re-elections to soviets to be held at the beginning of 1928, a broad campaign of reporting on the work of the soviets is to be launched, the poor peasant and middle peasant strata are to be involved to the maximum in the elections, the party must provide leader-ship throughout the pre-electoral campaign, and the standards for exclud-ing kulak and other anti-proletarian elements from electoral lists, as set forth in the appropriate electoral instruction (1926), are to be strictly applied.

c   The Central Committee is ordered to work on the question of improving the relations between the soviets and the land associations with a view to safeguard the leading role of the soviets and to take away the right to vote in land associations (at their assemblies) from persons who are excluded from the electoral lists of the soviets.

d   Measures must be adopted for the resolute implementation of universal compulsory primary education, and the initiative of the population and of the local soviets in this respect must be supported in every way.

Cultural, and especially school, construction in the national regions must be strengthened, with particular attention being directed to the most backward ones.

A considerable increase must be achieved in school attendance (all grades) of children of agricultural workers, farm labourers, and poor peasants, for which a special school fund must be set up to assist these children.

All measures must be adopted to give the children of poor peasants, and especially those under age, working as hired hands, adopted children, etc., a real opportunity to study in the schools.

e   Special attention must be directed to the development of professional and technical schools and various types of training work shops, and to the inclusion in school curriculums of courses in trades needed in agriculture.

f   More attention must be directed to the creation of new cadres of rural intellectuals and to raising the skills of the existing ones, making them into active and conscious agents of the socialist transformation of the village.

Particular attention must be directed to the creation of cadres of specialists in the organization of kolkhozes and model large sovkhozes in the village.

g   Political education work in the village must be strengthened and its quality heightened. Particular attention is to be directed at developing village radio stations and cinemas, at strengthening the library network, etc.

h   The network of schools for peasant youth is to be extended, and a series of measures must be adopted to strengthen in them the nucleus of farm labourer and poor peasant youth (increasing the number of scholarships, assigning funds for the upkeep of dormitories for the children of farm labourers and poor peasant smallholders, etc.).

i   Demobilized Red Army and Red Navy men must in every way be drawn into soviet and cultural construction in the village, for which the necessary improvements, in accordance with the present decisions, must be introduced into their socio-political training in the ranks of the Red Army and Navy.

j   The execution of the new tasks in the collectivization of agriculture requires the trade unions to intensify in every way their participation in the whole social life of the village. In particular, there must be a considerable strengthening, and improvement of supervisory work and work with associations of villagers, as well as a considerable expansion of cultural work by trade unions in the village (radio, cinema, libraries), especially among trade union members who for a considerable part of the year are involved in peasant farming (seasonal workers, etc.).

9 *Party organizational matters*

  a Existing groups of poor peasants in the soviets and co-operatives must be strengthened, and new ones formed, in order from time to time to hold meetings of these groups in the village and the volost (raion) for purposes of enriching their work experience.

  b Sections for village work are to be set up in party committees (from the okrug and guberniia levels to the Central Committee) and are to be entrusted, in particular, with the organization and preparation, as needed, of uezd and guberniia conferences of poor peasant groups.

  c Attention is to be concentrated on training and involving in party work primarily the farm labourer and poor peasant activists who are being developed in the agricultural workers' union, in poor peasant groups, in practical work in the soviets, the co-operatives, meetings of women peasant delegates, etc.

  d New party forces are to be assigned to co-operative and soviet organs in order to ensure correct implementation of the party line in their village work.

2.63
On the Opposition   18 December 1927

Having heard the report of the commission which had carefully studied all the materials concerning the opposition, the XV Congress states:

1   In matters of *ideology* the opposition has passed from tactical differences of opinion to *programmatic* ones, revising Lenin's views and sliding over to the menshevik position. Denial of the possibility of the victorious construction of socialism in the USSR and, consequently, denial of the socialist character of our revolution; denial of the socialist paths of development in the village under conditions of the proletarian dictatorship and the policy of alliance between the proletariat and the basic masses of the peasantry on the basis of socialist construction; finally, the actual denial of the proletarian dictatorship in the USSR ('Thermidor') and the capitulationism and defeatism connected with it – this whole ideological orientation has transformed the trotskyite opposition into an instrument of petty bourgeois democracy within the USSR and into an auxiliary detachment of international social democracy outside its borders.

2   In matters of *tactics*, the opposition is developing and intensifying its work against the party and has passed the limits not only of the party Rules,

but even of Soviet legality (illegal meetings, illegal presses, illegal publications, forcible occupation of buildings, etc.). The climax of this anti-Soviet tactic was the transition to an open struggle against the regime of the proletarian dictatorship, to the holding of street demonstrations against the party and the Soviet government on 7 November 1927. The opposition's anti-Soviet tactics, applied abroad as well, are associated with slanderous propaganda against the USSR and have in fact placed the opposition in the ranks of the open enemies of the land of the dictatorship of the proletariat.

3   In *organizational* matters the opposition relies on revising Lenin's views and has gone from factional activity to the creation of its own trotskyite party. The commission has made it entirely clear that the opposition has its own central committee, its oblast, guberniia, city, and raion centres, its technical staff, membership dues, publications, etc., etc. The trotskyite party abroad has established links not only with factional groupings of an anti-leninist inclination within the Comintern parties, but also with organizations, groups, and individual persons who have never belonged to the Communist International as well as with enemies and traitors to the communist movement who have been expelled from the Comintern (Maslow, Ruth Fischer, Korsch, Souvarine, Rosmer, Roland-Holst, Leibers, etc., etc.). Within the USSR this *organizational* practice of the opposition has led it to establishing ties with non-party bourgeois intellectuals (Shcherbakov and Co.) who are themselves associated with open counter-revolutionaries, and, outside the USSR, it has become the object of extensive support by the bourgeoisie of all countries.

On the basis of the above the XV Congress believes that the Central Committee and the Central Control Commission acted correctly in expelling Trotsky and Zinoviev from the ranks of the VKP(b) on 14 November 1927, and in expelling other opposition members of the Central Committee and the Central Control Commission from these latter bodies, and in submitting the question of the opposition as a whole to the Congress for discussion.

In its resolution on the Central Committee report the Congress stated that membership in the trotskyite opposition and the propagation of its views are incompatible with membership in the VKP(b). In this connection the Congress considers that the opposition must disarm itself both ideologically and organizationally, must resolutely condemn its above views as anti-leninist and menshevik, and must take on itself the obligation of defending the views and decisions of the party, its congresses, its conferences, its Central Committee.

The opposition, however, rejected this demand by the party. In the opposition document of 3 December 1927, which was signed by 121 active members of the opposition, it not only fails to recant but, on the contrary, insists on propagandizing its menshevik views.

After the Congress had adopted the resolution on the Central Committee report, the commission acquired two new opposition documents dated 10 December 1927, one (signed by Rakovsky, Muralov, and Radek) insisting on the necessity not only of maintaining these menshevik views but also on propagandizing them, the other (signed by Kamenev, Bakaev, Evdokimov, and Avdeev) insisting on preserving the opposition's menshevik views but agreeing not to propagate them, which is in contradiction with the demand for ideological disarmament and signifies a refusal to defend party decisions.

While noting a clear distinction between the two opposition groupings, the Congress is none the less of the view that both opposition declarations are entirely unsatisfactory.

On the basis of the above, and considering the opposition's two violations of its solemn promises to refrain from factional activities, the Congress resolves:

1   The following active members of the trotskyite opposition are hereby expelled from the party: [a list of seventy-five names follows].

2   To expel from the party Sapronov's group, as a clearly anti-revolutionary one: [list of twenty-three names follows].

3   The Central Committee and Central Control Commission are ordered to take all measures for exerting ideological influence upon the rank-and-file members of the trotskyite opposition in order to convince them of their error, and at the same time are to purge the party of all clearly incorrigible elements of the trotskyite opposition.

Pravda, 8 December 1927 (2.60); *KPSS v rezoliutsiiakh* IV, 13–74
20 December (2.61, 2.63); 21 December (2.62)

Plenum of the Central Committee   16–24 November 1928

When Molotov announced at the XV Party Congress that the slogan of the moment was '… forward – to a large-scale collectivization of agriculture,' he was announcing, on Stalin's behalf, a major shift in policy, away from the NEP, as well as declaring war on the rightists and their leader, Bukharin. Despite his successes, the General Secretary was uncertain of majority support in the nine member Politburo, in which he could count on opposition from Bukharin, Rykov, and Tomsky, and was doubtful of the loyalty of Kalinin and Voroshilov, whom he kept in line, according to Trotsky (*Stalin*, 388–9), only because he was blackmailing them for moral turpitude. Consequently, Stalin was compelled to start his campaign among the lower party ranks, a task which he accomplished once more with consummate skill (see for example his remarks in *Works* xi, 12–22, 50, 167). To appreciate the boldness and magnitude of this operation one must realize that Stalin was about to destroy the policy of caution and gradual change in the countryside, on the basis of which he defeated, only a few months before, the left opposition, whose policy he now advocated. Matters were approaching the culminating point at the July 1928 Plenum of the Central Committee, at which Stalin clashed openly with Bukharin (*Works* xi, 165–205). While the plenum was still in session, Bukharin approached Kamenev, evidently hoping that the latter and Zinoviev, both of whom were in the meantime readmitted into the party, might form an alliance with him against Stalin's forthcoming attack. In addition, Bukharin, Rykov, and Tomsky were putting pressure on Stalin in the Politburo for some change in leadership. When Stalin procrastinated they threatened with resignations. For the moment both sides preferred to keep the struggle from breaking into the open. Stalin, on his part, was content to deliver public attacks on anonymous proponents of the right policy, mentioning by name only one Frumkin, a relatively obscure party member, and to deny that there was any split in the Politburo, as he did at this plenum (*Works* xi, 231–48, 302).

Although the *KPSS v rezoliutsiakh* (iv, 122) does not refer to this meeting as a joint plenum of the Central Committee and the Central Control Commission, the communiqué on it states that members (perhaps not all of them) of the Central Control Commission and also the Central Revision Commission did attend. Apart from Stalin's attack on the policy of the right and perhaps some discussion of it, considerable part of this comparatively long plenum concerned economic matters, and passed resolutions on the control figures for 1928/29, the results of the seven-hour working day, and the agricultural situation in the North Caucasus grain region. It also passed a major resolution on party recruitment policy (2.64) taking into account the changed policy in favour of collectivization, with its emphasis on the liquidation of the kulak, a term which was beginning to be used very loosely, and on the recruitment of reliable agricultural workers into the party.

2.64
On the Recruitment of Workers and the Regulation of Party Growth

...

TASKS OF REGULATING THE PARTY'S COMPOSITION

The question of *party composition*, of regulating its growth, and of recruiting men and women workers into the party must be approached from the point of view of these tasks in the current period.

In the last several years, especially since the Lenin Enrolment, the party has grown rapidly. Hundreds and hundreds of thousands of progressive proletarians have joined the party, proletarians who now make up a substantial part of the leading Communist cadres. These new cadres of worker-communists have more than once given proof of their bolshevik steadfastness during the periods of especially sharp struggle between the party and the opposition, and at the same time they have been a most important addition to the ranks of the active builders of socialist society.

Even today the party is growing principally by taking in proletarians. At the same time, the inflow into the party of white collar workers, and especially of peasants, has also increased. The normal advancement and, in connection with it, the steady transition of a certain proportion of production workers to work in the organs of the proletarian state, and to study, is also reflected in the composition of the party. Consequently, while the proletarian component of the party predominates substantially (61 per cent), the proportion of workers employed directly in production is much smaller (42 per cent).

In the meantime, the party possesses huge reserves for growth in the working class. These reserves are – the broad and ever-growing *cadres of the non-party proletarian aktiv* in the trade unions, production conferences, soviets, co-operatives, the Komsomol, meetings of women worker delegates, voluntary organizations, clubs, etc. Some strata of industrial workers and skilled workers in particular, are represented quite inadequately in the party. An especially resolute change must be achieved in the recruitment of women workers into the party, since in this respect until recently the party has lagged behind, which is entirely inadmissible under present conditions. Great significance must be accorded to the intensified recruitment into the party of the worker youth which has passed through the serious school of Komsomol in industrial enterprises. The recruitment into the party of agricultural workers and hired hands remains an extremely backward sector, and the party must immediately direct its attention to this. The intensified recruitment of men and women workers must be combined with rigid observance of the conditions set for the admission of white collar workers and others into the party, and also with the necessary selections of peasants truly devoted to the party and, of the latter, especially the poor peasants and, in particular, those who have worked actively in the kolkhoz movement.

The goals of an intensified recruitment of workers into the party and the fundamental tasks of the period of socialist reconstruction demand that the party recruit genuinely *progressive elements* of the working class, able to become the vanguard of the working masses in practically surmounting the difficulties of socialist construction, in repelling petty bourgeois ideological wavering, in raising in every possible way the confidence in the party of the whole mass of workers and toilers in the countryside. Our task is – to bring into the party, in the most insistent and resolute fashion, those men and women workers who display the greatest political fortitude in periods of setbacks, who are genuine proletarian internationalists, whose personal example contributes to the increase in productivity and labour discipline, who heatedly and stubbornly fight against bureaucratism, who work actively on their own cultural development and thereby are capable of strengthening the leninist ranks of the proletarian vanguard. The party cannot fail to take into account the fact that during the years of war and revolution its proletarian composition was reinforced by substantial new strata, especially from the village, and also to a slight degree by persons from a social milieu which is alien to the working class. Hence the party has even better reasons for taking into its organizations all proletarian elements possessing revolutionary awareness and who are devoted to socialism, especially men and women workers who have long been employed in heavy industry. For us the practical task is to ensure that *not less than half of the party membership consists of production workers by the end of 1930.*

The broad recruitment of workers must be combined with strict verification of the present party composition and with the most resolute *purge* of its socially alien, bureaucratized, and degenerate elements, and other hangers-on. On the one hand, various measures, especially ideological ones, must be applied in the struggle to prevent the more backward workers, but who are devoted to the revolution, from leaving the party. On the other hand – intensified measures, considerably stronger than those of recent years, must be applied to purge the party organizations of elements who exploit their membership in the ruling party for their own selfish and careerist goals, degenerate bourgeois narrowminded elements, which have fused with the kulaks, etc.

In the composition of village organizations the relative proportion of proletarian elements is still completely negligible, and the cadres of kolkhoz members are absolutely insignificant. At the same time these, in some instances, contain a considerable portion of prosperous peasants and occasionally even elements which have become intimate with the kulaks, have degenerated, and are completely alien to the working class. This makes the task of a decisive improvement, a radical purge, and a considerable revitalization of these organizations, absolutely urgent. In the national republics and oblasts, where the proletarian cadres are still small, the intensified involvement of hired hands and agricultural workers, especially those of the local nationalities, and also a corresponding improvement of the social composition of the organizations, are the decisive conditions of socialist construction.

The *broadest non-party working masses* must be involved both in the intensified recruitment of workers and in the decisive purging of the party of ideologically and socially alien elements. This participation by non-party workers, and, in the countryside, by non-party peasants, especially the farm labourers and poor peasants, must be truly active and truly on a mass basis. For the party this support by the non-party mass of toilers is of exceptionally great significance, since it is very important support for the whole cause of socialist construction headed by the Communist Party ...

Pravda, 25 November 1928   *KPSS v rezoliutsiiakh* IV, 122–57

Joint Plenum of the Central Committee and the Central Control Commission   16–23 April 1929

The April Joint Plenum met to prepare for the XVI Party Conference, which opened on the last day of the plenum. A number of major theses submitted by the Politburo were approved at the plenum for presentation and adoption as resolutions at the Conference: on the Five-Year Plan, on agricultural improvement and the easing of taxes on the middle peasant, on the struggle with bureaucratism, and on the purge of the party. The plenum also launched a determined attack on the right by passing a resolution 'On Intra-party Affairs' which was kept secret at the time (2.65). This document extended the criticism contained in a secret resolution of the Politburo which met jointly with the presidium of the Central Control Commission on 9 February 1929 (2.66). This untitled resolution was ratified by the April Plenum.

Bukharin and his followers committed a number of errors, mainly because of their continued unwillingness to bring the dispute into the open. As is evident from the two resolutions below, Bukharin's joining of Stalin in public assurances that there were no disagreements in the higher party organs, made it possible for Stalin to expose him as a factionalist schemer. However, Stalin was not yet ready for the final assault. While, as he put it, 'some comrades' insisted on Bukharin's and Tomsky's expulsion from the Politburo (*Works* XII, 1–113, when the speech was published, in 1955, for the first time), he was for the moment satisfied with Bukharin's removal from his posts as editor of *Pravda* and as head of the Comintern, and with Tomsky's removal from his post as the head of the trade unions. However, officially, both were removed only after the XVI Party Conference – Tomsky in June and Bukharin in July 1929. Rykov, Chairman of the Sovnarkom, who wavered between defiance and capitulation, was for the moment spared.

2.65
On Intra-party Affairs   23 April 1929

The joint plenum of the Central Committee and Central Control Commission of the VKP(b) approves the 9 February 1929 resolution of the joint session of the Central Committee Politburo and the Central Control Commission Presidium on intra-party affairs.

Considering that the joint session of the Politburo of the Central Committee and the presidium of the Central Control Commission did not have an opportunity to evaluate the 9 February 1929 statement of Bukharin, Tomsky, and Rykov, which in itself introduced a factionalist platform; that in their interventions at the joint plenum of the Central Committee and Central Control Commission of the VKP(b) Bukharin, Rykov, and Tomsky continued to develop and defend their views, which run contrary to the party line and that Bukharin and Tomsky refused to submit to the decisions of the joint session of the Central Committee Politburo and the Central Control Commission Presidium on the repudiation of their resignations, the joint plenum of the Central Committee and Central Control Commission of the VKP(b), considers it necessary to adopt the following resolution:

1   The growth and formation of the right deviation in the party is very closely linked with features that are specific to the present stage in the development of the international proletarian revolution. The XV Congress of the VKP(b) and the VI Comintern Congress have already noted signs of a serious turning point in the situation of world capitalism and in the international revolutionary movement. The characteristic features of this turning point are: a sharpening of internal contradictions in the capitalist camp that is increasingly impairing and undermining its temporary and precarious stabilization and a growth of elements of a new revolutionary upsurge (the wave of strikes in a number of European countries, the radicalization of the working class and communist successes in parliamentary elections, the important victories in the elections to factory committees in Germany, the development of a revolutionary crisis in India, and the continuing revolutionary ferment in other colonies, the growth of contradictions and the danger of war both in the imperialist camp and between the capitalist world and the USSR).

In these conditions the most important tasks of communist parties are: further bolshevization of communist parties, freeing those parties of social democratic traditions, securing the leading role of the party in the growing revolutionary movement, and preparation of the broad masses for the approaching, decisive class battles.

Hence the need to intensify across the entire front the struggle of communist parties against social democracy, and in particular against its 'left' wing, and against reformist and bureaucratic leadership in the trade unions; hence the need for a broader and more energetic mobilization of organized, and in particular of unorganized, workers behind the slogans of the Comintern.

The reality of partial capitalist stabilization, the presence of a strong social democratic movement that exercises influence on certain elements of communist parties and, finally, the survivals of social democratic traditions in the communist parties themselves, feed right opportunist trends in the ranks of the Comintern sections, trends that, at the present time, represent the principal danger in the international communist movement.

In questions of international politics, the right deviation tends toward a social democratic appraisal of the stabilization of capitalism (the theory of capitalism's 'normalization'), which takes the form of papering over the constantly intensifying crisis of capitalism, of denying the fact of the unsteadiness of capitalist stabilization, of concealing the features of the 'third period.' Thus the rightists and the conciliators who are their hangers-on have arrived at the point of revising the leninist evaluation of the present era as a period of crisis for capitalism, as the era of wars and the world proletarian revolution. They underestimate elements of the growth of a new revolutionary upsurge and in this connection deny the tasks of mobilizing the working masses (particularly the unorganized working masses) for an independent struggle against the reformist trade union bureaucracy.

The link between the right deviation in the vKP(b) and these opportunistic trends in the ranks of the Comintern is quite apparent. Comrade Bukharin has, in fact, made common cause with the opportunistic position of the conciliators Humbert-Droz, Ewert, Gerhardt, and others. Comrades Bukharin, Rykov, and Tomsky are impeding the struggle of the Comintern against the right deviation and against conciliatoriness within the Comintern. The statement of these three comrades to the effect that the policy of our party 'demoralizes' the Comintern, weakens its ranks and leads to schisms and defections in foreign communist parties, not only signifies a philistine, opportunistic misunderstanding of the tasks of cleansing communist parties of the elements of social democracy, but also actual support for the rightist renegades. Thus, objectively, comrades Bukharin, Rykov, and Tomsky are increasingly becoming a centre of attraction for all the opportunistic and conciliatory groups in the Comintern sections.

2   The political position of the right deviation in the party means capitulation in the face of difficulties connected with the socialist reconstruction of the economy and the sharpening of the class struggle in the USSR. The reconstruction period signifies a serious turning point in the economic and political development of the USSR. The necessity to catch up with and surpass the advanced capitalist countries technically and economically in a brief historical period commits the party to conduct a policy of rapid

industrial development. In implementing socialist industrialization, the proletariat has at present undertaken the difficult job of destroying the roots of capitalism in the country's economy, the job of socialist reorganization of agriculture, which is our central task in the countryside for the period ahead. The union of the working class with the basic peasant masses has entered a new stage and is taking new forms, more and more assuming a production character (sovkhozes and kolkhozes, equipping of the farms with machinery, contractual arrangements, etc.). The task of eliminating the technical and economic backwardness of our country in rapid order under conditions of a hostile capitalist encirclement and of a predominantly small holding peasant agriculture, and setting directly to work on a fundamental, socialist reorganization of agriculture inevitably involves great difficulties. The party openly puts to the working masses the question of the necessity of overcoming these inevitable difficulties, as opposed to a policy of capitulating before them. The socialist and capitalist paths for the development of agriculture are in sharper opposition today then ever before. The growth of socialist forms of the economy, the exclusion of capitalist elements, and connected with it the growth of opposition from class forces that are hostile to us, inevitably give rise to a sharpening of the class struggle at the present stage, which represents a turning point in socialist construction. At the given stage, proletarian dictatorship means a continuation and sharpening (and not slackening) of the class struggle.

The capitalist elite in the countryside, which has been growing in strength over the years of the NEP, has at its disposal greater possibilities of economic character for manoeuver today than it did during the early years of the NEP (grain reserves, means of production). The kulaks are taking advantage of these possibilities for manoeuver in a fierce struggle against the advance of socialism, in attempts to thwart state regulation of the market and Soviet state price policy. These attempts to thwart the policy of Soviet authorities represent one of the most acute forms of the struggle for the basic demands of the country's capitalist elements, and above all for the path of a free capitalist development of agriculture.

The joint plenum of the Central Committee and the Central Control Commission states that in recent times the Bukharin group has gone over from a position of vacillation between the party line and the line of the right deviation in the basic questions of our policy to what is, in fact, a defence of the positions of the right deviation. Both Bukharin's 'Notes of an Economist' and, in particular, the platform of the three as enunciated at the 9 February joint session of the Politburo and the Central Control Commission presidium, as well as the statements of these comrades at the plenum of the Central Committee and the Central Control Commission are clearly directed toward a reduction in the rate of industrialization. The liberal interpretation of the NEP, which leads in fact to renunciation of regulation of market relations by the proletarian state, failure to attach proper significance to the new forms of the union of socialist industry with agriculture, failure to attach proper significance to the role of the sovkhozes and kolkhozes, while at the same time clearly overestimating the possibilities for the development of an individual, smallholding peasant economy – all this amounts, objectively, to a line of thwarting the advance of socialism and weakening the positions of the proletariat in the struggle against the capitalist forms of economy. Contrary to the party line, the Bukharin group, following in the footsteps of Frumkin, is in fact, counting on greater possibilities for the development of kulak economy. In line with this are the proposals to abolish individual taxation of kulaks, to further raise grain prices, and to put an end to pressure on the kulaks with regard to grain collection. In coming out against party measures to mobilize the poor and middle strata of the rural population for struggle against the kulaks' malicious concealment of, and speculation in, grain, the rightists are objectively assisting kulak attempts to thwart grain collections and the supply of grain to the working class and the poor peasants. Basic to this political line of the rightists is a theory of constant concessions to the peasantry, which attests to the fact that the rightists have forgotten about the leading role of the proletariat in the union with the peasantry and signifies an obvious revision of Lenin's teachings on the union with the middle peasants. The same political meaning attaches to the denial by Bukharin, Rykov, and Tomsky of the inevitable sharpening of the class struggle under present conditions of the reconstruction period and to their attempts to explain the fact of a sharpening of the class struggle not by socio-economic conditions, but by so-called planning oversights and by short-comings in the local apparatus, etc.

3   Fulfilment of the highly complex tasks of the reconstruction period, surmounting the difficulties connected with this period, intensification of the class struggle in the country require reorganization of the ranks and work methods of all organs of the proletarian dictatorship and of all organizations of the working class along the following lines: broadest mobilization of the activism of the proletarian and semi-proletarian masses, strengthening proletarian leadership of the peasantry, rallying and inciting the entire poor and middle peasantry against the kulaks, and assurance of consistent rebuffs to the pressures from petty bourgeois elements. Continued development of mass proletarian self-criticism, which is encountering resistance from bureaucratic elements in our apparatus, is the basis of this reorganization. In its struggle for socialism, the vanguard of the working class must be strengthened by a general party purge of elements of degeneration and by the development of self-criticism and intra-party democracy. *Reorganization* of the state apparatus and its continued improvement must be promoted by purifying *soviet institutions* of hostile

class elements and bureacuratic distortions, by revitalization of the soviets, by a decisive strengthening of the control of the masses from below over the work of all organizations of the working class, and by adapting the management system to the tasks of the reconstruction period. The *trade unions*, which are called upon to play a decisive role in the building of socialist industry, in increasing labour productivity and discipline, in organizing the production initiative of the working class and of socialist competition, and also in instilling class values in the new strata of the proletariat, must resolutely rid themselves of all remnants of guild exclusiveness and bourgeois trade-unionism, as well as of bureacratic lack of concern for the masses and disregard for the tasks of defending the day-to-day needs and interests of the working class. Stimulation of the cooperative movement and the complete freeing of certain of its organizations from the influences of the well-to-do and kulak elite in the villages, and strengthening of the proletarian direction of the movement are necessary to assure the socialist development of this most important mass organization of the peasantry.

The solution of these tasks is impossible unless the right deviation is decisively overcome. The slanderous statement of the Bukharin group to the effect that the party is spreading bureaucratism means discrediting the immense job that the party has done in combatting bureaucratism. The philistine denigration of self-criticism on the part of this group can have no other meaning than a direct struggle against the slogan of self-criticism. On the trade union question, comrades Bukharin, Rykov, and Tomsky have taken the highly dangerous course of setting off the trade unions against the party, they are, in fact, pursuing a policy of weakening party leadership of the trade union movement, they are concealing the short-comings in trade union work, covering up bourgeois trade-unionist tendencies and instances of bureaucratic petrification in a part of the trade union apparatus and representing the party struggle against these short-comings as a trotskyite 'shake-up' of the trade unions. But it is in the question of the role of the party apparatus and of the intra-party regime that the position of the Bukharin group completely reproduces the most malicious accusations that were ever levelled against our party by the trotskyite opposition. The party is fighting and will continue to fight for continued development of intra-party democracy and proletarian self-criticism within its ranks, 'without regard to individuals.' The party, however, resolutely rejects the sort of 'freedom' of criticism that the rightist elements seek in order to defend their antileninist political line. The leninist party resolutely repudiates the sort of 'democracy' that legalizes deviations and factional groupings within the party. Intra-party democracy serves the interests of strengthening the leninist unity of the party, it serves to rally the party behind the general line laid down by the XV Party Congress.

4   The right deviation has its roots in the petty bourgeois elements that surround the working class. The right deviation has as its basis within the party the least stable elements, the elements in the non-proletarian sector of the party that are most subject to petty bourgeois influence and to the danger of degeneration; it has as its basis the most backward strata of workers, the strata that have not undergone a prolonged schooling in the factories and that have ties with the petty bourgeoisie in the countryside and the towns. The 9 February platform of the Bukharin group and the views defended by members of the group at the plenum of the Central Committee and the Central Control Commission are an appeal to these unstable elements and objectively are an aid to the formation of a right deviation within the party.

In so far as the party has achieved a decisive success in exposing trotskyism both within its ranks as well as among the broad masses of the working class, the main task of intra-party policy in the present conditions must be to overcome fully the right deviation and conciliatory attitudes toward it. This task is to be solved both by systematically exposing the anti-leninist theory and policy of the right deviation and by mercilessly combatting manifestations of the right deviation in the everyday practical work of party, trade union, soviet, economic, co-operative, and other organizations. In the ranks of the leninist party, whose basic cadres have been strengthened by many years of struggle against opportunism, the openly opportunistic right deviation cannot hope to encounter any sort of extensive or open support. The greater the danger, then, of a covert form of the right deviation in which, hiding themselves behind public agreements with the decisions of the party, the opportunistic elements distort its class line in practice. Therefore, exposing the right deviation in practical work is, of necessity, an integral part of the struggle against opportunism within the party.

5   The joint plenum of the Central Committee and the Central Control Commission states that the Bukharin group has already begun a factional struggle against the party leadership. It is resorting to the most impermissible violation of party discipline (the refusal of comrades Bukharin and Tomsky to carry out repeated decisions by the Politburo concerning their work). It is attempting to impose its line on the party by means of resignations. It has instigated factional work against the Central Committee within the Moscow organization, attempted to set off against the Central Committee, the party fraction at the VIII Trade Union Congress, resorted to attempts to form an unprincipled, high-level bloc in opposition to the Central Committee (Comrade Bukharin's proposal to Comrade Kamenev to form a bloc against the Central Committee), etc. The unprecedented slander against the party concerning the alleged slipping to trotskyite positions, the slanderous attack on the party concerning a 'military-feudal

exploitation' of the peasantry, which was borrowed from the arsenal of Miliukov's party [the pre-revolutionary liberals], the accusation that the party is spreading bureaucratism and demoralizing the Communist International – all this unquestionably attests to the factional character of the Bukharin group and its deviation from the general line of the party. In so doing, the Bukharin group flagrantly violates leninist party unity, breaks bolshevik discipline, and subverts collective leadership in the Central Committee.

6   Guiding itself by the will of all party organizations, which unanimously support the line of the Central Committee and have decisively condemned the conduct and views of comrades Bukharin, Rykov, and Tomsky as basically reflecting right deviation; considering the fact that comrades Bukharin, Rykov, and Tomsky have not admitted their mistakes; finally, proceeding from the interests of party unity, which is particularly necessary under the present conditions, the plenum of the Central Committee and Central Control Commission of the vKP(b) resolves:

a to condemn the views of Comrade Bukharin's group set forth in Comrade Bukharin's statement of 30 January, in the 9 February statement of comrades Bukharin, Rykov, and Tomsky, and in the speeches of these comrades at the plenum of the Central Committee and Central Control Commission, as incompatible with the general line of the party and as basically in accord with the position of the right deviation, and to bind them to carry out unquestioningly the decisions of the party and its organs;

b to condemn Comrade Bukharin's behind-the-scenes talks with Comrade Kamenev as the most striking expression of Comrade Bukharin group's factionalism;

c to condemn comrades Bukharin and Tomsky's policy of resignation as a gross violation of party discipline;

d to remove Bukharin and Tomsky from their present positions (*Pravda*, the Comintern, the All-Union Central Council of Trade Unions) and to warn them that should they make the slightest attempt to violate the resolutions of the Central Committee and its organs, they will be immediately removed from the Politburo as violators of party discipline;

e that the Politburo must take steps to see to it that no divergences whatsoever from the party line and from the decisions of the leading party organs are permitted in statements by individual members and candidate members of the Politburo;

f to take all necessary measures to see to it that the party line and the decisions of the Central Committee are fully carried out in the press organs, both party and Soviet, in newspapers as well as in journals;

g to establish special procedures – up to and including exclusion from the Central Committee and from the party – capable of guaranteeing the secrecy of the decisions of the Central Committee and the Politburo and ruling out all possibility of informing the trotskyites about the affairs of the Central Committee and the Politburo;

h to disseminate the present resolution to all local party organizations and to members of the XVI Party Conference, without publishing it in the press.

2.66

[On the Bukharin Faction]   9 February 1929
                                                        (Ratified 23 April 1929)

Having become acquainted with the documents of, and taking account of the exchange of opinions at the 30 January 1929 joint session of the Politburo of the Central Committee and presidium of the Central Control Commission, the joint session of the Politburo and Central Control Commission presidium has come to the following conclusion.

I   COMRADE BUKHARIN'S BEHIND-THE-SCENES ATTEMPTS TO ORGANIZE
        A FACTIONAL BLOC IN OPPOSITION TO THE CENTRAL COMMITTEE

The joint session of the Politburo and Central Control Commission presidium asserts that:

I   During the July Central Committee Plenum (in 1928), unknown and contrary to the wishes of the Central Committee and Central Control Commission, Comrade Bukharin, together with Comrade Sokolnikov, conducted behind-the-scenes factional discussions with Comrade Kamenev on questions of changing the policy of the Central Committee and the composition of the Politburo;

2   Comrade Bukharin conducted these talks with the knowledge, if not the agreement, of comrades Rykov and Tomsky, and these comrades, knowing of the talks in question and understanding their impermissibility, kept this knowledge from the Central Committee and the Central Control Commission;

3   the aim of Comrade Bukharin's talks was to demonstrate to Comrade Kamenev that the Central Committee's policy on economic questions is incorrect, to reach agreement on changing that policy, to reach agreement on corresponding changes in the composition of the Politburo and in this way to substantiate the need for organizing a factional bloc of Comrade Bukharin and others together with Comrade Kamenev's group;

4   these factional talks took place at a time when there was already in existence a resolution on the economic situation and the policy for grain procurements that had been unanimously adopted by the Politburo (2 July) and the Central Committee plenum (10 July);

5   these factional talks of Comrade Bukharin took place at a time when

the Politburo, at the initiative of comrades Bukharin, Rykov, and Stalin, was working out the declaration of the Central Committee for the VI Comintern Congress on the absence of differences of opinion within the Politburo in which (i.e., in the declaration) there is the following categorical statement by all members of the Politburo: 'The undersigned members of the Central Committee Politburo of the vKP(b) declare to the senoren konvent of the Congress that they protest in the most resolute fashion against the dissemination of any and all rumours whatsoever concerning differences of opinion among members of the Central Committee Polit-buro of the vKP(b)'.

On the basis of the facts set forth, the joint session of the Politburo and Central Control Commission presidium resolves:

a   to condemn the conduct of comrades Bukharin and Sokolnikov (the talks with Comrade Kamenev) as a factional act that attests to the total lack of principle on the part of comrades Bukharin and Sokolnikov and that runs contrary to the elementary requirements of honesty and simple decency;

b   to declare the conduct of comrades Rykov and Tomsky, who concealed from the Central Committee and the Central Control Commission their knowledge of the behind-the-scenes talks between comrades Bukharin and Kamenev, to be absolutely impermissible.

II   WHERE COMRADE BUKHARIN'S FACTIONAL ACTIVITIES LEAD

The joint session of the Politburo and Central Control Commission presidium asserts that Comrade Bukharin's factional activities did not end with his behind-the-scenes talks with Comrade Kamenev's group but, on the contrary, they did not cease in the period since the July Plenum of the Central Committee but have continued, unfortunately, in one form or another, down to the present day. Such events as Comrade Bukharin's refusal to work in the Comintern; his refusal to work on the editorial board of *Pravda*; Bukharin's publication, without the knowledge of the Central Committee, of his 'Notes of an Economist,' which are an eclectic muddle impermissible for a marxist and which created a danger of discussion within the party; submission of their resignations prior to the November Plenum by comrades Bukharin, Rykov and Tomsky; Comrade Bukharin's 30 January 1929 statement confirming by and large the substance of his talks with Comrade Kamenev in July 1928; Comrade Tomsky's resignation in December 1928; the refusal of comrades Bukharin and Tomsky to submit to repeated Politburo resolutions demanding that they withdraw their resignations: all these events and others of a similar sort show that Comrade Bukharin continues to desire secretly to struggle against the Central Committee.

To justify his factional activities Comrade Bukharin is resorting to a series of highly impermissible slanders against the Central Committee, its domestic and foreign policy, and its organizational leadership, slanders whose aim is to discredit the party and its Central Committee. And while seeking to discredit party policy, Comrade Bukharin is slipping to a position of diplomatic defence of the rightist elements in the VKP (Comrade Frumkin and Co.), which are demanding the unleashing of the capitalist elements of town and countryside, and defence of the conciliatory elements in the Comintern (Humbert-Droz and Co.), that deny the precariousness of the capitalist stabilization, that are revising the decisions of the VI Comintern Congress on the struggle against rightist and conciliatory views, and that are opposing the decisions of the presidium of the ECCI on the expulsion of rightists from the German Communist Party.

In this connection the joint session of the Politburo and Central Control Commission presidium establishes the following facts:

I   Comrade Bukharin's statement to the effect that party policy since the July Plenum has allegedly been determined by the slogan set forth by Comrade Stalin in his speech at the plenum, 'the slogan of tribute, i.e., of the military-feudal exploitation of the peasantry,' is an intrinsically mendacious and thoroughly false statement. The party as a whole, as well as Comrade Stalin, have always combatted and will continue to combat the trotskyite theory of the 'military-feudal exploitation of the peasantry.' This is as well known to Comrade Bukharin as it is to the entire party. The party as a whole, as well as Comrade Stalin, proceed from the fact that the peasantry is still overpaying for manufactured goods and is being underpaid for agricultural produce, but that this surtax ('tribute') cannot be eliminated at once unless we wish to forego industrialization, that it must be reduced step by step, with a view of eliminating it completely in a few years. If this point is indeed a point of divergence between Comrade Bukharin and the party, then why did not Comrade Bukharin make a statement to this effect to the Politburo or the Central Committee plenum? It is a known fact that immediately after the July Plenum all members of the Politburo, including Comrade Bukharin, signed the 30 July 1928 declaration of the members of the Politburo to the VI Comintern Congress to the effect that 'the undersigned members of the Central Committee Politburo of the VKP(b) declare to the senoren konvent of the Congress that they protest in the most resolute fashion against the dissemination of any and all rumours whatsoever concerning differences of opinion among members of the Central Committee Politburo of the VKP(b).' How could Comrade Bukharin have signed that declaration if, in fact, he felt that his views differed fundamentally from those of Comrade Stalin or of the Politburo on the question of the 'military-feudal exploitation of the peasantry'? Is it possible that he was deceiving the party at that time? It is known that all members of the Politburo including Comrade Bukharin, adopted in November 1928, during the November Plenum, a unanimous resolution to affirm, both at the plenum and in reports, the unity of the Politburo and the absence of differences of opinion within it. How could Comrade Bukharin have voted for such a resolution if, in fact, he feels that his views differ fundamentally from those of Comrade Stalin or of the Politburo on the question of policy with respect to the peasantry? Is it possible, he was deceiving the party at that time? Is it not clear that Comrade Bukharin himself does not believe in the twaddle about 'tribute,' and that if he now resorts to such slander, it is to justify his factional activities, even if with fabricated tales and slander against the party.

Incidentally, this is not the first time that Comrade Bukharin has resorted to slander against the party. The history of our party knows instances from the period of the Treaty of Brest-Litovsk when Comrade Bukharin, himself bogged down in the petty bourgeois, opportunistic swamp, accused Lenin and his party of opportunism and petty bourgeois views, when he wrote in his theses of the 'Left' communists, which were presented to the VII Party Congress, that *the policy of the party's leading institutions was a policy of waverings and compromises,* and that *the social basis of such a policy was the process of our party's degeneration from a purely proletarian party to a party of the entire people,* and that *the party, instead of raising the peasant masses to its own level, itself sank to their level, was transformed from the vanguard of the revolution into a middle peasant*...

2   Bukharin's statement to the effect that the 'over-taxation' of peasantry is an integral part of party policy and that the party and Central Committee are allegedly not carrying out the decisions of the Central Committee plenum on providing incentives for the individual peasant holding and for increasing its yields is incorrect and false. The entire party as a whole recognized last year that taxes are insufficient, that the agricultural tax is low and must be increased. In this connection the Central Committee last year unanimously adopted a decision to increase taxes to 400,000,000 rubles. Practice this year has shown, however, that such an increase in taxes, with 35 per cent of holdings exempted from it and with the entire tax burden being borne by the remaining 65 per cent of holdings, places excessive burdens on certain strata of the middle peasants. On this basis the Politburo, at the suggestion of comrades Kalinin and Stalin, set up a commission as far back as December of last year to work out measures to relieve the tax burden on the middle peasant. On the same basis the Politburo, at the initiative of Comrade Stalin, has placed the question of tax relief for the middle peasant on the agenda of the forthcoming party conference. On the very same basis the Politburo on the strength of a report by Comrade Kalinin, has adopted a decision to reduce taxes to 375,000,000 rubles and to offer tax advantages to poor and middle peasant holdings that are expanding their sown areas.

These facts cannot be unknown to Comrade Bukharin.

As concerns the work of the party to raise the yields of the poor and middle peasant holdings, it is enough to note such instances as the extensive campaign by the entire party to raise yields, a campaign that has been particularly stepped up since the last session of the USSR Central Executive Committee, or the local and oblast conferences being convened in all the grain-growing regions to discuss grain problems, or the fact of the extremely widespread application of contractual methods, in order to understand the full intensity of the attention that the party is devoting to the grain problem, to the raising of crop yields, and to the provision of incentives for the individual peasant holding.

These facts must also be known to Comrade Bukharin.

The same must be said about supplying the villages with goods and about the state of affairs of grain procurements this year. It would be quite incorrect to deny that we have been able to improve both qualitatively and quantitatively on last year's results in supplying the countryside with consumer and production goods. It would be equally incorrect to deny that the party has been able to avoid application of extraordinary measures this year and that by and large it has been able to maintain what, for the USSR is a good rate of grain procurement if one takes into consideration such unfavourable circumstances as the very poor harvest in the Ukraine, the partial crop failure in the North Caucasus and in the Central Black-Earth raion, and the serious crop failure in the Northwestern raion. One can scarcely doubt that had it not been for these instances of poor harvests, particularly in wheat and rye, we would have had an even higher rate of grain procurements and would not have to resort to a certain reduction in the norm under which grain is supplied.

These facts must also be known to Comrade Bukharin.

If, despite the existence of all these facts, Comrade Bukharin none the less considers it necessary to discredit the work of the Central Committee and to wage a struggle against its policy on the peasant question by asserting unjustly that the Central Committee resolves to do one thing but carries out another, then this means that Comrade Bukharin does not subscribe to the party line and that he is developing a different line, distinct from that of the party.

But there cannot be two lines in the party. Either the party line is incorrect, in which case Comrade Bukharin is right in standing apart from the Central Committee. Or the party line is correct, in which case Comrade Bukharin's 'new' line on the peasant question can be nothing other than an approximation of Comrade Frumkin's line, which is predicated upon an unleashing of the capitalist elements. One cannot endlessly shuttle back and forth between the slogans 'enrich yourselves' and 'attack the kulaks.' The fact of the matter is that Comrade Bukharin has sunk to Comrade Frumkin's position.

3   Comrade Bukharin's statement to the effect that our currency situation is hopeless, that he 'predicted' that this would be the case, that no heed was paid him, etc., is completely incorrect. This statement of Comrade Bukharin is nothing but vainglory. In actual fact it was Comrade Rudzutak who spoke more than, and before, anyone else about currency difficulties. Comrade Bukharin evidently does not understand that this is an area in which not everything depends on us, that a great deal depends in this matter on the covert financial blockade imposed by Britain and France with a certain collaboration on the part of Germany and that has only in recent times begun to weaken. Comrade Bukharin does not understand that the situation cannot be helped through talk and exhortations, that to accumulate foreign currency reserves requires that very stern measures be taken to reduce imports of secondary importance, to increase exports of lumber, oil, etc., and to reduce foreign currency expenditures, etc., measures that are already being taken by the party without, incidentally, the slightest help on Comrade Bukharin's part. Comrade Bukharin cannot but know that these measures have already yielded their result, and that we now have certain foreign currency reserves at our disposal.

If, despite this fact, Comrade Bukharin none the less continues to bemoan the hopelessness of our foreign currency situation, this can only mean that he has succumbed to panic and is, in fact, demanding a reduction in our imports of equipment – that is a reduction in the rate of our industrial development.

4   Comrade Bukharin's statement to the effect that we have no intra-party democracy, that the party is being 'bureaucratized,' that 'we are spreading bureaucratism,' that there are no elected secretaries in the party, that we have allegedly established a system of political commissars in *Pravda*, in the Comintern and in the All-Union Central Council of Trade Unions, that the present party regime has become unbearable, etc., is a completely incorrect and thoroughly false statement. One cannot but note that Comrade Bukharin has sunk in this matter to Trotsky's position in his notorious letter of 8 October 1923. One has only to compare Trotsky's words in that letter on the 'intra-party regime,' on 'the bureaucratism of the Secretariat,' on the fact that 'the bureaucratization of the party apparatus has reached an unprecedented development with the application of the methods of secretarial selection' – one has only to compare these words of Trotsky's with Comrade Bukharin's statement to understand the full depth of Comrade Bukharin's fall. Only people who are dissatisfied with the existence of an iron intra-party discipline, only people who are dissatisfied with the fact that the party majority is not in agreement with these panicky 'platforms' and 'theses,' only people who are dissatisfied with the present composition of the leading organs of our party – only such people are capable of levelling a charge of bureaucratism and bureaucratization at our

party, with its method of self-criticism. Lenin was right when he called such comrades people afflicted with 'lordly anarchism.' Lenin was right when he said of such people: 'It seems clear that outcries concerning notorious bureaucratism are a simple cover-up for unhappiness with the staffs at the various centres, that they are a fig leaf ...'

Comrade Bukharin believes that if the party promoted him to the post of editor-in-chief of *Pravda* and secretary of the ECCI, and Tomsky to the position of chairman of the All-Union Central Council of Trade Unions, then that means that the party has turned *Pravda*, the ECCI, and the All-Union Central Council of Trade Unions over to them to be run as a mandate, and has surrendered the right to any supervision whatsoever over their day-to-day work by the organs of the Central Committee. This is absolutely incorrect. If that were the case, then we would have no unified, centralized party, but a formless conglomerate made up of feudal principalities, which would include a *Pravda* principality, an All-Union Central Council of Trade Unions principality, an ECCI secretariat principality, a People's Commissariat of Railroads principality, a Supreme Council of the National Economy principality, etc., etc. This would signify a break-up of the unified party and the triumph of 'party feudalism.' Therefore, Bukharin's howls about the political commissars merely betray the intrinsic unsoundness of his organizational position.

In his attacks on the 'intra-party regime,' Comrade Bukharin is, as a matter of fact, slipping to the very same position of 'freedom of ideological groupings' that was held by the trotskyite opposition in the initial stage of its development.

5   Bukharin's assertion to the effect that the policy of the ECCI, for which he is responsible, comes down to replacing conviction with shouts, that it has resulted in a disintegration of the Comintern sections, in defections and splits, etc., is completely incorrect. By this he means to say that he is opposed to the expulsion of the opportunists Thalheimer and Brandler from the German Communist Party. But he cannot muster the resolve to state this outright, since he knows that to defend Thalheimer and Brandler against the German Communist Party and the ECCI would mean to testify to his own opportunism. By this he means to say that he is opposed to the recall of the conciliators Ewert and Gerhardt from Germany. But he cannot muster the resolve to state this outright, since he knows that to defend Ewert and Gerhardt against the German Communist Party and the ECCI would mean to testify to his own waverings. In fact, what we are witnessing in the Comintern is a beneficial process of cleansing such parties as the German and Czechoslovak ones of social democratic filth and of opportunistic elements. Bukharin evidently does not understand that the Comintern sections cannot be strengthened and bolshevized without cleansing themselves of social democratic elements. Comrade Bukharin does not understand that the

present time of intensification of the class struggle in Europe and of growth in the conditions for a new revolutionary upsurge demand of the Comintern that it select for leading positions in communist parties the most steadfast and consistent revolutionary marxists, who are free of opportunistic waverings and unworthy panicking, that only leaders of this type are capable of preparing the working class for the coming battles with international capital and of leading it into battle for the dictatorship of the proletariat.

In fact, Comrade Bukharin has slipped to the position of diplomatic defence of the 'carriers' of the right deviation and conciliatory views within the Comintern.

Comrade Bukharin's statement to the effect that he accepts the decisions of the VI [Comintern] Congress on combatting rightists and conciliators is merely a fig leaf to avert the eye, for he accepts these decisions only in so far as they are not offensive to Brandler and Thalheimer, Ewert, and Gerhardt, Humbert-Droz and Serra. But not to offend them is impossible, for it is they, and they above all, who are keeping the ECCI from isolating the rightists and overcoming the conciliators in the Comintern sections.

6   There is no substance whatsoever in comrades Bukharin and Tomsky's statement to the effect that they are being 'picked to pieces' in the party, that they are the object of an 'organizational encirclement' and that as a result they are forced to insist on their right to resign, that the appointment of Comrade Kaganovich to the presidium of the All-Union Central Council of Trade Unions creates 'bicentrism,' that in such circumstances Comrade Tomsky is forced not to submit to the decisions of the Politburo rejecting his resignation, and that the resignation of comrades Tomsky and Bukharin is allegedly the best way out of the situation ...

On the basis of the materials set forth, the joint session of the Central Committee Politburo and the Central Control Commission presidium finds that:

1   Comrade Bukharin's completely incorrect criticism of the activities of the Central Committee, which found expression in such documents as Comrade Kamenev's 'record,' the article 'Notes of an Economist,' and Comrade Bukharin's 30 January 1929 statement, have as their aim to discredit the line of the Central Committee both in the field of domestic policy and in the field of Comintern policy;

2   in seeking to discredit the line of the Central Committee and in using all and sundry slanders against the Central Committee for that purpose, Comrade Bukharin is clearly leaning in the direction of working out a 'new' line, distinct from the party line, that can only mean drawing near the line of Comrade Frumkin (in the field of domestic policy), which is predicated on unleashing capitalist elements, and a duplication of the line of Humbert-

Droz (in the field of Comintern policy) predicated on a diplomatic defence of the rightist elements in the Comintern;

3   Comrade Bukharin's waverings in the direction of a 'new' line could be intensified in the near future in view of the difficulties confronting our party and in view of Comrade Bukharin's political instability, and this is not the first time in the history of our party that he has shown such instability, if the party does not take all measures incumbent upon it for Bukharin's preservation. Lenin was right when he said of Comrade Bukharin in a letter to Comrade Shliapnikov in 1916 that 'Nikolai Ivanovich is a working economist, and *in this* we have always supported him. But he is 1) credulous of slanders and 2) devilishly *unstable* in politics;'

4   Comrade Bukharin's waverings could be given new impetus if the party sanctions his and Comrade Tomsky's resignations.

Proceeding from the above, and with the aim of unconditionally maintaining party unity, the joint session of the Central Committee Politburo and Central Control Commission presidium resolves:

a   to declare Comrade Bukharin's criticism of the activities of the Central Committee to be absolutely groundless;

b   to advise Comrade Bukharin to resolutely renounce Comrade Frumkin's line in the field of domestic policy and Comrade Humbert-Droz' line in the field of Comintern policy;

c   to refuse to accept comrades Bukharin and Tomsky's resignations;

d   to advise comrades Bukharin and Tomsky to carry out loyally all decisions of the ECCI and of the party and its Central Committee...

VKP(b) v rezoliutsiiakh II   *KPSS v rezoliutsiiakh* IV, 180–99
(4th ed.), 515–30

XVI Party Conference   23–29 April 1929

The XVI Party Conference was something of an anti-climax in the stormy history of party congresses and conferences of the 1920s. Contrary to what one might expect, it was an orderly and (with one or two minor exceptions) dull meeting which sealed the fate of Bukharin and the right opposition, although the two sides in the power struggle continued their reticence about bringing it into the open.

By the time the Conference opened, Stalin had the situation well in hand and allowed Rykov, still at the time a member of the Politburo and Chairman of the Sovnarkom, to combine with Krzhizhanovsky and Kuibyshev, to deliver the major report on the Five-Year Plan, which declared that the maximal (most ambitious) version of the plan had been in force since October 1928. The resolution to this effect (2.67) was adopted unanimously. In fact, the proceedings were so well organized that the resolution was not even sent to a commission for final drafting, as was customary at previous conferences or congresses, but was put to a vote at once.

The determination not to allow the power struggle to break into the open could be seen from the resolution approving a general party purge (2.68) which did not cite 'rightists' among the elements to be eliminated, nor did it evoke any objections from them. The main attack on the opposition was launched at the evening session of 28 April, the day before the Conference closed, when Molotov delivered a two hour 'information report' on 'intra-party affairs,' which was not included in the stenographic report of the Conference and to this day has not been published. Molotov's report led to a short resolution which approved the resolution of the Central Committee and the Central Control Commission of 23 April 1929 (2.65), attacking the right. The resolution of the Central Committee and the Central Control Commission was, according to Molotov, distributed among the Conference delegates and also sent to all party organizations, as was decided at the plenum. Once again, the care taken in the preparation of the proceedings became apparent. At the suggestion of several delegations the resolution was not opened for discussion but put at once to a vote and, although Bukharin and his followers could hardly have agreed with it, no negative votes or abstentions were mentioned in the records of the Conference, which were not published until 1962.

Stalin's reluctance not to allow the struggle to break into the open at the Conference is not quite clear. Even if we allow for his usual caution the careful preparation of the Conference must have assured him that nothing would go wrong. The gathering was attended by 254 delegates with a deciding vote and 679 with a consultative vote, the largest number to attend a conference to that time. This was due to the increase in the membership of the Central Committee and the Central Control Commission. The new members were, of course, appointees of Stalin and therefore reliable. This far outweighed the possible opposition to Stalin in the Politburo.

In addition, Stalin had the resolutions approved three times during the period of the Conference. The opening day of the Conference (23 April), was also the closing day of the joint plenum of the Central Committee and the Central Control Commission. The latter body passed the resolutions first. They were then reconfirmed by the Conference. On the last day of the Conference, 29 April, a plenum of the Central Committee met as was customary, to approve the resolutions of the Conference once again. (This Central Committee plenum seems to have met secretly but its existence and function are referred to in the notes to the *KPSS v rezoliutsiiakh* IV, 200.) This threefold approval was by this time customary and it is most unlikely that it signifies a difficult struggle at the Conference. Certainly no evidence of it can be found in the published record. A more probable explanation is that Stalin wished to give his policies as great an appearance of legitimacy as possible.

Whatever the case, Stalin's victory at the Conference was complete, and he felt free to resort to an open attack on the opposition. As we saw the decision to remove Bukharin and Tomsky from their non-party posts was made in April but not implemented until after the XVI Conference, after Stalin's victory was assured. As soon as the announcement was made public, Stalin launched a large scale press campaign against the right, especially Bukharin.

It had become customary for defeated opposition groups to submit humiliating appeals and petitions to the Central Committee. The Bukharin troika was no exception. Stalin, patient as ever, resorted to a compromise. A terse resolution of the Central Committee plenum, meeting between 10 and 17 November 1929, announced the expulsion of Bukharin from the Politburo and issued a stern warning to Rykov and Tomsky, to the effect that 'appropriate organizational measures' would be applied to them in case of the smallest attempt on their part to prolong the struggle against the Central Committee line (see 3.3).

2.67
On the Five-Year Plan for the Development
of the National Economy   25 April 1929

...

II

Proceeding from the above-enumerated data on the Five-Year Plan and taking account of the fact that the plan makes complete provision for:

a maximum development of production of the means of production as the basis for the industrialization of the country;

b decisive strengthening of the socialist sector in town and countryside at the expense of capitalistic elements in the economy, enlistment of the millions-strong masses of the peasantry in socialist construction on the basis of a co-operative community and collective labour, and aid of every sort to the individual holdings of poor and middle peasants in the struggle against kulak exploitation;

c overcoming the excessive backwardness of agriculture with respect to industry and a basic solution of the grain problem;

d a significant rise in the material and cultural level of the working class and the toiling masses in the countryside;

e strengthening the leading role of the working class on the basis of the development of new forms of union with the basic masses of the peasantry;

f strengthening of the economic and political positions of the proletarian dictatorship in its struggle against class enemies both inside the country and outside it;

g an economic and cultural advance in the national republics and in backward raions and oblasts;

h a significant strengthening of the country's defence capability;

i a major step forward in realizing the party slogan: overtake and surpass the advanced capitalist countries in the technological and economic spheres –

the conference resolves to approve the Five-Year Plan of Gosplan in its optimal version, as confirmed by the Sovnarkom, as a plan that fully accords with the directives of the XV Party Congress.

III

The execution of the Five-Year Plan, which represents a programme of large-scale socialist advance, entails the overcoming of immense difficulties of both an internal and external character. These difficulties result from the strenuous goals of the plan itself, which are conditioned by the country's technical and economic backwardness, from the complexity of the task of reconstructing the many millions of scattered peasant holdings on the basis of collective labour, and finally, from the circumstances of the capitalist encirclement of our country. These difficulties are compounded by the intensification of the class struggle and the resistance of the capitalistic elements that are inevitably being squeezed out by the growing advance of the socialist proletariat.

It is possible to overcome these difficulties only by decisively improving work quality and labour discipline in all branches of the economy. Reducing the cost price of industrial production by 35 per cent over the course of the next five years; reducing the cost price of construction by 50 per cent; raising the productivity of industrial labour by 110 per cent; raising agricultural crop yields by 35 per cent; expanding the sown area by 22 per cent; unfailing fulfilment of the programme for kolkhoz and sovkhoz construction; a resolute struggle against absenteeism and laxity in production; strengthening labour discipline; socialist rationalization of production; providing industry and agriculture with the necessary managerial cadres and the creation of new cadres of red specialists from among the ranks of the working class; finally, reinforcement of the planning and regulatory principle in the economic system – such are the elementary conditions of a general economic nature that are necessary for overcoming the difficulties in fulfilling the Five-Year Plan.

The Conference considers it necessary to point out that it will be possible to overcome these difficulties and carry out the Five-Year Plan only on the basis of a vast increase in the activism and organization of the toiling masses in general and of the working class in particular, on the basis of enlisting by all possible means the millions-strong masses of the working class in socialist construction and in management of the economy, on the basis of the development by all possible means of socialistic competition and of a powerful development of self-criticism from below, by the millions-strong masses, directed against bureaucratic distortions in the state apparatus.

The difficulties of the period of socialist reconstruction, particularly in conditions of intensification of the class struggle, inevitably give rise to waverings among the petty bourgeois strata of the population, which are reflected among certain segments of the working class and even in the ranks of the party. These waverings, which reflect the influence of petty bourgeois elements, find expression in departures from the general party line in fundamental questions, and above all in the question of the rate of socialist industrialization, in the question of unleashing a socialist advance against the kulaks and against capitalist elements in general, and in the question of strengthening in every way the socialist forms of economic organization in the countryside.

In this connection, the greatest danger within the party in the given circumstances is the right deviation, as the expression of an outright repudiation of the leninist policy of the party, as the expression of a frankly opportunistic surrender of leninist positions under pressure from the class enemy. Only a merciless rebuff to all manner of waverings in the carrying out of the general bolshevik line, whose implementation signifies strengthening the leading role of the working class, can assure the solution of the tasks of socialist construction posed by the Five-Year Plan.

The Conference expresses its firm conviction that the party will deliver a crushing rebuff not only to the right deviation, but also to any other conciliatory sentiments with respect to deviation from the leninist line.

The party, at the head of the working masses, is moving ahead with confidence along the path of accomplishing the tasks of socialist reconstruction of the entire economy and is mobilizing the broadest masses of toilers under the leadership of the working class in order to surmount difficulties and implement the Five-Year Plan for economic construction.

2.68
On the Purge and Verification of Members and
Candidate Members of the VKP(b)   29 April 1929

I   Throughout its existence, the vkp(b) has conducted only one general purge, and that in 1921, at the beginning of the period of the restoration of the economy, after the Civil War had ended, a time when the party, having set itself the task of 'clearing the party of non-communist elements by means of a careful review of each member of the RKP(b) both in terms of work performance in his given capacity and as concerns his comportment as a member of the Russian Communist Party,' freed itself to a considerable extent of alien and corrupted elements, reinforced party ranks, and adopted a number of measures limiting the acceptance into the party of non-proletarian elements and assuring a more careful selection of those joining the party from the ranks of the working class and the peasantry.

2   Eight years have passed since that purge, a period during which the party has trebled in number. During this period a verification of the party members and candidates of party cells that were not associated with productive bodies was held between the XIII and XIV party congresses; the task of this review was above all to 'clear the party of socially alien and corrupted elements, and also to clear the party of those non-worker elements that during their period of membership in the party had failed to comport themselves like communists in the matter of improving the work of one or another state, economic, or other organization and who had no direct ties with the worker and peasant masses.' In all, about 25 per cent of the party membership was subjected to review, and of those checked, some 6 per cent were dismissed from the party. A partial check of rural party cells was conducted in 1926, and an all-Union census (re-registration) of party members and candidate members was held in 1927 ...

Moreover, during the reconstruction period the party regularly, on a day-to-day basis, kept a check on its ranks through the work of the control commissions and by means of calling to account members of the party who had violated the party Programme or party discipline as well as corrupt and alien elements; as a result, 260,144 members and candidates were expelled from the VKP(b) by the control commissions or voluntarily resigned and did not figure in the re-registration between 1922 and 1 July 1928 ...

4   In addition to the unquestionable improvement in the social make-up of the VKP(b) and the reinforcement of its proletarian core (44 per cent at the time of Lenin's death and 62 per cent as of 1 July 1928) and in addition to the fact that the number of workers in the party more than trebled in the same period, while the number and relative importance of worker party cells also increased, the social composition of the party is still not commensurate with the demands made on the party by the tasks of the socialist reorganization of the economy of the USSR. Nevertheless, the existence at almost all levels of the state, economic, trade union, and even party apparatus of bureaucratized elements, and in places, particularly at the lowest levels of the apparatus in the countryside, of elements of bourgeois-philistine degeneration, elements that have merged with the kulaks and that are distorting the party class line, is slowing down the enlistment of the best pro-

letarian elements of town and countryside into the party, is weakening the scope of socialist construction, and at times sows distrust among the broad masses of workers and peasants with respect to the measures of the party and the soviet authorities. Alongside the hundreds of thousands of proletarians that form the firm basis of the leninist party, there has been a penetration of party ranks by petty bourgeois elements, by carriers of rot in everyday life, people who are bringing corruption to the party ranks by the example of their personal and public life, people who hold the public opinion of the workers and toiling peasants in contempt, self-seeking and careerist elements of which the party is not sufficiently ridding itself through the regular, day-to-day work by the control commissions.

The purge presently being undertaken is to clear the ranks of the vKP(b) of those elements and in so doing to improve its mobilization readiness for the socialist offensive, to further strengthen the party's authority and faith in the party, and to attract new urban proletarian and rural labour strata to its cause.

5   In posing the question of a *general purge of the party*, it is necessary to keep in mind the fact that the make-up of the working class has considerably changed in recent years ...

While the party considers its factory cells the soundest, it must, none the less, check not only its cells outside the production sphere and its cells in the village; it is necessary to take account of the fact that the factory party cells have also been penetrated, although to a much lesser extent than the others, by elements that are incapable of fulfilling the role of a communist vanguard, elements that are in league with the kulak sector in the village and that are propagators of petty bourgeois influence on the proletariat, elements that consider work at a factory nothing more than a means for enriching their own, individual holdings, self-seeking elements who take no active part in increasing labour discipline, elements that take an indifferent view of such counter-revolutionary phenomena as anti-semitism, elements that have not made a final break with religious observances, etc.

Without a purge of the entire party, *production cells* included, the party will be unable to attract to its ranks the best elements from among the significant number of non-party proletarian activists in order to strengthen the basic proletarian core of the party. Without such a purge of their ranks, while at the same time making a systematic effort to recruit the best proletarian elements, the factory party cells will be unable to fulfil the large and complex tasks of the new stage, tasks that require maximum homogeneity, unity, consciousness, and proletarian leninist tenacity.

6   The party must review the composition of its *village cells* with particular care and resolutely cleanse them of the alien class elements that have penetrated their ranks or of those who have identified themselves with

kulak elements – with merchant, *bai* [rich Central Asian landowner] and clergy – of party members conducting a policy that repels farm labourers and poor peasants from the party, of party members who do not participate in implementing measures for the socialist reorganization of agriculture, of functionaries who are not carrying out the party's directives concerning reliance on support by the poor peasants in union with the mass of middle peasants, of party members for whom personal aggrandizement has taken precedence over the task of communist propaganda and organization in the village, of inveterate violators of revolutionary legality and of those who abuse power for personal gain ...

7   The verification of *non-production party cells* following the XIII Congress showed, in general, that their social composition had improved considerably. The composition of non-production cells by social origin proved to be: 39.4 per cent workers, 36.7 per cent peasants and 23.9 per cent employees and others. Although the non-production cells are continually being reinforced with new proletarian strata that the party is promoting from the working ranks, the non-production cells are often the most subject to the influence of non-proletarian elements and the most cluttered with them ...

It is precisely in the non-production cells that the broadest possibilities exist for exploiting one's party position for mercenary motives – for speculation, protectionism, careerism, and a bureaucratic attitude toward the masses; it is precisely here that one finds cases of 'rot in everyday life' that are particularly repellent to the masses; it is precisely in these cells that socially alien, bureaucratized and corrupt elements and hangers-on are doing the greatest harm to the party, it is precisely in the non-production cells that one finds the greatest number of former members of other parties, of people who have not adjusted in the Bolshevik Party and who have retained their ideologically alien views.

However, the faith of the broad masses of party and non-party workers and peasants in the apparatus of the Soviet state, the economic organs, the trade unions, and the party, as well as the success of their communist work depend on the composition of these cells, on the quality of their work, on the degree of their steadfastness as party members and on their ties with the masses.

Therefore there must be a particularly thoroughgoing purge of all non-communist, corrupted, alien, bureaucratized and self-seeking elements and hangers-on who take a functionary's view of their duties.

In so doing, it is necessary to exercise particular care with respect to those who have been advanced from the ranks of the workers, to take into account their difficulties during the initial period in mastering what are for them new forms of work, and to link the purge of non-production cells with a more energetic and carefully considered promotion of workers and women workers to the economic, party, and administrative apparatus.

8   In this way the verification and purge of the party ranks that is being undertaken is to make the party more homogeneous and to free it from everything non-communist. It goes without saying that such a verification is bound to entail immense difficulties and must be carried out in a most painstaking fashion, after a comprehensive explanation of the tasks of the purge and the verification both to party members and candidate members as concerns their moral level, their ties with the masses, their active participation in the party's work, in the building of communism, etc. The party warns against turning the review into a petty and carping investigation into the personal lives of party members, against a vulgarization of the review itself, and against conducting it from a standpoint other than that of the *class tasks* of the Communist Party. The purge must pitilessly eject from party ranks all elements that are alien to the party, that constitute a danger to its successes and that are indifferent to its struggle; it must eject incurable bureaucrats and hangers-on, those who are in league with the class enemy and are helping him, those who are cut off from the party by virtue of economic and personal aggrandizement, anti-semites, and covert adherents of religious cults; it must expose covert trotskyites, adherents of Miasnikov, and Democratic Centralists, and adherents of other anti-party groups and cleanse the party of them. But the purge must at the same time strengthen the work of organization, check the work of the cell, create more comradely relations between party members, increase each man's sense of responsibility for the policy and for the fate of the entire party, give impetus to raising the level of political knowledge, intensify the struggle against bureaucratism, increase the activism of all members of the organization, strengthen their ties with the masses of workers and peasants, intensify active participation in the socialist reorganization of the countryside, in the rationalization of production and management, in increasing labour discipline, in the elimination of all manner of excess, etc. Thus the verification must not assume either a narrowly inquisitorial or judicial-investigatory character. In cases where a party member qualifies for membership in all respects except for a lack of political literacy, this circumstance must in no case serve as a basis for expelling him from the party, but must be taken into consideration with a view toward creating conditions that would enable the given party member to make good this short-coming. While clarifying the fitness of each party member and candidate member for fulfilling party obligations, while helping to remedy their mistakes and short-comings, and leaving within the ranks of the party all elements that are devoted to communism, the verification must at the same time determine the extent to which the leadership of the given party cell is being correctly exercised and the extent to which the mistakes and short-comings of the party members are a reflection of that leadership ...

11   The party must devote *attention to the most painstaking preparation for the purge* so that the actual process of the purge and review can be

conducted in the shortest possible time. This requires the most painstaking preparatory work, elucidation of the purge's tasks in the press and at meetings, and the explanation of the demands that the party is making during the purge on every party member and candidate and, above and beyond the party mass, on those non-party members as well who will be enlisted to help the party in the verification of, and purge of, its ranks.

Bearing in mind the mistakes made during former verifications and the fact that the check-up applies to about 1,500,000 party members and candidates scattered across an immense territory and working under the most varied conditions, the party must be particularly painstaking in preparations for this verification. The party devotes exceptional attention to the *composition of the verification commissions*, to whose ranks it must attract, side by side with the most steadfast and irreproachable party members from the Bolshevik old guard, those party members who entered the party in 1917 and during the Civil War; the party must assure the most steadfast proletarian composition of these commissions, and the composition of these verification commissions must be made widely known to the working masses ahead of time so that workers and party members can rectify in good time the composition of the verification commissions in cases where they have been made up in an unsatisfactory fashion. These commissions must painstakingly prepare for their work; they must define precisely the tasks of the verification in each separate cell, depending on its composition, work conditions, level of development, etc.

12   The present verification will only avoid committing numerous mistakes if the party approaches each party member and candidate carefully, if derogatory accusations are thoroughly checked on, if the verifying commissions are able to prevent the settling of personal accounts during the verification, to prevent group struggles and to spot squabbles, intrigues, and intentional discrediting, and if the verification is conducted on a certain principled level, avoiding pettiness and callousness of approach and stereotypes. In particular, the party considers it necessary to warn against a formal attitude toward those who are the object of the verification. It is the job of the verification commissions to take into account all features peculiar to the work of party members and candidates in production work and in institutions, the everyday and material conditions in the life of party members, features peculiar to the nationalities, and the particular work conditions of comrades who are ill, of women, agricultural workers, peasants, young people, etc. The Central Control Commission must work out the most detailed guidelines for the local control commissions, guidelines that will rule out a number of mistakes. The Central Control Commission must constantly oversee the progress of the verification and correct mistakes as they occur in the work of the local control commissions or of the individual verification commissions.

13 Proceeding from these considerations, the joint plenum of the Central Committee and Central Control Commission resolves:

1 to conduct a general purge of the party such that the verification of party ranks will be completed by the time of the XVI Congress of the vKP(b). The calendar dates for the verification of particular categories of party cells (villages, production, teaching, etc.) must be set up with regard for features peculiar to their work (for the village party cells, at a time between the periods of the most important farm work; for the higher educational institutions, at times other than the examination periods, etc.). These dates must be set for each individual organization;

2 to assign to the Central Control Commission the job of working out highly detailed guidelines for the local control commissions on procedures for selecting the verification commissions, on procedures for conducting the actual verification and purge, for registering the work experience of the verification commissions, and for supervising their work, and to establish procedures for appealing the decisions of the local verification and control commissions, while assuring the most painstaking selection of the verification commissions and constant supervision of them on the part of the Central Control Commission and the responsible control commissions locally (the republic, krai, and oblast commissions);

3 to conduct the purge of the party openly with respect to non-party workers and the farm labour and poor and middle peasant masses in the village;

4 to conduct an extensive preparatory campaign both in the press and at party meetings, to acquaint all party members and candidate members – as well as non-party workers and peasants – with the tasks of the verification and purge.

Pravda, 30 April 1929 (2.67); *KPSS v rezoliutsiiakh* IV, 201–48
Izvestiia tsentral' nogo komiteta,
15 May 1929 (2.68)

Appendix

Members of the Secretariat 1917–29 Full Member —————— Candidate member ——————

Congress	VI 1917	VIII 1919	IX 1920	X 1921	XI 1922	XII 1923	XIII 1924	XIV 1925	XV 1927
Dzerzhinsky, F.E.	———								
Ioffe, A.A.	———								
Muranov, M.K.	———								
Stasova, E.D.	———————[2]								
Sverdlov, Ia.M.	———								
Krestinsky, N.N.			———[2,4]						
Preobrazhensky, E.A.			———						
Serebriakov, L.P.			———						
Molotov, V.M.					———[2]————————————————				
Iaroslavsky, E.M.				———					
Mikhailov, V.M.				———					
Stalin, I.V.					———[3]————————————				
Kuibyshev, V.V.					———				
Rudzutak, Ia.E.						———			
Andreev, A.A.							———		
Kaganovich, L.M.							to 30 IV 25 ———	from VII 28 ———	
Zelensky, I.A.							———		
Bubnov, A.S.							from 30 IV 25 ————————		
Uglanov, N.A.								to IV 29 ———	
Kosior, S.V.								to VII 28 ———	
Evdokimov, G.E.								to 9 IV 26 ———	
Shvernik, N.M.								———[5]	
Artiukhina, A.V.								———————	
Kubiak, N.A.								———	
Bauman, K.Ia.								from IV 28; from 29 IV 29	
Moskvin, I.M.								———	

1 It is not certain that the Secretariat actually functioned during the period up to the VIII Congress. The work was performed by Sverdlov and Stasova.
2 Responsible secretary.
3 General secretary.
4 Responsible secretary was not elected but the work was done by Krestinsky.
5 Appointed at the April 1926 Central Committee Plenum to replace Evdokimov.

Members of Politburo 1917–29

Full member ‾‾‾‾ Candidate member ‾‾‾‾

Congress	Central Committee meeting 23 X 17	VIII 1919	IX 1920	X 1921	XI 1922	XII 1923	XIII 1924	XIV 1925	CC and CCC* Plenum 14–23 VII 26	XV 1927
Bubnov, A.S.										
Kamenev, L.B.									to 23 X 26	
Lenin, V.I.						died 21 I 24				
Sokolnikov, G.Ia.										
Stalin, I.V.										
Trotsky, L.D.									to 23 X 26	
Zinoviev, G.E.										
Krestinsky, N.N.										
Bukharin, N.I.										to 17 XI 29
Kalinin, M.I.										
Molotov, V.M.										
Rykov, A.I.										
Tomsky, M.P.										
Rudzutak, Ia.E.										
Dzerzhinsky, F.E.								died 20 VII 26		
Frunze, M.V.								died x 25		
Voroshilov, K.E.										
Petrovsky, G.I.										
Uglanov, N.A.										to 29 IV 29
Ordzhonikidze, G.K.									to 3 XI 26	
Andreev, A.A.										
Kaganovich, L.M.										
Kirov, S.M.										
Mikoyan, A.I.										
Chubar, V.Ia.										
Kuibyshev, V.V.										
Kosior, S.V.										
Bauman, K.Ia.										from 29 IV 29

I Functioned to 3 November 1926, and reappointed after XV Congress.
* Joint Plenum of the Central Committee and the Central Control Commission.

Members of Orgburo, 1917–1929

Full member _____ Candidate member _____

Congress	12 XII 17[1]	VIII 1919	End of 1919[2]	IX 1920	X 1921	XI 1922	XII 1923	XIII 1924	XIV 1925	XV 1927
Lenin, V.I.										
Stalin, I.V.										
Sverdlov, Ia.M.										
Trotsky, L.D.							appointed autumn 23			
Sokolnikov, G.Ia.	from 22 I 18									
Krestinsky, N.N.										
Serebriakov, L.P.										
Beloborodov, A.G.										
Stasova, E.D.										
Muranov, M.K.										
Kamenev, L.B.		from VII 19								
Preobrazhensky, E.A.										
Rakovsky, Kh.G.										
Rykov, A.I.										
Dzerzhinsky, F.E.		from VII 19								
Tomsky, M.P.										
Molotov, V.M.										
Zalutsky, P.A.										
Mikhailov, V.M.										
Iaroslavsky, E.M.										
Komarov, N.P.										
Kalinin, M.I.										
Rudzutak, Ia.E.										
Kuibyshev, V.V.										
Andreev, A.A.									to IV 28	
Zelensky, I.A.										
Zinoviev, G.E.							appointed autumn 23			
Bukharin, N.I.							appointed autumn 23			
Korotkov, I.I.							appointed autumn 23			
Bubnov, A.S.										

Members of Orgburo, 1917–1929

Full member ———   Candidate member ┄┄┄

Congress	12 XII 17[1]	VIII 1919	End of 1919[2]	IX 1920	X 1921	XI 1922	XII 1923	XIII 1924	XIV 1925	XV 1927
Voroshilov, K.E.								———		
Dogadov, A.I.								———		———
Kaganovich, L.M.								———		from VII 28
Nikolaeva, K.I.								———		
Smirnov, A.P.								———		———
Frunze, M.V.								┄┄┄		
Chaplin, N.P.								———		———
Antipov, N.K.								———		
Lepse, I.I.								———		———
Uglanov, N A.									———	[3]
Kosior, S.V.									——— to VII 28	
Evdokimov, G.E.								4 ———		
Artiukhina, A.V.									———	———
Kviring, E.I.									———	
Shmidt, V.V.										
Ukhanov, K.V.										
Kubiak, N.A.										———
Moskvin, I.M.										———
Rukhimovich, M.I.										———
Sulimov, D.E.										———
Lobov, S.S.										
Kotov, V.A.										
Antipov, N.K.										from IX 28
Shvernik, N.M.									4 ———	from XI 29
Bauman, K.Ia.										from IX 28
Gamarnik, Ia.B.										from XI 29

1 This was the buro of the Central Committee which may have functioned as Orgburo.

2 The Central Committee elected a new Orgburo at the end of 1919 on the basis of the principle that only those members who were permanently in Moscow were to be members of that body; exception was made only in the case of Kalinin.

3 Although Uglanov was not officially relieved of his function in the Orgburo before the XVI Congress, it may be assumed that he remained in that post only to April 1929, when he was removed as candidate of the Politburo and as secretary of the Central Committee.

4 Although not announced officially, it is likely that Evdokimov, in addition to being relieved of his function as secretary, was also removed from the Orgburo and replaced by Shvernik.

The tables were derived from T. and M. Reiman, 'Přehled o složení nejvyšších orgánů KSSS ('Survey of the composition of the highest organs of the CPSU'), in *Revue dějin socialismu* (Review of the history of socialism), Prague 1968, no.3, 369–413.

Index